The English Elite in 1066

Gone but not forgotten

Donald Henson

Anglo-Saxon Books

BY THE SAME AUTHOR

A Guide to Late Anglo-Saxon England

First published 2001

Published by
Anglo-Saxon Books
Frithgarth
Thetford Forest Park
Hockwold-cum-Wilton
Norfolk, England

Printed by
Antony Rowe
Bumper's Farm
Chippenham
Wiltshire

British Library Cataloguing-in-Publication Data. A catalogue record for this book is available from the British Library.

ISBN 1–898281–26–2

Ure ieldran, ða þe ðas stowa ær hioldon, hie lufedon wisdom ⁊ ðurh ðone hi beȝeaton welan ⁊ us læfdon. Her mon mæȝ ȝiet ȝesion hiora swæð, ac we him ne cunnon æfterspyriȝan, forðæm we habbað nu æȝðer forlæten ȝe þone welan ȝe þone wisdom, forðamþe we noldon to ðæm spore mid ure mode onlutan.

Our forefathers, who formerly held these places, loved wisdom, and through it they obtained wealth and bequeathed it to us. In this we can still see their tracks, but we cannot follow them, and therefore we have lost both the wealth and the wisdom, because we would not incline our hearts after their example.

from King Ælfred the Great's preface to his translation of
Pope Gregory's *Regula Pastoralis* (Pastoral Care), c890

Table of Contents

List of Tables

List of Figures

Acknowledgements

Some of the references needed for this book have been hard to find, even with the resources of a university library to hand. Two people in particular were generous in their time to help me with this problem, and in providing useful advice and information: Phil Mernick and Veronica Smart.

Writing this book has meant delving into areas with which I was not previously familiar. While this has been a fascinating exercise, I have undoubtedly failed to cover every book and article written on the subject. Any omissions and inaccuracies are therefore very much my own responsibility. Readers are welcome to let me know of any modifications that can be made to improve upon this work.

INTRODUCTION

The total population of England in 1066 was probably between 1,600,000 and 2,000,000; 1,750,000 would be a reasonable estimate. Most of these people are invisible in the historical record. Society at the time (as before and since) was stratified and localised. That is, it was divided accorded to wealth and position, with those in the upper levels having disproportionate access to power. Also, most people would live and work in a small local area. Only those in the upper levels of the hierarchy would operate over a wider geographical scale. Describing such a society is not simple. It can be classified in a number of ways. The commonest way from a modern perspective would be by class; royal, noble, commoner and slave. Another way which was more contemporary was by function: warrior, priest and worker. Both of these would cut across the natural divisions of age and gender.

Social and political interaction would occur at several geographical levels, involving progressively fewer people overall. The most basic geographical unit was the township, which may or may not have been divided among more than one manor. The townships were grouped into larger units called hundreds (wapentakes in some parts of England), which were the basic judicial units of the crown with a court meeting every month. Above the hundred was usually the shire with its twice-yearly court and Sheriff appointed by the King. Earls were appointed over regional groupings of shires but these did not usually coincide with the regions defined by legal practice and tradition, or with the dioceses of the church. At the national level, social and political life revolved around the King and central administration through the King's household. Although this did not have a permanent base but moved around the country with the King, the treasury was kept at Winchester (the historical capital of Wessex). The commercial centre of the country however would have been the largest of the boroughs, London. As we move higher up the geographical scale, the number of people who could be considered to have been politically important would have become smaller and smaller, but our knowledge of them as individuals would become greater.

Our knowledge is greatest for the very highest levels, royalty and nobility, for the adult males within these and for the national, regional and shire scales of government. There has been a great deal of research done on the identities of the elite and their landed estates. Much of this work is available in dispersed articles and books. In many cases, studies focus only on one aspect of the elite, e.g. the lay landed aristocracy. A major reason for writing this book is to bring together the results of this research for the whole of the elite and present it in such a way as to be of use to anyone who wishes to research the people of England in 1066, and the social and political structures of the late Anglo-Saxon English state. This book should be of use both to those who are new to the period, the amateur historian and general reader, as well as to the serious researcher.

Sources

Primary sources for the period covering the reigns of Eadward III, Harold II, Eadgar II and Willelm I are, if not perfect, at least plentiful. They include charters, writs, chronicles, histories, biographies and material evidence such as coins. Also, the Domesday survey of 1086 provides a great deal of information on the England of 20 years earlier. We can reconstruct the ruling elite of England in the momentous year of the Norman Conquest with greater detail than at any time before.

The most important narrative historical source for the period is the Anglo-Saxon Chronicle (Chr), begun in 892. This was a monastic chronicle that survives in five versions for the reign of Eadward III, sharing many sections but also largely independent for some of their entries. The various versions of the Chronicle covering this period, with their manuscript dates (some are later copies of works originally written earlier), were:

> version A 1070? – written at Canterbury
> version C 1046-66 – written at Abingdon
> version D 1051-80 – written at Worcester & York
> version E 1121-54 – a Peterborough copy, originally written at Canterbury
> version F 1070? – written at Canterbury

Other contemporary 11th century sources include lives of saints and others, which shed a great deal of light on the period. These are overtly biased works and need to be treated with due caution. Two of the most important are the lives of Queen Ymme (EE) and of King Eadward III (VÆ). Saints and ecclesiastics for whom biographical information survives were Abbot Ægelwig of Evesham (Æ), Bishop Gisa of Wells (GW) and Bishop Leofric of Exeter (Lf). Other useful items can be found, including Osbeorn's account of the translation of St Ælfheah (TÆ), an account of the Acts of Lanfranc (AL) entered into version A of the Anglo-Saxon Chronicle, and Goscelin's Life of Wulfsige (Ws).

The English government machine was highly literate and it has left behind several types of administrative document of the greatest value for reconstructing the events and institutions of the periods. These include charters, writs, laws and wills. These have been intensively studied and can yield important information about particular people. They are referenced below under their appropriate catalogue number, e.g. S for Sawyer, H for Harmer (see References for details). Monastic Liber Vitae, e.g. Hyde Abbey (H), can also be used to flesh out information about individuals. Artefactual evidence comes in the form of coins. These preserve the place of minting and the moneyers' names, which allow an insight into the urban life largely ignored by the monastic chroniclers.

Two products of the Norman Conquest are crucial to our knowledge of the period, the Bayeux Tapestry (B) and the Domesday Book (DB). The former was produced for Bishop Odo of Bayeux and is an unrivalled pictorial source, which needs interpretation to yield all its secrets. The latter is a detailed and (almost) nationwide account of England and its ruling nobility that is unparalleled in Europe. It is however an imperfect document with gaps and inconsistencies, detailed analysis of which is still in progress.

Contemporary French writers, William of Jumieges (WJ), Guy of Amiens (GA) and William of Poitiers (WP) contribute much of value from the perspective of the victors. As their works are openly praising Duke Willelm and the Conquest, they need to be treated with care but cannot be ignored in helping to provide a full picture of events. Other continental writers of the time can also add useful information, e.g. Adam of Bremen (AB).

The generation after the Conquest was noted for its production of historical works preserving knowledge of a vanished Anglo-Saxon past written in the scholarly language of Latin used by the new elite. Works belonging the period of the 1090s to 1120s include versions of the Anglo-Saxon Chronicle produced at Worcester (W) and Durham (D), and various histories by Simeon of Durham (SD), William of Malmesbury (M), Orderic Vitalis (O), Eadmer of Canterbury (E). William of Malmesbury provided also his *Gesta Pontificum* (GP) and a Life of Wulfstan (VW), based on that of Wulfstan's friend Colman. Eadmer also left us with a letter to Glastonbury (EG) and a Life of St Dunstan (VD) which both contain useful information. The English Bishop Þurgod has left us a Life of St Margaret (VM). Also from the same period is the cartulary of Worcester cathedral drawn up by Hemming (Hm) and the inventory of knights of Canterbury cathedral, the *Domesday Monachorum* (DM).

By 1150, there was no longer any direct contact with the period of the Norman Conquest and sources need to be treated with greater care. Monasteries were keen assemblers of data about their own past and information about the late Anglo-Saxon period can be found in a number of later monastic histories mostly between c.1150 and c.1300, chiefly Abingdon (Ab), Crowland (Cw), Ely (LibE), Evesham (Ev), Peterborough (Pb), Ramsey (Ra), St Benet's (JO), St Edmund's (SE), Thorney (Ty), Waltham (Wþ), Westminster (Fl), Winchcombe (Wc) and Wilton (Wi). Some later histories of use include those of John of Fordun (JF), Thomas of Elmham (TE) and William Thorne (Th). The Welsh chronicles known as the *Brut y Tywysogion* (BT) can also be of use, and the French language chronicle of Geoffrey Gaimar (GG) can also shed extra light on events. Other works that provided useful information include two by Ailred of Rievaulx (AR, VSE), Osbert of Clare's Life of King Eadward (VBE), Hariulf of St Riquier's chronicle (HR), and the anonymous *Laws of Edward the Confessor* (LE).

Personal Names

The modern practice in printing of medieval personal names varies a great deal. Names after 1066 (most of which are still in use) are usually printed in their modern form. Thus, we have William instead of Willelm, Geoffrey instead of Goisfrið/Godefrið/Gaufrið etc. For names before 1066, this is not the case. Few Old English names survive into modern English as forenames, although many do as surnames. Those names that do survive as modern forenames are often spelled in the modern way, while the others are not. Using indexes thus becomes frustrating as Edward (Eadward) and Ethelred (Æþelred) may be widely separated from Eadwig and Æþelwold. This practice also tends to emphasise the difference between English history before and after 1066. That coming after being full of familiar names, while that before has names that seem outlandish and hard to pronounce. A further inconsistency is that modern editors of the Domesday survey, and others following this lead, have used 13th century Icelandic (so-called Old Norse) spellings for names of Norse origin used in England in the 11th century. So the name found on coins from York as Oþbeorn is printed by many modern editors as Auðbjorn, and Roscytel would be found as Hrossketill. Such practice ought to be discouraged as unhistorical, unnecessary, misleading and impractical for making a serviceable index. Thus emphasising the ethnic origin of a name by using spellings not in use at the time gives a false impression of the ethnic affiliation of the person holding the name (see below). To be consistent, all names should be either in their contemporary 11th century form, or all updated to their modern equivalent. In this work, I have chosen to show all names, whether English, Danish or Norman, in their standardised late Old English form. These are the forms found in most of the sources of the time. Variant 11th century spellings are noted in brackets after the name in the main entries.

There were a great many personal names in use among the English in 1066 (Reaney and Wilson 1997, Feilitzen 1937). The 405 native English listed in this book used 219 names of mostly Old English (74% of people) and Old Norse (25% of people) origin. This variety is accounted for by the way in which names were formed. Old English names were of three types (Clark 1992a). The commonest were formed of two elements, each a word in its own right but could be divorced from its meaning when used in names. For instance, Wulfstan was formed of Wulf (wolf) and stan (stone). Most elements were restricted to either first or second position. Only a few could be used in either. Elements could be put together in a large number of combinations, e.g. Ead + gar, mund, red, ric, ward, wig, wine or wulf.

The people listed here are not a representative sample of the whole population but their naming habits can be analysed to provide a picture of patterns in naming among the English elite of the day. A wide variety of first elements was in use but some were commoner than others. The following, listed with the number of people using the element (words also used as second elements are underlined), accounted for more than 41% of the people listed in this book:

Ælf 42, Ægel 29, Briht 16, Ead 30, God 22, Leof 29, Os 13, Wulf 35

The following were the second elements used most commonly, covering nearly 44% of people listed (those also used as first elements are underlined and feminine forms are in italics):

<u>man</u> 12, mær 16, noð 12, red 9, ric 50, <u>sige</u> 15, stan 15, ward 20, <u>wig</u> 14, wine 60, wold 11; *gyfu* 11, *gyð* 5

A second type of name was to use a word with the ending -ing or -ling, e.g. Bruning, Coling, Cypping, Duning, Hearding, Lyfing, Spræcling or Sweartling. The third type consisted of just one element, which may or may not have had an obvious meaning, e.g. Brun, Ceorl, Cild, Dunna, Heca, Leofa, Odda, Wine (Redin 1919).

This traditional stock of English names was increased by the Viking settlements and Danish conquest. Viking names were made in similar ways to English (Fellows Jensen 1968, Insley 1994), sometimes with the same elements but often with certain preferred words that were not found in English, e.g. Þor-, Ketil-, -sveinn. The elements were usually Anglicised in spelling, e.g. Þur-, Cytel-, -swegn. Cytel was commoner in East Anglia, while its shorter version, -cyll, was the version preferred in Yorkshire and eastern Mercia (Insley 1994). Elements that were shared with English included As/Es- (English Os-), Ulf- (Wulf-), -geirr (-gar), and -steinn (-stan). Common first elements included Arn- (4), Þor- (10), Auð-/Oð- (4), Kol- (3), Svart- (3) and second elements included -ketill/kell (11), -vard (6), -ulf (4). There were many single word names, often ending in -i (Anglicised as -a, -e or -ig), e.g. Beorn, Brand, Carl, Cytel, Gamal, *Gyða*, Gyrð, Orm, Tocig, Tofig, Tolig, Ulf. Unique combinations of elements among the elite included many well-known names, e.g. Ætsere, Harold, Healfdene, Mærleswegn, Morcere, Sihtric, Siward, Walþeof, Wicing, Wigod.

People from France and Germany had been in England among the ruling classes since the marriage of *Ymme* of Normandy to King Æþelred in 1002 and more had arrived under Eadward III. They usually had names of Germanic origin and often shared elements with both English and Norse names (Forssner 1916), e.g. Ans- (English Os-), -ard (-hard), -bert (berht), -elm (-helm), -ric, -ulf (-wulf), -wine. Names of Christian origin were also beginning to be used: *Agatha*, Alan, *Cristina*, Fitel (Uitalis), Iohan, *Margareta*, Peter, Spirites. One name of Celtic origin was common in Northumbria, Gospatric.

The commonest names listed in this book for English residents in 1066 are:

English origin (296 people): Godric 11, Ælfwine 9, Brihtric 9, Leofwine 9, Ægelwine 8, Godwine 8, Ægelric 7, Eadric 7, Eadwine 7; *Ælfgyfu* 5, *Eadgyð* 3
Norse origin (103 people): Siward 6, Ætsere 5, Þurcytel 5, Ulf 4; *Gunnhild* 2, *Gyða* 2
Continental origin (112 people): Willelm 9, Rodbert 6, Osbern 4

The English of this period seem to have had a great fondness for names ending in -ric or -wine. The figures given above find some support from Feilitzen (1976), who found that by far the commonest names of English origin in Winchester in 1066 were Godwine, Ælfwine and Leofwine.

Among the Normans and other Frenchmen who formed the bulk of the ruling class after 1066, names were usually of Norse or Germanic origin. Although there was a wide variety of names found among the French settlers, the choice of names was becoming more restricted. By 1066, relatively few names were becoming very common. The most popular were Willelm, Rodbert, Ricard, Raulf, Baldwine, Hugo, Goisfrið, Fitel, Durand. By 1154, among the 68 men in the royal family, earls, bishops and sheriffs just seven names accounted for 46 people (Goisfrið, Henri, Ricard, Rodbert, Roger, Walter, Willelm). This can be compared to 47 names used by the 48 English men in similar positions in 1066.

Studies of names of this period have in the past characterised names according to linguistic origin, and so have tended to over-emphasise their ethnic character (Bates 1997). It is important to emphasise that the use of a name does not imply ethnic affiliation. There are many examples. The English Earl Ælfgar had two sons, one with an English name (Eadwine) and the other with a Danish name (Morcere). The Breton Rodbert FitzWymarc gave his son the Danish name of Swegn. Tofig, a Danish follower of Cnut, gave his son the English name of Ægelstan. The English name Odda/Oda, was found among the Normans as Odo. The Norse Osbeorn occurred in Normandy as Osbern, and Osmund could be either English or Norman. The Viking name Þurstan was also used both in Normandy and in England. The Norse name Stigand was shared by the English Archbishop of Canterbury and a later Norman Bishop of Rochester. Archbishop Stigand's brother had the English name of Ægelmær. Bishop Ulf of Dorchester was a Norman, but with a common Norse name found in England. Most of those listed in Domesday with Norse names were English born, who may or may not have had a Viking ancestor. Where such an ancestor existed, he would have been either a grandfather coming over with Cnut, or more likely came over with the Viking settlers of the late 9th or early 10th centuries, some 5 to 7 generations earlier. Such people may have been of Viking descent but that does not mean they saw themselves as Danish or Norwegian rather than English. All the evidence shows that they were as loyal (or disloyal) to the same degree as any native English.

Variation in spelling

Writing conventions in English had been fixed in the middle of the 10th century. However, by 1066, pronunciation was changing and spellings sometimes tried to reflect this. Variations in spelling could also be the result of other factors, e.g. inadequately educated scribes, miscopying between documents, dialectal differences. The largest source for names of the period is the Domesday Book, whose main scribe was most likely English but writing according to Latin spelling conventions (Bates 1997). For the sake of consistency, names below are given in their full standard Old English form. Variants found in English documents of the 11th century are noted in brackets after the name. Forms have been taken only from manuscripts belonging to the 11th century. These include the A, C, D and F versions of the Anglo-Saxon Chronicles, charters and writs, the Vita Ædwardi, the Bayeux Tapestry and the

Domesday Book. Later copies of 11th century material have not been used. Since most Anglo-Saxon names are unfamiliar to most modern English readers, women's names are printed in italics below to distinguish them from similar men's names. For instance, Eadgar and Wulfwine were men's names but *Eadgyð* and *Wulfwynn* were women's.

The spelling and pronunciation of names were often simplified during the 11th century. For example, Ælf-, Eald-, Ealh- and Æþel- often appear as Al-. Æþel- had been changed to Ægel- (its standard spelling by this time and so used as the standard form in this book) and thence to Æil/Ail-. Furthermore, the different dialects of English often had alternative forms. Eald- (pronounced *aild*) was the West Saxon form of Anglian Ald-, so Bishop Aldhun of Durham would be known as Ealdhun in a Winchester document. Second elements were also affected by changes in pronunciation, e.g. -frið becoming -ferð, -briht becoming -berht, -wulf simplified to -ulf, -sige to -si. Sometimes vowels were added between elements, e.g. Leofenoð for Leofnoð. Double consonants were often simplified, e.g. Mana for Manna. Names of foreign origin were also affected by spelling variation, e.g. Rodbert appearing also as Rotbeard. For further discussion see Dodgson and Palmer 1992.

Some of the more important variations in spelling are:

Ælf-	Alf, Æl, Al	-bein	begen
Ægel-	Ægl, Æl, Al	-beorn	bern, bearn
Briht-	Bryht, Byrht, Birht, Brict, Berht	-cytel	citel, cetel, cyll, cill
Cyne-	Cyn, Cin/e	-ferð	frið
Ead-	Ed, Æd	-ing	inc
Eald-	Ald, Æld	-mer	mær, mar
Earn-	Arn, Ern, Ærn	-noð	nað
Leof-	Liof	-sige	si, sie
Os-	Æs, Es	-swegn	swegen
Oþ-	Ouþ	-ward	werd
Sæ-	Se	-wig	wi
Seolh-	Seolc	-wold	wald
Sige-	Si	-wulf	ulf
Sweart-	Swart		
Wulf-	Wul		
Lyfing	Lifing, Leofing		

Pronunciation

Pronunciation of names is straightforward. In the middle of words, *f, þ, s* had the 'hard' sounds of modern *v*, the *th* of *bathe* and *z*. The letter *g* was pronounced as either *g* or *y* (next to *i* or *e* and in *-gyfu, -gyð*). The letter *c* was either *k* or *ch* (next to *i* or *e*, except in *Cent-*). *Æ* was either *ai* (as in *air*) or a short *a* (as in *cat*). The combination *eo* was like the *er* in *herd*. The letter *y* has no modern equivalent but is found in Scots *ü* in words like *hus (house)* and *foot*.

15

Examples of pronunciations are:

Ælfred ....*Alvred*
Ægelmær ....*Ayelmair*
Eadgyfu ....*Airdyüver*
Ecgfriþ ....*Edgevrith*
Leofsige ....*Lervzeeyer* or *Lerfseeyer*
Wulfric...................*Wulvrich*

The Structure of the Book

The people listed in this book formed the topmost section of the ruling elite in 1066. It includes all those who held office between the death of Eadward III and the abdication of Eadgar II. There are 455 individuals in the main entries and these have been divided according to their office or position: the royal family, earls, bishops, abbots and abbesses, the greater thanes (with lands over £40 and officials in the King's household), sheriffs, royal chaplains, moneyers, foreigners settled in England and Englishmen in exile. For many of these individuals, we have only the barest outline of their existence, but for some we can provide some detail. Four types of information are listed where possible. First is given what is known of their life, followed by an account of their landed wealth, the source of much of their power. The final two entries list the early sources in which information about the individual can be found (unless stated otherwise, a major source for the landed estates of all individuals is the Domesday Book) and then any modern references that give details about his or her life. A series of appendices provide more detailed information about particular topics or groups of people.

Where charters are listed under early sources, no attempt has been made to differentiate between genuine and altered or faked documents. The complexities of charter production and history are such that many genuine witness lists were used to add authenticity to faked materials, and the identification of many charters as genuine or not is still a subject of lively academic debate. Quotations from documents written in Old English are included in some sections. In these, the Old English letter forms have been used as follows: ȝ = g, þ = th, ð = th, ƿ = w, ⁊ = &.

THE KING AND HIS KINSMEN

The government of England (Loyn 1984) was based on the King, his family and household. Although it was less well developed than it would become in the 12th century, the English monarchy was one of the most powerful in Europe and had created a sophisticated government machine. The King took an oath at his coronation to protect the church, punish wrongdoers and promote justice. Both King Ælfred and Archbishop Wulfstan of York left in their writings views of the ideal kingship. The simplest statement is to be found in King Ælfred's translation of the *Cura Pastoralis* of Pope Gregory (Sweet 1871-72):

> ꝛ hu þa kyninȝas þe ðone anpald hæfdon ðæs folces Gode ꝛ his ærendprecum hirsumedon; ꝛ hie æȝðer ȝe hiora sibbe ȝe hiora sido ȝe hiora anpald innanbordes ȝehioldon, ꝛ eac ut hiora oeðel rymdon

> and how the kings who had power over the nation obeyed God and his ministers; and they preserved peace, morality and order at home, and at the same time enlarged their territory abroad

In his translation of the *De Consolatione Philosophiae* of Boethius, Ælfred provided an analysis of what the King needed in order to rule effectively in terms of the ideal social order (Sedgefield 1899 & 1900):

> Þæt bið þonne cyninȝes andpeorc ꝛ his tol mid to ricsianne, þæt he hæbbe his lond fullmonnad; he sceal habban ȝebedmen ꝛ fyrdmen ꝛ peorcmen. Hpæt, þu past þætte butan þissan tolan nan cyninȝ his cræft ne mæȝ cyðan. Þæt is eac his ondpeorc, þæt he habban sceal to ðæm tolum þam þrim ȝeferscipum bipiste. Þæt is þonne heora bipist: land to buȝianne, ꝛ ȝifta ꝛ pæpnu ꝛ mete ꝛ ealo ꝛ claþas ꝛ ȝehpæt þæs ðe þa þre ȝeferscipas behofiað. Ne mæȝ he butan þisum þas tol ȝehealdan, ne buton þisum tolum nan þara þinȝa pyrcan þe him beboden is to pyrcanne.

> Thus a king's raw material and instruments of rule are a well-peopled land, and he must have men of prayer, men of war and men of work. As you know, without these tools no king may display his special talent. Further, for his materials he must have means of support for the three classes above spoken of, which are his instruments; and these means are land to dwell in, gifts, weapons, meat, ale, clothing, and what else so ever the three classes

need. Without these means he cannot keep his tools in order, and without these tools he cannot perform any of the tasks entrusted to him.

In other words, the King not only ruled over the people but he also had to be concerned for the people's welfare. More developed ideas on this theme were expressed by Archbishop Wulfstan. Naturally, he stressed the Christian values of kingship and the moral character of the ruler. However, it is noteworthy he was fully aware of the secular responsibilities of kingship and that he expressed the purpose of kingship in terms of the well-being of the people. His views can be found in his *Institutes of Polity* (Jost 1959, Swanton 1975):

> *Cristenum cyninȝe ȝebyreð on cristenre þeode þæt he sy ealspa hit riht is folces frofer ⁊ rihtpis hyrde ofer cristene heorde. And him ȝebyreþ þæt he eallum mæȝne cristendom rære ⁊ Godes cyrican æȝhpær ȝeorne fyrðrie ⁊ friðie, ⁊ eall cristen folc sibbie ⁊ sehte mid rihtre laȝe spa he ȝeornost mæȝe, ⁊ ðurh ælc þinȝ rihtpisnesse lufie for Gode ⁊ for porulde. Forðam þurh þæt he sceal sylf fyrmest ȝeþeon ⁊ his þeodscipe eac spa þe he riht lufie for Gode ⁊ for porulde. And him ȝebyreð þæt he ȝeornlice fylste þam þe riht pillan ⁊ a hetelice styre þam ðe þpyres pillan. He sceal mandæde menn þreaȝan þearle mid poruldlicre steore ⁊ he sceal ryperas ⁊ reaferas ⁊ ðas poruldstruderas hatian ⁊ hynan ⁊ eallum Godes feondum styrnlice piðstandan. And æȝðer he sceal beon mid rihte ȝe milde ȝe reþe, milde þam ȝodum ⁊ styrne þam yfelum. Ðæt bið cyninȝes riht ⁊ cynelic ȝepuna ⁊ þæt sceal on þeode spyðost ȝefremian.*
>
> *And seofon þinȝ ȝedafeniað rihtpisum cyninȝe. An ærest þæt he spyðe micelne Godes eȝe hæbbe ⁊ oðer þæt he æfre rihtpisnesse lufiȝe ⁊ þridde þæt he eadmod sy pið ȝode ⁊ feorðe þæt he stiðmod sy pið yfele. And fifte he Godes þearfum frefriȝe ⁊ fede. And syxte þæt he Godes cyrican fyrðriȝe ⁊ friðiȝe. And seofoðe þæt he be freondan ⁊ be fremdan fadiȝe ȝelice on rihtlican dome.*

It behoves the Christian King in a Christian nation to be, as is right, the people's comfort and a righteous shepherd over the Christian flock. And it behoves him to raise up the Christian faith with all his power and zealously advance and protect God's church everywhere, and with just law to bring peace and reconciliation to all Christian people, as diligently as he can, and in everything cherish righteousness in the sight of God and the world. For if he cherish justice in the sight of God and the world, through that he himself foremost shall prosper and his subjects similarly. And it behoves him diligently to support those who desire righteousness, and strictly punish those who desire perversity. He must severely correct wicked men with worldly punishment, and he must loathe and suppress robbers and plunderers and despoilers of the world's goods, and sternly resist all God's foes. And with justice he must be both merciful and austere: merciful to the good and stern to the evil. That is the king's right and a kingly custom, and that shall accomplish most in the nation.

And seven things befit a righteous king: first that he have a very great awe of God and second that he always cherish righteousness; and third that he be humble before God; and fourth that he be resolute against evil; and fifth that he comfort and feed God's poor; and sixth that he advance and protect the church of God, and seventh that he order correct judgement for friend and stranger alike.

The power of the King came from various sources. He was the largest single landowner in the kingdom, drawing rents and services, along with a personal following from his lands. Under Eadward III, the family of Earl Godwine and his sons together had lands that exceeded those of the King in extent. However, this concentration of wealth and power was exceptional, and Godwine's sons were Eadward's brothers-in-law, given their lands by Eadward himself. Anyway, the unity of the family was broken by the northern revolt of 1065 and the King still had more land than any one earl. With the accession of Harold, his own possessions were united to those of the crown, giving him a vast superiority over all others. The Earls were the King's representatives over large regions. The office tended to be passed on within families but was not strictly speaking hereditary. Earls held office at the King's whim and could be removed at any time, as Godwine's eldest son Swegn had found when he was dismissed and exiled for abducting an abbess. The King also had an army of lesser officials whom he appointed to carry out the functions of government. Of these, the local sheriffs were perhaps the most important, carrying the King's will into every shire. Royal control over the church was also important and although bishops and abbots were in theory freely elected, their appointments were in fact under royal control. Any government needs military forces to enforce its authority and the King had both his own household troops and the right to summon the national army for service (which stood Eadward III in good stead during the crisis of 1051). The basis of social and economic life was the law, a body of traditional custom and declared provisions. Kings both declared and created laws throughout the period and acted as the enforcers of these, with the royal court itself able to act as a primary court and court of appeal. However, Kings were not omnipotent and had to rule within the law, and with the support of the aristocracy and church. Forfeiting the support of either could make a King's position difficult, as Eadwig had found in 957 when his attempt to create a new political following independent of the old established elite led to the placing of his brother as King in Mercia and Northumbria. King Eadward's father Æþelred had also found this out in 1013 when his alienated nobility accepted the invader Swegn of Denmark as King in his stead.

The King's wife or mother played an especially important role (Stafford 1981). It would seem that the eldest surviving wife of a King took precedence over other royal wives. Hence, the King's mother would take precedence over his wife and be responsible for the upbringing of the King's children. Eadward's mother *Ymme* had been dominant for most of the period since 1002 until he disgraced her in 1043. Although, she was reinstated the following year, following his marriage in 1045, the dominant figure was his wife *Eadgyð*. This dominance arose from her family connections as the daughter of Earl Godwine. She shared her family's fall in 1051, but was restored in 1052. However, she did seem to have a secure place in her husband's affections and played an important political role of her own.

The succession of a new King often culminated in his coronation. However, some Kings are not known to have been crowned, and yet this did not impair their title as King nor their power (e.g. Eadmund II, Harold I). Eadward waited 10 months before his own coronation. No writer of the time suggested that this was in any way unusual or that he was any the less King until his coronation. Church writers were keen to stress that coronation increased a King's status and that a crowned King could not be overthrown. Such theory was of little use to Æþelred in 1013, yet it is notable that he was recalled as soon as possible after the death of Swegn, and that his son Eadmund had trouble raising an army to fight the Danes two years later in the absence of his father.

THE KING

EADWARD III (Eadward, Eadweard, Eadwerd, Edward, Eduuard, Eadwardus, Ædwardus, DB Eduuard)

Life: Eadward was born probably in 1005 (he was first mentioned in charters of that year), the son of King Æþelred and his second wife *Ymme* of Normandy. He was sent to Normandy in 1013 with the Bishop of London to join *Ymme* during the Danish invasion of Swegn, but returned to England for the negotiations over Æþelred's return in 1014. However, the Danish conquest of England by Cnut was completed on the death of Eadmund II in November 1016 and Eadward went into exile again. His mother *Ymme* married Cnut in 1017, leaving Eadward and his brother and sister in Normandy. While in exile, he built up his own retinue of followers including priests, e.g. Leofric (later Bishop of Exeter), and laymen, e.g. the Constable Rodbert FizWymarc, and his own nephew Earl Raulf. Eadward attempted to visit *Ymme* in England in 1036 after the death of Cnut but was repulsed at Southampton (his brother Ælfred landed elsewhere, and was captured and killed). *Ymme* was expelled from England and fled in 1037 to Bruges where Eadward visited her. She returned to England in 1040 with Harðacnut, her son by Cnut. Eadward returned to England in 1041 and was recognised as heir, succeeding Harðacnut on 8th June 1042. He was crowned at Winchester on 3rd April 1043. An early act of his reign was to deprive his mother of her lands and wealth, in November 1043 (relations with his mother cannot have been good since she abandoned him to marry Cnut in 1017). She was restored in 1044 but does not seem to have played much of a political role thereafter. His early years as King were dogged by the threat of attack from Magnus of Norway and he regularly gathered the fleet at Sandwich to forestall this attack. Magnus had inherited

Denmark by treaty from Harðacnut who had also been King of England. Hence, Magnus considered that he also had a claim to Eadward's crown. His successor as King of Norway, Harald Hardrada, made peace with Eadward in 1048. Eadward showed no favour to the Danes in England who had prospered under Cnut and his sons, reducing their status and gradually eliminating them from court. Neither did he show favour to Cnut's family. He expelled Cnut's niece *Gunnhild* from England in 1044 and refused to help Swegn of Denmark (Cnut's nephew) fight against Magnus of Norway in 1047 and 1048. This was in spite of the fact that Swegn's uncle by marriage was Earl Godwine, whose daughter *Eadgyð* Eadward married on 23rd January 1045. From 1049, foreign affairs were dominated by relations with the continent, rather than Scandinavia. In that year he agreed to help the Emperor Henry III by stationing his fleet off the coast of Flanders, which was at war with Henry. He also sent representatives to the reform synod at Rheims convened by the Pope. An influential member of Eadward's retinue was Rodbert, Abbot of Jumieges in Normandy, whom he made Bishop of London. In 1051, he promoted Rodbert to be Archbishop of Canterbury. Rodbert immediately came into conflict with both Eadward, over the appointment of a new Bishop of London, and with Earl Godwine, over land. A visit by Eustatius of Boulogne provided the flash point that brought conflict to a head. There was violence between Eustatius's men and the citizens of Dover. Earl Godwine refused to punish this and led a general attack on the foreign faction centred on Rodbert. Eadward insisted on the Earl carrying out his instructions to punish Dover and gathered support against Godwine. The Earl and his family were isolated and fled. They were outlawed on 24th September 1051, and *Eadgyð* was sent to the nunnery at Wherwell. As part of the events leading up to this, Rodbert may have conveyed a promise of the succession to Willelm II of Normandy, one of Eadward's nearest living relatives. Two members of Godwine's family were probably sent to Willelm as hostages to ensure their acceptance of this, as Godwine was known to favour instead his nephew Swegn of Denmark. It is not known whether *Ymme* played any role in all this but she died on 6th March 1052. Soon afterwards, Godwine and his sons began their campaign to be reinstated by attacking the south coast and winning over supporters from their lands in the south east. Although Eadward again gathered his supporters, they seemed unwilling to fight and a settlement was reached on 15th September 1052, which restored Godwine and his family. Archbishop Rodbert, two other bishops (one of whom was later recalled) and two French landowners in Herefordshire fled. Rodbert's place was filled by the Bishop of Winchester, Stigand. This was an irregular appointment, which was not recognised by the Papacy (thus he was unable to perform the functions of a metropolitan). Stigand was in his 50s and cannot have been expected to hold office for the next 18 years. However, Eadward stood by him and English bishops had to seek consecration elsewhere. Eadward allowed followers and relations of the nobility to secure appointments in the church but he listened to local feeling on occasion and also appointed his own chaplains to office. All factions would feel that the King was open to their requests. In this, Eadward may have consciously learned from the mistakes of his father Æþelred. From 1052, relations with the Welsh became strained with repeated Welsh attacks on the border. Some of these were undertaken in support of Earl Ælfgar, an opponent of Godwine's son, Harold. Godwine had died in 1053, leaving Harold as head of the family. After Ælfgar's death, Harold led a major invasion of Wales in 1063 and succeeded in having Griffin of Gwynedd killed and replaced by more acceptable rulers. Relations with Scotland were relatively good after 1054 when an English force defeated Macbeth in support of his opponent Mælcolm III. As Eadward and *Eadgyð* were childless, a dominant feature of the later years of the reign was the search for a successor. Willelm of Normandy's position as heir would have been revoked by the return of Godwine in 1052. Eadward's only paternal kinsmen (Princes Eadmund and Eadward) had been in exile since the Danish conquest and from 1054, efforts were made to secure their return from Hungary. This was hampered by the enmity between Eadward's ally Henry III of Germany and Andras I of Hungary. It was not until Henry III's death that Prince Eadward and his family did return but Eadward died shortly after on 19th April 1057. Eadward's only son Eadgar was under age (probably only 13 in January 1066) and by 1062, on the death of Ælfgar, Earl Harold was so dominant as to be a serious contender for the crown himself as the King's brother in law. His position was threatened by a revolt in October 1065 in the north against his brother Earl Tostig. It is notable that Harold negotiated a settlement that involved his brother being exiled and that Harold at some point married the sister of Earl Eadwine (Ælfgar's son), whose brother was chosen as Tostig's replacement. Eadward died on 5th January 1066 and was buried in his newly rebuilt Westminster Abbey. His portrait in the Bayeux Tapestry backs up his description in the *Vita Ædwardi* as being tall, white haired with rosy cheeks and long thin hands. This of course is how he appeared in 1066 when he was over 60, not how he appeared at his accession 24 years earlier. Eadward was canonised in 1161 after a campaign led by Osbert of Clare of Westminster Abbey.

Family: Eadward had a full brother, Ælfred (born 1013?), and full sister, *Godgyfu*. Ælfred died after being blinded when captured on the orders of Harold I while visiting England in 1036. *Godgyfu* married firstly Count Drogo of the Vexin who died in 1035, and secondly Count Eustatius of Boulogne, probably in 1036. She was dead by 1049. Her second son, Raulf, was brought over to England and was made an Earl by Eadward, but was dead by 1066.

Lands: As King, Eadward held land worth £5,310 in all shires except, Cheshire, Essex, Hertford, Lincoln and Rutland. He was the major secular landowner in Bedford, Berkshire, Cambridge, Derby, Dorset, Gloucester, Hampshire, Huntingdon, Kent, Northampton, Oxford, Somerset, Suffolk and Warwick. This represented a widely spread power base, not restricted only to the ancestral heartlands of Wessex.

Early sources: EE, VÆ, WJ, WP, B, AB, W, E, SD, O, M, VBE, VSE: Chr C (1013, 1014, 1041-1066), D (1013, 1014, 1041-1066), E (1013, 1014, 1041-1066): as a Prince, Eadward witnessed the charters S910, S911, S912 (1005), S915, S918 (1007), S923 (1011), S931 (1013), S933 (1014), S934 (1015), F69, F70, F85 (1031/35), F111 (1035/41), *S993* (1042): while in exile, he granted a charter at Ghent on 25th December 1016 (Barlow 1970 p36) and granted a charter to Mont St Michel

S1061 (1027/35): as King, he granted charters S998-S999, S1001, S1003-S1010, S1012-S1025, S1027-S1029, S1031-S1032, S1034, S1037-S1038, S1044, S1047, S1050-S1051, S1058 and issued writs H1-H2, H4-5, H7-H25, H31-H35, H38-H47, H49-H51, H54-H55, H58-H62, H64-H69, H73-H106, H109-H120, S1162: DB.

Modern references (major ones only): Freeman 1869-75, Barlow 1970, Keynes 1990.

THE KING'S FAMILY

The English royal family had been badly damaged by the Danish conquest of 1016. The only one of King Æþelred's sons to have any descendants was Eadmund II (Fig. 1), and they were in exile – at first in Russia and later Hungary. Eadward and his sister *Godgyfu* were the children of Æþelred's second marriage and had no contact with Eadmund's children. Æþelred's daughters by his first wife did provide descendants (Fig. 2), but these do not seem to have been considered for inheritance of the crown. Eadward made little effort to cultivate a faction to support him based on his wider half-family relations. Instead, he was happy to rely on his wife's family, and since 1057 the dominant faction in power was that led by her brother Earl Harold. Eadward did show favour to his sister's son, the half French Raulf, making him an Earl. However, Raulf never seems to have become a major political figure and was not promoted above Eadward's relations by marriage.

Only Eadward's wife and the family of Eadmund II are listed in this section. His in-laws and nephew are described under the Earls.

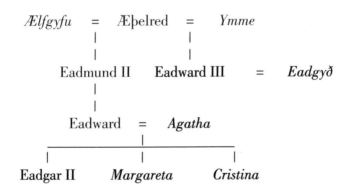

Fig. 1: Eadward III's nearest kin in 1066
Those living in 1066 are in bold

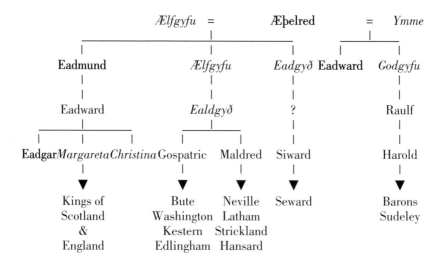

Fig. 2: Descendants of King Æþelred
Kings of England are shown in **bold**
▼ shows families descended from the individual above

AGATHA (Agathes)

Life: *Agatha* was probably the daughter of Liudolf, Margrave of West Friesland (half-brother of Emperor Henry III). She married Prince Eadward (Eadward III's nephew), perhaps in Russia in 1043. The family moved to Hungary with Andras I when he returned from exile in Russia to take over the throne in 1046. She accompanied Eadward on his return to England as heir to his uncle in 1057. *Agatha* went to Scotland with her family in 1068, which is the last that is heard of her. If Eadgar had succeeded Eadward then *Agatha* would have been an important person, the mother and guardian of a King under age. As such she would have been rival for the ambitious Queen *Eadgyð*. Could this have been a source of friction between the King and Eadgar's family? *Agatha* is an otherwise shadowy figure of whom we would dearly like to know more. She would have been in a key position to influence events as the mother of the heir presumptive to the throne but seems to have been unable to build up a power base for her son.
Early sources: W, LE, VSE: Chr D (1057, 1068).
Modern references: de Vajay 1962, Ronay 1989.

CRISTINA (Cristina, DB Cristina)

Life: *Cristina* was born in Hungary, daughter of Prince Eadward (son of Eadmund II) and *Agatha*. She came to England in 1057, fleeing to Scotland with her brother Eadgar in 1068. She later returned to England, and retired to Romsey nunnery in 1086 where she became tutor to the daughters of her sister *Margareta*: *Eadgyð*, who later married Henry I, and *Maria*, who later married Eustatius of Boulogne. She was said to be a strict tutor and determined in protecting the girls from unwanted attention.

Land: She is credited with lands worth £58 in Warwick and Gloucester. Lands that had been granted to her were later held by Radulf of Limisei (after her withdrawal to Romsey).

Early sources: E, LE: Chr D (1068), E (1086): DB.

Modern references: Ronay 1989, Wilson 1993.

EADGAR (Eadgar, DB Edgar)

Life: Eadgar was born probably in 1052 in Hungary, the son of Prince Eadward (son of Eadmund II) and *Agatha* of Friesland. He came to England with his father in 1057, and would have been heir presumptive to Eadward III after his father's death on 19 April the same year. However, he was only 13 at Eadward III's death and as there was no faction built up around his family, he was passed over in favour of the dominant lay figure Harold II. His selection as King, Eadgar II, came after the death of Harold II at the Battle of Hastings on 14th October 1066. The surviving English leadership were either unable or unwilling to mount a serious military campaign against the Normans and Eadgar abdicated in favour of Willelm of Normandy in December. He was taken to Normandy by Willelm in 1067 along with the other English leaders and returned to England in 1068. Eadgar soon fled to Scotland with his cousin Gospatric and others in May 1068 in opposition to Willelm I. The marriage of his sister to the King of Scotland guaranteed support for his ambitions. He and his supporters invaded Northumbria and he was again acclaimed as King, taking York in April 1069. However, they were defeated by Willelm, and retreated to back Scotland. He later joined the Danish fleet that had arrived in the Humber and again took York on 21st September, but was forced to retreat northwards as Willelm advanced into Yorkshire. Eadgar returned to Scotland with Mælcolm III in 1071. Willelm's invasion of Scotland in 1072 forced Eadgar into exile in Flanders but he returned in 1074. The same year, he was offered Montreuil by France, but was shipwrecked on the way there, and made peace with Willelm, abandoning his claim to the throne. He presumably spent the years after 1074 at court but was not listed as a witness on any surviving charters and does not seem to have played any role in the events of the time. Eadgar left England in 1086, complaining about his treatment by Willelm, going to Apulia, and later joined Rodbert III of Normandy in opposition to his brother Willelm II. Forced by Willelm to leave Normandy for Scotland in 1091, he made peace with Willelm and mediated peace between Willelm and Rodbert in 1093. He acted as ambassador to Mælcolm III from Willelm II but could not prevent Mælcolm's invasion of England, defeat and death (1093). In 1097, he invaded Scotland and put his nephew Eadgar (Mælcolm's son) on the throne, and in the same year, left to join the first crusade. His niece *Eadgyð* married Henri I in 1100, Eadgar thereby becoming Henri's uncle (she died in 1118). At the Battle of Tinchebrai in 1106, he joined his old friend Rodbert III of Normandy against Henri I and was captured. Eadgar was said to be still living in retirement in the country in 1125 when he was in his 70s. He was described as handsome, eloquent and generous but also indolent. His life however shows him seeking activity and honour. He only abandoned his claim to the throne when all means of opposing Willelm I had gone. He sought adventure in Apulia and on the crusade, and successfully put his nephew on the throne of Scotland. He seems to have had strong affections for people and place. His closest friend was Rodbert III, the son of his supplanter. His supposed indolence was a judgment based on his acceptance of Norman rule after 1074. He would be better described as a realist, willing to come to terms when all hope had gone. He was said to be unwilling to live in exile from England and this meant accommodating himself to the new regime. Eadgar is not known to have married. Any attempt to perpetuate his line would have had important political implications for the succession, which the new Norman dynasty could only have viewed with alarm.

Lands: Eadgar presumably surrendered his lands in 1086 when leaving for Apulia. In the Domesday survey he is recorded as the lord of only two manors, worth £10 in Hertfordshire. Two manors in Huntingdon worth £8 were held by an Eadgar in 1066 who may or may not be the Prince. He must have held more than this but there seems no way of estimating just how much land he had been given by Willelm. Three pipe rolls of Henry II mention Prince Eadgar rendering taxes in Northumberland. These are anachronistic since he could not be still living in 1166. Before 1091, he held lands also in Normandy given to him by Duke Rodbert.

Early sources: GA, WJ, WP, DB, W, SD, O, M, LE, AR, JF: Chr D (1066, 1067, 1068, 1069, 1074), E (1066, 1068, 1069, 1074, 1086, 1091, 1097, 1106): witnessed charters R318 (1091), R363 (1095): Pipe Rolls – 4 Henry II (1157-58), 5 Henry II (1158-59), 13 Henry II (1166-67).

Modern references: Freeman 1869-75, Hooper 1985, Ronay 1989, Wilson 1993.

EADGYÐ (Eadgyð, Ædgith, Ædgit, Eadgyða, DB Edid, Eddid, Eddeua)

Life: *Eadgyð* was the daughter of Earl Godwine and *Gyða*, born possibly in 1020, and educated at Wilton Abbey, being skilled in literature and needlework. She married Eadward III on 23rd January 1045 (being 15 years younger than he), was separated from Eadward and sent to a nunnery on 24th September 1051 on the disgrace of her father, but was restored on 15th September 1052. She and Eadward had no children but the marriage was said to be a happy one. *Eadgyð* was a strong character, influential at court, whose favours were worth securing through bribery. She could also be dangerous, having an opponent of her brother Tostig murdered. Her religious life was expressed by her avid collection of relics, and her rebuilding of Wilton Abbey. After the Battle of Hastings, she submitted to Willelm on his approach to Winchester (before the surrender of Eadgar II). She was treated with respect as Eadward's widow and left unmolested. However, her position was one of retirement, especially after the coronation of Willelm's wife *Mathild* in 1068. It has been suggested that the exile of Tostig caused a breach between her and her brother Harold II. In any case, her position might have been threatened by Harold's new Queen, *Ealdgyð*. She died on 18th December 1075 and was buried beside Eadward at Westminster.

Lands: *Eadgyð* had lands worth £1,667 in half the shires in England.

Early sources: VÆ, DB, GA, W, VBE, Pb, Ab, Ra, BT, HR: Chr C (1043, 1052), D (1051, 1052, 1075), E (1043, 1051, 1052, 1075): witnessed charters S1007, S1008, S1010, S1012 (1045), S1013, S1016 (1046), S1479 (1058/62), S1028 (1059), S1029, S1031 (1060), S1033 (1061), S1238 (1061/62), S1426 (1061/65), S1059 (1061/66), S1036 (1062), S1480 (1062/66), S1037a, S1038, S1040, S1041, S1042, S1043 (1065), P56 (1072): witnessed writ H112 (1053/66): mentioned in writs H79 (1049), H112 (1053/66), H69 (1061/66), H94 (1065/66): granted writs H70 (1061/66), H72 (1065/66): DB.
Modern references: Freeman 1869-75, Cutler 1973, Stafford 1997.

MARGARETA (*Margareta*)

Life: *Margareta* (known usually as Margaret) was born, in Hungary, the daughter of Prince Eadward (son of Eadmund II) and *Agatha*. She came to England with her father in 1057. Her marriage to Mælcolm III of Scotland took place after her family's flight there in 1068. Sources are divided about the motive for the marriage. Some noted that Mælcolm actively courted her and had to overcome the reluctance of Eadgar to part with his sister. The author of her life has the marriage arranged at the urging of her family. There was also a tradition that the marriage had been promoted by King Eadward. She would certainly have met Mælcolm on his visit to Eadward in 1059. It was undoubtedly politically useful in giving Eadgar a brother in law able to provide military and financial help. However, the marriage seems to have been close and Mælcolm devoted to her. *Margareta* was described as very devout, sober and prudent, avoiding excess. She zealously observed religious fasts and was always generous to the poor. Although affable, she could be severe towards wayward behaviour. She was also intelligent, with a good memory and eloquent. Her acts as Queen in Scotland included the building of a new church at Dunfermline and setting up a ferry service for pilgrims across the Forth to St Andrews (modern Queensferry). *Margareta* strove to reform the practices of the church in Scotland to bring them more into line with orthodox western practice, asking Archbishop Lanfranc for advice. She fostered the import of costly goods and dress for the court, and was anxious to increase the status and ceremonial of the King. Her English origins were not forgotten. English captives were often held in Scotland, taken in raids on Northumbria. *Margareta* took pains to find and ransom them. Her first five children were named after her English royal ancestors rather than Mælcolm's. She died after a long illness on 16 November 1093 (three days after her husband and eldest son had been killed invading Northumbria) and was buried at Dunfermline. *Margareta* was canonised in 1249.
Early sources: VM, O, M, AL: Chr D (1068, 1074), E (1068, 1093): see also sources for Eadgar.
Modern references: Freeman 1869-75 (Vol. 4), Anderson 1922, Ronay 1989, Wilson 1993.

THE EARLS AND THEIR KINSMEN

Earls stood at the summit of lay society under the King and royal family. An earldom was an office, rather than a hereditary title, and the earls were the King's chief representatives in the regions of the kingdom. The title of earl was Danish in origin and the office was known before 1016 as alderman. The aldermen were originally officers responsible for one shire within Wessex. After the unification of England under Ælfred, Eadward I and Æþelstan, aldermen were given groups of shires to control. The laws of Cnut laid down the heriot (death duties) of an earl as 8 horses (4 saddled), 4 helmets, 4 mailcoats, 4 swords, 8 spears, 8 shields and £25 (2 Cnut c.71). This was double the fighting equipment of a King's thane and four times the amount of money. We have evidence for their activities and duties in four spheres; military, judicial, financial and in providing the King with advice. To reward them in their work, they received a third of the profits of justice from the courts, as well as income from the boroughs (Loyn 1984) and were given manors by the King to support their position as earl (Clarke 1994: 18-21). Indeed, the earls were the greatest lay landowners in the kingdom after the King, and far wealthier than even the most important thanes. However, the earl was still a royal official and could be dismissed by the King at any time. This might be for actual transgressions of the law, e.g. the dismissal and exile of Earl Swegn in 1047, or because of political intrigue, e.g. the dismissals of Earl Ælfgar in 1055 and 1058. Although holders of the office were appointed by the King, and there was no automatic inheritance of the position, there was a strong tendency for Kings to appoint earls from a restricted group of families.

Military Leadership

At a time when the military forces of the kingdom were needed not just for defence but also for enforcing the King's rule (what we may loosely call police work), the earl played a key role in defending the kingdom and upholding the King's authority by leading the military forces of the district under his control. Armies are mostly portrayed in the Anglo-Saxon Chronicle as led by either the King or by alderman/earl. The earls thus acted in defence of their own district, e.g. Bryhtnoð at Maldon in 991. They could also lead armies in a national defensive capacity. The 'Peterborough' Chronicle explicitly mentions that the King gave command of a naval force in 992 jointly to two aldermen and two bishops. Earls could also lead their forces in support of the King's authority against malcontents at home. During the crisis of 1051, King Eadward ordered Earl Godwine to punish Dover for its acts against Count Eustatius of Boulogne. When Godwine, refused to do this, the King then had the other earls gather their forces against Godwine. Earls would also act in an offensive capacity, attacking lands outside England. The successful invasion of Wales in 1063 was led by Earls Harold and Tostig. Likewise, the defeat of Macbeth of Scotland in 1054 was led by Earl Siward. While a system of delegating military leadership could provide for powerful local responses to emergencies, it could be a form of weakness. Cnut conquered England largely through defeating or allying separately with various of Æþelred's aldermen (Abels 1988: 180-181). It may be that the earls also had other military functions such as supervising the repair of fortifications.

Judicial Supervision

A major function of the earl was to preside, alongside the bishop, over the twice yearly shire and thrice yearly borough courts. This was laid down in law by the statute of 3 Eadgar I c5 (Andover, 959/63). The actual sitting of courts was more complex than the law suggests, e.g. it was possible to summon joint meetings of several hundreds or even shires for particular purposes (Fleming 1998). Given that earls might be responsible for many shires, they (and the bishops) must have delegated this work to others on occasion, but there is no doubt that both did actually sit presiding over these courts (Robertson 1939: 150-153, Loyn 1984: 139). Surviving writs of the period, sent to the shire court, are addressed to the earl alongside the bishop and usually the sheriff. Their task was not to pass judgement on offenders or decide the outcome of civil suits but to ensure that the workings of the court ran in accordance with law and local custom. However, the earl would also have had what we would now call police functions, being responsible for ensuring that justice was done and the laws observed (Faith 1997: 116-117). In practice, much of the day-to-day work in the localities would be done by the sheriff, a royal official in each shire.

Financial Supervision

It has been suggested that aldermen and earls played an important role in supervising the minting of coins (Loyn 1974: 125). There is no direct evidence for this but such supervision would have worked best when die cutting for new coins was decentralised to regional centres. Any supervision may have been simply a reflection of the earl's duty to uphold the law. Laws against the minting of false coins were very strict. Further financial duties may have stemmed from the receipts of borough customs and court fines. If the earls received a third of these, then it may be that this was most easily achieved by having them be responsible for collecting the whole, and passing on two thirds to the King's treasury. There is no evidence however that they were also responsible for collecting the land tax (the geld).

Providing Advice

Earls were prominent witnesses to charters, a fact which betrays their presence at court at times when solemn business was conducted, during *gemotas* (moots). As senior members of a moot, they were key advisers of the King in the major affairs of state (Oleson 1955). However, specific mention of the advice given by earls is rare in the sources of the time. In 1047, the Anglo-Saxon Chronicle noted the different advice given by Earls Godwine and Leofric about whether to give military help to Swegn of Denmark.

Earls would naturally attract their own personal following of thanes and have a network of clients in their district bound to them by personal ties of lordship. Their role at court as royal advisers and military assistants meant that they connected their local areas with national affairs, acting as a bridge between the crown and the locality. This may have been important in the crisis of 1051/2. The earls had responded to the King's summons in 1051 by bringing forces to enforce his commands against the recalcitrant Earl Godwine. The following year, the now banished Godwine had landed with his troops hoping to force his return from exile. One version of the Chronicle mentions that military support for the King in opposing Godwine's return was slow in coming. Moreover, when the support did arrive there was great reluctance to engage in fighting on the grounds that Englishmen fighting each other would weaken the kingdom's defences against foreign invasion. Given that one cause of the conflict was the dispute between Godwine and the King's foreign supporters, this seems like the support of the earls and political society in the localities swinging against the foreign faction, in opposition to the King. The earls would have been subjected to a conflict of interests between their role as King's officials and as regional magnates (Stafford 1989: 157).

The number of earls and the boundaries of earldoms fluctuated through time. There had been four at the accession of Eadward III in 1042 but for most of his reign there were five or six earls at any one time. By January 1066 this number had risen to seven, drawn from three families. Eadward had made his nephew, Raulf (son the Count of the Vexin in France) an earl earlier in the reign. Raulf's son was under age in 1066 and would presumably expect promotion when he reached adulthood. From 1057 to 1065, four out the five earldoms had been held by Harold and his brothers; an unprecedented accumulation of power. However, the northern revolt against Tostig broke this dominance and by January 1066, Harold's family only held three out of seven earldoms.

THE EARLS

EADWINE (Eadwine, Edwine, DB Eduin)
Earl of Mercia (area included Chester, Lincoln, Shrewsbury, Stafford, Worcester)
Life: Eadwine was the son of Earl Ælfgar and elder brother of Morcere. He succeeded his father as Earl, who last appeared in documents in 1062. Eadwine is perhaps the most enigmatic figure of the period. After the death of Harold, he was the one English leader who could have rallied support against the Normans, but failed to do so until it was far too late. Unfortunately, we do not have enough evidence to decide if he was a self-serving traitor, politically inept or simply too young and inexperienced. The

evidence of the chroniclers (mostly written long after the events) is too contradictory. A complicating factor might have been the existence of his newly born nephew, Harold's son, as a potential claimant to the throne. During 1066, he and his brother beat off an attack in the Humber by the exiled Tostig but were themselves beaten by Harald of Norway at Fulford outside York on 20th September. He was the senior surviving earl after the Battle of Hastings and promised his support for Eadgar II. However, he was either unwilling or unable to bring together forces to further the campaign and surrendered along with Eadgar in December. He was taken by Willelm to Normandy in 1067, with all the English leaders. During 1068, Willelm built a castle at Warwick, which effectively forestalled any potential military forces advancing south from Mercia. Eadwine's loyalty must have been suspect as Normans were appointed as earls in Shrewsbury and Chester, part of Eadwine's heartland, possibly in 1068 but certainly by 1069. This would make more difficult Eadwine's continuation of his father's alliance with the Welsh. Eadwine remained at court though and took no part in the northern campaign against Willelm under Eadgar, or in the Mercian revolt of 1069-70, from which he stood to benefit if it were successful. It was not until 1071 that he left court, with Morcere, shortly after which he was killed by his own men. A later tradition reported that Eadwine was hoping for a marriage to one of Willelm's daughters. Given that another earl, Walðeof, did marry Willelm's niece, this was not an impossible expectation.

Land: in Shrewsbury, Chester, York, Warwick, Oxford, Worcester, Lincoln, Derby, Hereford and Stafford worth £690, with £710 ascribed to his father in Stafford, Middlesex, Essex, Lincoln, Cambridge, Buckingham, Huntingdon, Derby, Oxford, Northampton, Suffolk, Warwick and Nottingham, and £20 ascribed to his grandfather in Shrewsbury and Warwick.

Early sources: WP: Chr C (1066), D (1065, 1066, 1071), E (1065, 1066, 1071): witnessed charters B181, B286 (1068), B138 (1069): addressed in writs H96 (1065/6), B292 (1066/8): DB.

Modern references: Williams 1995.

GYRÐ (Gyrð, Gyrth, Gerð, DB Guerd, Guert)

Earl of East Anglia (Norfolk, Suffolk and Oxford)

Life: the son of Earl Godwine, and brother of Earls Harold and Leofwine, he went into exile with his father and brother Tostig in Bruges in 1051, returning to England in 1052. Gyrð was appointed when still young (probably succeeding Ælfgar in East Anglia and then Raulf in Oxford) in 1057. Tostig took him to Rome in 1061. He may have been at Stamford Bridge with Harold on 25th September 1066 and was killed at Hastings on 14th October 1066.

Land: in Norfolk, Sussex, Bedford, Suffolk, Cambridge, Berkshire, Southampton and Essex worth £250.

Early sources: VÆ: Chr C (1051), D (1051, 1066), E (1066): witnessed charters S1027, S1028 (1058), S1031 (1060), S1033, S1034 (1061), S1037a, S1038 (1065): addressed in writs H23, H24, H25 (East Anglia 1065/66), H95, H103, H104 (Oxford 1065/66): DB.

Modern references: Harmer 1952, Barlow 1962 (VÆ).

HAROLD (Harold, Harald, Haroldus, Haraldus, DB Harold, Herold, Herald)

Earl of Wessex (area included Berkshire, Devon, Dorset, Somerset, Southampton, also Hereford after 1057)

Life: Harold was born c1022, the second son of Earl Godwine and was brother-in-law to Eadward III. He headed the list of thanes witnessing charters in 1045 and may have been a Steward of the King's household. However, promotion came quickly and he was appointed Earl of East Anglia (included Cambridge, Huntingdon, Essex) in the same year. In 1049, his elder brother Swegn returned to England hoping to be reinstated in his earldom, from which he had been dismissed. It is noteworthy that Harold opposed this, breaking the unity of the family. He was expelled with his father on 24th September 1051 and fled to Ireland. As part of the family's campaign to be reinstated, he attacked the coasts of Somerset and Devon before winning back his earldom with his father on 15th September 1052. Godwine died on 15th April 1053 and Harold succeeded his father as Earl of Wessex. He defended Hereford against Welsh attack in 1055, after the defeat of Earl Raulf. He then had his priest Leofgar appointed as Bishop of Hereford the following year, but Leofgar's death fighting the Welsh forced Harold to mediate a settlement. A visit to Flanders was recorded in late 1056 and he may have gone on to Germany to accompany Prince Eadward (Eadward III's nephew) on his return to England early in 1057, also visiting Rome at the same time. By the end of 1057, Harold was the senior earl as well as the King's brother in law, and had three of his brothers as earls alongside him. The only earl not of Harold's family at this time was Ælfgar who had been exiled in 1055 before returning the same year with the military help of the Welsh. Ælfgar was again exiled, and again returned, in 1058. Probably after Ælfgar's death, Harold invaded Wales with his brother Tostig and toppled Ælfgar's ally Griffin of Gwynedd in 1063. In 1064, he was captured by the Count of Ponthieu while on a mission to the continent and had to be 'freed' by Willelm II of Normandy. While with Willelm, he accompanied the Normans on a military campaign to Brittany and swore an oath to help Willelm in his bid to succeed Eadward in England. During the revolt against his brother Tostig by the northern thanes, he negotiated a settlement with them that exiled Tostig and broke the unity of the family. At Eadward III's death on 5th January 1066, Harold was the senior earl and King's brother in law, the most experienced and successful layman in the country, by far the wealthiest man in England, and of proven loyalty to the Eadward. At the age of 44, he could claim the status of an elder statesman. His oath to Willelm was set aside, as was the claim of the King's great nephew Eadgar who was just 13 years old, when Eadward nominated Harold on his deathbed as his successor. Despite having a long-term common law marriage to a lady named *Eadgyð*, he married *Ealdgyð*, the sister of Eadwine and Morcere, and Griffin's widow. On 25th September 1066, he defeated a Norwegian invasion at Stamford Bridge, killing Harald Hardrada and his own brother Tostig. He then headed south to deal with the Norman invasion and was himself killed at the Battle of Hastings on 14th October. His body was buried at Waltham Abbey, which he had patronised. In the

Vita Ædwardi Regis, commissioned by his sister *Eadgyð*, Harold was described as a good soldier, open and affable but also cautious and wily, capable of following long-term plans. He was said to be physically strong but mild of temper, able to take criticism but not readily forthcoming about his plans. Although keen for success, this was not at any price and he was said to value happiness as much as being successful. Harold quickly became the subject of legend, with the growth of a tradition that he escaped the battle of Hastings to die at a great age as a hermit in Chester!

Land: worth £2,850 in 28 shires, with £720 ascribed to his father in 4 shires. Harold was by far the wealthiest man in England under the King. Most of his lands lay in Wessex (including the family's ancestral shire of Sussex) and the shires immediately north of the Thames, together with Hereford. In most of this area, the King was also a major landholder. One exception is Essex, where Harold was dominant, and it was here that Harold patronised Waltham Abbey.

Early sources: VÆ, B, E, W, D, WJ, WP, O, VH, Wþ, Chr C (1049, 1051, 1052, 1053, 1055, 1056, 1065, 1066), D (1051, 1052, 1053, 1063, 1065, 1066), E (1049, 1051, 1052, 1053, 1063, 1065, 1066): witnessed will S1531 (1043/45): witnessed charters S1003 (1044), S1007, S1012 (1045 as thane), S1008 (1045 as earl), S1015 (1046), S1017 (1048), S1018, S1019 (1049), S1025 (1049/50), S1020, S1021, S1022 (1050), S1023 (1052), S1060 (1057/60), S1027, S1028 (1059), S1029, S1031 (1060), S1033, S1034 (1061), S1059 (1061/66), S1037a, S1038 (1065), H62: addressed in writs H13 (1045/47), H14 (1046/47), H84 (1052/53), H1 (1053/58), H35 (1053/61), H5, H39, H40, H41, H85, H98, H112 (1053/66), H49 (1057/60), H2, H42 (1058/66), H120 (1060/66), H50, H64, H65 (1061), H66, H68, H69, H70 (1061/66), H115 (1062): as King, sent writ H71: DB.

Modern references: Freeman 1869-75, Harmer 1952, Barlow 1962 (VÆ), Hart 1975, Walker 1997.

LEOFWINE (Leofwine, Levvine, Leofwinus, DB Leuuin)

Earl in the South East (area included Essex, Middlesex, Hertford, Kent? and Surrey?)

Life: he was the son of Earl Godwine and brother of Earls Harold and Gyrð. Leofwine shared exile with Harold in Ireland in 1051-52, and with Harold attacked Somerset and Devon as part of their campaign to be reinstated. He was probably appointed earl in 1057, when he would have received part of the earldom vacated by Ælfgar (moving from East Anglia to Mercia in succession to his father). He was killed with Harold II at Hastings on 14th October 1066.

Land: in Kent, Middlesex, Sussex, Devon, Essex, Buckingham, Surrey, Dorset and Somerset worth £290.

Early sources: VÆ: Chr C (1051), D (1051, 1066), E (1066): witnessed charters S1027, S1028 (1059), S1033 (1061), S1037a, S1038 (1065): addressed in writs H86, H88, H89 (Middlesex), H90, H91 (Hertford), H76 (Kent), H92, H93 (Surrey).

Modern references: Harmer 1952, Barlow 1962 (VÆ).

MORCERE (Morkere, DB Morcar)

Earl of York (area included Nottingham as well as York)

Life: Morcere was the son of Earl Ælfgar and brother of Earl Eadwine. He was chosen by the rebels against Tostig in October 1065 to be their new earl, which was later confirmed by the King. Morcere was probably very young and later tradition stated that he might have been appointed jointly with his elder brother (Eadwine held important estates in Yorkshire). He and Eadwine were defending the north against possible invasion in 1066, and were beaten by Harald of Norway at Fulford on 20th September. They both agreed to support Eadgar II in October 1066 after Harold II's death. However, they made no military move against Willelm. Their defeat at Fulford may have weakened them, or their support for Eadgar II was less than fulsome. It may also have been merely their youthful inexperience. They surrendered along with Eadgar in December, and were taken to Normandy by Willelm I in 1067. Willelm forestalled possible revolt in the north by establishing a castle at York in 1068. Eadgar had fled to Scotland that summer and might have been expecting Morcere's support in an invasion through Northumbria. However, Morcere is not known to have joined any of the outbreaks against Norman rule until he joined the rebels against Willelm at Ely in 1071, where he was captured. He was kept in prison, in the custody of Roger de Beaumont, until Willelm freed him at his death in September 1087. However, he was immediately rearrested by Willelm II in October the same year. It is not known when he died.

Land: in York, Lincoln, Shrewsbury, Nottingham, Leicester, Northampton, Chester, Stafford, Hereford and Derby worth £970, and may have held £150 ascribed to his predecessor in York and Nottingham.

Early sources: Chr C (1065, 1066), D (1065, 1066, 1071), E (1065, 1066, 1071): witnessed charters B181 (1068), B138 (1069), a charter of Roger de Beaumont (Lewis 1991): DB.

Modern references: Lewis 1991, Williams 1995.

Oswulf

Earl of Northumbria (covering Northumberland and Durham)

Life: Oswulf belonged to the powerful family of earls whose power base lay north of the River Tees. He was the son of the last member of the family to hold office, Eadwulf, who had been dispossessed in 1041. Little is known of him and he only fleetingly held the stage. The northern revolt against Earl Tostig gave the opportunity for him to recover the family's office at the end of October 1065. Willelm I appointed Copsig, a follower of the now dead Tostig, as earl in February 1067, but he was killed by Oswulf on 12th March. Oswulf then held the earldom unchallenged until he himself was killed while arresting a robber in the autumn of the same year.

Land: he would have held lands in Northumbria, which was not covered in the Domesday Book.

Early sources: SD.

Modern references: Freeman 1869-75, Kapelle 1979, Higham 1993.

Walþeof (Walþeof, Wælþeof, Waldþeof, DB Waltef, Walteif, Wallef, Walleu)

Earl of Mid Anglia (area included Huntingdon and probably Northampton)

Life: Walþeof was the son of Earl Siward of York and cousin of Oswulf of Northumbria. His father had held an earldom in south east Mercia as well as York. Both earldoms were given to his successor Tostig, and Walþeof was probably appointed to this southern earldom on Tostig's exile in October 1065, although it has also been suggested that he was appointed by Harold during 1066. Walþeof continued to hold office under Willelm I. Willelm perhaps showed his distrust of Walþeof by building castles at Cambridge and Huntingdon in 1068 as part of his attempt to prevent rebellion. The following year, Walþeof joined the claimant against Willelm, Eadgar II in the north. He submitted to Willelm again in 1070 on the failure of the revolt. It was probably after this that he married Willelm's niece, Judith. He recovered his father's earldom at York in 1072 and was the senior surviving native-born Englishman at court (and the last to hold high office for a very long time). He was regarded favourably by the midland abbeys of Ely, Crowland and Thorney but was in dispute over land with Peterborough. In the north, he was closely allied to the Bishop of Durham, Walcher. In 1074, he prosecuted an old family feud by killing the two brothers Þorbrand and Gamal. He became involved in the plot against Willelm by Earls Raulf of East Anglia and Roger of Shrewsbury in 1075. Although, he did not raise arms against Willelm, he confessed his involvement and threw himself on the King's mercy. However, Willelm was an unforgiving man and Walþeof was executed on 31st May 1076 at Winchester, and buried at Crowland.

Land: in Rutland, Middlesex, York, Northampton, Essex, Leicester, Derby, Bedford and Huntingdon worth £140, with £240 ascribed to his father in York and Derby.

Early sources: SD, O, Cw: Chr D (1067, 1069, 1070 1075, 1076), E (1069, 1070 1075, 1076): witnessed charters S1033 (1061), B159 (1067), B181, B286 (1068): granted a charter at Durham 1072/75: mentioned in S1481: DB.

Modern references: Freeman 1869-75 (Vol. 4), Scott 1952, Williams 1995, Walker 1997.

THE EARLS' KINSMEN

This section covers the wives, widows, siblings, children and important cousins of the earls. It thus includes people who might in their turn expect an earl's appointment. The widows of earls held land in their own right and could be powerful figures, while under-age sons or cousins might expect an earl's appointment in the future.

ÆLFGYFU (DB *Alveva, Ælueua*)

Life: the wife of Earl Ælfgar (died 1062?), she might have been the daughter of Morcere and *Ealdgyð*, the niece of Alderman Ælfhelm. Ælfhelm was prominent under King Æþelred and his daughter (also *Ælfgyfu*) was the wife of Cnut. Morcere was killed by Alderman Eadric in 1015 and his estates seized by Æþelred.

Lands: in Suffolk, Hertford, Leicester and Northampton worth £66.

Early sources: DB.

Modern references: Sawyer 1979, Williams 1995.

ÆLFGYFU (*Ælfgyva?*, DB *Alueue*)

Life: the sister of Earl Harold. There was a tradition at Canterbury that Harold had promised to send his sister to Willelm of Normandy for him to arrange her marriage to a Norman noble, in return for Harold marrying one of Willelm's daughters. This was supposedly arranged when Harold was in Normandy shortly before the death of Eadward III. When Willelm asked, after the death of Eadward, for the agreement to be implemented, he was told that the sister in question was now dead. It has been argued that *Ælfgyfu* was the figure portrayed under that name on the Bayeux Tapestry, but this is by no means certain.

Lands: she had £1 worth of land at Waldridge in Buckinghamshire and probably more elsewhere.

Early sources: DB, E.

Modern references: Freeman 1869-75 (Vol. 3), McNulty 1980, Walker 1997.

ÆLFWIG

brother of Godwine, see under Abbots and Abbesses.

EADGYÐ

sister of Harold, see under The King and His Kinsmen.

EADGYÐ SWANNESHALS

Life: the common-law wife of Harold, she may have met him while he was Earl of East Anglia, their marriage being part of his attempt to consolidate his interests in the area as an outsider. Their children were old enough to be militarily active in 1068. According to a 13th century account, she may have given lands to the monastery of St Benet in Norfolk, although her name is given as '*Edgyve*' (*Eadgyfu*). This has led to her being confused with the wealthy landowner *Eadgyfu* the Fair (Walker 1997). There was a tradition that she identified Harold's body on the battlefield at Hastings.

Lands: the Domesday Book assigns her some houses in Canterbury but we cannot identify her as owning any lands. An *Eadgyð* had £19 worth of lands in Suffolk and may be her.

Early sources: JO, VH: DB.

Modern references: Freeman 1869-75 (Vol. 3), Walker 1997.

EADGYÐ (DB *Eddied*)

Life: the sister of former Earl Odda (1051-56).

Lands: owned the estate of Upleadon in Herefordshire worth £14.

Early sources: DB.

Modern references: Thorn et al 1983 (Domesday Book Vol. 17).

EALDGYÐ (DB *Aldgid*)

Life: she was the sister of Earls Eadwine and Morcere and married Harold, possibly after his accession. They had a son, also called Harold. She had before this been the wife of King Griffin of Gwynedd, who had been killed as a result of Harold's invasion of Wales in 1063. After the Battle of Hastings, she was taken to Chester by her brothers and nothing further is heard about her after this. It has been suggested that she retired to France where she might have made a donation to the monastery of La-Chaise-Dieu in the Auvergne.

Lands: she can be identified as the *Ealdgyð* who held £3 worth of land at Binley in Warwickshire, and presumably held land elsewhere in addition to this.

Early sources: W, O, DB.

Modern references: Freeman 1869-75 (Vol. 3), Williams 1995, Walker 1997.

GODGYFU (DB *Godeua, Godeva*)

Life: the wife of Earl Leofric (died 1057), *Godgyfu* died 1057/66 but was still listed as a landowner in the Domesday Book. Along with her husband she had helped to found Coventry Abbey.

Lands: in Nottingham, Warwick, Shrewsbury, Stafford, Worcester and Leicester worth £110.

Early sources: W, Pb, Hm: DB.

Modern references: Fleming 1991.

GODWINE (DB Goduin)

Life: the son of Harold. As the only son holding land, he was presumably Harold's eldest son by his common law wife, *Eadgyð*. He fled to Ireland after the Norman Conquest but returned to attack the south west with his brothers in 1068 and 1069.

Lands: in Somerset worth £5, possibly with other lands elsewhere among the numerous other Godwines of the time.

Early sources: W, O, WJ: Chr D (1068, 1069): DB.

Modern references: Clarke 1994.

GOSPATRIC (Gospatric, Gaius Patricius)

Life: Gospatric was the son of Maldred (brother of King Duncan of Scotland) and grandson of Earl Uhtred of Northumbria, and hence cousin of Earls Oswulf and Walðeof, as well as Eadgar II. He might have been associated with Earl Tostig, accompanying him on his journey to Rome in 1061. He was appointed Earl of Northumbria by Willelm in 1067 but supported Eadgar in 1068 and in the northern campaigns of 1069-70. After his submission to Willelm, he was reappointed Earl of Northumbria in 1070 but was dismissed in 1072 and fled to Scotland. He was granted lands by King Mælcolm and was the ancestor of the Earls of Dunbar.

Early sources: VÆ, SD: Chr D (1068, 1069).

Modern references: Freeman 1869-75 (Vol. 4), Gibbs & Doubleday 1916, Anderson 1990, Walker 1997.

GUNNHILD (DB *Gunnild*)

Life: *Gunnhild* was the sister of Earl Harold. Little is known of her other than she retired to St Omer in Flanders, where she died in 1087.
Lands: in Somerset worth £22.
Early sources: DB.
Modern references: Clarke 1994, Walker 1997.

GYÐA (*Gyða*, DB *Gida*)

Life: The wife of Earl Godwine (died 1053) and mother of Earls Harold, Leofwine and Gyrð, she was the sister of Ulf (father of King Swegn of Denmark). She was in Exeter leading its revolt against Willelm in 1068, and left England on its collapse, going into exile in Flanders. *Gyða* offered money to Willelm for her son Harold's body after the Battle of Hastings; an offer that was refused.
Lands: in Devon, Wilton, Sussex, Somerset, Southampton, Dorset, Surrey, Gloucester and Cornwall worth £590, and may have held also some of the £720 ascribed to her husband.
Early sources: W, O: Chr C (1052), D (1051, 1052, 1068): DB.
Modern references: Freeman 1869-75, Fleming 1991, Williams 1995, Walker 1997.

GYÐA (DB *Gueth, Gethe, Godæ*)

Life: *Gyða* was the wife of Earl Raulf (died 1057). She might have been connected with the family of Burgred and his sons, Eadwine, Ulf and Wulfsige, important landowners in south east Mercia and benefactors of Peterborough Abbey.
Lands: in Northampton and Buckingham worth £55.
Early sources: DB.
Modern references: Williams 1989a.

HACON

Life: the son of Harold's elder brother Swegn. He had been a hostage in Normandy since 1051 but was freed by Willelm to accompany Harold back to England after the latter's visit to Normandy in 1064.
Early sources: WP, E.
Modern references: Freeman 1869-75, Walker 1997.

HAROLD (DB Harold, Herald)

Life: the son of Earl Raulf and great nephew of Eadward III through his sister *Godgyfu*, he was still underage in 1066, in the wardship of Queen *Eadgyð*. Harold was granted additional lands by Willelm and became the ancestor of the later Barons Sudeley.
Lands: in Warwick, Middlesex and Worcester worth £30, with £85 ascribed to his father in Gloucester (Sudeley £40), Leicester, Berkshire, Warwick and Northampton.
Early sources: DB.
Modern references: White 1953, Williams 1989a.

TOSTIG

see under Exiles Abroad

WULFNOÐ

see under Exiles abroad

CHILDREN OF HAROLD II

Information about the children of Harold is contained in few early sources (Chr D 1068, 1069; W and some Scandinavian sources, see Freeman 1869-75, Vol. 4, Walker 1997). Harold seems to have had four sons by his common law wife *Eadgyð*: Godwine, Eadmund, Magnus, and Ulf. The three elder sons had fled to Dublin after William's defeat of their mother, *Gyða*, at Exeter. They returned to attack Bristol and Somerset in 1068, and Devon and Cornwall in 1069. The local inhabitants were unwilling to risk William's wrath by giving them their support and they went back to Ireland on each occasion after being defeated by local forces. They later attempted to gain Danish support against William, but without success. The youngest son, Ulf was held captive by Willelm to be freed in 1087, being knighted by Willelm's son Duke Robert. Harold and *Eadgyð* also had two daughters: *Gunnhild* and *Gyða*. *Gunnhild* was at Wilton Abbey after the Conquest, leaving in 1093 to marry the Breton Alan of Richmond (Alan the Red). After his death, she married his brother, also called Alan (Alan the Black). *Gyða* ended up in Denmark after the Conquest and was married to Vladimir of Smolensk in Russia (and is the only one of Harold's children to have known descendants). She died on 7 May 1107. By his legal wife, *Ealdgyð*, Harold had a son, also called Harold, who was later to be with Magnus of Norway on his invasion of western Britain in 1098. It has been suggested that Ulf was the son of *Ealdgyð*, but if so then he and Harold must have been twins.

The names of Harold's children give a clue to Harold's own political and personal stance. The eldest was named after his father, the youngest after his Danish maternal uncle, and one of his daughters was named after his sister (who shared the name with both King Cnut's daughter and niece). The other daughter was named after his mother. His third son seems to have been named after Magnus of Norway, the long-standing enemy of Swegn of Denmark. So far, Harold's affiliations seem to be both strongly familial and Scandinavian. However, his second son was given the name of the King who did more than most to resist the Danish conquest of 50 years earlier. This may reflect a long-standing affinity between Harold's family and the family of King Æþelred and his first wife. Æþelred's eldest son, Æþelstan (Eadmund II's elder brother) restored to Harold's father, Godwine, an estate once held by the family in Sussex. It may be that Eadmund was named after St Eadmund of East Anglia, but in this case the anti-Danish sentiment would be just as strong. This seemingly marked anti-Danish bias would have been in marked contrast to the later political affiliations of his father.

FAMILY TREES
(Earls are given in **bold**)

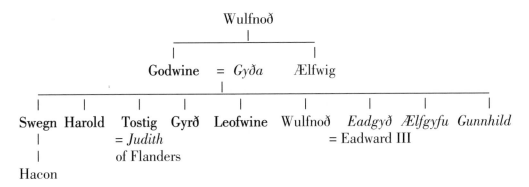

Fig. 3: The family of Godwine of Wessex

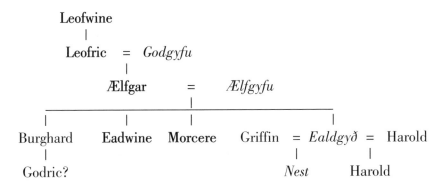

Fig. 4: The family of Leofric of Mercia

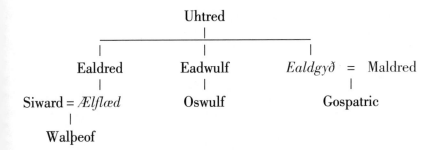

Fig. 5: The family of the Earls of Bamburgh

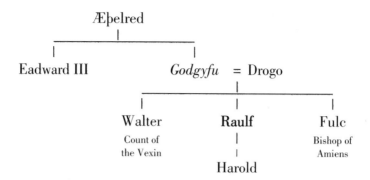

Fig. 6: The family of *Godgyfu*, Eadward's sister

THE BISHOPS

Bishops had an important dual role, as officials of the King but also as leaders of the church. The English church in 1066 was integrated with the state in a way that was unacceptable to the Papal reformers in power at Rome since 1049. Their ideal of freeing the church from secular control would not have made sense in Eadward's England. Bishops had both clerical and secular responsibilities. Their clerical duties were: 1. to administer baptism and confirmation, 2. to ordain priests and consecrate churches, 3. to instruct the clergy and laity in a Christian way of life and duties, 4. to administer canon law and legislate for their diocese (Barlow 1979). Although there were no national synods of the church at this time, there could be local diocesan synods attended by the priests of the diocese, and presided over by the bishop. The main assistants to the bishop in administering the diocese were the archdeacons, although there is no evidence that they were as yet assigned to geographical areas (Godfrey 1962).

Bishops had an important part to play in secular affairs. At local level, they were co-presidents of the shire courts along with the earls; ecclesiastical and secular law being considered together in the same judicial forum. As major landowners, they contributed to the taxation and defence of the kingdom, and formed part of the network of political alliances through patronage and lordship, as well as being subject to the same political rivalries as their secular colleagues. At national level, Kings relied on them for advice. It was Archbishop Sigeric whom the Anglo-Saxon Chronicle credited with advising Æþelred to make the first payment of geld to the Danes in 991. Bishops could also be useful for diplomatic work. For instance, Bishop Ealdred of Worcester was sent by Eadward to Germany in 1054 to try to arrange the return of his half nephew and potential heir, Prince Eadward, the son of Eadmund II. Bishops could even be found leading military forces. Bishop Leofgar of Hereford was killed in 1056 leading an army against an incursion into Hereford by the Welsh.

After the monastic reform under Eadgar I (959-75), many bishops were monks and had links with monasteries outside their sees. However, the trend since Cnut's time had been for the promotion of the King's chaplains as bishops and the episcopate in 1066 was only partly monastic. Some cathedral chapters were themselves monastic, with the bishop acting as abbot (Canterbury, Sherborne, Winchester, Worcester). Others had colleges of secular canons, some with a communal rule (Durham, Exeter, Hereford?, London, Wells, York). Appointment as bishop was by a pragmatic mixture of royal appointment and election by the chapter, which sometimes came into conflict. The cathedral chapter at Canterbury had elected a relative of Earl Godwine, Ælfric, as their new archbishop in 1050 but the King insisted on his own favourite, Rodbert of Jumieges, being appointed. However, even the King's appointment to office could not guarantee a bishopric. Archbishop Rodbert refused to consecrate the King's choice, Spearhafoc, as Bishop of London in 1051 because of Papal opposition to the appointment. It is noteworthy that Spearhafoc did occupy the see nevertheless. The appointment of a new bishop would be announced in writs sent to the shire courts. An example of such a writ is that for Wulfstan of Worcester in 1062 (Harmer 1989: 410-411):

> *Eadƿard kyninȝ ȝret Harold eorl ⁊ Ælfȝar eorl ⁊ ealle þa ðeȝnas on Ƿiȝeraceastrescire ⁊ on Gleaƿeceastrescire ⁊ on Ƿærinȝƿicscire freondlice. ⁊ ic cyðe eoƿ þæt ic habbe ȝeunnen Ƿulstane munuce þæt bisceoprice into Ƿihȝeraceastre mid sace ⁊ mid socne, toll ⁊ team, binnan burhȝe ⁊ butan, ƿa full ⁊ ƿa forð ƿa hit æniȝ his foreȝenȝa fyrmæst on handa stode on eallan þinȝan for þan ic nylle ȝeþafian þæt him æniȝ mann æt æniȝan þinȝan misbeode, oððe him of hande drahȝe æniȝ þæra ðinȝa þe he mid rihte into his biseoprice ahȝe to habbanne.*
>
> King Edward sends friendly greetings to Earl Harold and Earl Ælfgar, and all the thanes in Worcestershire, Gloucestershire and Warwickshire. And I inform you that I have granted to the monk Wulfstan the bishopric of Worcester with sake and soke, toll and team, within borough and without, as fully and as completely in all things as ever any of his predecessors held it. Therefore I will not allow anyone in any matter to do him wrong, or to deprive him of any of the things that he ought lawfully to have for his bishopric.

An innovation of Eadward's was the promotion of the head of the King's chancery, Reinbald, to the status of bishop but without an appointment to a bishopric (Harmer 1989: 213).

ÆGELMÆR (Ægelmær, Ægelmærus, DB Ailmar, Almar, Almer, Ælmar, Ælmer)
Bishop of Elmham

Life: Ægelmær was the brother of Archbishop Stigand, whom he succeeded as Bishop of Elmham in 1047. He was married, a relatively common practice at the time for priests but one which the Papal reformers after 1049 were trying to outlaw. He was deposed in 1070 as part of Willelm's purge in the aftermath of the English revolts in 1069-70. It is not known when he died, but he bequeathed part of his property to Bury St Edmund's Abbey. Norfolk seems to have been the home shire of Stigand and Ægelmær, and Stigand retained estates and influence there after his departure for Winchester. By having his brother succeed him as bishop he would have protected his power base and made Elmham into a dependant see with Ægelmær on the spot to protect the family's interests.

Lands: in Norfolk and Suffolk worth £220.
Early sources: witnessed charters S1028 (1059), B286 (1068): addressed in writs H15 (1051), H16 (1051/52), H17 (1052), H18, H19, H20, H21, H22 (1052/57), H60 (1053/57), H23, H24, H25 (1065/66), B37, B38, B36, B35, B41 (1066/70): bequeathal of land S1499: DB.
Modern references: Harmer 1952, Oleson 1955, Barlow 1979.

ÆGELRIC (Ægelric, Aielricus, DB Alric)

Bishop of Selsey

Life: Ægelric was a monk of Canterbury Cathedral, and so presumably a follower of Archbishop Stigand. He was appointed Bishop of Selsey in 1058 and was deposed on 23rd May 1070 after the depositions of Stigand and his brother, and imprisoned at Marlborough. His deposition was controversial at the time (being ineffectually condemned by the Pope) and was probably carried out because of his link with Stigand rather than for any personal shortcomings. It has also been suggested that he was the monk being put forward as the new Archbishop of Canterbury with the support of Earl Godwine in 1051, his association with the Godwine family being grounds for his deposition. The source for this (VÆ) gives the monk's name as Ælric (representing Ælfric?) rather than a form that would represent an original Ægelric. However, given that the two names could be easily confused this is not an impossible identification. Sometime between 1072 and 1076, his advice was sought in a land dispute involving Canterbury Cathedral. He was then described as an old man and very learned in the law. He also helped the English monk Eadmær when writing his life of St Dunstan after 1066.
Lands: in Sussex worth £160.
Early sources: VD: Chr D, E, F (1058): witnessed charters S1033 (1061), B286 (1068), B254 (1069): DB.
Modern references: Oleson 1955, Barlow 1979, Williams 1995, Walker 1997.

ÆGELRIC (Ægelric)

former Bishop of Durham

Life: Ægelric was a monk of Peterborough who was consecrated bishop on 11th January 1042. It was later said that he had been appointed Archbishop of York but deprived of office and given Durham instead. However, this is probably a false tradition based on a misreading of an entry in the Anglo-Saxon Chronicle. He retired from Durham to Peterborough Abbey in 1056 and was succeeded by his brother Ægelwine. During the revolts of 1069-70, he was arrested by Willelm I and imprisoned at Westminster. However, he excommunicated the rebels under Hereward for their attack on Peterborough in 1071. Ægelwine died on 15th October 1072.
Early sources: SD: Chr D (1042, 1056, 1070, 1072), E (1069, 1071, 1072): witnessed charter S1011 (1045).
Modern references: Freeman 1869-75 (Vol. 4), Barlow 1979, Williams 1995.

ÆGELWINE (Ægelwine, DB Aluuin)

Bishop of Durham

Life: Ægelwine was a monk of Peterborough and succeeded his brother Ægelric as Bishop of Durham in 1056. The appointment of monks from outside Durham was not popular in the cathedral chapter and Ægelwine owed his appointment to Earl Tostig's influence. When Mælcolm III of Scotland visited England in 1059, Ægelwine acted as escort to bring him to Gloucester. He was also sent to negotiate with Mælcolm in 1068 by Willelm I. Ægelwine had submitted to Willelm earlier in the year after the building of the castle at York forestalled a possible northern revolt. During the northern campaign of Eadgar II in 1069-70, Ægelwine took shelter with the body of St Cuþberht on Lindisfarne. He does not seem to have been associated with the opposition to Willelm I, providing accommodation for the new Norman Earl Rodbert in 1069. However, his brother Ægelric was arrested by Willelm in 1070 and although Ægelwine had returned to Durham (25th March 1070), he soon fled to Scotland. He afterwards joined the rebels in Ely, where he was captured in 1071. He had been deposed in early 1071 and after his capture was imprisoned at Abingdon. It is possible that the Pope protested to Willelm about his imprisonment and his deposition. He was probably a devout man who took his clerical role seriously. There was a story about him refusing to become involved in lay judicial matters in sentencing criminals, even when the crime was against his own church. This would be in accord with the prevailing reforms initiated by the Papacy.

Early sources: SD, GG: Chr D (1056, 1070, 1071), E (1070, 1071): DB.

Modern references: Freeman 1869-75 (Vol. 4), Harmer 1952, Oleson 1955, Barlow 1979, Williams 1995.

EALDRED (Ealdred, Aldred, Aldret, Aldredus, DB Eldred, Ældred)

Archbishop of York

Life: Ealdred was a monk of Winchester who later became Abbot of Tavistock (1027). He was appointed Bishop of Worcester in 1046 (possibly after acting as assistant bishop to his predecessor), and acquired a considerable ecclesiastical empire. He administered Winchcombe Abbey from 1053 to 1054, the sees of Ramsbury from 1055 to 1058, and Hereford from 1056 to 1060. He may also have administered Gloucester Abbey in the 1050s, having a kinsman of his appointed its abbot in 1058, and Abbot Ægelwig of Evesham was appointed at Ealdred's request. Although made Archbishop of York at Christmas 1060 he held on to Worcester until 1062. As Bishop of Worcester, he led an unsuccessful military expedition against the Welsh in Hereford in 1049. In 1051, he was sent to intercept Earl Harold fleeing to Ireland, but probably by design failed to stop him. He was a widely travelled man and diplomat who visited Rome for a Papal council in 1050, brought Godwine's son Earl Swegn back from exile to arrange his reinstatement in the same year, acted as ambassador to Germany from 1054 to 1055 (trying to arrange the return of Prince Eadward), helped mediate a peace between Eadward and Griffin of Gwynedd in 1056, visited Hungary and Jerusalem in 1058, and received the archbishop's pallium at Rome in 1061 (on condition that he surrender the see of Worcester, although he kept hold of some manors within the see and ensured the appointment of Wulfstan as a pliable subordinate). The lack of Papal recognition for Stigand's position as Archbishop of Canterbury meant that Ealdred was the only Archbishop able to perform metropolitan functions in England. Accordingly, it may have been he who crowned Harold II and he certainly crowned Willelm I. After Harold's death he was one of those supporting Eadgar II but submitted along with Eadgar and the other English leaders. The submission of the northern nobility in 1068 may have been brought about by Ealdred's mediation. He died on 11th September 1069 opposing the revolt against Willelm I while the Danes, allied with Eadgar II, were moving on York. His later reputation was as a good administrator, and a vigorous and courageous man. He remained loyal to Willelm I but apparently did not hesitate to publicly rebuke perceived Norman irregularities, such as high taxation or land seizures. As Archbishop, he continued the building programme at Beverley Minster and improved and strengthened the chapters of canons at York, Beverley, Ripon and Southwell. Ealdred also held diocesan synods to improve the standards of the clergy in York. He commissioned literary works from the Flemish monk Folcard of St Bertin's and may well have been responsible for the compilation of the D version of the Anglo-Saxon Chronicle while at Worcester.

Lands: in York, Gloucester, Warwick, Worcester, Hampshire, Devon and Leicester worth £350.

Early sources: Chr C (1050, 1054, 1056), D (1046, 1050, 1051, 1053, 1054, 1056, 1058, 1060, 1061, 1066,1068, 1069), E (1050, 1060, 1066): witnessed charters S1014 (1046), S1025 (1049/50), S1020 (1050), S1021 (1050), S1022 (1050), S1028 (1059), S1029 (1060), S1031 (1060), S1033 (1061), B295 (1066/69), B216, B345 (1067), B181, B286 (1068), B254 (1069): addressed in writs H49 (1057/60), H7 (1060/65), H102, H118, H119, H120 (1062/66): issued charters S1405 (1058), S1406 (1046/53), S1407 (1053/56), S1408 (1052/56), S1409 (1051/55): granted lands in S1027 (1059): DB.

Modern references: Robertson 1939, Harmer 1952, Oleson 1955, Hart 1975, Barlow 1979, Williams 1995, Cubbin 1996, King 1996.

GISA (Gisa, Giso, Gyso, DB Giso)

Bishop of Wells

Life: Gisa was one of Eadward's chaplains and came from Liege in Lotharingia, Germany. He was appointed Bishop of Wells in 1060 and consecrated in Rome on 15 April 1061. While in Rome, he obtained a Papal privilege protecting the possessions of the see from outside interference. It has been suggested that his appointment was arranged by, or rewarded with, a gift of land to Queen *Eadgyð*. He was certainly favoured by *Eadgyð* with land after his appointment. Gisa took over the wealthy abbey of Bath as his episcopal seat in 1085, and died in 1088. He was much concerned to strengthen the finances of the see and reformed and strengthened the organisation of the cathedral chapter. He may also have been the author of a section on early Wells history (his so-called autobiography) incorporated in a late 12th century account of the bishopric.

Lands: in Somerset worth £200.

Early sources: GW: Chr D, E (1060): witnessed charters B181 (1068), B254, B138 (1069), B68 (1072): addressed in writs H64 (1060, appointment), H65 (1061), H66, H68, H69, H70 (1061/66), H6 (1061/82), H71 (1066), H72 (1066/75), B11 (1067), B160 (1078/83), H67: DB.

Modern references: Robertson 1939, Harmer 1952, Oleson 1955, Barlow 1979, Keynes 1997.

HEREMAN (Hereman, Heremann, Herimann, Herimannus, Heremannus, DB Hermann, Herman)

Bishop of Ramsbury & Sherborne

Life: Hereman came originally from Flanders, and was one of Eadward III's chaplains. He either came to England with Eadward in 1041, or had already come over before this. He was appointed to Ramsbury in 1045. It has been suggested that, like Gisa, his appointment was arranged by, or rewarded with, a gift of land to Queen *Eadgyð*. After failing in his attempt to transfer the see to Malmesbury Abbey, he resigned and retired to become a monk at St Bertin's in Flanders in 1055. Hereman was clearly trusted by the King, visiting Rome in 1050 for a Papal council and was persuaded to come back to England in 1058 by Queen *Eadgyð* with the offer of combining the sees of Ramsbury and Sherborne. Goscelin of St Bertin's, the monastic writer of saints' lives, came to England to join Hereman's household. Hereman planned the transfer of the joint see to Salisbury after 1075 and died in 1078.

Lands: in Wiltshire, Dorset, Berkshire and Oxford worth £450 with £65 held also by the cathedral monks of Sherborne in Dorset.

Early sources: Chr C (1045, 1050), D, E (1045, 1050, 1078): witnessed charters S982 (1040/42), S993 (1042), S999 (1043), S1007, S1008, S1012 (1045), S1013, S1014, S1016, S1018 (1046), S1019 (1049), S1025 (1049/50), S1020, S1021, S1022, S1023 (1050), S1028 (1059), S1031 (1060), S1033, S1034 (1061), S1037a, S1038 (1065), B181, B286 (1068), B254, B138 (1069), B68 (1072): addressed in writs H3 (1045/48), H5 (1053/66), H2 (1058/66), B223 (1067), B1, B2 (1066/78): DB.

Modern references: Robertson 1939, Harmer 1952, Oleson 1955, Barlow 1979, Keynes 1997.

LEOFRIC (Leofric, Leofricus, Liuricus, DB Leuric, Liuric)

Bishop of Exeter

Life: Leofric was a close associate of the King, being one of Eadward's chaplains who had come with him to England in 1041. He seems to have been an Englishman who was educated abroad, in Lotharingia. Eadward appointed him Bishop of Crediton and Cornwall in 1046, and he moved the see to Exeter in 1050 reorganising the cathedral chapter. The new cathedral was inaugurated on 29th June 1050. He was later reputed to have been Chancellor of Eadward, although here is no contemporary evidence for this. Leofric died on 10th February 1072. He built up a collection of manuscripts, which he left to the cathedral, and this included an important collection of Old English poetry known today as the Exeter Book.

Lands: in Devon, Cornwall, Berkshire and Oxford worth £250.
Early sources: Lf: Chr C, D, E (1046): witnessed charters: S993 (1042), S999 (1043), S1018 (1046), S1019 (1049), S1025 (1049/50), S1020, S1022 (1050), S1023 (1052), S1027 (1059), S1031 (1060), S1033, S1034 (1061), S1037a, S1038 (1065), B181, B286 (1068), B254, B138 (1069): granted land in S1003 (1044): S1021 (1050, the moving of the see): DB.
Modern references: Harmer 1952, Oleson 1955, Barlow 1979.

LEOFWINE (Leofwine, DB Leuuin)

Bishop of Lichfield

Life: Leofwine was a monk who became Abbot of Coventry (c.1043) before being appointed Bishop of Lichfield in 1053. As Coventry was founded by Earl Leofric, he may have been a follower of the Earl and his family, possibly, given his name, even a kinsman. His father might well have been the Wulfwine who held £13 of land in Worcestershire in 1066. Leofwine is known to have married and had a child. He resigned in 1070, probably in advance of dismissal because of this, and retired to Coventry.
Lands: in Stafford, Derby, Shropshire, Warwick and Worcester worth £70.
Early sources: Chr C, D (1053): addressed in writs H46 (1043/53), H96 (1065/66), B292 (1066/68): DB.
Modern references: Robertson 1939, Harmer 1952, Oleson 1955, Barlow 1979, Thorn et al 1982.

SIWARD (Siward, Sihward)

Bishop of Rochester

Life: Siward was another of the monk-bishops common in England. He had been Abbot of Chertsey (c.1042) before being appointed Bishop of Rochester in 1058. He escaped deposition in 1070 but the see of Rochester was poor and subordinate to Canterbury. The cathedral chapter Rochester had to be reformed after his death in 1075.
Lands: in Kent worth £100.
Early sources: Chr D, E, F (1058): witnessed charters S1044 (1042/44), S1012, S1010 (1045), S1471 (1045), S1033 (1061), B68 (1072).
Modern references: Oleson 1955, Barlow 1979.

STIGAND (Stigand, Stigant, Stigandus, DB Stigand)

Archbishop of Canterbury and Bishop of Winchester

Life: Stigand had been one of Cnut's chaplains and was entrusted with the minster at Assandun in 1020, built to commemorate the battle which gave Cnut mastery over England. He had a long career, prospering in its early stages from the patronage of Queen *Ymme*. Stigand was appointed Bishop of Elmham on 3rd April 1043 but was soon deposed for being a supporter of *Ymme*. Both *Ymme* and Stigand were restored in the following year. From 1047, he was Bishop of Winchester and after the flight of

Rodbert of Jumieges in 1052 was appointed to hold also the Archbishopric of Canterbury. His appointment (a neutral choice perhaps, acceptable to both the King and Earl Godwine) while his predecessor was still living was condemned by the Papacy. He was only recognised as metropolitan by Benedict X in 1058. However, Benedict represented an anti-reform faction at Rome and his grant of the pallium to Stigand was annulled in January 1059, after his deposition. Stigand was a career minded cleric rather than a spiritual man and was careful to keep his position by accommodating the powers in charge. It is no surprise that he was the first of the English leadership to submit to Willelm of Normandy after the Battle of Hastings. Willelm I supported his position as metropolitan but Stigand was deposed after the English revolts of 1069-70, along with his brother Ægelmær (Bishop of Elmham) on 11th April 1070. By this time he must have been an old man, well into his 70s, or even 80s, and he died on 22nd February 1072. His wealth was matched by his ecclesiastical power. As well as being Archbishop of Canterbury and Bishop of Winchester, the see of Rochester was traditionally subordinate to Canterbury, he consecrated a monk of Canterbury as Bishop of Selsey and his brother was Bishop of Elmham. In addition, he had some sort of authority over the abbeys of Ely, St Alban's and St Augustine's by the 1060s. In contrast to his later reputation, he was well remembered by both Winchester and the Abbeys already mentioned.

Lands: in Kent, Sussex, Surrey, Middlesex and Oxford worth £805 for Canterbury, with £400 being held by the cathedral monks in Kent, Essex and Suffolk. He also held lands worth £830 for Winchester in Hampshire, Wiltshire, Somerset, Surrey, Berkshire, Oxford, Buckingham, Cambridge and Hertford with £340 held by the cathedral monks in Hampshire. Stigand personally held lands worth £450 in Suffolk, Dorset, Hertford, Hampshire, Gloucester, Kent, Cambridge, Bedford, Oxford and Norfolk. This made him the second wealthiest of Eadward's subjects behind Earl Harold of Wessex with £2,085.

Early sources: Chr C (1043, 1047, 1053), D (1047, 1058, 1066), E (1043, 1044, 1047, 1052, 1058, 1061), F (1020): witnessed charters S979 (1029/32), S967, S969 (1033), S975 (1035), S993 (1042), S1014, S1018 (1046), S1019 (1049), S1025 (1049/50), S1020, S1021, S1022 (1050), S1023 (1052), S1027, S1028 (1059), S1029, S1031 (1060), S1033, S1034 (1061), S1037a, S1038 (1065), B181, B286 (1068), B254, B138 (1069), writ H62: addressed in writs H13, H14 (1044/47), H111 (1052/53), H33, H34 (1052/66), H60 (1053/57), H35 (1053/61), H39, H40, H41, H85, H112 (1053/66), H92 (1057/66), H42, H93 (1058/66), B291 (1066/70): issued charters S1402, S1403 (1047/52): DB.

Modern references: Robertson 1939, Harmer 1952, Oleson 1955, Hart 1975, Barlow 1979, Brooks 1984, Smith 1994, Williams 1995.

WALTER (Walter, Waltere, Walterius, DB Walterius, Walterus)

Bishop of Hereford

Life: Walter was a Lotharingian chaplain of Queen *Eadgyð* and was appointed Bishop of Hereford in 1060. He was consecrated at Rome on 15 April 1061. Walter was one of the English leaders who submitted to Willelm at Berkhampstead in 1066. He was reputedly killed while attempting to rape a seamstress in 1079!

Lands: in Hereford, Shropshire, Gloucester, Essex, Worcester and Hampshire worth £270.

Early sources: Chr D, E (1060): witnessed charter B68 (1072): addressed in writ H50 (1061, appointment): DB.

Modern references: Harmer 1952, Oleson 1955, Barlow 1979, Keynes 1997.

WILLELM (Willelm, Willem, Wyllelm, Willhelm, Willelmus, DB Wiħ.)

Bishop of London

Life: Willelm was a chaplain of Eadward's from Normandy. He was given the see of London in September 1051 after the Norman Archbishop of Canterbury, Rodbert of Jumieges, refused to consecrate the King's original nominee. His association with Rodbert caused him to flee England on 14 September 1052 when Rodbert's opponent Earl Godwine secured his return from exile. However, he was not really part of Rodbert's faction and was soon recalled and resumed his office. Willelm is known to have been at Bergues in Flanders in May 1060, but the purpose of the visit is unknown. After the Norman Conquest, he was one of the officials who supervised the redemption by the English of their lands in East Anglia. He died in 1075.

Lands: in Essex, Middlesex and Hertford worth £320, with £170 also held by the cathedral canons in Essex, Middlesex, Hertford and Surrey.

Early sources: Chr C (1052), D (1051, 1052), E (1051): witnessed charters S1025 (1049/50), S1020, S1022 (1050), S1028 (1059), S1034 (1061), S1037a, S1038 (1065), B181, B286 (1068), B254, B138, B232 (1069), B14, B15, B16 (1070/71), B68 (1072): addressed in writs H86, H88, H89, H105 (1051/66), H84 (1052/53), H98 (1053/66), H43 (1058/66), H106 (1065/66), B180 (1067), B107, B299, B300, (1066/75): DB.

Modern references: Harmer 1952, Oleson 1955, Barlow 1979, Williams 1995.

WULFSTAN (Wulfstan, Wulstan, Wlstan, DB Wlstan, Vlstan)

Bishop of Worcester

Life: The son of Æþelstan and *Wulfgyfu*, Wulfstan was born c1009 at Itchington in Warwickshire, and educated at Evesham and Peterborough before becoming priest of Hawkesbury and then a monk at Worcester under Bishop Brihtheah (1033/38). He rose through various offices to become provost before his appointment as bishop in 1062 and he was consecrated on 8 September 1062 by Archbishop Ealdred. His rival for the office was Abbot Ægelwig of Evesham. Wulfstan was a close friend of Harold II and went north with Harold to secure the allegiance of the northern nobility early in 1066. After Hastings, he was in London and submitted to Willelm along with Eadgar II at Berkhampstead. He was given the administration of Lichfield after the resignation of Leofwine from 1070 to 1072. After 1075, he was the only surviving native-born Englishman of the rank of bishop or earl. Wulfstan survived into the reign of Willelm II, dying on 20th January 1095. He organised the defence of the King's interests in Mercia during the revolt of 1075 and also organised the defence of Worcester in 1088 in support of Willelm II. He sponsored the writing of a chronicle at Worcester and the diocese of Worcester became a noted centre for the preservation of the English literary tradition. He began the rebuilding of the cathedral in the new Romanesque style, although deploring the ornate fashion that was at odds with traditional architecture. This accorded with his dislike of worldly show and vanity. He was devout and respected for his character and abilities as a diocesan bishop, being a good administrator and disciplinarian as well as tirelessly travelling and preaching throughout the diocese. A priory at Westbury was established and he was a stern enforcer of priestly celibacy. He took care to defend and increase the authority of the see, successfully excluding the sheriff from the episcopal liberty of Oswaldslaw. Although Wulfstan accepted the position of Worcester as part of Canterbury province, the traditional ties with York were kept. He acted as an assistant to the Archbishop of York in 1073 and 1081 at the consecration of bishops in the north. Wulfstan organised a confraternity of abbeys in 1077, which included Worcester, Gloucester, Winchcombe, Evesham, Pershore, Bath, Chertsey and perhaps Malmesbury. A friend of his later years was the Bishop of Hereford Rodbert Losinga. He was canonised in 1203.

Lands: in Worcester and Warwick worth £210, with £230 held also by the cathedral monks in Gloucester, Worcester and Warwick.

Early sources: VW: Chr E (1088): witnessed charter B68 (1072): addressed in writs H115 (1062, appointment), H116, H117 (1062), H102 (1062/66), B223 (1067), B295 (1066/69), B152 (1070), B132 (1066/77), B133 (1072/77), B136 (1066/87), B137 (1080/87): DB.

Modern references: Lamb 1933, Harmer 1952, Oleson 1955, Barlow 1979, Mason 1990, Williams 1995.

WULFWIG (Wulfwi, Wlfwinus, DB Vluui)

Bishop of Dorchester

Life: Little is known about Wulfwig who was appointed in 1053 in place of the Norman Ulf who had fled abroad with Rodbert of Jumieges in 1052. His two brothers Ælfwine and Godric were King's priests, as was Wulfwig. He died in 1067. A forged charter of the 12th century listed Wulfwig as Chancellor, which may or may not reflect genuine tradition. He was certainly authorised to draw up his own charter for a land grant to St Denis (H55), but then so were Bishops Ealdred and Gisa (Keynes 1988).

Lands: in Oxford, Huntingdon, Buckingham, Lincoln, Cambridge and Bedford worth £360.

Early sources: Chr C (1053), D (1067): witnessed charters S1028 (1059), S1029, S1031 (1060), B216 (1067), B159 (1067): addressed in writs H55 (1053/57), H90, H91 (1053/66), H102 (1062/66), H94, H95, H103, H104 (1065/66): recorded agreement S1478 (1053/55): DB.

Modern references: Harmer 1952, Oleson 1955, Barlow 1979.

bishop	appointed	English	foreign	from	priest	monk	monastery
Stigand	1043	x	–		x	–	
Hereman	1045	–	x	Flanders	x	–	
Ealdred	1046	x	–		–	x	Winchester
Leofric	1046	x	–		x	–	
Ægelmær	1047	x	–		x	–	
Willelm	1051	–	x	Normandy	x	–	
Leofwine	1053	x	–		–	x	Coventry
Wulfwig	1053	x	–		x	–	
Ægelwine	1056	x	–		–	x	Peterborough
Ægelric	1058	x	–		–	x	Canterbury
Siward	1058	x	–		–	x	Chertsey
Gisa	1061	–	x	Lotharingia	x	–	
Walter	1061	–	x	Lotharingia	x	–	
Wulfstan	1062	x	–		–	x	Worcester

Table 1: The Bishops in 1066

Abbots and Abbesses

Monasteries had been founded in the early decades of Christianity in England. They followed varying rules and by the 9th century the status of many would have been regarded as uncertain by the standards of later times. The reign of Eadgar I (959-75) saw a major monastic reformation. This was an English adaptation of the continental Cluniac revitalisation of monastic life, through the inspiration of Fleury and Ghent. It led to the founding of many new monasteries and the reorganisation of existing ones on stricter lines. No more than one major monastery occurred in any one shire although some shires also had a major nunnery, and a monastic cathedral. The wealthiest abbeys were concentrated in four areas: East Anglia and the Fens, the Thames Valley, central Wessex, and the see of Worcester. By the 11th century the monastic hierarchy consisted of the abbot and his deputy the provost (the post-Conquest prior), several deans and other officers. Some cathedrals adopted collegiate rules and some became monastic chapters headed by the bishop. Communal religious life in regions without monasteries was often provided for by secular minsters (colleges of canons); especially in the sees of Lichfield and Selsey. In Eadward's reign, the patronising of secular minsters seems to have become more popular than making gifts to monasteries. The most famous instance was that of Waltham by Harold. However, the monasteries were generally wealthier than the minsters and have left abundant documentary materials for the historian, and so tend to dominate our picture of religious life at the time.

Abbots were supposed to be elected by the monastic community with the permit and advice of the King. This allowed a variety of practice to be followed from free election to royal appointment, depending on circumstances. In abbeys founded by an important layman his family might keep a strong influence in the choice of abbot. Consecration by a bishop completed the process of appointment. Just as bishops sometimes held more than one see, so some abbots likewise held more than one abbey, often appointing deputies. Such an arrangement may have had advantages. The great monastic pluralist Abbot Leofric was a member of the family of the Earls of Mercia, and so had access to powerful lay patrons, which could have benefited the monasteries in his care. A 12th century copy of a writ of 1055-66 records the appointment of an abbot (Wulfric) to Ely (H47 in Harmer 1989: 224):

> *Eadpard kynȝ ȝret ealle mine biscopes ꝺ mine eorlas ꝺ mine scirȝereuan ꝺ ealle mine þeȝenas on þam sciran þer þa lande to liȝȝað into Ely freondlice, ꝺ ic kyþe eop þæt ic habbe ȝeunnen Plfrice þæt abbodrice in Hely, on eallan þinȝan, binnan burȝan ꝺ butan, toll ꝺ*

*team, ꝺ infanꝤenþeof, fyhtpite ꝺ fyrdpite, hamsocne ꝺ Ꝥryþbryce, sitte
his man þer þar he sitte, pyrce þæt he pyrce, ꝺ nelle ic Ꝥeþauian þat
æniꝤ man of handa ateo nan þæra þinꝤa þæs ic him Ꝥeunnen hæbbe.
God eop Ꝥehælde.*

King Edward sends friendly greetings to all my bishops and my earls
and my sheriffs and all my thanes in the shires in which the lands
belonging to Ely are situated. And I inform you that I have granted to
Wulfric the abbacy at Ely with everything within the boroughs and
without, toll and team, and infangentheof, fihtwite and fyrdwite,
hamsocn and grithbreach, wherever his man may dwell, whatever he
may do. And I will not permit anyone to take from him any of the
things that I have granted him. God keep you.

Abbots were often at court and took their place among the *witan*, being found as
signatories to royal charters. As a general rule, the wealthier the abbey, the more
important was its abbot, being found more often at court (Oleson 1955). In time, an
abbot might gain promotion to a bishopric, e.g. Leofwine of Coventry who was made
Bishop of Lichfield in 1053.

By 1066, the abbeys were major cultural institutions and were the main schools of the
kingdom. It was the monastic reformation that had led to the creation of a relatively
standard written form of English for official use (Gneuss 1972). It was also the abbeys
and monastic cathedrals that kept up the tradition of historical writing in the Anglo-
Saxon Chronicle. The wealthiest abbeys (with lands as valued in Domesday Book for
1066) were Ely £730, Glastonbury £670, Abingdon £430, St Augustine's £420,
Ramsey £390, Westminster £390, St Edmund's £320, New Minster £280 and St
Alban's £260 with the nunneries of Wilton £310 and Shaftesbury £280. It is known
that Glastonbury and Ramsey obtained Papal privileges giving them independence of
episcopal or lay control, and that the Abbot of St Augustine's was granted the right to
wear a bishop's mitre. Ely was outside the control of the diocesan Bishop of
Dorchester.

Most of the information about the abbots and abbesses below is contained in
Knowles, D, Brooke, C N L & London, V C 1972 *The Heads of Religious Houses
England and Wales 940-1216*. Other references are given where appropriate. The
heads of nunneries are less well known than the monasteries and there is no
information for 1066 on the following: Amesbury, Chatteris, Wherwell, Winchester.

ÆGELNOÐ (Ægelnað, Ægelnoðus)

Abbot of Glastonbury

Life: Ægelnoð had been a monk at Glastonbury before becoming Abbot in 1053. He
was taken to Normandy by Willelm along with other leaders of the English in 1067.
Archbishop Lanfranc had him deposed on 28th May 1078 and he retired to
Canterbury Cathedral.

Lands: in Somerset, Wiltshire, Dorset, Berkshire, Gloucester, Devon and Hampshire worth £670.

Early sources: EG, Chr D (1053, 1067), TÆ: witnessed charters S1027 (1059), S1031 (1060), S1037a, S1038 (1065), B68 (1072): issued a charter in Glastonbury cartulary (1079): addressed in writs H6, H66, H68 (1061/66), H64 (1060/61), H65 (1061), H71 (1066), B286 (1068), B287 (1066/82), H67.

Modern references: Robertson 1939, Harmer 1952, Oleson 1955.

ÆGELSIGE (DB Elsi)

Abbot of St Augustine's

Life: Ægelsige was a monk of Winchester, appointed to St Augustine's through the influence of Archbishop Stigand in 1061. He was administering Ramsey by 1066 during the illness of Abbot Ælfwine, and was involved against Willelm I in 1068/70. He may have sought refuge in Denmark. His successor was appointed in 1070. Ægelnoð later returned to England and was appointed Abbot of Ramsey in 1080, dying in 1087.

Lands: in Kent worth £420.

Early sources: TE, Th: Chr E (1061): witnessed charters S1479 (1058/62), S1041 (1065), B181 (1068): DB.

Modern references: Freeman 1869-75 (Vol. 4), Robertson 1939, Oleson 1955, Williams 1995.

ÆGELWIG (Ægelwig, DB Eluui, Aluuin, Æluuin)

Abbot of Evesham

Life: he was provost of Evesham and had been chosen by Abbot Mannig to succeed him in 1058 when he became too ill to continue as abbot. Ægelwig was connected with Archbishop Ealdred and may have administered the diocese of Worcester in Ealdred's absence, e.g. in 1054. He was a candidate for the bishopric of Worcester when Ealdred was forced to step down to concentrate on York in 1062 but lost out to Wulfstan. He administered Winchcombe Abbey 1067-69 and 1075-77, was given the power of a justice within Mercia in 1068, gave shelter to refugees from the north in 1070, and helped to command the military forces against Earl Roger of Hereford in the revolt of 1075. Ægelwig died on 16th February 1077. He was learned in the law, loyal to Willelm but gave protection to English victims of Norman rule.

Lands: in Worcester, Gloucester and Warwick worth £140.

Early sources: Æ: Chr D, E (1078): witnessed charters S1057 (1044/59), S1405 (1058), S1426 (1061/65), S1041, S1043 (1065), B345 (1067), B181 (1068), Wilkins (1075): addressed in writ B131 (1072): DB.

Modern references: Darlington 1933, Oleson 1955, Barlow 1970, Williams 1995, King 1996.

ÆGELWINE? (Ægelwine, Ageluine)

Abbot of Cranborne?

Life: references to him may be to Ægelwig of Evesham or Ælfwine of Ramsey but if not then Cranborne was the only vacant abbacy to which he could be assigned.
Lands: in Dorset, Wiltshire and Devon worth £40.
Early sources: witnessed charter S1034 (1061), S1480 (1062/66), S1043 (1065), B68 (1072).

ÆLFGYFU

Abbess of Wilton

Life: She was abbess from 1065 to 1067, and was succeeded by her sister *Godgyfu*.
Lands: in Wiltshire, Sussex, Dorset and Hampshire worth £310.
Early sources: Wi.
Modern references: *Analecta Bollandiana* 56.

ÆLFGYFU?

Abbess of Barking

Life: she may have died on 11th May (year unknown but possibly as late as 1122).
Lands: in Essex, Bedford, Buckingham, Middlesex and Surrey worth £170.
Early sources: mentioned in writ B10 (1066/87).

ÆLFGYFU?

Abbess of Romsey

Life: Ælfgyfu was the name of the later of two abbesses known from Romsey in the 11th century. It is not at all certain that she would have been abbess in 1066.
Lands: in Wiltshire and Hampshire worth £120.
Early sources: H.

ÆLFWIG

Abbot of New Minster

Life: Ælfwig was said to be the brother of Earl Godwine and was killed at Hastings on 14th October 1066. As Ælfwig was appointed in 1063 and Godwine died in 1053, he must have been a much younger brother or only promoted in his old age.
Lands: in Hampshire, Wiltshire, Sussex, Berkshire and Surrey worth £280.
Early sources: H.
Modern references: Freeman 1869-75.

ÆLFWINE (Ælwine, Ælfwinus, DB Aluuin)

Abbot of Ramsey

Life: Ælfwine was the son of Eadberht (a priest in Essex). He became provost of Ramsey before being appointed abbot in 1043. He was sent to the Council of Rheims in 1049, and also went abroad to Germany and Denmark on the King's business. It was probably while he was in Rome in 1062/65 that he obtained Papal privileges for Ramsey. He was the senior English abbot by 1066, although by then he was in ill health and the external affairs of Ramsey were entrusted to Abbot Ægelsige of St Augustine's. After the Norman Conquest, his advice was sought in a legal dispute between St Edmund's and the Bishop of Elmham. He died in 1081.

Land: in Huntingdon, Cambridge, Bedford, Norfolk, Hertford, Suffolk, Northampton and Lincoln worth £390.

Early sources: Ra: Chr D, E (1049): witnessed charters S999 (1043), S1004, S1006 (1044), S1007, S1008, S1010, S1012 (1045), S1015 (1046), S1017 (1048), S1019 (1049), S1021 (1050), S1023 (1052), S1025 (1054), S1027 (1059), B68 (1072): addressed in writs H59 (1050/52), H60 (1053/57), B181 (1068), H61, H62.

Modern references: Harmer 1952, Hart 1975, Oleson 1955, Williams 1995.

ÆLFWINE

Abbot of Buckfast

Life: He was abbot by 1045/46 and was still in office during 1066.

Lands: in Devon worth £15.

Early sources: witnessed charter S1474 (1046), DB.

Modern references: Robertson 1939, Oleson 1955.

ÆLFWOLD (DB Aluuold, Aluold)

Abbot of St Benet's

Life: Abbot since 1064, Ælfwold was put in charge of the defences of East Anglia by Harold II in 1066, and was outlawed for a while by Willelm I (fleeing to Denmark) but came back to resume his office. He died on 14th November 1089.

Lands: in Norfolk worth £80.

Early sources: SB: DB.

Modern references: Williams 1995.

ÆSWARD

Abbot of Abbotsbury

Life: Æsward witnessed a charter of 1075 and was presumably appointed before 1066, although this is not certain.

Lands: in Dorset worth £70.

Early sources: Wilkins 1 364 (1075).

BALDWINE (Baldwine, DB Balduin)

Abbot of St Edmund's

Life: Baldwine was born at Chartres in France, and was a monk of St Denis (France), before becoming provost of Leberau (Germany) and Deerhurst. He was physician to Eadward III who appointed him abbot in 1065. He died on 29th December 1097.

Lands: in Suffolk, Norfolk, Essex, Bedford, Northampton, Cambridge and Oxford worth £320.

Early sources: GP, SE: Chr E (1097): witnessed charters S1041, S1043 (1065), B181 (1068), B138 (1069), B68 (1072), R315 (1091), R318 (1091), R328 (1092):

addressed in writs H23 (appointment), H24, H25 (1065/66), B34 (1067), B41 (1066/70), B226 (1071), R296 (1087), R301 (1088), R395 (1087/97): DB.
Modern references: Harmer 1952, Oleson 1955.

BRAND (DB Brand)

Abbot of Peterborough

Life: he was monk and provost of Peterborough, before being chosen as abbot in 1066. The appointment was approved by Eadgar II, and Peterborough was fined by Willelm for accepting Eadgar's authority. He died on 27th/29th November 1069. By later tradition, Brand was the uncle of Hereward, and was certainly brother of Godric (abbot 1098-1102). His father Tocig and his other brothers (Oscytel, Ælfnoð, Sigeric, Siward and Fencyll) were landowners in Lincolnshire and Holderness.
Lands: in Northampton, Lincoln, Huntingdon, Nottingham and Bedford worth £130.
Early sources: Pb: Chr E (1066, 1069): witnessed charter B181 (1068): DB.
Modern references: Fleming 1991.

BRIHTRIC

Abbot of Malmesbury

Life: Brihtric was sponsored by Earls Godwine and Harold in opposition to Bishop Hereman's attempt to transfer his see to the abbey in 1052/53. He was deposed by Willelm I and transferred to Burton in 1067 where he ruled until 1085.
Lands: in Wiltshire, Gloucester and Warwick worth £170.
Early sources: GP: witnessed charters S1479 (1058/62), S1038 (1065).
Modern references: Oleson 1955.

EADMUND (Eadmund, DB Edmund)

Abbot of Pershore

Life: Eadmund had succeeded to Pershore by 1058 and was one of the abbots who entered into confraternity with Bishop Wulfstan of Worcester in 1077. He died on 15th June 1085.
Lands: in Worcester and Gloucester worth £105.
Early sources: W, Wc: witnessed charters S1405 (1058), S1479 (1058/62), S1036 (1062), S1041 (1065), Wilkins 1 364 (1075), Thorpe 615 (1077): DB.
Modern references: Oleson 1955.

EADWARD

Abbot of Cerne

Life: Eadward witnessed a charter of 1075 and may have been appointed before 1066, although this is not certain.
Lands: in Dorset worth £170.
Early sources: Wilkins 1 364 (1075).

EADWINE (Eadwine)

Abbot of Westminster

Life: Eadwine had been a monk of Westminster, and was appointed through the influence of the King in 1049. He may have died on 12th June 1068, although his successor seems to have been appointed in 1072 and he may have lived until then.
Lands: in Middlesex, Worcester, Hertford, Gloucester, Essex, Northampton, Buckingham, Wiltshire, Surrey, Bedford, Berkshire, Sussex and Stafford worth £390.
Early sources: witnessed charters S1033 (1061), B181 (1068), writ H62: addressed in writs H79 (1049), H81 (1049/66), H87 (1057/66).
Modern references: Harmer 1952, Oleson 1955.

EALDRED

Abbot of Abingdon

Life: Ealdred had been a monk and provost of Abingdon before succeeding as abbot in 1066. He was deposed and imprisoned at Winchester, where he died, for conspiracy against Willelm I in 1071 (possibly involved in the Ely revolt of 1071?).
Lands: in Berkshire, Oxford and Gloucester worth £430.
Early sources: W, Ab.
Modern references: Williams 1995.

EALDWINE

Abbot of Milton

Life: Ealdwine witnessed a charter of 1075 and was presumably appointed before 1066, although this is not certain.
Lands: in Dorset and Hampshire worth £90.
Early sources: Wilkins 1 364 (1075).

ECGFRIÐ

Abbot of St Alban's

Life: knowledge of the history of the abbey is hazy for this period and it is not certain that Ecgfrið really existed. However, it is likely that he did and was appointed by Stigand, possibly in 1064, retiring to Ely in 1070 at the fall of the Archbishop.
Lands: in Hertford and Buckingham worth £260.
Early sources: LibE.

GODRIC (Godric)

Abbot of Winchcombe

Life: Godric was the son of the King's priest Godeman. Appointed in 1054, he was removed by Willelm I, being imprisoned at Gloucester and then Evesham from 1066 to 1069, staying there voluntarily afterwards.
Lands: in Gloucester, Oxford and Warwick worth £80.
Early sources: W, Wc, Ev: witnessed charters S1405 (1058).

Modern references: Oleson 1955.

LEOFGYFU (DB *Leueua*)

Abbess of Shaftesbury

Life: She probably died before 1074.
Lands: in Wiltshire, Dorset, Sussex and Somerset worth £280.
Early sources: DB.

LEOFRIC (Leofric, DB Leuric)

Abbot of Burton, Coventry, Peterborough & Thorney

Life: Leofric was a nephew of Earl Leofric and was a monk at Peterborough. He became successively abbot at Burton in 1051, Peterborough in 1052, Coventry in 1053 and Thorney c1058 holding them jointly and ruling through deputies. He possibly also held Crowland for a while. He was at the Battle of Hastings and died shortly afterwards on 31st October 1066. His accumulation of abbeys was spectacular and gave a status befitting his social rank. It may also have benefited the monasteries by giving them an abbot with powerful relations.
Lands: £20 from Burton in Stafford, Derby and Warwick, and £100 from Coventry in Warwick, Gloucester, Northampton, Worcester and Leicester with £130 from Peterborough in Northampton, Lincoln, Huntingdon, Nottingham and Bedford (£260 in all). (see Siward for Thorney)
Early sources: Chr E (1052, 1066): witnessed charter S1037a (1065): addressed in writs H45, H62: DB.
Modern references: Harmer 1952, Oleson 1955.

LEOFWARD (DB Liuuard)

Abbot of Muchelney

Life: Leofward was Abbot by 1066 and may have still been ruling in 1102 when an unnamed Abbot of Muchelney was deposed. If this was Leofward then the grounds for deposition may have been old age.
Lands: in Somerset worth £40.
Early sources: DB: witnessed charter B286 (1068), Wilkins 1 364 (1075).
Modern references: Robertson 1939, Oleson 1955.

ORDRIC

Abbot of Abingdon

Life: he had been a monk at Abingdon and was freely elected by the community in 1052. Ordric died on 22nd January 1066 and was succeeded by Ealdred.
Lands: in Berkshire, Oxford and Gloucester worth £430.
Early sources: W, Ab: witnessed charters S1033 (1061), S1038 (1065): mentioned in writs H4, H5 (1052/66).
Modern references: Harmer 1952, Oleson 1955.

OSRIC

Abbot of Horton

Life: the abbey was reformed c1050 and as he witnessed a charter of 1075, Osric may have been the first or second of its abbots.
Lands: in Devon and Dorset worth £15.
Early sources: Wilkins 1 364 (1075).

SÆWOLD

Under-Abbot of Bath

Life: Sæwold held Bath under Abbot Wulfwold of Chertsey from at least 1065. He had retired to St Vaast in Arras by 1075.
Lands: in Somerset and Gloucester worth £70.
Early sources: occurred in document Wells 1 428-9 (1065), in manumission Kemble 1351, DB.
Modern references: Grierson 1940, Oleson 1955.

SIHTRIC (DB Sitric)

Abbot of Tavistock

Life: Sihtric died on 6th April 1082 and had been Abbot since 1043/46. He was possibly involved against Willelm I in 1070-71, having been granted land by Countess *Gyða*.
Lands: in Devon, Cornwall and Dorset worth £70.
Early sources: GP: witnessed charters S1474 (1046), S1019 (1049), S1036 (1062), B181 (1068): DB.
Modern references: Robertson 1939, Finberg 1942-46, Oleson 1955, Walker 1997.

SIWARD

Under-Abbot of Thorney

Life: he held Thorney under Abbot Leofric as provost from c1058, and then succeeded him as abbot but was never consecrated. Siward may have been Danish. He was succeeded by Folcard c1068 and was reputed to have served for c10 years.
Lands: in Huntingdon, Cambridge, Northampton and Bedford worth £60.
Early sources: Ty, MS BM Add. 40,000 (14th century, see Knowles, Brooke, & London 1972), mentioned in writ H62.
Modern references: Harmer 1952.

ÞURSTAN

Abbot of Ely

Life: Þurstan was a monk at Ely, and was appointed by Harold II in succession to Wulfric who died on 19th August 1066. He called in Hereward to defend the abbey in 1071 and acted as the centre of the last Anglo-Saxon revolt against the Normans, paying a heavy fine to keep office afterwards. He died on 7th July 1072.

Lands: in Cambridge, Suffolk, Norfolk, Essex, Hertford and Huntingdon worth £730.
Early sources: LibE: witnessed charter B68 (1072).
Modern references: Williams 1995.

ULFCYTEL (DB Vlchel)

Abbot of Crowland

Life: he was a monk of Peterborough, appointed by Abbot Leofric in 1061, and was deposed in December 1085, retiring to Peterborough.
Lands: in Cambridge, Northampton, Lincoln, Huntingdon and Leicester worth £50.
Early sources: DB, AL, O.
Modern references: Williams 1995.

WILSTAN (Wilstan, Wlstan)

Abbot of Gloucester

Life: a monk of Worcester, he became abbot in 1058 and died on 9th February 1072 on pilgrimage to Jerusalem. Some sources have his name as Wulfstan.
Lands: in Gloucester, Hereford and Worcester worth £50.
Early sources: W: witnessed charters S1479 (1058/62), S1480 (1062/66), B345 (1067), GC.

WULFGEAT

Abbot of Athelney?

Lands: in Somerset worth £20.
Early sources: witnessed charter B286 (1068), occurs in Kemble 897 (1066).
Modern references: Robertson 1939.

WULFRIC (DB Uluric)

Abbot of Ely

Life: Wulfric was a kinsman of Eadward III appointed abbot in 1045. He died on 19th August 1066.
Lands: in Cambridge, Suffolk, Norfolk, Essex, Hertford and Huntingdon worth £730.
Early sources: LibE, Ra: witnessed charters S1010 (1045), S1017 (1048), S1033 (1061), S1036 (1062), S1038 (1065): addressed in writ H47 (1045? writ of appointment):DB.
Modern references: Harmer 1952.

WULFWOLD (DB Wluuold, Vluuard)

Abbot of Chertsey and Bath

Life: his predecessor at Chertsey became Bishop of Rochester in 1058. Wulfwold added Bath to Chertsey in 1061. He signed the association of abbeys under Bishop Wulfstan in 1077 and died on 19th April 1084.

Lands: for Chertsey in Surrey and Berkshire worth £200, and for Bath in Somerset and Gloucester worth £70 (£270 in all).
Early sources: Chr E (1084): witnessed charters S1002 (1044), S1026 (1055), S1033 (1061), S1035 (1062), B181, B286 (1068), Wilkins 1 364 (1075), B314 (1076/84): addressed in writs H42, H43, H93 (1058/66), B98 (1067): sent writ H6 (1061/66): granted land in S1034 (1061):DB.
Modern references: Harmer 1952, Oleson 1955.

CATHEDRAL PROVOSTS

There were four monastic cathedral chapters: Canterbury, Sherborne, Winchester and Worcester. Each was under the bishop as nominal abbot. In practice, the day-to-day running of the chapter must have devolved onto the provost. As the chapter would have its own lands, independently of the bishop, this could have made the provost a power to be reckoned with. Promotion from provost to bishop was not unknown, e.g. Wulfstan of Worcester in 1062.

ÆLFSTAN

Provost of Worcester

Life: Ælfstan was the brother of Bishop Wulfstan, serving as Provost 1062-77.
Lands: in Gloucester, Worcester and Warwick worth £230.
Early sources: Hm, WC, Thorpe 1 615 (1077): mentioned in writs H116 (1062), B346 (1066/87).

GODRIC

Provost of Canterbury

Life: Godric had been present at the translation of Archbishop Ælfheah's body in 1023, and was the source of the post-Conquest writer Osbern's account of the affair. He had been Provost since at least 1044 and died on 8th July 1074/75.
Lands: in Kent, Essex and Suffolk worth £400.
Early sources: TÆ: witnessed S1471 (1045), S1473 (1044/48), S1234 (1052/70).

WULFRIC

Provost of Sherborne

Life: Wulfric was Provost sometime between 1058 and 1078.
Lands: in Dorset worth £65.
Early sources: Ws.

WULFSIGE

Provost of Winchester

Life: He was Provost in 1065 but nothing else known about him.
Lands: in Hampshire worth £340.
Early sources: Wharton, H 1691 *Anglia Sacra*.

Major Thanes

The hierarchy of early medieval England was expressed through social and legal distinctions that marked off thanes from commoners. To be a thane was to hold land in return for service, either directly from the King or from another landowner. A King's thane might also hold some of his land from someone else. This might be an earl, bishop, abbey or another thane. He might also lease land or have a life interest in an estate that would pass to the church on his death. In practice, many people will have had lands by a variety of tenures and from a variety of landlords. Thanes could also commend themselves in their personal capacity to some more powerful lord. This would create a kind of patron and client relationship but would not involve transferring ownership of land. The amounts of land held by thanes varied a great deal, and the term covered people that in later times would be divided into barons, knights and other types of lesser gentry. The lowest grade of thanes would in later times have held land by serjeanty, the level below that of knight. It was said that a thane had to have at least five hides of land (a hide being a way of rating land for tax and services, reckoned nominally at 120 acres). This was the amount that commonly provided one soldier for the King's army and it is clear that thanes were expected to fulfil a military role. However, with the descent of land to heirs and the transfer of land by will, lease and purchase, many thanes held less than five hides and contributed financially to finding soldiers for the army, or shared the duties on an agreed basis with their co-holders of the five hide unit. A tract on the various grades of person to be found on an estate, written in the early 11th century, gave an account of the thane as follows (Liebermann 1903-16, Swanton 1975):

> Ðeȝenlaȝu is þæt he sy his bocrihtes pyrðe ꝉ þæt he ðreo ðinc of his lande do: fyrdfæreld ꝉ burhbote ꝉ brycȝȝepeorc. Eac of maneȝum landum mare landriht arist to cyniȝes ȝebanne, spilce is deorheȝe to cyniȝes hame ꝉ scorp to friðscipe ꝉ sæpeard ꝉ heafodpeard ꝉ fyrdpeard, ælmesfeoh ꝉ cyricsceat ꝉ mæniȝe oðere mistlice ðinȝe.

> The law of the thane is that he be entitled to his chartered estates, and that he perform three things in respect of his land: military service, the repair of fortresses and work on bridges. Also, in many estates further land duties arise by order of the king, such as the deer fence at the king's residence, equipping a guard ship and guarding the coast, attendance on his superior, military guard, almsgiving and church dues, and many other different things.

A treatise, associated with Archbishop Wulfstan of York, allowed for the possibility of prosperous commoners rising to become thanes. The list of attributes he gave for the thane shows what was expected of the 11th century nobility (Liebermann 1903-16, Whitelock 1955: 432):

> *ʒif ceorl ʒeþeah, þæt he hæfde fullice fíf hida aʒenes landes, cirican ꝛ cycenan, bellhus ꝛ burhʒeat, setl ꝛ sunder note on cynʒes healle, þonne pæs he þanon forð þeʒenrihtes peorðe.*

> if a churl prospered, so that he had fully five hides of his own land, a church and kitchen, a bell tower and burgh gate, a seat and special office in the king's hall, then was he thenceforth worthy of thaneright.

There is evidence that thanes with over £40 of land could be seen as constituting an upper class within the nobility. In terms of their wealth and in numbers, they would roughly equate with later medieval barons. They would be absentee landlords from most of their estates during the year, and would have an important role in national politics. Most thanes would have lesser amounts of land and their importance was more local. All thanes had certain privileges and responsibilities. Their *wergyld* was 1200 shillings compared with a commoner's 200 shillings. This was payable as compensation for their murder and many other compensations and judicial penalties were also graded accordingly. Their oath in court also carried more weight in the same proportion. The more important thanes might be granted the right to hold court over certain men or lands, or receive the fines from those men in the public courts. On their death, a *heregeat* (heriot) or form of death duties was payable. The King's thane would owe four horses, two swords and four spears with shields and armour, and £6¼. Other thanes, those under other lords, would pay one horse and his weapons, or £2. Different rates applied in the Danelaw. All lands held by the thanes that had been granted by the King owed three particular services that were only rarely granted away: army service, bridge repair and maintenance of fortress or city walls.

An important group of thanes were the officers of the King's household. It seems as though the greater offices were held jointly at this period. King Ælfred is said to have organised the household into three shifts. There were certainly three Chamberlains nearly 200 years later in 1066. There were also three names associated with the office of Steward, although this is based on unreliable evidence. There is one person who is known to have been a Butler. Two other names occur with the title of 'consiliarius'. No office is known with this title and they might have been be the two other Butlers, assuming the threefold division still operated in 1066. However, this may be stretching the evidence further than it would warrant. An office that was created after Ælfred's time was that of Constable. Five holders of this can be identified for 1066. The Constables may have had command over the housecarls, the King's paid military retainers.

Thanes' estates were constantly shifting in size and distribution through all the normal processes of sale, leasing, inheritance, marriage, forfeiture and new grants. Thanes could hold land directly of the King while also leasing lands from the church, farming manors or holding as dependants of other thanes. What the Domesday survey provides is merely a snapshot in time. It should always be remembered that social classes were not closed groups. Families in medieval times seldom managed to perpetuate themselves in the male line for any length of time. The chances of fertility, war and politics meant the eclipse of many and the rise of others. There were two ways of assessing land: by value and by rating. The values given in the Domesday survey are assumed to have represented the yearly income of the land (Welldon Finn 1973). Rating of lands involved assessing land at so many hides or ploughlands. This is thought to have born some relationship to the arable agricultural potential of the land.

A major problem with identifying individual thanes is the general lack of surnames. Old English naming practices could create a huge variety of names and in any one region men sharing the same name could be rare. Surnames were thus uncommon and only used to prevent confusion where necessary. Nationally the same name could be born by a number of thanes. Criteria for identifying thanes have been suggested by Lewis (1997).

The following section relies heavily on the work of Clarke 1994. This has not gone uncriticised (see Lewis 1997 for a particularly unsympathetic view of Clarke's work). However, Clarke's is by far the most detailed national account of possible landowners in 1066 and should form the starting point for any identification of thanes. All the thanes listed below can be found in either Clarke 1994 or in the relevant volumes of the Domesday Book published by Philimore. Other works with more detailed information than simply a listing of lands are also given under each thane as modern references. The thanes listed below are those identified by Clarke (1994) as having lands worth over £40 (rounded up to the nearest £), along with those in Yorkshire who may also belong to this group (the uncertainties of the Yorkshire Domesday making accurate assessments of wealth difficult) and the leading officials of the King's household. Very few were still holding lands in 1086 and the history of the dispossession of the majority is poorly known. Fleming (1991) has suggested that where lands were handed to a single Norman successor this was done soon after the Conquest. Instances of this are noted where appropriate.

ÆGELFERÐ (DB Aieluert, Ailuert, Aeluert, Aluerd, Aluert)

Life: he was probably the brother of Ælfmær (see below). His lands were given with those of his brother to Roger of Arundel by 1068.

Lands: in Dorset £38 and Somerset £16, overall worth £54. His main manors were Piddletrenthide and Worth Maltravers (Dorset), and Beckington (Somerset). Worth Maltravers however, might well have belonged to a thane named Ælfward instead, reducing his holding to £38.

Early sources: witnessed charters S1034 (1061), S1042 (1065).

Modern references: Clarke 1994, Williams 1995.

ÆGELGYÐ (DB Ailith, Ailid, Ailida, Ailed, Ailiet)

Life: she was the widow of Þurstan, son of Lustwine. Her own ancestry was illustrious in that she was the granddaughter of Alderman Brihtnoð, killed at the Battle of Maldon in 991. *Ægelgyð* was an important local figure, with at least 26 men in Suffolk commended to her.
Lands: in Essex £53, Norfolk £42 and Suffolk £16, overall worth £111. Her main manors were Henham, Pentlow and Wimbish (Essex), and Shimpling (Suffolk).
Early sources: will of Þurstan S1531 (1043/45).
Modern references: Clarke 1994.

ÆGELMÆR MELC (DB Agelmar, Ailmar, Almar)

Lands: in Essex worth £63. His main manors were Elmdon and Hatfield Peverel.
Modern references: Clarke 1994.

ÆGELNOÐ CILD (Ægelnað, DB Alnod Cilt, Cild, Cit)

Life: Ægelnoð was allied to Earl Harold and his family. Harold had helped him gain land from St Martin's in Dover at advantageous terms. He was described as governor (satrap) of Kent, and was taken to Normandy by Willelm I in 1067. His lands were in Norman hands by 1078.
Lands: in Kent £71, Sussex £58, Oxford £50, Surrey £40, Hampshire £25 and Buckingham £16, overall worth £260. His main manors were Alciston (Sussex) and Bramley (Surrey).
Early sources: W: witnessed charters S1036 (1062), S1041, S1043 (1065).
Modern references: Fleming 1991, Clarke 1994, Williams 1995.

ÆGELRIC (Ægelric, DB Æilric, Ailric, Eilric, Alric, Ælric)

Life: his father was Mærgeat. He had been with the fleet guarding the south coast against Norman invasion during the summer of 1066.
Lands: in Lincoln £60, Leicester £6, Warwick £3 and Essex £2, overall worth £71. His main manors were Caythorpe and Doddington (Lincoln).
Early sources: witnessed charter? S1405 (1058).
Modern references: Clarke 1994.

ÆGELSIGE (DB Alsi, Elsi)

Lands: in Somerset £32 and Devon £17, overall worth £49. His main manor was Castle Cary (Somerset). An Ægelsige was a member of the Hampshire or Wiltshire shire court after the Conquest. There is no record of a landowner of that name in either shire. Was he Ægelsige of Somerset?
Early sources: witnessed charter S1034 (1061): addressed in writ B339? (1070/87).
Modern references: Clarke 1994, Williams 1995.

ÆGELSTAN (DB Adestan, Alestan)

Life: He was the son of Godram.
Lands: in Lincoln worth £45. His main manor was Fishtoft.
Early sources: witnessed charter S1059 (1061/66).
Modern references: Clarke 1994.

ÆGELWIG (DB Aluui)

Life: he was a local official of the King, being described as King's reeve in the Domesday Book and was the son of Bana.
Lands: in Somerset £46, Devon £10, Dorset £6 and Wiltshire £3, overall worth £65. His main manor was Arlington (Devon). His lands went to Ælfred of Spain after the Conquest.
Early sources: witnessed charter S1042 (1065).
Modern references: Thorn & Thorn 1980, Clarke 1994.

ÆLFMÆR (DB Ailmar, Almar)

Life: he probably had a brother Ægelferð. His lands were given to Roger Arundel by 1068.
Lands: in Dorset £27 and Somerset £17, overall worth £44. His main manors were Piddletrenthide (Dorset) and Whitelackington (Somerset).
Modern references: Clarke 1994, Williams 1995.

ÆLFRIC CAMP (Ælfric, DB Aluric)

Life: Sheriff of Huntingdon. Two freemen in Suffolk who had commended themselves to Ælfric were taken over by another English lord after the Conquest, suggesting that Ælfric was an early casualty of the Conquest itself, or a later revolt. His wife and sons however were treated favourably by Willelm.
Lands: in Essex £46, Cambridge £20, Suffolk £6, Bedford 4/- and Berkshire £4, overall worth £77. His main manors were Fowlmere (Cambridge), Delham, Ramsey and Tendring (Essex).
Early sources: witnessed charters S1027 (1059).
Modern references: Freeman 1869-75, Green 1990, Fleming 1991, Clarke 1994.

ÆLFRIC (DB Alric)

Life: his father was Goding. Although not among the greatest of landowners, he must have been locally very important since a large number (15) of local men had commended themselves to him.
Lands: in Buckingham £46 and Bedford £15, overall worth £61. His main manor was Woburn (Bedford). Clarke mistakenly lists his Buckingham lands under Hertford.
Modern references: Clarke 1994.

ÆLFSIGE (DB Alsi, Elsi)

Life: most of his lands were granted out as part of large territorial fees.

Lands: lands in Yorkshire, West Riding £60 10/- (+ 5 ploughlands) and North Riding 10/- (+ 2 ploughlands), overall worth £61 (+ 7 ploughlands). His main manors were Branton and Maltby. He was still holding £6 10/- under Ilbert de Laci in 1086.
Modern references: Faull & Stinson 1986.

ÆLFSTAN OF BOSCOMBE (DB Alestan)

Life: he was related to the former Constable Ælfstan and had been made Sheriff of Bedford. Ælfstan may have been a officer in the King's household (perhaps Butler), although the evidence for this is far from certain. It is possible, though unlikely, that he and the Constable Ælfstan were actually the same man. Most of his lands went to Willelm of Eu.
Lands: in Wiltshire £89, Hertford £47, Somerset £43, Gloucester £36, Bedford £37, Dorset £30, Hampshire £5 and Berkshire £3, overall worth £289. His main manors were Weston (Hertford), Durnford (Wiltshire) and Sundon (Bedford).
Early sources: witnessed charters S1235 (1053/66), S1036 (1062), S1042 (1065): the earlier Constable Ælfstan had been granted a manor in S999 (1043) which was in Ælfstan of Boscombe's hands in DB.
Modern references: Green 1990, Clarke 1994.

ÆLFWINE (DB Aluuin)

Life: also called Æþelwine by modern writers, Sheriff of Warwick (Gloucester according to Clarke), he was the father of Þurcyll (holding land in chief in 1086) and Guðmund, and ancestor of the Arden and Le Notte families. He was a benefactor of Coventry Abbey, giving it the township of Clifton in Warwickshire before the Conquest.
Lands: in Gloucester £54, Warwick £7, Hereford £2 and Huntingdon £2 worth £63 (Clarke only lists his lands in Gloucester). His main manors were Guiting Power and Farmcote (Gloucester).
Modern references: Williams 1989b, Green 1990, Clarke 1994, Williams 1995 (Þurcyll).

ÆLFWOLD THE BALD (DB Aluiold)

Lands: in Somerset £50, Gloucester £7 and Dorset £3, overall worth £60. His main manor was North Cadbury (Somerset).
Early sources: witnessed charter S1480 (1062/66).
Modern references: Clarke 1994.

ÆLFWOLD OF STEVINGTON (DB Aluuold, Adelold)

Life: he was allied to Earl Harold and his family.
Lands: in Bedford worth £50. His main manor was Stevington (Bedford).
Early sources: witnessed charter S1036 (1062).
Modern references: Fleming 1991, Clarke 1994.

ÆTSERE (Azor, DB Azor)

Life: Ætsere was allied to Earl Harold and his family. He might have been the King's Steward. If so, he was still living in 1086.
Lands: in Sussex £163, Surrey £61, Wiltshire £23, Hampshire £17 and Gloucester £7, overall worth £271. His main manors were Shoreham and Slindon (Sussex) and Chitterne (Wiltshire).
Early sources: witnessed charters? S1036 (1062), S1480 (1062/66), B286 (1068).
Modern references: Fleming 1991, Clarke 1994, Williams 1995.

ÆTSERE (DB Adzor)

Life: he was the son of Þored, and was still alive in 1072 when he sold some land to Bishop Gisa. It has been suggested that his estate was of fairly recent creation, possibly built up through royal service. Might he have been the Ætsere who was the King's Steward?
Lands: in Wiltshire £47, Dorset £40, Oxford £15, Northampton £12 and Buckingham £2, overall worth £116. His main manors were Gussage St Michael (Dorset), Elcombe and Stratford Tony (Wiltshire).
Early sources: witnessed charter? B286 (1068): sold land P56 (1072).
Modern references: Clarke 1994, Williams 1995.

ÆTSERE (DB Azor, Azer)

Life: the son of Totig, he was a housecarl of Eadward III and a tenant of Queen *Eadgyð*. It has been suggested that he was a commander of the King's housecarls, recently granted land in return for his service.
Lands: in Buckingham £34, Middlesex £19, Warwick £11 and Northampton £2, overall worth £66. His main manors were Stanwell (Middlesex) and Leamington Hastings (Warwick).
Modern references: Fleming 1991, Clarke 1994, Stafford 1997.

ÆTSERE (DB Azor, Azer)

Life: the son of Godwine and *Swalufu*. His father was recorded as holding the Lincolnshire lands of the family but he was probably dead by 1066 leaving Ætsere as the actually holder on the day King Eadward died.
Lands: Lincoln £37, Nottingham £3, overall worth £40. His main manor was Welbourne (Lincoln).
Modern references: Clarke 1994.

BALDWINE (DB Balduin, Baldeuin)

Life: the Steward of Bishop Ealdred at Worcester, he was the son of Eorlwine (Herluin) a Norman follower of Bishop Brihtheah. He was also a tenant of Archbishop Stigand for some of his land. He might have been a godson of Eadward III, and still held land in 1086.

Lands: in Gloucester £38, Warwick £37, Berkshire £27, Northampton £20, Wiltshire £14 and Leicester £1, overall worth £136. His main manors were Bradley and Childs Wickham (Gloucester), Marston and Pillerton (Warwick).
Early sources: granted land in S1407 (1053/56).
Modern references: Clarke 1994.

BARÐ (DB Baret)

Life: he was still holding some of his manors under Ilbert de Laci in 1086 (Smeaton, Roall, Eggborough, Kellington, Beal) and Hensall as King's thane. He had a son, Gamal, who succeeded to his lands and was a benefactor of Selby Abbey.
Lands: lands in Yorkshire, West Riding £36 (+ 3.4 ploughlands) and East Riding £2, overall worth £38 (+ 3.4 ploughlands). His main manors were Campsall, Darrington, Hensall and Knottingley.
Modern references: Faull & Stinson 1986.

BONDIG (DB Bondi, Bundi)

Life: he was one of King Eadward's Constables. His name was common in Norfolk, and the northern part of the east Mercia (Insley 1994), yet he held no land in these areas. Does this mean that he was a newly made man deriving his fortune from service to the King rather than inheritance?
Lands: in Dorset £40, Hampshire £28, Wiltshire £25, Essex £23, Oxford £22, Berkshire £20, Buckingham £12, Northampton £6, Somerset £5, Gloucester £1, overall worth £182. His main manors were Fisherton (Wiltshire), Broadwindsor and Compton Valence (Dorset), and Woodham Ferrers (Essex).
Early sources: witnessed charters S1235 (1053/66), S1033, S1034 (1061), S1426 (1062/66), S1036 (1062), S1040, S1041, S1042, S1043 (1065), B286 (1068): addressed in writ B296 (1067).
Modern references: Larson 1904, Oleson 1955, Robertson 1939, Clarke 1994.

BONDIG (DB Bundo, Bund, Bond)

Life: his lands went to Hugh de Montfort and he may have been dispossessed of them soon after the Conquest.
Lands: in Norfolk worth £49. His main manors were Raynham and West Binley.
Modern references: Clarke 1994.

BRIHTMÆR (DB Brismar, Brismer)

Lands: in Cornwall £62 and Devon £46, overall worth £109. His main manor was Rillaton (Cornwall).
Modern references: Clarke 1994.

BRIHTRIC (Brihtric, Byrhtricus, DB Brictric)

Life: the wealthiest of all the thanes, he was the son of Ælfgar Mæw (a supporter of Earl Eadric and Cnut) and grandson of Æþelward Mæw (the founder of Cranborne Abbey). The family might have been connected with the royal family in the time of

Eadward I. Brihtric had been an associate of the former Earl Odda in the 1050s, himself connected with the family of Alderman Æþelward (a descendant of King Æþelred of Wessex, brother of King Ælfred). An unreliable story reported that Brihtric had rejected the hand of *Mathild* of Flanders while on an embassy there, and that after 1066 *Mathild* (who was now wife of Willelm I) took her revenge by having him deprived of his lands. He had certainly lost Tewkesbury to Willelm Fitz Osbern by 1071. He may have had an office in the King's household, perhaps that of Butler, being titled 'consiliarius' in one charter of 1061. He was also Sheriff of Gloucester.

Lands: in Gloucester £237, Devon £164, Dorset £95, Cornwall £30, Hereford £15, Wiltshire £15, Worcester £3 and Hampshire £1, overall worth £560. His main manor was Tewkesbury (Gloucester).

Early sources: witnessed charters S993, S994 (1042), S1406 (1046/53), S1409 (1051/55), S1408 (1052/56), S1405 (1058), S1027, S1028 (1059), S1033, S1034 (1061), S1037a, S1036 (1062), S1480 (1062/66), S1042 (1065), B286 (1068): addressed in writ B223 (1067).

Modern references: Freeman 1869-75 (Vol. 4), Hart 1975, Clarke 1994, King 1996, Williams 1997.

BRIHTRIC (DB Brictric)

Life: he was a tenant of Queen *Eadgyð*. His lands went to Miles Crispin after the Conquest.

Lands: in Buckingham £79, Bedford £12, Hertford £3, Oxford £2 and Worcester £1, overall worth £101. His main manors were Marshworth and Waddesdon (Buckingham).

Modern references: Robertson 1939, Clarke 1994, Stafford 1997.

BRIHTRIC (DB Brictric)

Life: one of three brothers, including Osgod (£88) and Eadmund (£27). He and Osgod were tenants of Harold.

Lands: in Berkshire £32, Hampshire £15, Buckingham £6, Hereford £4 and Gloucester £3, overall worth £60. His main manors were Newton Valence (Hampshire), Upton and Childrey (Berkshire).

Modern references: Clarke 1994.

BRIHTRIC (DB Brictric)

Life: his lands went to Odo FitzGamelin and he may have lost his lands early in Willelm's reign.

Lands: in Devon worth £43. His main manor was Great Torrington.

Modern references: Clarke 1994.

BRIHTSIGE CILD (DB Bricsi, Brixi, Brixe)

Life: he might have been given one of his manors (Plumstead) by Earl Godwine. If so then he was another of the many followers of Godwine's family.

Lands: in Kent £47, Sussex £38 and Surrey £22, overall worth £107. His main manors were Seal (Kent) and North Stoke (Sussex).
Early sources: witnessed charters S1036 (1062), B286 (1068).
Modern references: Fleming (as Beorhtric) 1991, Clarke 1994.

BURHRED (DB Burgered, Burgret, Borgerete, Burred, Burret, Borred, Bored, Borret)

Life: he was the father of two thanes, Eadwine (£48) and Ulf (£8). He might have been related to *Gyða* the widow of Earl Raulf (Eadward III's nephew). It has been suggested that he was dead by 1066 and that the lands assigned to his name had in fact been divided between his two sons.
Lands: in Northampton £19, Bedford £15 and Buckingham £12, overall worth £46. His main manor was Olney (Buckingham).
Early sources: witnessed charter S1235 (1053/66).
Modern references: Williams 1989a, Clarke 1994.

CARLA (DB Carlo, Carle)

Lands: in Wiltshire £92, Surrey £20, Hampshire £10, Sussex £9, Berkshire £8 and Somerset £5, overall worth £144. His main manors were Norton Bavant (Wiltshire) and Send (Surrey). Most of his lands had passed to Ælfred of Marlborough by 1086.
Modern references: Clarke 1994.

CARLA (DB Carle)

Life: this may be one landowner or several. If one, then his lands had been split by 1086 between the King, Count Rodbert of Mortain, Willelm Perci, Drogo, Gislebert de Gant and Roger of Poitou. This may be the Carl, son of Þurbrand, who murdered Earl Ealdred of Bamburgh in 1038 as part of a longstanding feud. Þurbrand had murdered Ealdred's father Earl Uhtred in 1016 and had himself been killed in vengeance by Ealdred. His sons were active in the revolts of 1069-70, two of whom (Gamal and Þurbrand) were themselves killed by Earl Walþeof (Ealdred's grandson) in 1073. A Carla still held 4/- worth of land in 1086 (at Bolton, East Riding). This is unlikely to have been the same man.
Lands: in Yorkshire, East Riding £34 (+ 7.4 ploughlands), North Riding £3 (+ 1 ploughland) and West Riding 10/- (+ 5.6 ploughlands), overall worth £37 (+ 14.2 ploughlands). His main manors were Hunmanby, Nafferton and Burton Fleming. Carla's sons may be identified (though not with certainty) with the following who held various lands in 1066 – Þurbrand £10 (+17.3 ploughlands) in all three ridings, Gamal £6 8/8 (+27.6 ploughlands) in all three ridings, Cnut £6 in the East Riding, Sumorled 2/- in the North Riding.
Modern references: Faull & Stinson 1986.

CYPPING (DB Cheping)

Life: Cypping was one of the thanes allied to Earl Harold and his family, holding two manors from Harold himself.

Lands: in Hampshire £128 and Berkshire £9, overall worth £137. His main manor was Headbourne Worthy (Hampshire).
Early sources: witnessed charter S1476 (c1053).
Modern references: Fleming 1991, Clarke 1994.

CYTEL ALDER (DB Kitel, Ketel, Chetel)

Life: the son of Ælfwine and *Wulfgyð*. He had two brothers, Godric and Ælfcytel, and three sisters *Gode, Bote* and *Ealdgyð*. His wife was *Sæflæd*, and she had a daughter by a previous marriage *Ælfgyfu*. He was the man of Archbishop Stigand. His will was made shortly before he set out on a pilgrimage to Rome. He presumably came back alive and well since the will was not acted upon.
Lands: in Norfolk £41, Suffolk £3 and Essex £2, overall worth £46. His main manors were Great Melton and Walsingham (Norfolk). His lands were divided between a number of Norman successors.
Early sources: will S1519, mother's will S1535, uncles' will (Eadwine and Wulfric) S1516.
Modern references: Fleming 1991, Clarke 1994.

DUNNA (DB Dunne, Donno, Donne, Duns)

Life: he was a tenant of Earl Harold. His lands went to Osbeorn Giffard.
Lands: in Gloucester £24, Wiltshire £12 and Somerset £5, overall worth £41. His main manor was Brimpsfield (Gloucester).
Early sources: witnessed charter B286 (1068).
Modern references: Clarke 1994, Williams 1995.

EADGYFU FÆGER (DB *Edeua, Eddeua, Eddeue, Eddeuæ, Æideua*)

Life: *Eadgyfu* might have been the wife of the Constable Raulf. Both their estates passed to Count Alan and were administered by Godric the Steward by 1086. Both were connected with Exning in Cambridge. She was known as either *Eadgyfu* the Fair or *Eadgyfu* the Rich. Although Cambridge was the centre of her influence, she is known to have had 76 men commended to her in Suffolk. She must have been a powerful presence in the region, and an attractive match for Raulf. She has often been confused with *Eadgyð Swanneshals* (see above).
Lands: in Cambridge £235, Hertford £57, Suffolk £34, Essex £26 and Buckingham £14, overall worth £366. Her main manors were Exning and Brassingbourne (Cambridge), and Cheshunt (Hertford).
Modern references: Clarke 1994.

EADMÆR ATRE (Eadmær, DB Edmer, Edmar)

Life: he was connected with Earl Harold and his family.
Lands: in Dorset £38, Hertford £28, Devon £24, Buckingham £20, Somerset £17, Middlesex £10 and Northampton £6, overall worth £143. His main manors were Berkhampstead (Hertford), Bledlow (Buckingham) and Gussage All Saints (Dorset).
Early sources: witnessed charters S1027 (1059), S1034 (1061).

Modern references: Fleming 1991, Clarke 1994.

EADNOÐ (Eadnoð, DB Ednod, Alnod)

Life: Eadward's Constable and ancestor of the later families of Berkeley (FitzHarding) and Meriet. He was killed repelling an attack on Somerset by the sons of Harold in 1068, although he had been allied to Earl Harold and his family before the Conquest. His son Hearding was living in 1125, having been employed as a justice in Devon and Cornwall in 1096.

Lands: in Gloucester £20, Hampshire £16, Somerset £14, Wiltshire £11 and Berkshire £6, overall worth £64. His main manors were Ampney (Gloucester) and Freefolk (Hampshire). Clarke does not list Knowle in Somerset, held by Alnod the Staller, most likely a mistake for Eadnoð (although this is disputed by Lewis).

Early sources: Chr D (1068): witnessed charters S1041, S1043 (1065): addressed in writs H85 (1053/66), B11 (1067).

Modern references: Freeman 1869-75 (Vol. 4), Larson 1904, Oleson 1955, Fleming 1991, Lewis 1991, Clarke 1994, Williams 1995.

EADRIC OF ELHAM (DB Edric, Ederic)

Life: he might have been associated with Osbeorn Bicga, from whom he held some of his lands. It has been suggested that he was still living in 1086, farming his land from Bishop Oda of Bayeux.

Lands: in Kent worth £66. His main manor was Elham.

Early sources: witnessed charter S1400 (1038/50).

Modern references: Clarke 1994, Williams 1995.

EADRIC OF LAXFIELD (Eadric, DB Edric)

Life: he was the son of Ingold and had been exiled some time before 1066 but allowed to return (was he associated with the exile of Earl Ælfgar or even the earlier exile of the Constable Osgod?). His lands were in the hands of Willelm Malet by 1069. Eadric was clearly a major power in East Anglia and had the commendations of a great many men.

Lands: in Suffolk £199 and Norfolk £33, overall worth £232 (Clarke's total for Eadric is only £192 but the manors listed for him add up to £232). His main manor was Dunwich (Suffolk).

Early sources: witnessed charter? S1405 (1058).

Modern references: Fleming 1991, Clarke 1994.

EADRIC WILDE (Eadric Cild, DB Edric Saluage)

Life: Eadric was the son of Ælfric (possibly nephew of Alderman Eadric who died in 1017). His son Ælfnoð may have been the ancestor of the later Savage family. He attacked Hereford in alliance with the Welsh in 1067, and attacked Shrewsbury with Welsh help in 1069, before submitting to Willelm in 1070. He went on Willelm's invasion of Scotland in 1072, and was still living in 1086. Eadric seems to have become a figure in local folklore. A later fictional tradition represented him as Earl of Shropshire, being attacked and captured by Ralph Mortimer at Wigmore Castle.

Lands: in Shropshire £98 and Hereford £3, overall worth £100 + 20 hides waste. His main manors were Clun, Hopesay and Lydham (Shropshire). His landholdings were much reduced by 1086 and he was no longer a tenant in chief of the King. He held his 1086 lands under Raulf de Mortimer, the Bishop of Hereford and Much Wenlock.

Early sources: O, W: Chr D (1067).

Modern references: Freeman 1869-75 (Vol. 4), Reynolds 1981, Clarke 1994, Williams 1995.

EADRIC (Eadric, DB Edric)

Life: Sheriff of Wiltshire, he was dead by 1086 when his widow was living, and held lands under his successor Arnulf of Hesdin.

Lands: in Gloucester £27, Somerset £14, Hampshire £11, Wiltshire £7 and Dorset £4, overall worth £63. His main manors were Oldbury and Great Badminton (Gloucester).

Early sources: witnessed charters S1028 (1059), S1036 (1062): addressed in writ B223 (1067).

Modern references: Clarke 1994, Williams 1995.

EADWARD CILD (DB Eduuard)

Life: he was connected to Earl Harold and his family.

Lands: in Buckingham £73, Lincoln £14 and Northampton £6, overall worth £93. His main manor was Wing (Buckingham). His Buckinghamshire lands are listed under Hertfordshire by Clarke.

Modern references: Fleming 1991, Clarke 1994.

EADWINE (DB Eduin)

Life: son of Burhred (see above).

Lands: in Northampton £16, Buckingham £16, Middlesex £10 and Somerset £6, overall worth £48. His main manor was Kensington (Middlesex).

Modern references: Clarke 1994.

EARNCYLL (DB Archil, Archel)

Life: he submitted to Willelm in 1068, giving his son Gospatric as a hostage but took part in the risings of 1069-70. Most of his lands were taken by the King or given to Count Alan and Erneis de Burun.

Lands: North Riding £17 (+ 3 ploughlands), West Riding £7 and East Riding £1, overall worth £25 (+ 18.3 ploughlands). He may also have held other lands in Yorkshire, later given to Count Robert (North Riding £6), Ilbert de Lacy (West Riding £9) or Roger of Poitou (19.6 ploughlands). His main manor may have been Bolton (in Morley Wapentake).

Early sources: O.

Modern references: Faull & Stinson 1986.

EARNSIGE (DB Ernesi)

Life: Earnsige's father was the Danish Oca (presumably a follower of Cnut) but he had an English mother, *Ealdgyð*. Moore raises the possibility that he was in reality a Norman, Erneis. However, an Anglo-Danish origin is still the most likely identification.

Lands: in Gloucester £60 and Worcester £10, overall worth £70. His main manors were Painswick and Siddington (Gloucester), and Astley (Worcester).

Early sources: Ev: witnessed charter S1026 (1055).

Modern references: Moore 1982, Clarke 1994.

ESGAR (Esgar, Esegar, DB Esgar, Asgar, Ansgar)

Life: Esgar was the grandson of the Constable Tofig the Proud. He was probably the most senior of the Constables and was allied to Earl Harold and his family. Esgar organised the defence of London against Willelm after Hastings, at which he may have been wounded. His lands were in the hands of Goisfrið de Mandeville possibly by 1067 and he died in captivity shortly after the Conquest. Esgar had many dependant landowners and was one of the most powerful of the greater thanes.

Lands: in Essex £148, Middlesex £102, Hertford £68, Berkshire £52, Buckingham £19, Northampton £18, Oxford £17, Warwick £15 and Suffolk £11, overall worth £448. His main manors were Sawbridgeworth (Hertford), Enfield (Middlesex) and Waltham (Essex).

Early sources: GA, LibE: witnessed charters S1476 (c1053), S1026 (1055), S1060 (1055/60), S1028 (1059), S1029, S1030, S1031 (1060), S1033, S1034 (1061), S1426 (1061/66), S1036 (1062), S1480 (1062/66), S1040, S1041, S1042, S1043 (1065), S1000, writ H62: addressed in writs H75 (1042/44), H91 (1057/66), H98 (1065/66), H76.

Modern references: Larson 1904, Robertson 1939, Oleson 1955, Fleming 1991, Clarke 1994.

FITEL (DB Vitel, Phitelet, Fitheus)

Life: he bore the French name of Vitalis and was presumably a Norman follower of Eadward III. Fitel was still living in 1086. It is possible that he was the Fithel, husband of *Restra*, whose name was entered into the *Liber Vitae* of New Minster, Winchester. Moore (1997) identified this name as Irish in origin.

Lands: in Wiltshire £23, Somerset £20 and Hampshire 15/- worth £44 (including Luccombe, omitted by Lewis). His main manors were Charlton Horethorne (Somerset) and Fittleton (Hampshire).

Modern references: Lewis 1995, Moore 1997.

GAMAL (DB Gamel, Game)

Life: Gamal, son of Osberht, may have taken part in the campaign of Eadgar in the north in 1069-70, or fallen at Fulford or Stamford Bridge in 1066 since some of his lands were held by Willelm Malet in 1069. Neither he nor his descendants held lands

in 1086. His holdings had been split by 1086 between the King, Count Rodbert of Mortain, Rodbert Malet, Hugo FitzBaldric and Osbern d'Arches.
Lands: in Yorkshire, East Riding £39 (+ 13.2 ploughlands), North Riding £4 (+ 14.6 ploughlands) and West Riding £3, overall worth £49 (+ 32.2 ploughlands). His main manor was South Cave.
Modern references: Faull & Stinson 1986.

GAUTIG (DB Gouti, Couta, Goti)
Life: he was a housecarl of Earl Harold.
Lands: in Essex £25, Suffolk £12, Hertford £7 and Middlesex £6, overall worth £50. His main manor was Freckenham (Suffolk).
Modern references: Fleming 1991, Clarke 1994.

GODRIC (Godric, DB Godric)
Life: Sheriff of Berkshire and possibly Buckingham, he was killed at Hastings in 1066. He seems to have been particularly grasping, enriching himself at the expense even of the King. If he was the Godric who witnessed S1029 then his mother's name was *Eadgyfu*.
Lands: in Berkshire £31, Wiltshire £9 and Buckingham £5, overall worth £45. His main manor was Fyfield (Berkshire).
Early sources: witnessed charters S1235 (1053/66), S1028 (1059), S1029 (1060), S1041, S1043 (1065): addressed in writ H5 (1053/66).
Modern references: Freeman 1869-75 (Vols 3 & 4), Clarke 1994.

GODWINE (DB Goduin)
Life: he was a priest, allied to Earl Harold and his family, connected with the family's estate and church at Bosham.
Lands: in Sussex £58 and Hampshire £15, overall worth £73. His main manor was Plumpton (Sussex).
Modern references: Fleming 1991, Clarke 1994.

GODWINE (DB Goduin)
Life: his lands went to Eudo Dapifer and he may have lost them soon after the Conquest.
Lands: in Suffolk £22 and Essex £20, overall worth £42. His main manor was Eriswell (Suffolk).
Modern references: Clarke 1994.

GOSPATRIC (DB Gospatric)
Life: he was the son of Earncyll (see above), sent as a hostage to Willelm in 1068, and therefore did not take part in the rising of 1069-70. Some of his lands were taken by the King, some were given to Count Alan and Erneis de Burun, but he was still a major landowner in 1086. However, later evidence shows that he still held some of his land as tenant of the new Norman lords.

Lands: in Yorkshire, North Riding £23 (+ 28 ploughlands), West Riding £35 (+ 41.6 ploughlands) and East Riding (3.4 ploughlands), overall worth £58 (+ 69.6 ploughlands). He may also have held other lands in Yorkshire, later given to Count Robert (North Riding £26), Ilbert de Lacy (West Riding £2) and Roger of Poitou (10 ploughlands). His main manors may have been Hutton Rudby and Seamer (North Riding), and Bingley (West Riding).

Early sources: O.

Modern references: Michelmore 1981, Faull & Stinson 1986.

GUÐMUND (DB Gudmund)

Life: his brother was Abbot Wulfric of Ely. He was clearly a powerful local landowner and had the commendations of various freemen in Suffolk. He had leased land from his brother in order to raise his holdings above 40 hides, the least that he needed in order to marry a richer woman according to local custom.

Lands: in Essex £39 and Suffolk £34, overall worth £73. His main manor was Haughley (Suffolk). His lands were allotted to Hugo de Montfort after the Conquest.

Early sources: LibE.

Modern references: Clarke 1994.

HEARDING OF WILTON (DB Harding)

Life: Queen *Eadgyð's* Butler, he has often been confused with the Hearding who was son of Constable Eadnoð (who was a landholder in 1086, and was still living in c1120, and so unlikely to have been a major landowner in 1066). He was Sheriff of Derby and probably Nottingham. A close associate of his was Wulfward Hwit, another follower of Queen *Eadgyð*. Hearding was still living in 1086.

Lands: in Wiltshire £58, Leicester £18, Warwick £7, Somerset £4 and Dorset £3, overall worth £90 (ascribed to Hearding son of Eadnoð by Clarke, but identified as the Queen's Butler by Williams). His main manors were Knighton and Compton (Wiltshire). He still had lands worth £25 in Dorset and Wiltshire in 1086, worth £4.

Early sources: witnessed charters S1036 (1062), S1042 (1065), B286 (1068), P56 (1072), VCH Som 1 399: addressed in writ B33 (1066/86).

Modern references: Clarke 1994, Williams 1995, Stafford 1997.

INGWARE (DB Inguuara, Inguuar, Inguar, Ingeuuar, Ingar)

Lands: in Essex £71, Huntingdon £10 and Cambridge £8, overall worth £79. His main manors were Burstead and Chrishall (Essex).

Modern references: Clarke 1994.

IOHAN (DB Ioħs = Iohannes)

Life: he was of Danish origin and might have been an old follower of Cnut, or a later housecarl, rewarded for service. His son Norðman was active in 1072, associated with Queen *Eadgyð*. Iohan's lands went to Matthew of Mortagne, along with those of Strang (£15) and Purcyll (£2), also Danes and perhaps relatives of Iohan.

Lands: in Dorset £20, Somerset £17 and Gloucester £5, overall worth £42. His main manors were Owermoigne (Dorset) and Yatton (Somerset).
Modern references: Clarke 1994.

LEOFNOÐ (Leofnoð, DB Leuenot)
Life: he was the son of Osmund.
Lands: in Bedford £62, Northampton £46 and Buckingham £10, overall worth £118. His main manors were Totternhoe and Segenhoe (Bedford).
Early sources: witnessed charter S1027 (1059).
Modern references: Clarke 1994.

LEOFNOÐ (DB Leuenot)
Life: brother of Leofric (£22), both were succeeded early by Raulf FitzHubert. It has been suggested that they might have been related to the family of Alderman Ælfhelm, and the important thane Morcere who was killed in 1015, since they held estates that had once been Morcere's.
Lands: in Derby £47 and Nottingham £11, overall worth £58. His main manors were Eckington, Barlborough and Palterton (Derby), and Barton (Nottingham).
Modern references: Sawyer 1979, Clarke 1994.

LIGULF (DB Ligulf)
Life: it is not known whether the Ligulf holding lands in 1066 was one man or several. A Ligulf still held nearly £3 of land in 1086, under Ilbert de Laci and as King's thane. This again might have been more than one man.
Lands: lands in Yorkshire, West Riding £31, North Riding £11 (19.4 ploughlands), East Riding 15/4 (+ 25 ploughlands), overall worth £44 (+ 46.2 ploughlands). His main manors might have been Bramham and Featherstone (West Riding).
Modern references: Faull & Stinson 1986.

MÆRLESWEGN (Mærleswegen, Mærlaswegen, DB Merlesuain, Merlesuen, Merlosuen)
Life: Sheriff of Lincoln, he was left in charge of the north by Harold II after the Battle of Stamford Bridge. He fled to Scotland with Eadgar II in 1068 and took part in the campaign in the north 1069-70. He presumably returned to Scotland with Eadgar in 1070. Nothing is known of his later career. His lands were given to Raulf Pagenel.
Lands: in Lincoln £62, Somerset £41, Devon £36, Cornwall £32 and York £29, overall worth £214. His main manors were Rasen, Tealby and Irnham (Lincoln), and Quantoxhead (Somerset).
Early sources: O, SD: Chr D (1068, 1069), E (1068): witnessed charters S1060 (1055/60), S1029 (1060), B216 (1067).
Modern references: Fleming 1991, Clarke 1994, Williams 1995.

NORÐMAN (DB Norman, Normann)
Lands: in Kent £34, Sussex £23 and Surrey £12, overall worth £68. His main manors were Mereworth (Kent), Annington (Sussex) and Camberwell (Surrey).

Early sources: witnessed charter? S1042 (1065).
Modern references: Clarke 1994.

ORDWULF (Ordulf, DB Ordulf)

Life: the son of Ordgar, an important thane in the earlier part of Eadward's reign, Ordwulf belonged to an old established and important family in the south west. The founder of the family's fortunes was Ordgar, whose daughter *Ælfþryð* had married Eadgar I. His son Ordwulf was the founder of Tavistock Abbey. The Ordwulf of 1066 might have been the grandson of the latter.
Lands: lands in Devon £50, Cornwall £13 and Somerset £4, overall worth £67. His main manors were Frithelstock and Bratton Fleming (Devon), and Tehidy (Cornwall). After the Conquest, most of his lands went to Count Rodbert of Mortain. His uncle Ælfgar might still have been living in 1066 holding £4 of land in Devon (Bradford and Lashbrook).
Early sources: witnessed charter S1027 (1059).
Modern references: Finberg 1943, 1964, Hart 1975, Clarke 1994.

ORM (DB Orm)

Life: son of Gamal, his lands went to Hugo FitzBaldric. An inscription records that he bought and renovated St Gregory's church at Kirkdale (North Riding). He might have had a son Gamal who was one of the hereditary lawmen of York, listed in a document of 1106. If so, he must have either inherited at least part of his father's lands as Hugo's tenant.
Lands: lands in Yorkshire North Riding £36, East Riding £13 and West Riding £1, overall worth £50 (+23 ploughlands). His main manors were Kirby Moorside, Hovingham and Langton.
Modern references: Faull & Stinson 1986, Clarke 1994, Williams 1995.

OSBEORN BICGA (DB Esber, Sbern, Sberne)

Life: he was the son of Ægelric Bigga.
Lands: lands in Kent worth £49. His main manors were Birling, Thurnham and Postling.
Early sources: mentioned in charter S1471 (1045): witnessed charter S1400 (1038/50), S1036 (1062).
Modern references: Robertson 1939, Clarke 1994.

OSCYLL OF WARE (DB Aschil, Aschi, Anschil, Anschill)

Lands: lands in Bedford £60 and Hertford £50, overall worth £109 (succeeded by Raulf Taillebois). His main manor was Ware (Hertford). Oscyll was lord of a great many local thanes and sokemen.
Modern references: Clarke 1994.

OSFERÐ (DB Offers)

Life: Osferð was still living in 1086, holding his Cornish lands under Count Rodbert of Mortain.
Lands: lands in Devon £22 and Cornwall £19, overall worth £41. His main manor was Okehampton (Devon).
Modern references: Clarke 1994.

OSGOD (DB Osgot)

Life: his brothers were Brihtric (£60) and Eadmund (£27). He and Brihtric were tenants of Earl Harold. His son Leofric still held some of his lands in 1086 and seems to have accommodated himself to the new regime by taking the Norman name Willelm.
Lands: lands in Gloucester £45, Berkshire £28, Buckingham £8, Essex £6 and Wiltshire £1, overall worth £88. His main manor was Kempsford (Gloucester).
Early sources: witnessed charter S1480 (1062/66).
Modern references: Clarke 1994, Williams 1995.

OSMUND (DB Osmund)

Life: Osmund was either a brother or brother-in-law of Wigod of Wallingford. His son Þurold (described as Wigod's nephew) was still holding his father's lands in 1086, but as a tenant of Earl Roger of Shrewsbury.
Lands: lands in Surrey £20, Wiltshire £19 and Hampshire £9, overall worth £47. His main manors were Castle Eaton (Wiltshire) and Worplesdon (Surrey).
Early sources: witnessed charter? S1042 (1065).
Modern references: Clarke 1994, Williams 1995.

OSWARD OF NORTON (DB Osuuard)

Life: Sheriff of Kent.
Lands: lands in Kent £65, Surrey £26, Sussex £12 and Essex £6, overall worth £109. His main manors were Walkingstead (Surrey) and Harrietsham (Kent).
Early sources: addressed in writs H35 (1053/61), H39 (1053/66).
Modern references: Clarke 1994.

OSWULF (DB Osulf)

Life: the son of Frane he was succeeded before 1076 by Rodbert de Tosni.
Lands: lands in Bedford £16, Buckingham £11, Hertford £11 and Northampton £4, overall worth £42. His main manors were Miswell (Hertford) and Studham (Bedford).
Early sources: witnessed charters S1010 (1045), S1019 (1049).
Modern references: Fleming 1991, Clarke 1994.

RAULF (Raulf, Rodulfus, DB Radulf)

Life: he was born in Norfolk of a Breton father who may have come to England with *Ymme* of Normandy in 1002. Raulf had a brother (or brother in law) Godwine and sons Raulf and Heardwine. He might have married the wealthy *Eadgyfu Fæger*, and was Eadward's Constable, being promoted to Earl of East Anglia by Willelm, and died 1068/70. He was succeeded as Earl by his son Raulf, who lost his title and lands rebelling against Willelm I in 1075. After the Norman Conquest, he was one of the officials who supervised the redemption by the English of their lands in East Anglia. Hereward, the Ely rebel, was reputed to have been his great-nephew. He still had interests in Brittany and was a benefactor of St Riquier Abbey.

Lands: lands in Lincoln £137, Norfolk £43, Cornwall £12 and Suffolk £11, overall worth £201 (£216 according to Lewis 1995). His main manors were Drayton and Longbennington (Lincoln). His brother Godwine held £7 in Norfolk in 1066, while Godwine's son Ælfsige held £13 in Norfolk and Suffolk.

Early sources: Chr D, E (1075): witnessed charters S1476 (c1053), S1028 (1059), S1029, S1031 (1060), S1033, S1034 (1061), S1426 (1061/66), S1036 (1062), S1040, S1041, S1042, S1043 (1065), charter of Duke Alan of Brittany in 1034, S1000.

Modern references: Freeman 1869-75 (Vols. 3 & 4), Larson 1904, Robertson 1939, Oleson 1955, Clarke 1994, Williams 1995, Lewis 1995.

RODBERT (Rodbt, Rotbert, Rodbertus, DB Rodbert, Rotbert, Robert, Robt fili Wimarc, Wimarch)

Life: he was named after his Breton mother as son of *Wymarc* and was said to be a kinsman of Eadward III. Rodbert came to England with Eadward in 1041, and became one of Eadward's Constables. He was at the deathbed of Eadward III and attempted to dissuade Willelm from fighting Harold II. He gained lands from Willelm I after the Conquest, and was appointed Sheriff of Essex. Rodbert died 1068/75 and his son Swegn inherited his position as Sheriff, and most of his lands.

Lands: lands in Essex £104, Suffolk £53, Huntingdon £32, Somerset £15, Wiltshire £1, Hereford (waste) and Shropshire (waste), overall worth £204 (£163 according to Lewis 1995). His main manors were Eynesbury (Huntingdon) and Clavering, at the latter of which he built one of the earliest castles in England (Essex).

Early sources: VÆ, WP, witnessed charters S1028 (1059), S1030, S1031 (1060), S1000, S1033, S1034 (1061), S1036 (1062), S1037a, S1040, S1041, S1042, S1043 (1065), B286 (1068), B232 (1069): addressed in writs H84 (1052/53), H93 (1058/66), H76.

Modern references: Freeman 1869-75 (Vol. 4), Larson 1904, Oleson 1955, Fleming 1991, Clarke 1994, Williams 1995, Lewis 1995.

ROLF (DB Rolf, Rolft)

Life: he was the son of Scyldware.

Lands: in Lincoln £58, Nottingham £2 and Leicester 1/6, overall worth £59. His main manor was Manton (Leicester).

Modern references: Clarke 1994.

SEAXIG (DB Saxi, Sexi)

Lands: lands in Hampshire £40 and Berkshire £14, overall worth £54. His main manors were Upper Clatford and Thruxton (Hampshire).
Modern references: Clarke 1994.

SIGERED OF CHILHAM (DB Sired, Siret)

Life: he might have been associated with Osbeorn Bicga, from whom he held some of his lands.
Lands: lands in Kent worth £66. His main manor was Chilham.
Modern references: Clarke 1994.

SIWARD BARN (Sigwarð, DB Siuuard, Seuuard)

Life: Siward joined the opposition to Willelm under Eadgar II in 1069-70, and took part in the resistance at Ely in 1071 where he was captured. He was imprisoned in Normandy, and his lands were given to Henri de Ferrers, but was released in 1087 and ended up in Scotland. It may be that he eventually joined the Varangian Guard at Constantinople, in the service of the Byzantine Emperors. It has been suggested that he was the brother or half-brother of Gospatric, son of Maldred (Earl after the Conquest and co-supporter of Eadgar).
Lands: Berkshire £48, Derby £35, Gloucester £20, Lincoln £15, Warwick £8, Nottingham £6, Norfolk £6 and Yorkshire West Riding £4, overall worth £142. His main manors were Stanford (Berkshire) and Lechlade (Gloucester).
Early sources: W, SD: Chr D, E (1071): witnessed charters? S1480 (1062/66), S1041, S1043 (1065).
Modern references: Fell 1973, Godfrey 1978, Faull & Stinson 1986, Fleming 1991, Hart 1992, Clarke 1994, Williams 1995.

SIWARD THE FAT (Siward, DB Siuuard, Seuuard, Seuuar)

Life: a kinsman of Eadward III, he and his brother Ealdred (£19 + 1½ hides) were sons of Ægelgar who may have married the daughter of Eadward's half sister *Eadgyð* and Alderman Eadric of Mercia (died 1017). He took part in the submission of the Mercian magnates to Willelm in 1067 at Barking. Siward was a benefactor of St Peter's church in Shrewsbury, and was still living in 1086, although with reduced lands (he probably took part in the revolt of 1069-70 in Mercia with his cousin Eadric Wilde). He may be the ancestor of the later Seward family in Shropshire. His son Eadward may have become Constable of Scotland under his cousin King David.
Lands: lands in Shropshire £68 and Hereford £4, overall worth £72. His main manor was Stanton Lacy (Shropshire). He was no longer a tenant in chief in 1086 but held his land from Earl Roger, Roger de Lacy and Osbeorn FitzRicard.
Early sources: O, DB.
Modern references: Clarke 1994, Williams 1995.

SIWARD OF MALDON (DB Siuuard, Seuuard)

Life: he took part in the revolt at Ely with Hereward in 1071. Siward held land of the Abbey of Ely (and Barking Abbey in Essex) and had made donations to the abbey.
Lands: lands in Essex £113 and Suffolk £34, overall worth £147. His main manors were Debden (Essex) and Acton (Suffolk).
Early sources: witnessed charters? S1036 (1062), S1041, S1043 (1065).
Modern references: Hart 1992, Clarke 1994, Williams 1995.

SIWARD (DB Siuuard)

Life: he may have been an early casualty of the Conquest since his lands went to Baldwin of Exeter.
Lands: lands in Somerset £29, Devon £16 and Dorset £15, overall worth £60 (Clarke omits his Dorset lands). His main manors were Hemington (Somerset) and Iwerne Courtney (Dorset).
Early sources: witnessed charter S1042 (1065).
Modern references: Clarke 1994.

STORIG (DB Stori, Estori)

Life: his lands went to Ivo Taillebois.
Lands: lands in Lincoln worth £46. His main manor was Bolingbroke.
Modern references: Clarke 1994.

SWEGN (DB Suuen)

Life: he may have been involved in the northern resistance to Willelm. Most of his lands were granted out as part of large territorial fees, but he was still holding part of his lands in 1086 and had exchanged some for others under Ilbert de Laci.
Lands: lands in Yorkshire, West Riding £33 (+ 5.6 ploughlands), East Riding £10 and North Riding £9 (+ 2 ploughlands), overall worth £52 (+ 7.6 ploughlands). His main manors may have been High Melton and Sprotbrough (West Riding).
Modern references: Faull & Stinson 1986.

TOCIG (DB Tochi)

Life: he was the son of Otta (Autig) and was either killed in 1066 or took part in the revolts of 1069-71 as he was succeeded early by Goisfrið Alselin.
Lands: lands in Lincoln £50, Derby £38, Nottingham £28, Yorkshire West Riding £23, Leicester £8 and Northampton £4, overall worth £151. His main manors were Ruskington and Westborough (Lincoln).
Modern references: Fleming 1991, Clarke 1994.

TOCIG (DB Toca, Toka, Tocha, Toche, Tohe, Tochi, Tochil)

Life: his lands had been given to Frederic. This must have been soon after the Conquest as Frederic was one of the Normans killed by Hereward in 1070. Tocig's lands then passed to Frederic's brother-in-law, Willelm de Warenne. Perhaps Tocig

was one of those who fell at Hastings. Hart (1992) identifies him with Þurcyll of Harringworth, partially dispossessed after the Conquest and so goaded into joining Hereward's rebellion.
Lands: lands in Norfolk £59, Cambridge £38 and Suffolk £5, overall worth £103. His main manors were West Walton (Norfolk), Kennet and Weston Colville (Cambridge).
Modern references: Fleming 1991 (Frederic), Clarke 1994, Williams 1995.

TOLIG (DB Toli, Tholi, Tol, Thol, Toul, Tou)
Life: he was a Dane by birth.
Lands: lands in Dorset £42, Hampshire £24, Somerset £7, Wiltshire £2 and Devon 6/-, overall worth £75. His main manors were Somborne and Deane (Hampshire), and Bradford Peverel (Dorset).
Modern references: Clarke 1994.

TONNIG (DB Tonna, Tunna, Tonne, Tunne, Tona)
Lands: lands in Lincoln £60, Northampton £21, Oxford £10, Berkshire £6 and Yorkshire West Riding £1, overall worth £93. His main manors were Culverthorpe and Lusby (Lincoln). His lands went to Gislebert de Gand after the Conquest.
Modern references: Clarke 1994.

ÞOR (DB Tor)
Life: he may have taken part in the resistance to Willelm in 1069-70, his lands being forfeited to the King but then given out as part of large territorial fees. He may still have held Wombwell and West Melton as King's thane.
Lands: lands in Yorkshire, North Riding £30 (+ 27 ploughlands), East Riding £6 (+ 1 ploughland) and West Riding £5, overall worth £41 (+ 28 ploughlands). His main manors may have been Thirsk, Constable Burton, Carperby, Harmby and Kiplin (North Riding).
Modern references: Faull & Stinson 1986.

ÞURCYLL HWIT (DB Turchil)
Life: Þurcyll was a Dane, probably a follower of Cnut, and had married an English wife, *Leoflæd* (£19). His lands were given to Hugo the Ass by Earl Willelm FitzOsbeorn, possibly in 1067. He was allied to Earl Harold and his family.
Lands: lands in Hereford £50 and Gloucester £6, overall worth £56. His main manor was Fownhope (Hertford).
Early sources: witnessed charters S1462 (1016/35), S1469 (1043/46).
Modern references: Fleming 1991, Clarke 1994.

ÞURCYLL (DB Turchil, Torchil)
Life: Willelm Malet held lands of a Þurcyll by 1069, who may have been killed at Fulford or Stamford Bridge. Another Þurcyll was still holding 23/- and 1 ploughland

in 1086. The earlier Þurcyll may well have held most of the lands attributed to that name in 1066.

Lands: lands in Yorkshire, East Riding £30 (+ 17.2 ploughlands), West Riding £19 (+ 4.4 ploughlands), North Riding £13 (+ 27 ploughlands), overall worth £62 (+ 48.6 ploughlands). His main manors may have been Scrayingham (East Riding), East Appleton, Rainton and Well (North Riding), Whiston and Woolley (West Riding).

Modern references: Faull & Stinson 1986.

ÞURCYLL OF HARRINGWORTH (DB Turchill, Torchill, Turchil)

Life: also known as Þurcyll Cild, he was a Dane and was active late in the reign of Cnut, most likely being the son of one of Cnut's followers. His wife was *Þurgun* and both were patrons of Ramsey and Thorney Abbeys. Þurcyll took part with Hereward in the revolt against the Normans at Ely in 1071, and his lands were given to Earl Walþeof.

Lands: lands in Northampton £26, Huntingdon £19, Leicester £3 and Buckingham £2, overall worth £49. Hart (1992) has a different list of his lands, including those of Tocig, predecessor of Frederic, and others, which would give him a total of over £150. Þurcyll's main manors were Sawtry (Huntingdon) and Harringworth (Northampton).

Modern reference: Hart 1966, Fleming 1991, Hart 1992, Clarke 1994, Williams 1995.

ÞURGOD LAH (DB Turgot)

Life: he was one of the lawmen of Lincoln, dispossessed and replaced by the Tosni family. In 1068, he was held as a hostage for the loyalty of Lindsey. He later entered the service of Bishop Walcher of Durham and then joined the new monastery at Jarrow, later travelling to Melrose before settling down at Wearmouth. In 1087, he became Prior of the Cathedral at Durham and, in 1107, he was chosen as Bishop of St Andrews, returning to Durham to die in 1115. He spent some time with Queen *Margareta* in Scotland and wrote a life of her between 1100 and 1107.

Lands: lands in Lincoln £36, Oxford £19 and Yorkshire East Riding £5, overall worth £59. His main manor was Broughton (Oxford).

Early sources: VM.

Modern references: Robertson 1939, Fleming 1991, Clarke 1994, Williams 1995.

ULF FENISC (Ulf, DB Vlf)

Life: one of the most powerful of thanes before 1066. He was probably dispossessed early in Willelm's reign. His byname probably indicated that he came originally from the Fens (although it has also been suggested that he came from Fjon in Denmark). A surviving inscription records that he built a church at his manor of Aldborough in Yorkshire. He was succeeded early by Gislebert of Ghent and Drogo de Bevrere, which suggests that he might have taken part in Eadgar's northern rising against Willelm.

Lands: lands in Lincoln £189, Yorkshire East Riding £88, Nottingham £45, Huntingdon £17, Buckingham £14, Bedford £10, Northampton £10, Derby £8,

Oxford £6, Rutland £4 and Cambridge £3, overall worth £394. His main manors were Folkingham and Barton on Humber (Lincoln), and Aldborough (York).

Early sources: witnessed charters? S1060 (1055/60), S1028 (1059), S1029 (1060), S1059 (1061/66), S1037a (1065).

Modern references: Fleming 1991, Clarke 1994.

ULF (DB Vlf)

Life: Ulf was a housecarl of Eadward III, and might have been one his military commanders recently enriched in return for his services. His lands passed to Rodbert de Tosni.

Lands: lands in Gloucester £38, Suffolk £9, Buckingham £8 and Cambridge £8, overall worth £57. His main manors were Sapperton, Horton and Rissington (Gloucester).

Modern references: Clarke 1994.

WIGOD OF WALLINGFORD (Wiggod, DB Wigot)

Life: the King's Butler, his daughter *Ealdgyð* married Rodbert d'Oilly (who thereby acquired Wigod's lands), and his nephew Ælfred and brother-in-law Þurold were landholders in 1086. His son Tocig (holding £16 in 1066) had been one of Eadward's housecarls and was killed fighting in the Norman army at Gerberoi in 1079. Eadward III addressed him as his kinsman in a writ (H104), but it is not known how he was related to the King. His name is of Norse origin, common in Norfolk and Lincoln (Insley 1994). He seems to have become wealthy through his service to the King.

Lands: lands in Sussex £23, Oxford £20, Middlesex £18, Buckingham £18, Berkshire £15, Wiltshire £8, and Gloucester £5 overall worth £116. His main manors were Broadwater (Sussex) and Letcombe (Berkshire). Clarke includes Clyst St Mary in Devon, in reality held by Wigod the priest, a different man.

Early sources: witnessed charters S1036 (1062), S1041, S1042, S1043 (1065): addressed in writ H104 (1065/66).

Modern references: Freeman 1869-75 (Vols. 3 & 4), Fleming 1991, Clarke 1994, Williams 1995.

WIHTGAR (DB Wisgar, Wiscar)

Life: the son of Ælfric (son of Wihtgar) was a follower of Queen *Ymme*, and founder of the minster at Clare. His father was related to two important landowners, Ægelwine Niger and *Leofgyfu*. The latter had left him land in her will. Some of Wihtgar's lands were due to be given to Bury St Edmund's at his death (eg Clare). His lands passed to Ricard of Clare, with whom he might have reached some sort of agreement before the transfer took place. Wihtgar was clearly a powerful local lord with a number of dependant landowners.

Lands: lands in Suffolk £107 and Essex £76, overall worth £182. His main manors were Clare, Hundon and Desming (Suffolk), and Thaxted (Essex).

Early sources: father mentioned in will S1521 (1035/44): father witnessed S1228 (1042/49).

Modern references: Fleming 1991, Clarke 1994, Williams 1995.

WULFGYFU OF BETTESLAU (DB *Vlueua, Vlueue*)

Life: she may have been the widow (*laf*) of Bette, and was connected to the household of Queen *Eadgyð*.

Lands: Hampshire £66, Somerset £11, Berkshire £10, Dorset £10 and Wiltshire £1, overall worth £98. Her main manors were Mapledurham and Sherborne St John (Hampshire).

Modern references: Clarke 1994, Stafford 1997.

WULFMÆR OF EATON (DB Vlmar, Vlmer)

Lands: lands in Bedford £43, Essex £36 and Cambridge £20, overall worth £99. His main manors were Gamlingay (Cambridge), Eaton Socon and Sandy (Bedford).

Modern references: Clarke 1994.

WULFWARD HWIT (DB Wluuard, Vluuard)

Life: he owed his fortune to the patronage of Queens *Ymme* and *Eadgyð*, and was possibly still living in 1084. His wife *Eadgyfu* held £38 of land in Buckinghamshire in 1066, and his son Wulfward Cild held £11 in the same shire. His daughter married Ælfsige (*Eadgyð's* steward) who was a landholder in 1086.

Lands: lands in Middlesex £42, Bedford £30, Hampshire £15, Somerset £15, Oxford £15, Dorset £13, Berkshire £12, Lincoln £10, Gloucester £9, Kent £8 and Wiltshire £7, overall worth £225. His main manors were Ruislip (Middlesex), Toddington (Bedford), Chipping Norton (Oxford) and Hayling Island (Hampshire).

Early sources: recorded an agreement in S1476 (c1053): witnessed charters S1041 (1065), B286 (1068), P144 (1066/86), P56 (1072), VCH Som 1 399: involved in a record of sale P107.

Modern references: Robertson 1939, Fleming 1991, Clarke 1994, Williams 1995, Stafford 1997.

WULFWINE (DB Wluuin, Wluin, Vluuin)

Life: the son of Ælfwine, his lands were given to Alberic de Vere.

Lands: lands in Essex £74 and Cambridge £62, overall worth £136. His main manors were Silverley and Camps (Cambridge), Belchamp and Hedingham (Essex).

Modern references: Fleming 1991, Clarke 1994, Williams 1995.

WULFWYNN OF CRESLOW (DB Wluuen, Vluuen, Wluuene)

Life: it is likely that she was the mother of Eadward of Salisbury who was the wealthiest surviving native English landholder in 1086, and ancestor of the Earls of Salisbury. Her estates might have been only recently brought together before she acquired them from her father or husband.

Lands: lands in Dorset £50, Buckingham £28, Hertford £25, Wiltshire £16, Berkshire £11 and Middlesex £9, overall worth £137. Her main manors were Cranford Magna (Dorset), Great Gaddesden (Hertford) and Aston Sanford (Buckingham).

Modern references: White 1949, Clarke 1994, Williams 1995.

THE KING'S HOUSEHOLD

Wealth was not the only way of exercising power. A powerful weapon in the hands of the King was the appointment to various offices which gave power, either directly or through having access to the King. Among the latter, the most important were probably the chief offices of the royal household. The household officials would be well placed to exercise influence over the King. Many, but not all, of these were important landowners. The most important offices (Larson 1904) seem to have been the constable, chamberlain, steward, and butler (see later under *The King's Priests* for the post of chancellor). The constable was known in English as a *steallere* (staller) and the office seems to have been an introduction of Cnut. One of the holders of this office was identified in the Latin of the Domesday Book as *constabularius*, although other terms were also used to describe the post, e.g. *procurator*, *dapifer* (Larson 1904: 151). The other three offices had a longer history and were referred to in the will of King Eadred as the *discþegn* (steward, in Latin *dapifer* or *discifer*), *hræglþegn* – elsewhere as *burþegn* – (chamberlain, in Latin *camerarius* or *cubicularius*) and *biriele* (butler, in Latin *pincerna*). The duties of the officials were to oversee the various secular activities of the household. The butler had care of the cellar, the chamberlain of the chamber and wardrobe (and the King's money kept within the chamber), the steward of provisioning for the table. The constable may well have been the main military official, in charge of the household troops, the housecarls. Offices were shared between several holders, usually only three at any one time for the civilian offices (which may reflect the division of the court into three shifts by King Ælfred). Identification of the holders of these offices depends on the evidence of charters and the Domesday survey. Attribution of people to an office is often either confused, e.g. Eadnoð the constable is termed in the Domesday Book *dapifer* (the Latin term for steward), or unsecure, e.g. Brihtric and Ælfstan who are referred to as *consiliarius* or *princeps* in charters of the period which, if meant to signify office at court, would leave them to be fitted into the two positions not already known to be filled, i.e. as butlers.

Constable		Chamberlain		Steward		Butler	
Esgar	£448	Wynsige	£19	Ætsere	£9	Brihtric?	£560
Rodbert	£204	Hugo	£13	Alan	£1	Ælfstan?	£289
Raulf	£201	Ælfric	£1	Yfing?	?	Wigod	£117
Bondig	£182						
Eadnoð	£64						

Table 2: The King's household

Some of the people identified (Table 2) seem to have been quite lowly while others were among the wealthiest thanes of the kingdom, often holding several offices, e.g. Brihtric who was also Sheriff of Gloucestershire, and Ælfstan, Sheriff of Bedfordshire. Presumably, the latter might have delegated their day-to-day duties in the household to deputies. The wealthier office holders are listed above among the thanes. Those with less than £40 of land are as follows:

ALAN (DB Alan)

Life: he was a French or Breton Steward of Eadward III who was still living in 1086.
Lands: in Suffolk worth £1 (Wyken).
Early sources: DB.
Modern references: Larson 1904, Lewis 1995.

ÆLFRIC (DB Aluric)

Life: an Ælfric is mentioned in the Domesday Book as King Eadward's Chamberlain.
Lands: in Buckingham worth £1, and probably others elsewhere. Unfortunately, his name is rather common which makes it difficult to further identify his lands.
Early sources: DB.
Modern references: Larson 1904.

ÆTSERE (DB Azor)

Life: identified as Steward (*dispensator*) in the Domesday Book, in an entry in Berkshire. His name was fairly common and he might well have been one of the Ætseres listed among the greater thanes. He was still living in 1086, one of his estates having been restored to him by Willelm.
Lands: in Berkshire worth £9 (Eddington and Ardington).
Early sources: DB.
Modern references: Oleson 1955.

HUGO (Huhgelin, DB Hugo)

Life: a Frenchman, the King's Chamberlain who was buried at Westminster, where there was a tradition that he was unjustly disgraced and executed, possibly after the Conquest. He was reputed to have had charge of the treasury and royal archives, although this is known to have been a function of the King's chaplains.
Lands: in Oxford £8, Berkshire £4 and Warwick £1, overall worth £13.
Early sources: Ra, Fl, DB: witnessed charters S1002 (1044), S1030, S1031 (1060), S1033 (1061), S1426 (1061/66), S1480 (1062/66): witnessed writ H62.
Modern references: Larson 1904, Harmer 1952, Barlow 1970.

WYNSIGE (Wynsi, DB Wenesi)

Life: one of the King's Chamberlains.
Lands: in Buckingham (£5) and Bedford (10 hides). Possibly also in Berkshire, Cambridge, Hampshire, Shrewsbury and Surrey, overall worth £19 + 15 hides.
Early sources: DB: witnessed charters S1480 (1062/66), S1042 (1065).

Modern references: Larson 1904.

YFING

Life: a Steward of the King is identified as Yfing in a forged document supposedly of 1062. This may reflect genuine tradition although the name is unusual and may be a mistake for Lyfing. There was a Constable called Lyfing signing charters from 1043 to 1053/55.
Early sources: witnessed charter S1036 (1062).
Modern references: Larson 1904.

THANES INVOLVED IN REVOLTS 1065-71

It is clear from the numbers of thanes replaced by Normans that many must have been dispossessed as a result of taking part in revolts against Willelm. There are simply too many to have been all casualties at Fulford, Stamford Bridge or Hastings. However, the sources for the period reveal only the leading campaigners against Willelm. Fleming (1991) suggests others can be added for the northern revolt by identifying their Norman successors. Known rebels are listed in Table 3. For the sake of completeness those who rebelled against Tostig in 1065 are also given. Some achieved later notoriety and a place that may have been out of proportion to their original importance, e.g. Hereward in the 19th century (Hart 1992, Head 1995), whose revolt was arguably nowhere near as much a threat to Willelm's position as the opposition of Eadgar in the north, and whose status was that of a relatively minor noble.

Date	Place	Names
1065	Northumbria	Dunstan c£10, Gamalbarn c£30-40, Glunier £10
1069-70	Northumbria	Ælfwine ?, Eadgyfu £22, Earncytel c£60-80, Gamal £21, Gamal £3, Gamalbarn 32 ploughlands, Gamalbarn £8, Mærleswegn £210, Norðman £20, Orm £50, Siward Barn £140, Tocig Otta's son £151, Ulf Topi's son £15, sons of Carl Cnut £25-35 Gamal £15-30, Sumorled 2/-, Þorbrand £20-25
1069-70	Mercia	Eadric £100+, Siward? £70
1070-71	The Fens	Godric of Corby £4 (possibly the nephew of Earls Eadwine and Morcere), Hereward £3, Sheriff Ordgar of Essex £13, Siward of Maldon £150, Siward Barn £140, Tostig of Daventry £5, Þorberht, Þurcyll of Harringworth £49

Table 3: Thanes involved in revolts 1065-71

THE SHERIFFS

Sheriffs (from *scir gerefa*, shire reeve) were the King's officials in the shires. The earliest known sheriff was Wulfsige of Kent 964/88. The origins of the office have been sought in the administration of hundreds under Eadgar I (Morris 1927) or the administration of royal rights and collection of taxes (Green 1990). However, there are early references to King's reeves and it is probable that the sheriff evolved out of reeves appointed to look after royal estates. Judicial and financial functions would be a natural extension to their existing duties since the King's estate would act as a convenient central point for both functions. A key period for the growth of the office was the reign of Æþelred who may have been using the sheriffs as administrative and political counterweights to the aldermen, leading to inevitable tension between the two. In 1002, Alderman Leofsige was dismissed and exiled for killing the King's reeve Æfic.

Appointments as sheriff were made by the King, perhaps influenced by earls or other powerful interests, although a strong King would ensure that he had his own nominees in post. There was no set term of office and we do not have enough information to know whether they served for long or short periods of time, or whether sons could expect appointment in succession to fathers. The men appointed sheriffs seem mostly to have been lesser nobility, only rarely were they drawn from the ranks of the wealthiest thanes. Even priests could be appointed as sheriffs. Unfortunately, we do not have enough information to determine how their composition compared with that of post-Conquest sheriffs (Green 1983). They would play a key role in the shire and be important channels of communication between the King and the localities. The effective functioning of the machinery of justice and administration depended on their abilities. They presumably had staff to help them carry out their duties but we know little of who these might have been at this period.

The sheriff's duties were various. Managing the King's lands and receiving their income on behalf of the King remained important. Collecting taxes and fines was an extension of this. Accounting for the King's finances involved a twice-yearly journey to the exchequer in the 12th century. Earlier arrangements are unknown but may have involved similar visits using wooden tallies rather than the exchequer counting table (John 1982). It has been argued however that any centralised system of financial accounting like this was introduced after the Conquest (Green 1986: 42). Other tasks included supervising the judicial work of the hundreds (king's reeves were ordered to hold courts every 4 weeks in the law code of 2 Eadward I in 923/24) and enforcing the decisions of the courts (what we might call police work). In later times, the sheriff is known to have supervised the system of frankpledge, which bound all free men into associations of ten individuals with mutual liability for enforcing the law upon each other. These ten men tithings are evident in the Anglo-Saxon law codes (Loyn 1984: 142) and so the sheriff's responsibilities for this may date back to this period. The sheriff must also in practice have presided over the shire courts as their nominal heads, the earl and bishop, must often have been called away by other business. The final task of the sheriff was to lead the military forces of the shire, most likely in its own defence. The Anglo-Saxon Chronicle noted the names of two 'high reeves' who were killed opposing the Danes with the *fyrd* of Hampshire in 1001. In many of these functions, the sheriff was subordinate to the earl but he remained a royal official, appointed by, and responsible to, the King. No doubt the interplay of factional rivalries and power politics at local level made such a line of responsibility less clear-cut.

Much of the evidence for sheriffs comes from writs sent by the King to the shire court where the sheriff is addressed alongside the earl and bishop. Not all included the sheriff's name and in some a name is given without the title of sheriff (writs shown below with *). Some of these may not be sheriffs but other officials. However, some of these names were identified as sheriff in the Domesday survey. Officials of the King's household, the constables, were sometimes addressed in writs instead of the sheriff. In Middlesex, the portreeves of London may have acted at times also as sheriffs. The pre-Conquest Latin terms used for sheriff were *praefectus* or *praepositus*. After the Conquest, the Norman preference was for *vicecomes*.

For the sake of completeness, all the sheriffs are listed below, even though some have already been listed in the section on thanes (indicated with * after the name). In these cases, only a summary of them is given and fuller details can be found in their earlier entry. No names of sheriffs are known for the following shires: Chester, Cornwall, Leicester, Northumberland, Shrewsbury, Surrey and Sussex. The list relies heavily on Green 1990, augmented by evidence from the writs of the period. In some cases exact identification of a sheriff with a particular shire cannot be certain.

ÆGELWIG (DB Alwi, Ailuin, Aluuin)
Sheriff of Norfolk
Life: he was certainly reeve of Thetford under Harðacnut and then or later had jurisdiction throughout Norfolk, and was still in office until sometime after 1075. His son Stanhard inherited only a small part of his father's lands. Ægelwig gave lands to St Benet's Abbey, where was later buried.
Lands: in Norfolk worth at least £16.
Evidence: H56* (1040/42), DB.
Modern references: Williams 1995.

ÆLFGEAT
Sheriff of Middlesex
Early sources: witnessed charter S1034 (1061).

98

Evidence: H86, H87 (1057/66).

ÆLFRED (DB Alured)

Sheriff of Dorset
Life: he was replaced sometime after 1066 by Hugo FitzGrip.
Lands: in Dorset worth £20 and possibly elsewhere.
Evidence: H1 (1053/58), DB.

ÆLFRIC*

Sheriff of Huntingdon
Life: Ælfric was appointed also to Cambridge after 1066. He was replaced in Huntingdon before 1080 by Eustatius and in Cambridge c1071 by Picot.
Lands: in Huntingdon £11, perhaps the same as Ælfric the thane with lands in Essex, Cambridge, Suffolk, Bedford and Berkshire worth £77.
Early sources: witnessed charter S1027 (1059).
Evidence: H59 (1050/52, Huntingdon), DB (Huntingdon and Cambridge).

ÆLFSIGE

Portreeve of London
Life: he, or his colleague Leofstan, was probably replaced by Goisfrið de Mandeville in 1067. Ælfsige was likely to have been the moneyer of that name minting at London during this period.
Evidence: H105, H106 (1065/66).

ÆLFSTAN*

Sheriff of Bedford
Life: Ælfstan may have held office in the King's household. By 1075/81 he was replaced by Raulf Taillebois.
Lands: in Wiltshire, Hertford, Somerset, Gloucester, Bedford, Dorset, Hampshire and Berkshire worth £289.
Evidence: in a private charter S1235 (1053/66).

BLACWINE (DB Blacuin)

Sheriff of Cambridge?
Life: replaced soon after 1066 by Ælfric of Huntingdon.
Lands: in Cambridge worth £11 and 4 hides.
Evidence: DB.

BRIHTRIC*

Sheriff of Gloucester
Life: Brihtric was the wealthiest of the thanes, possibly with an office in the King's household, but was replaced before 1079/83 by Roger de Pîtres. Roger had been granted land in Gloucester by Earl Willelm before the latter's death in 1071.

Lands: in Gloucester, Devon, Dorset, Cornwall, Hereford, Wiltshire, Worcester and Hampshire worth £560.
Early sources: witnessed charters S1027, S1028 (1059), S1033, S1034 (1061), S1036 (1062), B286 (1068).
Evidence: B223* (1067).
Modern references: Hart 1975.

CYNEWARD (DB Chenuard, Cheneuuard, Keneuuard)

Sheriff of Worcester
Life: he was replaced by 1069 by Urse d'Abetot. Cyneward might have a member of the family of Archbishop Wulfstan of York (1002-23).
Lands: in Gloucester, Warwick and Worcester worth £15.
Evidence: Hm (before 1069).
Modern references: Williams & Erskine 1988, Williams 1995.

EADMUND (DB Edmund)

Sheriff of Hertford
Life: Eadmund was a follower of Earl Harold, who was replaced by 1072/75 by a Norman named Ilbert.
Lands: in Hertford worth £2 and possibly others elsewhere.
Evidence: B297 (1067).

EADRIC*

Sheriff of Wilton
Life: Eadric was replaced by 1081 by Eadward of Salisbury and was dead by 1086.
Lands: in Gloucester, Somerset, Hampshire, Wiltshire and Dorset worth £63.
Early sources: witnessed charters S1028 (1059), S1036 (1062).
Evidence: B223* (1067), DB.
Modern references: Williams 1995.

EADSIGE (DB Ezi)

Sheriff of Hampshire
Lands: in Hampshire worth £8, and possibly others elsewhere.
Evidence: in a private contract S1476 (1053), DB.

EADWINE (DB Eduin)

Sheriff of Warwick
Life: Eadwine was probably replaced by 1072 by Ægelwine, certainly before 1077 by Rodbert d'Oilly.
Lands: in Warwick worth £16.
Evidence: DB (1066).

GAMAL

Sheriff of York
Life: He was the son of Osbeorn, and was replaced probably in 1068 by Willelm Malet.
Evidence: Farrer 88 (1066/69).

GODRIC*

Sheriff of Berkshire, possibly also of Buckingham
Life: Godric was killed at Hastings.
Lands: in Berkshire, Wiltshire and Buckingham worth £45.
Early sources: witnessed charters S1028 (1059), S1029 (1060), S1041, S1043 (1065).
Evidence: H5* (1053/66, Berkshire), DB (Berkshire and Buckingham).
Modern references: Freeman 1869-75, Williams 1995.

HEARDING*

Sheriff of Derby, and possibly Nottingham
Life: Queen *Eadgyð's* Butler. Derby and Nottingham shared a common shire court at this period and he was most likely the sheriff for both shires.
Lands: lands in Wiltshire, Leicester, Warwick, Somerset and Dorset worth £90.
Evidence: B33 (1066/86).
Modern references: Williams 1995.

HECA (DB Heche)

Sheriff of Devon
Life: He was replaced by 1069 by Willelm de Vauville.
Lands: in Devon worth £17.
Evidence: DB.

LEOFSTAN

Portreeve of London
Life: He, or his colleague Ælfsige, was probably replaced by Goisfrið de Mandeville in 1067. A Leofstan was brother of the prominent moneyer Deorman. It is possible this might have been the same man. He had two sons, one of whom he gave the Norman name of Rodbert, showing that he accommodated himself to the new regime.
Evidence: H105, H106 (1065/66).
Modern references: Freeman 1869-75, Williams 1995.

MÆRLESWEGN*

Sheriff of Lincoln
Life: Mærleswegn supported Eadgar II against Willelm 1068-70.
Lands: in Lincoln, Somerset, Devon, Cornwall and York worth £214.
Early sources: O, SD: Chr D (1068, 1069), E (1068): witnessed charters S1060 (1055/60), S1029 (1060).

Evidence: S1060 (1055/60), B216 (1067), DB.
Modern references: Williams 1995.

NORÐMAN (DB Normann)

Sheriff of Northampton
Lands: in Northampton worth £6 and possibly other lands elsewhere.
Evidence: H94 (1065/66), H62.

ORDGAR (DB Orgar)

Sheriff of Essex?
Life: An Ordgar, identified as a sheriff, was a follower of the Constable Esgar and had been given some land by Earl Harold in Cambridge. However, the Sheriff of Cambridge may have been Blacwine and Ordgar's shire could have been Essex where he also held land. Ordgar was probably involved in Hereward's uprising at Ely in 1071. The Constable Rodbert may have been appointed to Essex soon after 1066, his son Swegn was certainly Sheriff by 1075.
Lands: in Cambridge worth £12 (+ 4 hides) and in Essex worth £13.
Evidence: DB.
Modern reference: Hart 1992.

OSBEORN (DB Osbern)

Sheriff of Hereford
Life: Osbeorn was the son of Ricard FitzScrob, a Norman follower of Eadward III. He was probably replaced by Raulf de Bernai, appointed by Earl Willelm FitzOsbeorn before 1071. He married Nest, the daughter of Queen *Ealdgyð* by her first husband, King Griffin of Gwynedd.
Lands: with his father in Hereford, Shropshire and Worcester worth £22, with another 31 hides as waste.
Evidence: H50* (1061).
Modern references: Freeman 1869-75, Williams 1995.

OSWARD*

Sheriff of Kent
Life: Haimo the Steward had replaced him by 1077, and possibly Hugo de Port before then.
Lands: lands in Kent, Surrey, Sussex and Essex worth £109.
Evidence: H35 (1053/61), H39* (1053/66), DB.

SÆWOLD (DB Sawold, Sauuold)

Sheriff of Oxford
Life: he was replaced by 1069 by Roger d'Ivry and may have been still living in 1086.
Lands: in Oxford, Warwick, Wiltshire and Worcester worth £7.
Evidence: B296 (1067).

TOFIG (DB Toui)

Sheriff of Somerset
Life: may have been succeeded by 1076 by Willelm de Courseilles.
Lands: in Devon and Somerset worth £18.
Early sources: witnessed charter R23 (1068).
Evidence: H68, H69, H70* (1061/66), H71* (1066), DB, B11 (1067), B287 (1066/82).

TOLIG (Tolig, DB Toli, Tohli)

Sheriff of Suffolk
Life: Tolig was replaced in Suffolk by Norþman, who was replaced in turn by Rodbert Malet by 1071. A dubious writ named him as Sheriff also in Norfolk.
Lands: in Suffolk worth £19.
Evidence: H10*, H18 (1052/57), H20 (1051/57), H23, H24, H25 (1065/66), H61 (Norfolk), DB.
Modern references: Clarke 1994.

ÞURCYLL

Sheriff of Stafford
Life: Þurcyll was a common name but there was no landowner with this name in the Staffordshire Domesday. The name is common but he could have one of the greater thanes, or perhaps son of Ælfwine of Warwick.
Evidence: B292 (1066/68).
Modern references: Freeman 1869-75.

CONSTABLES ACTING IN PLACE OF SHERIFFS

In some writs addressed to the shire court, a constable is found in the place where a sheriff's name would normally be. The implications of this are unknown. It may be that the constable was appointed to the shire for a particular purpose, or during a vacancy in the sheriffdom. In one case, there is evidence that the constable was sheriff of the shire after 1066 (Rodbert in Essex). In other cases, we have the names of the appropriate sheriff during the period of the writ (e.g. Eadsige in Hampshire) and in a writ of Willelm I (R18) the Constable Bondig is addressed alongside the sheriff. It should be noted that few of the writs involved are authentic beyond any doubt.

EADNOÐ

Hampshire: H85 (1053/66)
Somerset: R7 (1067)

ESGAR

Hertford: H91 (1057/66)
Kent: H76
London: H75 (1042/44)
Middlesex: H98 (1065/66)

RODBERT

Essex: H84 (1052/53)
Kent: H76
Surrey: H93 (1058/66)

THE KING'S PRIESTS

We know little about the ecclesiastical side of the King's household. There must have been two components, his chapel and the writing office. The former would have been staffed by priests; the latter perhaps more by deacons and clerks in lesser orders, who also had charge of the chapel's relics. The will of King Eadred (died 955) makes plain this division of the chaplains into two sorts, and their relatively high status:

> *And ælcan ȝesettan discðeȝne and ȝesettan hræȝlðeȝne and ȝesettan biriele, hundeahtatiȝ mancusa ȝoldis. And ælcan minra mæssepreosta þe ic ȝesette hæbbe in to minum reliquium, fiftyȝ mancusa ȝoldes, and fif pund penenȝa. And ælcan þæra oþerra preosta fif pund.*

> And to each appointed steward, chamberlain and butler, eighty mancuses of gold. And to each of my chaplains, whom I have appointed to my reliquary, fifty mancuses of gold and five pounds of pennies. And five pounds to each of the other priests.

A list of King's priests (chaplains) during the reign of Eadward III can be found in Barlow 1979: 156-158 (the modern reference for all those listed here). Becoming a King's priest was a to be at the centre of power and influence. Being high in the King's favour could result in promotion and a number of chaplains were rewarded with bishoprics and lands; some were very influential and wealthy men. Other rewards included appointment to benefices. Being made a canon of a local minster gave rights to lands held by that minster. There seems to have been a strong link between the chapel and St Martin's Minster in Dover. One feature of the chapel under Eadward III was the proportion of foreigners. The church in England was in full communication with the church elsewhere and there had always been a flow of people back and forth between England and the continent. Eadward's upbringing in Normandy ensured that he had strong contacts in northern Europe, and Normans, Germans and Lotharingians were all present in his chapel.

The King would need some sort of writing office to handle incoming correspondence and to send the numerous letters and writs that would have been part of the administrative activity of government. Educated clerics were the best-qualified people to staff such an office at the time. Keynes (1980) has suggested that such a central agency was also responsible for the writing of charters at least since the time of Æþelstan. Charters and other documents could be validated as coming from the King by use of the great seal. After the Conquest, the official responsible for the great seal and for supervising the writing office was the chancellor, the office itself becoming known as the chancery. There is evidence that documents were kept with the religious relics of the chapel before the Conquest (Keynes 1980: 146-149) but the evidence for the existence of a chancellor before 1066 is not as secure. However, there seems little doubt that the official did in fact exist (Keynes 1980, 1988). The position had the potential to become an important one in the administration, and it is significant that there is a writ in favour of one holder of the office, Reinbald, allowing him the same privileges as a bishop (Harmer 1989: 213).

ÆLFGEAT (DB Aluiet)

Life: Ælfgeat may have been a clerk in the writing office.
Lands: in Cambridge and Somerset worth £1.
Early sources: DB, may have witnessed S1041 (Ælfgeat notarius).
Modern references: Barlow 1979.

ÆLFWINE (DB Aluui, Aluuin)

Life: an Ælfwine who was a canon of St Martin's in Dover may have been a brother of Bishop Wulfwig of Dorchester and another of the canons of St Martin's, Godric.
Lands: in Kent (the canon £4), Buckingham and Bedford (Wulfwig's brother £7), and Suffolk and Warwick (the priest £2) worth £13.
Early sources: DB, S993 (1042).
Modern references: Barlow 1979.

ALBERT (DB Albert)

Life: from Lotharingia in Germany.
Lands: in Bedford and Rutland worth £14 (£6 according to Lewis 1995).
Early sources: DB.
Modern references: Barlow 1979, Lewis 1995.

BERNARD (DB Bernard)

Life: he had held St Mary's church in Huntingdon with Vitalis, but sold it to the Chamberlain Hugo.
Lands: in Gloucester worth £3.
Early sources: DB.
Modern references: Barlow 1979, Lewis 1995.

ENGELRIC (DB Engelric, Ingelric, Engelri)

Life: Engelric was either German or French, and had a brother Eirard/Gerhard. After the Norman Conquest he was one of the officials who supervised the redemption by the English of their lands in East Anglia. He and his brother were the founders of St Martin's church in London, and profited from the Conquest receiving further grants of land after 1066.
Lands: in Hertford £25, Essex £19, Oxford £12 and Suffolk £5 worth £60.

Early sources: witnessed charter B216, B159 (1067), B138 (1069): mentioned in writs B35-B38: DB.
Modern references: Freeman 1869-75 (vol 4), Barlow 1979, Clarke 1994, Williams 1995.

GODRIC (DB Godric)

Life: a Godric was a canon of St Martin's in Dover and may have been a brother of Bishop Wulfwig of Dorchester and Ælfwine.
Lands: in Buckingham (Wulfwig's brother £10), Kent (the canon £8), Cornwall, Hampshire and Huntingdon (the priest £4) worth £22.
Early sources: DB.
Modern references: Barlow 1979.

LEOFA (DB Leue)

Life: a Leofa was a King's clerk holding land in Somerset and may have been the same as the priest holding land in Huntingdon.
Lands: in Somerset and Huntingdon worth £2.
Early sources: DB.
Modern references: Barlow 1979.

LEOFWINE (DB Leuuin)

Life: Leofwine was a canon of St Martin's, Dover and may have been the priest who earlier witnessed charters of the King.
Lands: in Kent worth £4.
Early sources: DB: witnessed charters S1020, S1022 (1050).
Modern references: Barlow 1979.

OSBEORN (DB Osbern)

Life: Osbeorn was a Norman, the brother of Willelm FitzOsbern who was one of Duke Willelm's closest supporters. He was given a wealthy manor based on Bosham, a harbour opposite Normandy and within Earl Harold's sphere of influence. This may have been a political act of Eadward III's to help Willelm. On the other hand, it could simply have been a way of giving Osbeorn facilities for trading and communicating with his native land. He was well placed to benefit from the Norman Conquest and was appointed Bishop of Exeter in 1072. However, he was no simple apologist for the new order, and defended traditional English church practices. Osbeorn died in 1103.
Lands: in Cornwall, Sussex and Wiltshire worth £28, and the wealthy holding of £300 at Bosham in Sussex (£362 according to Lewis 1995).
Early sources: witnessed S1033 (1061), S1036 (1062), S1037a, S1041 (1065), B181 (1068).
Modern references: Barlow 1979, Lewis 1995.

PETER (DB Petrus)

Life: he was appointed Bishop of Lichfield in 1072, and administered the diocese of Dorchester after the death of Bishop Wulfwig in 1067. Peter died in 1085.
Lands: in Berkshire, Somerset worth £7.
Early sources: witnessed charters S1021 (1050), S1036 (1062), S1037a, S1041 (1065).
Modern references: Barlow 1979.

REINBALD (DB Reinbald, Reimbald, Rainbald)

Life: also called Reinbald of Cirencester, he was credited with being Eadward's chancellor. The evidence for this is disputed, but a powerful case for accepting his position as chancellor before 1066 has been made out by Keynes (1988). He was certainly Willelm's first chancellor, and had been given the status of a bishop by Eadward (*"þæt his pite beo eallspa muchell spa þæt leodbisceopes æt ællan þinʒan"*, "that the fine payable to him be equivalent to that of a diocesan bishop in all things", H44). The evidence of the Domesday Book shows that he had a son, Ælfward. Judging by his name, he was originally from Germany. He was buried at Cirencester church, and his estates were later used by Henri I to endow the same church. Reinbald was replaced as chancellor by Herfast shortly after December 1067.
Lands: in Berkshire, Buckingham, Dorset, Hereford and Somerset worth £32 or £38, also several churches.
Early sources: witnessed charters S1025 (1049/50), S1020, S1022 (1050), S1023 (1052), S1037a (1065): witnessed as chancellor S1030 (1060), S1033 (1061), S1036 (1062), S1041, S1043 (1065): mentioned in writ H44 (1042/66), H112 (1053/66 as chancellor): lands listed R1782.
Modern references: Round 1895, Larson 1904, Robertson 1939, Barlow 1979, Keynes 1980, Keynes 1988, Harmer 1989.

RODBERT (DB Robert)

Life: a Lotharingian, Rodbert was appointed Bishop of Hereford in 1079, and was a close friend of Bishop Wulfstan of Worcester. He was a noted mathematician and astronomer who was familiar with the relatively new technology of the abacus. He died on 26th June 1095.
Lands: in Lincolnshire worth 10/- according to Lewis 1995.
Early sources: witnessed charters S1025 (1049/50), S1020, S1022 (1050), S1023 (1052), S1041 (1065), B181 (1068).
Modern references: Barlow 1979, Lewis 1995, Keynes 1997.

SMELT (DB Esmellt, Esmeld, Esmund)

Life: he had been appointed a canon of St Martin's, Dover.
Lands: in Kent and Sussex worth £23. (Barlow mistakenly places his Sussex lands in Dorset)
Early sources: DB, S975 (1035).
Modern references: Barlow 1979.

UITALIS (DB Vital, Vitalis)

Life: he held St Mary's church, Huntingdon with Bernard, but sold it to the Chamberlain Hugo. Uitalis may have been still living in 1086.
Early sources: DB.
Modern references: Barlow 1979, Lewis 1995.

WULFMÆR (DB Vlmer)

Lands: in Bedford, Buckingham and Sussex worth £2.
Early sources: DB.
Modern references: Barlow 1979.

English	Lands	Position	Foreign	Lands	Position
Ælfgeat	£1 3/-	'notarius'	Albert	£14	
Ælfwine	£13 6/-	St Martin's	Bernard	£3	
Godric	£21 10/-	St Martin's	Engelric	£60?	
Leofa	£1 10/-		Osbeorn	£328	
Leofwine	£3 10/-	St Martin's	Peter	£6 10/-	
Smelt	£22 10/-	St Martin's	Reinbald	£38	'chancellor'
Wulfmær	£2 9/-		Rodbert	10/-	
			Uitalis	?	

Table 4: Summary of the King's priests

THE MONEYERS

The English monetary system in 1066 was probably the most centralised and well administered in Europe. Reforms under Eadgar I had produced a coinage based on the silver penny of a common design throughout the kingdom. This was periodically redesigned, with all current coins being handed in for melting down and reminting with the new design. The dating of remintings is not yet generally agreed, but it seems that at first it happened every six years, later reduced to every two years. By 1066 it was taking place every three years and at the change of a reign (Dolley 1964). This interpretation of the coinage has not gone undisputed (Stewart 1990). See Appendix 3 for the scheme of dating adopted in this book, and upon which the dating of the careers of moneyers is based.

Mints

The minting of coins was carried out in a variety of centres throughout the country, always in a borough. Each borough was allowed a certain number of licensed moneyers, depending on its size. The number of mints was large, ensuring that no one was too far from a source of currency. Moneyers would be issued with the new dies for every issue, sometimes from a regional die cutting centre but often from a central source. For this, they would pay but would expect to recover their costs and make a profit by charging locally for the new coin issue. In a few cases, local churchmen had the right to appoint and receive profits from one or more moneyers. Legal codes mention moneyers in the hands of the Archbishop of Canterbury (three moneyers), the Bishop of Rochester and Abbot of St Augustine's. The Domesday Book notes that the Bishop of Hereford had one moneyer in the borough. According to later tradition, the Archbishop of York was entitled to a third of the total moneyers in the city of York (Craig 1953). There survives a 13th century copy of a writ of Eadward III issued in 1065-66 granting the right to a moneyer to the Abbot of St Edmund's (H25 in Harmer 1989:165):

> Eadpard cynʒ ʒret Æiʒelmer b. ꝥ Georð eorl ꝥ ealle mine þeʒenas on Æstenʒle freondlice, ꝥ ic cyðe eou þæt ic habbe ʒeunnen Baldpine abbe. onne menetere piðinne Seint Eadmundes byriʒ, alspa freolice on ealle þinʒ to habben, alspa me mine on hande stonden oper on eniʒ minre burʒe alre freolukeost. God seo eop alre freond.

> King Edward sends friendly greetings to Bishop Ægelmær and Earl Gyrð and all my thanes in East Anglia. And I inform you that I have

granted to Abbot Baldwine one moneyer within St Edmund's borough, to have with the same freedom from restriction as I have my own anywhere in any of my boroughs, where I have them more freely than anywhere else. May God be the friend of you all.

The boroughs were an important part of English life, containing almost 10% of the population and generating wealth through trade, markets and craft industry. The boroughs were not large, averaging only 1,700 people. However, boroughs varied greatly in size, the evidence of the Domesday Book being combined with the number of moneyers at work and its place as a regional die cutting centre to determine the largest and most important of them. Only London was of any size with perhaps 15,000 people. The other large boroughs with between 5,000 and 10,000 people were York, Winchester, Norwich, Lincoln, Oxford and Thetford. Those that had been used in the past as major regional die cutting centres were Canterbury, Chester, Exeter, Gloucester, Lincoln, London, Norwich, Thetford, Winchester and York (Blackburn & Lyon 1986). The peak of regional die cutting was late in the reign of Æþelred and early under Cnut, c. 1009-24 but the same boroughs were still among the largest mints in England in 1066 (of the other mints only Hereford, Oxford and Shrewsbury were of similar size). The term borough covered many types of settlement. Market rights, minting rights, having tenements for rent were among the features that could be found in a borough. However, a group of more important boroughs can be identified. These were towns with urban landholdings of several lords and could be thought of as 'county towns' (most were listed separately in the Domesday survey of 1086). In the 11th century, they were liable for taxation separately from the shires. There were also some large towns on royal or private land. They would also have a mint, a borough court and burgage tenure (tenements for rent). Lesser boroughs in private hands might have only some of these features.

It has been suggested Nightingale (1982) that there were four varieties of mint. In some cases the burgesses of the borough would farm the mint from the King, paying a fixed sum in return for appointing the moneyers and sharing in the profits. Sometimes the moneyers themselves would be the farmers of the mint, taking all the minting profits for themselves. However, some mints appear to have been under the control of the King himself (including the important mints of London, Canterbury and York). In these cases the King would take the profits of minting and appoint his own moneyers, possibly from among his officials and so not be resident within the borough. Some mints might have been of mixed character, with the resident moneyers or burgesses sharing the minting rights with moneyers appointed by the King or favoured churchman.

Status of Moneyers

The social status and/or wealth of the moneyer may have been quite high (Smart 1968, Loyn 1984: 123, Loyn 1991: 129-130). The laws of Æþelred (IV Æþelred 9) show that moneyers were expected to have employees who did the actual striking of the coins (Liebermann 1903-16, Robertson 1925: 76-77).

Et illi habeant suboperarios suos in suo crimine, quod purum faciant et recti ponderis, per eandem witam quam praediximus.

And they shall be responsible for the production by their employees of pure money of the proper weight, under pain of incurring the same fine as we have fixed above.

One of Æþelred's moneyers at York was known as 'Osulf Thein', while a moneyer of Eadward III, also at York, was known as Ulfcytel ðaginc, which may represent 'þegning' or 'son of the thane' (Smart pers. com.). A moneyer of Cnut, Hunwine, may well have been the same man who signed charters as a King's thane (Stewartby 1988). Three of the moneyers of London under Eadward III were very likely to have been addressed in writs to the city, holding the position of port reeves (Wulfgar 1042/44, Ælfsige 1051/66 and Swetman 1058/66). At Lincoln, three (possibly as many as six) of the lawmen of the borough were also moneyers there (Smart 1968). The evidence of surveys of Winchester from the early 12th century also suggests high status for moneyers (Biddle & Keane 1976). At Winchester, they formed a distinct group in the urban mercantile elite, with economic interests limited to the borough, and having links with other occupations like goldsmithing and money changing. The Domesday Book (Smart 1968: 213) sometimes recorded the sums of money that moneyers paid to the King, e.g. those of Colchester and Ipswich paid £4 a year for the right to mint, no small sum in 1066. It also noted that moneyers had the duty of serving with the fyrd, and had sake and soke (rights of jurisdiction over others). Resident moneyers and King's moneyers might have formed distinct types of person, with the latter being liable to accrue minting rights in a number of possibly unrelated boroughs. Instances of the same name occurring at widely separated and unrelated mints might indicate this but without other evidence there is no way to establish whether this was the case and I have made no attempt to identify 'official' moneyers below.

It is possible that the position of moneyer was held by particular families, the right to the position itself passing from father to son (Dolley 1966). One particular family has been studied in detail, that of Deorman of London (Nightingale 1982). It is only by combining the evidence of the coins with documentary evidence that such a study is possible. Sadly, only rarely can such a combination be used for 1066. In the case of Deorman, the family was engaged in minting for several generations, held land and eventually married into the landed aristocracy

It is possible that the lines between the urban mercantile elite and landed gentry should not be drawn too tightly. In the entries for moneyers below, I have listed holdings of land by persons of the same name in the shires in which the moneyer was based. Identification of moneyers with landholding thanes can only be tentative at best and misleading at worst. However, the rare name of Sigered was used in Kent by a thane, Sigered of Chilham, and a moneyer at Canterbury. The fact that dwellings in the city were attached some of the thane Sigered's manors suggests that the two might have been the same man. If so, then it is possible that minting rights were granted to powerful thanes and some of the moneyers listed below were in fact local landowners. It was also possible for moneyers to gain land and enter the ranks of the lesser landed nobility, e.g. the family of Deorman. Unfortunately, there is seldom evidence to support such identifications of moneyers with landowners, and I have inserted a list of lands held by men of the same name merely as a reminder of possibilities. Identity of moneyer and landowner is more likely in the case of those with rarer names, e.g. Snæbeorn in Yorkshire. Accordingly, I have not usually listed lands where the name is relatively common, e.g. Godwine.

The moneyers of Eadward, Harold and Willelm have been examined and listed in detail by Freeman (1985), Jonsson & Van Der Meer (1990), Pagan (1990) and Harris (1983-88). This section relies heavily on their work. However, new finds of coins are always liable to alter the picture presented below.

Freeman (1985) suggested that moneyers were of two kinds: the 'established' and the 'single-type'. The former would mint several issues of coins at the borough, and be more prolific in each issue, while the latter appear only fleetingly minting coins of only one type in relatively small numbers. Freeman himself provides many exceptions to his scheme and it is perhaps preferable to see moneyers as forming a continuum of old, well established moneyers to newcomers at the beginning of a career. Some of the latter would prosper and become established in their turn while others would not, being subject to changing fortunes and mortality before becoming major players in the borough economy. Some of Freeman's single-type moneyers were characterised by irregularities in die and the occurrence of several together at particular mints, which might indicate temporary arrangements for expanded coin production. However, the effect may be no more than random effects of an imperfect sample of coins that survive from the mints concerned. Freeman (1985) also raises the possibility that there might have been a position of 'senior moneyer' belonging to the longest serving of the moneyers and which allowed the man concerned a higher output of coins, or some administrative role in relation to the mint (Freeman 1985). The moneyer Godwine Socche was given the title master of the mint in the Winchester survey for the 1050s (Biddle & Keene 1976).

Identification of Moneyers

A difficulty in identifying the moneyers active in 1066 is the incomplete survival of coins from the various boroughs. The Domesday Book only tells us in a small number of cases how many moneyers there were in a borough. This can occasionally be matched by the coin evidence. At Bridport there was one moneyer, and coins of Harold from there only bear one name, Hwateman. Shaftesbury is listed with three moneyers in the Domesday Book and, sure enough, there are three names on Harold's coins: Ælfnoð, Ægelwine and Godric. In other cases we cannot quite find the evidence for full complement of moneyers. For example, there should have been seven moneyers at work in Hereford but we only have five names on surviving coins of Harold II from there (Ælfwig, Ægelric, Eadric, Eadwig and Leofnoð). The evidence of the early coin issues of Willelm I suggests that the two missing moneyers might have come from among Ægelwine, Brihtric or Earnwig. For most mints, the number of moneyers at work in 1066 must be reconstructed by looking at the pattern of minting throughout the reigns of Eadward, Harold and Willelm. It is immediately striking that the number of moneyers at the larger mints was being drastically reduced during this period, e.g. the largest mint, London, appears to go from 59 moneyers in 1048 down to 17 in 1066.

In some cases a moneyer can be definitely identified as having minted in 1066. Their names occur on coins of Harold II. Some can be shown to have minted every coin issue in their career, e.g. Anderboda at Winchester or Brand at Wallingford. Others minted only the single issue of Harold II, e.g. Wulfred who is found on coins from 1066 at Canterbury but not from earlier or later coin issues there. It is more usual to find gaps in the evidence. It can be assumed that minting took place in 1066 in cases like that of Wulfwig at Oxford who minted coins of the last issue of Eadward III and the first issue of Willelm I, or of Baldric of Worcester who is found on sporadic issues of both Eadward III and Willelm I but is the only likely candidate to complete the complement of moneyers to the right number for 1066. Besides these definite and probable moneyers, there is a group of possible moneyers whose attribution to minting under Harold II is less secure. For example, Owig's earliest coins are the first issue of Willelm I at Worcester but he would be prime candidate for minting in 1066, assuming that the Ælfwine who minted there under Eadward and Willelm was in fact two people leaving a gap in the complement to be filled. The final category of moneyer in 1066 is that of the alternative. These are those from whom a choice of men has to be made to bring the mint up to its complement, e.g. Southwark had two moneyers, one of whom was Osmund, leaving the second place to be filled either by Godric (on coins of 1062-65) or Leofwine (on coins of 1068-71).

If each moneyer minted only at one borough then there would be 243 individuals in all four of the above categories. However, this is unlikely to be the case. Some moneyers undoubtedly moved from one mint to another as suggested by Freeman (1985), e.g. Cenric occurs on coins of Harold II from Norwich but then appears on coins of Willelm I at Thetford. Many moneyers probably also minted at two or more boroughs at the same time, e.g. Osmund at London and Southwark, or Hwateman at Bridport and Dorchester. To identify the moneyers as particular people, I have made certain assumptions. The chief of these is that moneyers would have been more likely to have a second workshop in, or move to, nearby boroughs than distant ones. Regional links between boroughs have been suggested by Freeman (1985). In some cases a group of names links two mints, e.g. London and Canterbury. The other assumption is that most long-serving moneyers would have had a career of up 35 years with a small number living to great age and having careers up to 45 or in rare cases 50 years. These figures are based on an analysis of earls, bishops and abbots between 871 and 1066. Most long serving holders of these positions held office for 30-35 years. Only eight men had careers longer than this, including Ealdred of York with 42 years as Abbot and Bishop, Bishops Ægelstan of Hereford, Ægelwulf of Hereford, Brihtwold of Ramsbury and Wærferð of Worcester with 40-43 years. The only men serving over 45 years were Archbishop Dunstan of Canterbury with 48 years as Abbot and Bishop, Archbishop Stigand of Canterbury with 50 years as priest and bishop, and possibly Bishop Godwine of Rochester, although it has been suggested that that was in fact two men of the same name.

Moneyers in 1066

There are 102 unique moneyers' names identified as definitely, probably or possibly minting under Harold II which occur at just one mint, and which can thus be identified as individual moneyers, e.g. Leofred at Cricklade. This leaves 140 individuals who might have worked at more than one mint. These share 42 names between them. Using the evidence of minting between 973 and 1135, together with the assumptions stated above, the 140 potential multi-mint moneyers can be reduced to 74 individuals likely to have worked at just one mint, and 32 who probably worked at more than one borough, giving a total of 210 moneyers listed below (a more generous identification of multi-mint moneyers would reduce the total to 197). Identification of individuals on this basis cannot be assured and should not be taken as certain. For instance, the relatively common name Swegn occurred at three widely separated mints between 1042 and 1087 (Bristol, Ipswich and York) and most likely represents three separate men, as could Wulfmær, occurring at Lincoln, Romney and Shrewsbury. On the other hand, the rare name Gilcrist occurred on coins of 1042-44 from Taunton and Lincoln and might represent separate men since the boroughs have no obvious link, or one man minting in the King's service wherever he was needed. Between these two extremes there is room for considerable debate about how to interpret the data. For example, is the Godsunu who minted early in Eadward's reign at London, Canterbury and Cambridge one man or three? Given the frequent name links between London and Canterbury moneyers we might suggest two men as a likely interpretation. In the listing of moneyers below I have tried to be honest about the limits of certainty in identification. There are 132 definite moneyers, 40 probable moneyers and 7 possible moneyers. The remaining 31 individuals are alternatives for 18 minting places.

A full list of moneyers for each mint between 1042 and 1087 can be found in Appendix 3 so that readers can make their own interpretation of the evidence if they so wish. All spellings on coins of the moneyer's name are noted in brackets (except for five I have been unable to trace), with spellings of thane's names from the Domesday Book. In some cases the name has obviously been mis-spelled, or inaccurately copied in capitals on the die, e.g. Areytel for Arcetel at York. In other cases, letters have been left out, e.g. Brhtric, or doubled, e.g. Brandd.

AGAMUND (Agemund, Ahemund, Ahmund; DB Agemund)
Career: minted at Lincoln 1062-71. An Agmund was listed in 1086 as a lawman of Lincoln, son of Walrafn, having sake and soke over his own property. Was this the same man?
Early sources: DB.

ALEIF (Aleif, Alef, Aleof, Aleigf)
Career: at York 1065-96.

ANDERBODA (Anderboda, Anderbode)
Career: at Winchester 1053-83. His name is continental, probably German.

AUTIG (Auti, Autti, Outti, Utti, DB Outi)
Career: at Lincoln 1050-66 and possibly under Harold II.
Lands: he had held meadowland at Lincoln in 1066.
Early sources: DB.

ÆGELBERHT (Ægelbriht)
Career: minted at Ipswich 1068-80 and might have been a new moneyer under Willelm I.

ÆGELMÆR (Ælmer, Almær)
Career: at Lincoln 1065-67.

ÆGELRIC (Ægelric, Aglric, Eglric, Ælric, Ælrie)
Career: began his career at Hereford 1046-68 and soon minted also at Shrewsbury 1056-77.

ÆGELRIC (Ægelric, Æglric, Ælric)
Career: minted at Leicester 1053-66 and might have continued under Harold II.

ÆGELRIC (Ægelric, Æglric, Æielric, Egelric)
Career: there was most likely to have been an older man minting at London 1044-56 and a younger one 1068-74. The younger Ægelric might have minted under Harold II, but no coins have yet been found.

ÆGELRIC (Ægelric, Æglric, Æglrc, DB Agelric, Egelric)
Career: at Wareham 1067-87 and might have minted there under Harold II.
Lands: an Ægelric held Athelhampton, Corfe Mullen (½) and Bardolfeston (Dorset) worth £14 10/- (13h).
Early sources: DB.

ÆGELWINE (Ægelwine, Eilwine, Iielwine)

Career: he probably began at Langport in 1053 and then transferred to Ilchester 1053-83 (the senior moneyer under Harold II) when the Langport mint closed down. He is also likely to have been the same man who minted at Shaftesbury 1066-67. Pagan notes that he used three obverse dies while at Ilchester in 1066, more than would be normally expected and put forward the idea that he was the only moneyer in the borough where there should have been two. However, Wihtsige might have been minting there also in 1066.
Modern references: Pagan 1990.

ÆGELWINE (Æglwine)

Career: he was at Hereford 1068-96, and either he or Brihtric might have minted there under Harold II.

ÆGELWINE (Ægelwine, Æglwine, Elwine)

Career: minted at Leicester 1056-86.

ÆGELWINE (Ægelwine, Æglwin, Æglwne, Ælwine)

Career: at least two, but more likely three, men of this name minted at London 991-97 and 1003-77. The second of the three might have ended in 1062/65, and the third have begun in 1068/71 (with either possibly minting under Harold II). It is possible that one of these men was the son of Brihtmær (moneyer up to 1056). Ægelwine son of Brihtmær was a listed as knight of Archbishop of Canterbury, Brihtmær had given a house and church to Canterbury Cathedral in 1054.
Early sources: DM.
Modern references: Douglas 1944, Nightingale 1982.

ÆGELWINE (Ægelwine, Æglwine, Æielwine, Ælwinee)

Career: likely to have minted at Oxford 1036-77 where he became the senior moneyer. However, there could have been two men of this name at Oxford, the elder finishing in 1059/62 and the younger beginning in 1068/71. If so, then either or both might also have minted at London.

ÆGELWINE

Career: minted at Thetford 1062-67. It is possible this could be the Ægelwine who minted at Leicester.

ÆLFGEAT (Ælfgeat)

Career: had a short career at Lincoln 1065-67.

ÆLFMÆR (Ælmar, Almar)

Career: known from coins at Lincoln 1066-71.

ÆLFNOÐ (Ælfnoð, Ælfnað, Ælfnot, Ælnoð, Ælnot, Elfnoð, Alfoð)

Career: likely to have minted at Lincoln, there might have been two people of that name minting there between 1018 & 1074.

ÆLFNOÐ (Ælnoð, DB Alnod, Elnod)

Career: at Shaftesbury 1066-87. He was definitely 'on the make', receiving Earl Harold's help in taking land at Islington, buying estates from the church and taking land from another thane after 1066. Ælfnoð appears to have been a landed thane who added minting rights to his estate, rather than a moneyer moving into landed society.
Lands: in Catsley, Fifehead, Islington, Morden, Nutford, South Perrott, Tyneham and Wyndlam (Dorset) worth £17 15/-.
Early sources: DB.

ÆLFSIGE (Ælfsige, Ælfsig, Ælfsie, Ælfsi, Ælfsiie, Ælesige, Elfsige, Elfsie, Elfsi, Elfsiie, Elfsig, DB Alsi)

Career: likely to have minted at Chester in 1066, there were at least two men minting under this name 1018-87.
Lands: half of two townships in Cheshire worth 16/-, Leftwich and Wharton.
Early sources: DB.

ÆLFSIGE (Ælfsige, Ælfsie, Ælfsi, Ælfsiie, Ælesii, Elfsie)

Career: minted at Gloucester 1036-67 where he was the senior moneyer by 1066.

ÆLFSIGE (Ælfsige, Ælfsie, Ælfsi, Æolfsi, Ælfsise)

Career: likely to have minted at London in 1066, with a career between 1044 and 1074. He was probably the same man addressed on writs as one of the two port reeves of the city.
Early sources: H105, H106 (1065/66).

ÆLFWARD (Ælfward, Elfwered, DB Aluuard)

Career: might have minted at London, probably at least 1044-66, although this was a common name at London and he might have begun his career earlier than this. Most likely also minted at Canterbury 1059-66. Not certain to have minted under Harold at either place. If he is identical with the Ælfward holding lands in Kent then he had a brother Godwine.
Lands: Charlton, Dean Court (¼), Horton Kirby, Otterden and Ruxley (Kent) £12 10/- (3s 30a).
Early sources: DB.

ÆLFWIG (Ælfwig, Ælfwi)

Career: at Hereford 1053-68.

ÆLFWIG (Ælfwig, Ælfwi, Ælfwii, Elfwig, Elfwi)

Career: at Oxford 1044-80. Was this the same man as Ælfwig of Hereford? An Ælfwig was recorded as having a house in the borough in 1086.
Early sources: DB.

ÆLFWINE (Ælfwine, Ælfyn, Elfwine, Elvwine, Elfine, DB Aluuin)

Career: at Canterbury 1062-67, but might also have been at London where the name occurs 1040-62 & 1067-77 or even later. Ælfwine was a commonly occurring name at London between 979 and 1141.

ÆLFWINE (Ælfwine, Ælfwne, Ælwine, Ælefwine, Eilfwine)

Career: minted at Winchester 1036-71 (probably the senior moneyer), and might be the same man as the Ælfwine at Chichester 1046-67 (definitely the senior moneyer). If not, then he might have begun his career at Hythe 1044-46.

ÆLFWINE (Ælfwine, Alfwine, Elfwine)

Career: he might have begun minting at Norwich in 1059 and then transferred to Thetford 1059-67, as well as minting at Ipswich 1062-71. He shared an obverse die at Ipswich in 1066 with Leofsige and Wulfgar of London (both ended in 1067).
Modern references: Pagan 1990.

ÆLFWINE (Ælfwine)

Career: the senior moneyer at Bristol, 1042-66, and most likely finished minting in 1066, to be replaced by Leofwine.

ÆLFWINE (Ælfwine)

Career: he minted at Lincoln 1046-66 and might have continued under Harold II.

ÆLFWOLD (Ælfwold, Alfwold, Alwold; DB Aluuold)

Career: at Wilton 1050-67, and the senior by 1066. He most likely came from Salisbury where he minted 1046-50. His output at Wilton in 1066 was exceptionally heavy but no reason for this has been put forward.
Lands: an Ælfwold held lands in Broughton, Grafton and Sutton worth £12.
Early sources: DB.
Modern references: Pagan 1990.

ÆRE(ORB?)-NNE (Ære(orb?)-nne)

Career: he minted at Sandwich 1068-71, and either he or Godric was minting there under Harold II. The name appears hopelessly garbled.

BALDRIC (Baldric, Balderic)

Career: likely to have minted at Worcester 1062-86.

BLACMAN (Blacaman)
Career: the senior moneyer at Dorchester 1042-67.

BRAND (Brand, Brad, Brandd)
Career: began at Winchester 1050-53 but then moved his operations to Wallingford 1050-83, becoming senior moneyer.

BRIHTMÆR (Brihtmær, Brihtnar, Brihtiær)
Career: minted at Winchester 1044-62 and then moved to Wallingford 1059-74. He appears to have shared a workshop with Sweartling since they both used the same obverse dies in 1066.
Modern references: Pagan 1990.

BRIHTNOÐ (Brihtnoð, Brihtoð)
Career: minted at Gloucester 1059-93.

BRIHTRED (Brihtred, Brihtræd)
Career: likely to have minted at Oxford under Harold II with a career extending from 1059 to 1093. A Brihtred, who might have been the moneyer, shared a dwelling worth 16d in Oxford with Deorman in 1086.

BRIHTRIC (Brihtric, Brhtric; DB Brictric)
Career: his main base might have been at Colchester 1046-71 (possibly as the senior monyer), before moving to London 1071-80.
Lands: there were two men called Brihtric in Colchester in 1086, one with one house, and the other with one house and 9 acres. He might have held Finchingfield and Cornish Hall in 1066, worth £4.
Early sources: DB.

BRIHTRIC
Career: at Cambridge 1066-67, he might have moved from Ipswich where he minted 1053-65, and possibly in 1066. This Brihtric could have been the same as the man minting at Colchester and London.

BRIHTRIC (Brihtric, Brihric, Brfhtric)
Career: at Taunton 1056-77 and Exeter 1066-68.

BRIHTRIC (Brihtric)
Career: minted at Hereford 1068-77 and might have minted also under Harold II.

BRIHTWIG (Brihtwi, DB Bristuui)
Career: minted at Malmesbury 1050-80.
Lands: a Brihtwig held 15/- worth of land at Bradfield.

Early sources: DB.

BRIHTWOLD (Brihtwold, Brihtwal, Brihw)
Career: minted at Oxford 1042-67.

BRUNING (Bruning, Bruninc, Brunic, Brunnic)
Career: likely to have been the senior moneyer at Chester under Harold II, with a career 1036-68.

BRUNING (Bruninc, Brnic, Brihinc)
Career: a Bruning is named on occasional coins from Tamworth 1044-93 (though not yet of Harold II), and is likely to be the senior among the moneyers. He is unlikely to have been the Bruning at Chester 1036-68.

BRUNING (Bruninc, Buninc, Bruing, Bruinne)
Career: the senior moneyer minting at Ipswich 1044-65, and might have minted under Harold II.

BRUNMAN (Brunman, Brumman, Bruman, Brumn)
Career: known to have been at Chichester 1067-99, and possibly also at Dover 1068-80. Might have begun at Chichester under Harold II.

BRUNMAN (Brunman, Brman, Brunm, Brum, DB Bruman)
Career: minted at Ipswich 1056-67. A freeman, Brunman of Burgh (the borough = Ipswich?), was attached to the manor of Stratton sometime after 1066, having been under the patronage of Eadric of Laxfield at the time of the Conquest.
Early sources: DB.

BRUNWINE (Brunwine, Brunwinne, Bruwine)
Career: found on coins from Stamford 1030-74, where he was senior moneyer.

BURHWINE (Burewine, Burwne)
Career: minted at Wallingford 1053-67.

CENRIC (Cinric, Cunwic)
Career: began his career at Norwich 1066-67 and then moved to Thetford 1067-86.

CENTWINE (Centwine, Kentwine, Kæntwine)
Career: minted at Wilton 1065-67. He produced an exceptionally large number of coins in 1066, for which there has been no satisfactory explanation.
Modern references: Pagan 1990.

CEOLWIG (Ceolewi, Cilwi)

Career: likely to have minted under Harold II at Dover, found on coins 1050-66.

CEORL (Ceorl, Coiiirl)

Career: was based at Bristol 1065-80.

CILD (Cild, Cilda)

Career: minted at Bedwyn 1046-68, although no coins of Harold II have yet been found. He moved to the new Marlborough mint in 1071, continuing there until 1090.

COLBEIN (Colbegen, Colbin)

Career: likely to have been at Derby 1062-74.

COLING (Colling, Collinc, Cullinc, Colinc, Colic, Coleinc)

Career: is found on coins from Tamworth 1056-93 (but not yet on one of Harold II). He also minted at Stafford 1059-62 and either he or Wulfnoð was the second moneyer there in 1066.

COLSWEGN (Colswegen)

Career: minted at Hastings 1062-68. A Colswegn also minted at London 1074-77 and might be the same person.

CYNSTAN (Cinstan, Cnstan)

Career: minted at Dover from at least 1030 to 1067 (senior moneyer by 1066), and might have also minted there 1083-86.

DEORMAN (Deorman, Diorman, Dermon, Direma; Deormann, DB Derman)

Career: a Deorman minted in London 1009-15, 1030-38 and 1044-59. This could have been one man, or two, or three. If more than one, the latest of them might also be the Deorman who minted at Colchester 1053-87 (but only sporadically on surviving coins, with none of Harold II), and at Steyning 1059-87. He had a brother Leofstan, and may have been the son of Ælfgar who was the previous holder of his land in Middlesex in 1066. He is known to have had four sons: Ælfgar (a canon of St Paul's), Ordgar, Þeodric, Eadwine, all of whom became moneyers themselves at London or Hertford.

Lands: Deorman was among the knights of the Archbishop of Canterbury and held land in Essex and Middlesex, and possibly Hertford. As well as inheriting Ælfgar's land in Middlesex, he would gain the lands of Ælfwine Horn in Hertfordshire by 1086, to have an estate worth £13. His interests might have been even wider than this. A Deorman shared a dwelling worth 16d with the moneyer Brihtred at Oxford in 1086, and had a further dwelling of his own worth 12d. He also had a house in Colchester in 1086.

Early sources: DM, DB.

Modern references: Nightingale 1982.

DUNING (Dunning, Duninc, Dunic, Dicnnig, DB Dunning, Donning)
Career: minted at Chester 1056-66, and likely under Harold II.
Lands: worth £4 17/- (7h 1½y) at Bartington, Greasby, Kingsley, Oulton, Sandbach and Storeton. By 1086, he only held Kingsley (1 hide), worth 6/-, from Earl Hugo.
Early sources: DB.

DUNING (Dunning, Dunninc, Dunnic, Duning, Dunic, Duinnc)
Career: this might have been one long-lived (and the senior) moneyer at Hastings 1048-1100, with a second Duning 1111-34.

EADRIC (DB Edric, Ederic)
Career: minted at Canterbury 1062-65, and might have continued under Harold II.
Lands: the thane Eadric of Elham held £66 of land in Kent (see above). This might have been the same man.
Early sources: DB.

EADRIC (Eadric)
Career: minted at Hereford 1056-67.

EADRIC (Edric, Edricc)
Career: was based at Lincoln 1036-67.

EADWARD (Eadward, Edward, Edwerd, DB Eduuard)
Career: a series of signatures on coins from London with gaps in between that represent at least three or four men 991-97, 1009-35 & 38-42, 1050-62, 1077-83. The third of these might have minted under Harold II. He might also have been the Eadward who was minting at Canterbury 1044-68.
Lands: an Eadward (of Stone?) held land in Kent – Knowlton, Ringleton and Teston £17 (+2s). An Eadward Snoc held Swalecliffe worth £1 1/- (2y).
Early sources: DB.

EADWIG (Edwicg)
Career: minted at Hereford 1050-71.

EADWINE
Career: minted at Cambridge 1066-67.

EADWINE (Eadwine, Edwine, Edwne)
Career: occurred at Norwich 1059-87 (not yet on a coin of Harold II). It is possible that he is the same Eadwine as at Cambridge although he is not found on coins from intervening borough of Thetford.

EADWINE (Eadwine, Edwine, DB Eduuin, Eduin, Eduun)

Career: there were at least three moneyers of this name at London 985-1096, one of whom is likely to have been at Canterbury 1066-67, and may have been at Rochester 1044-59.

Lands: an Eadwine held Upper Hardres, Wormshill and Wrotham Heath (½) in Kent worth £12 (3s 3y). An Eadwine also held land in Cornilo hundred worth £4 (85a), and was still holding it in 1086, worth £3. Another Eadwine held Hougham £5 (1s), which was held by his brother Baldwine in 1086, worth £4.

Early sources: DB.

EALDGAR (Ealdgar, Ealdgær, Ealgar, Aldgar)

Career: minted at London 1030-77, but this might have been two moneyers beginning 1003.

EALHSIGE (Ealcsi, Alhsie, Alcsie, Alcsi, Alsiie, Alesige, Alxxi)

Career: minted at Chester 1050-71.

EARNCYTEL (Arncetel, Arncil, Arncel, Arnctel, Erncytel, Erncetel, Erncil, Earcil, Arcytel, Arcetel, Arketel, Arcetl, Arcill, Arcil, Arcel, Arctel, Arctl, Areytel)

Career: was based at York 1018-71. It is just possible that this was one man, and if so would easily be the senior moneyer in the borough.

EARNWIG (Earnwi, Eornwi, Ærnwi, Ærnewi, Earwi)

Career: was at Hereford 1046-66 (and possibly under Harold II) before moving to Shrewsbury 1056-96.

EASTMÆR (Estmær)

Career: minted at Worcester 1065-93.

EORLWINE (Eorlewine)

Career: minted at Bath 1059-65, and might have continued under Harold II. His name is continental, possibly French (Herluin).

FOLCARD (Folcærd, Folerd, Folciiierd)

Career: was at Thetford 1074-1100, but might have begun there in 1059. The name Folcard was continental, possibly Flemish or Lotharingian.

FOLCWINE (Folcwine)

Career: minted at Sudbury 1053-71. He might have been continental in origin.

FORNA (Forna, Forne, Forn, Corna)

Career: was based at Nottingham 1053-77, where he was the senior of the borough's moneyers.

FROMA (Froma, Frome, Froam)
Career: minted at Derby 1044-80 (senior moneyer). Is this the same man as Forna who was at Nottingham 1053-77? To complicate identification further, a Frana (DB Frane) held lands worth £4 17/6 (+1 oxgang) in Nottingham in 1066.

GARFIN (Garfin, Garvin)
Career: minted at Lincoln 1062-68.

GARWULF (Garulf)
Career: was at Worcester 1050-80.

GIFEL (Gifel, Givel, Gife)
Career: minted at Lincoln between 1059 and 1074.

GODA (God)
Career: was based at Thetford 1067-74, and also probably under Harold II.

GODESBRAND (Godesbrand, Godsbrand, Godesbran)
Career: minted at Shrewsbury 1050-87. The name is continental, most likely German.

GODFERÐ (Godefurð, Godeverd)
Career: was at Norwich 1062-68. It is possible that the name represents Norman Godfrið, but more likely to have been an Anglicised version of Norse Guðfrið.

GODLEOF (Godeleof, Godelif, Godlef, Godelf, Odelif)
Career: minted at Thetford 1050-1107 (senior moneyer), although there might have been two men, with the younger beginning at Thetford and Stamford in 1086. The name could be continental.

GODRIC (Godric, DB Godric)
Career: minted at Huntingdon 1050-77 (where either he or Godwine was the senior moneyer), and may be the same Godric who minted also at Cambridge 1067-8.
Lands: from the Bishop of Dorchester and Abbot of Ramsey at Denton and Hemingford Abbots (Huntingdon) worth £5 10/- (6h).
Early sources: DB.

GODRIC (Godric, Gdric)
Career: was based at Thetford 1059-1107.

GODRIC (Godric)
Career: the name occurs between 979 and 1093 at London, probably representing at least four different people, one of whom was definitely minting under Harold II. The same man might also have minted at Southwark 1062-65 (with a second Godric 1083-

87). A Godric also minted at Sandwich 1062-65 (after an earlier Godric 1044-46) and this might well have been the same man, possibly continuing there under Harold II.

GODRIC (Godric)

Career: minted at Salisbury 1056-86 (the senior among the moneyers), and probably also at Wilton 1068-77. He might have begun at Bath 1046-59.

GODRIC (Godric, Godricc)

Career: minted at Shaftesbury 1062-67, and might have moved there from Ilchester 1053-62, possibly having begun at Winchester 1044-53. He could also have been the Godric who minted at Salisbury 1056-86.

GODRIC

Career: was based at Droitwich 1062-67.

GODRIC (Godric, Godricc, DB Godric)

Career: minted at Leicester 1046-93, where he might have been the senior moneyer. Was he the same Godric who minted at Huntingdon?
Lands: a Godric held South Croxton, Great Dalby, Swinford £3 6/- (12p 2o). Another Godric held land in 1086 – Burton on the Wolds, Houghton on the Hill and Loughborough worth £1+ (14p 4o).
Early sources: DB.

GODWIG (Godwi, Goddi)

Career: minted at Thetford 1065-66, and likely minted under Harold II.

GODWINE (Godwine, DB Goduin)

Career: the senior moneyer at Cambridge 1053-67 & possibly since 1040. He may be the same Godwine who minted at Hertford 1044-50, Huntingdon 1050-83 (where either he or Godric was the senior) and Maldon 1053-67.
Lands: Orton Waterville (Huntingdon) worth £2 (3h 2y).
Early sources: DB.

GODWINE (Godwine)

Career: there were several men of this name at Winchester between 991 and 1135. One of these could be the same man who minted at Chichester 1053-1100 and Lewes 1050-67. A Godwine, with the byname Socche, minting in 1056/59, was described as the master of the mint in the eleventh century Winton Domesday, but it is not known whether this position carried with any authority over fellow moneyers. The Godwine of 1066 was most likely not to have been the same man if he was the moneyer whose career continued long after the Conquest.
Modern references: Biddle & Keene 1976.

GODWINE (Godwine, Godwwne)
Career: most likely to have minted both at Norwich 1062-96 and Thetford 1062-74.

GODWINE (Godwine, Godwinne, Godwne, Godwinc)
Career: minted at Shrewsbury 1059-66 and may have continued under Harold II. Alternatively, he might have moved to Stafford where a Godwine minted 1065-87.

GODWINE (Godwine)
Career: most likely to have been two men minting at Oxford 1018-80, the younger perhaps beginning in 1066.

GOLDMAN (Goldman; DB Goldman)
Career: was based at Colchester 1056-71.
Lands: he had one house in Colchester in 1086.
Early sources: DB.

GOLDSTAN (Goldstan; DB Goldstan)
Career: minted at Colchester 1066-71. Were he and Goldman related since they share a relatively uncommon name element?
Lands: he had a house and 5 acres of land in Colchester, along with lands in Essex worth £1 17/-, some of which he had held in 1066.
Early sources: DB.

GOLDWINE
Career: minted at Hythe 1059-62 and might have continued under Harold II. He could have come from London where a Goldwine minted 1044-59.

GOLDWINE (Goldwine, Goldewine, Goldwin)
Career: was at Winchcombe 1048-87. Could this be the same as the Goldwine who had a dwelling the borough of nearby Oxford (DB)?

GYLDWINE (Gyldewine, Gyldiwine, Geldewine)
Career: the senior moneyer minting at Canterbury 1036-66, and likely to have continued under Harold II.

HEAÞUWULF (Heaðewulf)
Career: the senior moneyer at Droitwich 1059-67, probably then moving to Worcester 1074-77.

HEREGOD (Heregod, Hæregod, Haregod, Hergod, Hærgod, Hargod, Æregod)
Career: minted at Oxford 1044-86. His name was continental, probably German.

HUSCARL (Huscarl, Huscalr, Huscar, Hruscar)
Career: was based at Chester 1044-67.

HWÆTMAN (Hwateman, DB Wateman)
Career: minted at Bridport 1036-80, although only found so far in 5 out of 19 possible issues. He probably also minted at Dorchester 1046-56, and might have been that mint's second moneyer under Harold II.
Lands: at Wey (Dorset) worth £1 10/- (2h 2y).
Early sources: DB.

IOCYTEL (Iocytel, Iocitel, Iocetel, Ioccetel, Iocetl, Ioctel, Ioctl, Iucetel, Iokel, Iughtel, Gocil, Ioeetl, Iukelel)
Career: minted at York 1044-67.

LEISING (Leising, Leigsing, Leisinc)
Career: minted at York 1066-99.

LEOFNOÐ (Leofnoð, Leofenoð, Leofnað, Liofnoð, Liofenoð, Leofþnoð, Leonoð, Lienoð, Leofenð, Eofnað, DB Leuenot)
Career: could have been two men minting at Chester 1003-30 and 1038-66 (continuing as senior moneyer under Harold II), the second perhaps having begun at Hereford 1030-67.
Lands: a Leofnoð held lands widely in Cheshire in 1066: Antrobus, Broughton, Caldy, Cogshall (½), Gayton, Leadbrook (½), Leighton, Meols, Minshull, Moulton and Thurstaston worth £8 1/- (14h ½y).
Early sources: DB.

LEOFRED (Leofred, Liofred, Lefred)
Career: was based at Cricklade 1053-80.

LEOFRIC (Leofric, Leofrc, Liofric, Lefric, Lefricc, DB Leuric)
Career: the Leofric at Stamford 1036-74 might have been the same man who minted at Leicester 1059-71. Freeman (1985) identifies him as the same as the Leofric minting at Huntingdon 1059-62, and might have continued there under Harold II. He might have transferred from Northampton where he minted 1053-59, and could also be the Leofric who minted at Norwich 1059-62.
Lands: in Huntingdon – Orton worth £1 (3h 1y), in Leicester – Bosworth, Bottesford, 'Plotelei', Stathern, 'Stormesworth', Swepstone worth c£11 15/10 (50p 1½o). A Leofric Leofwine's son held Melton Mowbray and Stathern in Leicester worth £11 (110p 7o).
Early sources: DB.

LEOFRIC (Liofric, Lifric)

Career: this could have been one man at Worcester 1024-74, or up to three men 1024-30, 1036-42, 1048-74 (and possibly the senior moneyer).

LEOFSIGE (Leofsi)

Career: minted at London 1050-67. He shared an obverse die in 1066 with Wulfgar of London (also ended 1067) and Ælfwine of Ipswich (1062-71).
Modern references: Pagan 1990.

LEOFSTAN (Leofstan, Liofstan, Lefstan, Lifstan, DB Lefstan)

Career: at least two of this name at Canterbury, one possibly 979-1030 and this Leofstan probably 1038-65 and carrying on under Harold II.
Lands: a Leofstan had a sixth share of £5 worth of lands in Pising and Pineham. A Leofstan also held Eddintone worth £4 (2y) but had died, the land going to Ægelnoð Cild, most likely before the Conquest.
Early sources: DB.

LEOFSTAN (Lifstan, Liftan)

Career: minted at Rochester 1056-87. This is probably not the same as the Leofstan at Canterbury.

LEOFSTAN (Leofstan)

Career: at Ipswich 1066-83. An earlier Leofstan minted here 1040-44.

LEOFSTAN (Leofstan; DB Lefstan)

Career: minted at Northampton 1065-67. Did he transfer to Ipswich in 1066?
Lands: a Leofstan held one house in Northampton in 1086 worth 4d. This could have been the same man. He might have held land at Evenley in 1066 worth £3.
Early sources: DB.

LEOFWARD (Liofwærd, DB Leuuard)

Career: was based at Lewes 1059-67.
Lands: at Willingdon (Sussex) worth 10/- (2y).
Early sources: DB.

LEOFWINE (Leofwine, Leofwne, Liowine, Lfwine, DB Leuuin)

Career: possibly the same man who was minting at Canterbury 1018-65 (and maybe under Harold II), and at Rochester 1056-67.
Lands: a Leofwine held Frinsted, Monk's Horton, 'Leueberge', Siffleton worth £4 5/- (2s), also a sixth share of £5 worth of lands in Pising and Pineham. Leofwine was a common name and this might not have been the same man as the moneyer.
Early sources: DB.

LEOFWINE (Leofwine, Liofwine, Lefwine, Lifwine)
Career: minted at Gloucester 1050-80 and at Bristol 1066-87.

LEOFWINE (Leofwine, Lifwine, Leowine, DB Leuuin)
Career: might have been three moneyers at Exeter 1024-42, 1059-68 & 1086-1100.
Lands: a Leofwine held Knowstone and West Putford, worth 15/-, and another
Leofwine held Blackborough worth 10/-.
Early sources: DB.

LEOFWINE (Lifwine, Lioifine)
Career: at Southwark there is most likely to have been an earlier Leofwine 1046-50
and perhaps two later men covering 1068-1134, the former of whom might have
minted under Harold II.

LEOFWINE (Leofwine, Liofwine, Lefwine, Lifwine, Liifwine, DB Leuuine)
Career: most likely at least three moneyers at Stamford between 997 and 1083. One
of whom probably also minted at Huntingdon 1059-62 and might have continued
there under Harold II.
Lands: at Winwick in Huntingdon worth £1 6/8. He seems to have been a wealthy
burgess holding 10 residences in Stamford.
Early sources: DB.

LEOFWINE HORN (Lifwine Horn)
Career: was at Rochester 1059-87, alongside another Leofwine for part of this time.

LEOFWOLD (Leofwold, Liofwold, Lifwold, Lifwod, Liafwold, Liefwold, Læfwold,
Lofold)
Career: minted at Guildford 1065-67, and might have moved there from London
where he minted 1062-65. The Leofwold who minted at Winchester 1059-90 was
likely to have been the same man.

LEOFWOLD (Leofwold, Liofwold; DB Leuolt)
Career: minted at Ipswich 1050-65, and might have continued under Harold II.
Lands: a Leofwold held 4/- worth of land at Akenham in 1086.
Early sources: DB.

LEOFÞEGN (Lioeðegen)
Career: this name occurs on coins from Bedford 1036-40 and 1059-66 (and possibly
under Harold II). This might be the same man or two separate, perhaps related, men
(the name is rare).

LYFING (Lifing, Lifinc)

Career: the senior moneyer minting at Exeter 1042-68. Was he also a moneyer at Winchester?

LYFING (Lyfinc, Lyffinc, Lyfic, Lifinc, Lufinc, Luffinc)

Career: most likely to have been two people at Warwick 1018-59 & 1066-87.
Lands: a Lyfing held the manor of Offord worth 10/-.
Early sources: DB.

LYFING (Lifinc, Lifincc, Livinc, Liifinc, Lfinc, Lfine, Lifind; DB Leuing)

Career: might have minted at Winchester 1040-96 but is more likely to have been two men. An earlier Lyfing was based at Winchester 1018-24.
Lands: a Lyfing held lands at Coombe, Exton, Lymington and Utefel worth £5.
Early sources: DB.

MANNA (Manna, Manne, Mana, Man)

Career: minted at Canterbury 1042-80.

MANNA (Manna, Mana, Man; DB Manna)

Career: was based at Nottingham 1066-87 and Norwich 1066-68. A Manna at Leicester 1048-59 might have been the same man.
Lands: he held land at Little Snoring in Norfolk worth £2.
Early sources: DB.

MANWINE (Manwine)

Career: minted at Dover 1062-80.

MORCERE (Morcere, Morcre, Morcereee)

Career: minted at Bury St Edmunds 1048-65 and is likely to have continued under Harold II.

ORDRIC (Ordric)

Career: minted at Gloucester 1056-71.

OSBEORN (Esbern, Esbn)

Career: at Lincoln 1067-68, possibly beginning under Harold II. He might have gone to Thetford where he minted 1068-80.

OSMÆR (Osmær, DB Osmer)

Career: minted at Bath 1053-93 (senior moneyer).
Lands: the father of an Osmær held 1 yardland in Otterhampton in 1066.
Early sources: DB.

OSMUND (Osmund, Omund)

Career: minted both at London 1053-67 and Southwark 1053-93 (where he might have been the senior moneyer).

OSWARD (Osward, Oswarde)

Career: worked at Stamford 1059-66 and might have continued under Harold II. An earlier Osward minted there 1024-38.

OSWOLD (Oswold)

Career: was based at Lewes 1044-87 (as senior moneyer by 1066).

OÞBEORN (Oðbeorn, Oðbern, Oðborn, Oðboren, Oðbrn, Oðbron, Oðben, Ouðbeorn, Ouðbearn, Ouðbern, Ouðborn, Ouðboen, Awðbern, Awðbrn, Uðbrn, Otbern, Æwtbrn)

Career: minted at York 1059-1100, and might have begun at Lincoln 1050-56.
Lands: an Autbert held land at North Dalton (East Riding) worth 10/-. Was this the same man?
Early sources: DB.

OÞGRIM (Oðgrim, Odgrim, Ouðgrim, Oeðgrim; DB Outgrim)

Career: minted at Lincoln 1038-71 (the senior moneyer), and might have minted also at York 1056-77.
Lands: he possibly held Withcall worth £2.
Early sources: DB.

OÞWULF (Ouðolf)

Career: worked at Leicester 1065-66, possibly continuing under Harold II.

OÞWULF (Oðolf, Ouðulf, Ouððulf, Ouðolf, Ouðoif, Oudulf, Auðolf, DB Oudulf, Audulf)

Career: minted at York 1062-71. Did he also mint at Leicester?
Lands: an Oþwulf held land at Coulton and Leyburn in North Riding worth +10/-, Eddlethorpe in East Riding worth 10/-.
Early sources: DB.

OWIG (Owi)

Career: minted at Wilton 1067-71, and maybe under Harold II also.

ROSCYTEL (Roscetel, Rozcetel, DB Roschil, Roschel, Ruschil)

Career: worked at York 1066-71.
Lands: at Kirklington and Wath in North Riding worth £1 10/-; Alwoodley, Linton, Lofthouse, Ryther, Stockton in West Riding worth £3 13/4.
Early sources: DB.

SÆCOLL (Sæcol, Sæcolf)
Career: minted at Cambridge 1056-67.

SÆFARA (Sævara, Sefar)
Career: began at Salisbury 1067-68, and then moved to Wilton 1068-93. Either he or Sigeboda minted at Salisbury under Harold II.

SÆMAN (Seman)
Career: most likely began at Newport (Pagnell) 1059-62 and then moved to Hertford 1062/67, minting there 1067-96.

SÆWINE (Sæwine, Sewine)
Career: possibly three moneyers at Exeter 1009-30, 1050-93 & 1101-16. Sæwine appears to have been a common name in Devon, with a number of landowners bearing it, who may or may not have been the moneyer.

SÆWINE (Sæwine, Sewine, Sæwi, Sewi; DB Sauuin)
Career: most likely an earlier Sæwine minted at Leicester 1038-53 and moved to Northampton 1056-80, becoming senior moneyer, with a later Sæwine at Northampton 1086-1103.
Lands: he might have held Braunston in 1066 worth £1.
Early sources: DB.

SÆWINE (Sæwine, Sewine, Sæwi, Swwine; DB Sauuin)
Career: worked at Wilton 1056-96. Was he also the Sæwine who worked at Exeter?
Lands: a Sæwine held £2 worth of land at Smithcot in Wiltshire.
Early sources: DB.

SEOLCWINE (Seolcwine, Silcwine)
Career: minted at Gloucester 1056-67.

SIBWINE (Sibwine)
Career: worked at London 1065-66 and might have continued under Harold II.

SIDUMAN (Sideman)
Career: the senior moneyer at Wareham 1038-74. Used the large number of three obverse dies in 1066, which has been interpreted as meaning that he was the only moneyer at the time (but see Ægelric).
Modern references: Pagan 1990.

SIGEBODA (Sibode)

Career: was based at Salisbury 1065-66 and either he or Sæfara minted there under Harold II. He most likely moved to London 1071-74. His name was continental and he might have been German.

SIGEBRAND (Sibrand)

Career: minted at Bedford 1067-87 and might have begun under Harold II. Judging by his name, he might have come from Germany.

SIGEFERÐ (Siferð, Siffarð, Siifrð, Sihfeorð, Sihforð, Sifreð, Sigfeorð, Sigverið, Sigvewið, Sefward, Seifward, Segwarð, Segwarað, Sigworð, Sighwerð, Sigewið)

Career: minted at Lincoln 1067-87 and possibly under Harold II.

SIGEGOD (Sigod)

Career: worked at Bedford 1059-80.

SIGELAC (Silac, Silach, Silæc)

Career: was based at Gloucester 1056-90.

SIGERED (Sired, DB Sired)

Career: worked at Canterbury 1062-66 and is likely to have continued after this.
Lands: the thane Sigered of Chilham held £66 of land in Kent (see above). Attached to his main manor of Chilham were 13 dwellings in Canterbury. Did these include workshops for minting coins? Plots in Canterbury were also attached to his lands at Luddenham and Wickhambreux (held from Ælfred Bicga).
Early sources: DB.

SNÆBEORN (Snæbearn, Snæborn, Snebern, Sneborn, Snebrn, Sneaburn, Senebrn, DB Esnebern)

Career: worked at York 1056-66. He seems to have died or retired under Harold II, sharing obverse dies with Leising who began in 1066 and presumably replaced him.
Lands: at Studley Royal, West Riding worth 10/-.
Early sources: DB.
Modern references: Pagan 1990.

SPRÆCLING (Spræclinc, Spracling, Spraclinc, Spracline, Spralinc, Spracelnc)

Career: was based at Winchester 1056-99 but might have moved there from London where he worked 1050-53.

SUTERE (Sutere)

Career: minted at York 1066-67.

SWEARTCOL (Sweartcol, Swearcol, Swartcol, Swartc, Swertcol, Swrtcol, DB Suartcol, Suardcol, Sortcol, Sortcolf)

Career: minted at York 1050-71.
Lands: at Harome, Sproxton in North Riding worth +3/4; Askham Richard, Bordley, Hetton, Sprotbrough in West Riding £2+.
Early sources: DB.

SWEARTCOL (Swarcolf, Swarculf, Swarcole)

Career: worked at Stamford 1062-66, continuing under Harold II perhaps. Is he the same as the Sweartcol who was minting at York? The difference in spellings of his name suggests not.

SWEARTLING (Sweartlinc, Swartlinic, Sweortinc, Sweortnc, Swirtlic, Swirtinc, Swirtic, Swrtic, DB Soarding)

Career: minted at Wallingford 1066-87. He shared obverse dies (and presumably workshops) with Brihtmær in 1066. Sweartling owned a plot of land within the borough that was exempted from payment of dues, which had passed by inheritance into the hands of a Frenchman, Nigel, by 1086.
Early sources: DB.
Modern references: Pagan 1990.

SWETMAN (Swetman)

Career: minted at London 1044-68, and also at Southwark 1053-62. He was addressed in a writ sent to London as one of its port reeves but had given up this post by 1065.
Early sources: H43 (1058/66).

SWETMAN (Swetman, Swwetman, Setman, DB Suetman)

Career: based at Oxford 1050-87, and could have been the same man as the Swetman who minted at Northampton 1062-71. He could have been the Swetman of London.
Lands: in 1086, he had a free house in Oxford paying 40d, 2 wall dwellings paying 3/- and a further dwelling paying 8d. He might have held land in Croughton (Northamptonshire) worth 3/-.
Early sources: DB.

ÞEODRED (Ðeodred, Ðreodred)

Career: minted at Hastings 1059-68. His name was continental and he might have come from Germany.

ÞOR (Ðorr, Ðor, Ðour, Ðuri, DB Tor)

Career: worked at York 1046-71.
Lands: he might have been an important thane, based mainly in North Riding (see above) with lands worth at least £41.

Early sources: DB.

ÞROND (Ðrond)
Career: minted at Chester 1065-67.

ÞURCYTEL (Ðurcil, Ðurkil, Ðiurcil, Drcil)
Career: was based at Warwick 1055-87 (as senior moneyer in 1066).

ÞURGOD (Ðurgod)
Career: minted at Thetford 1066-67.

ÞURGRIM (Ðurgrim, Ðuregrim, DB Turgrim)
Career: he was based at Norwich 1065-77.
Lands: he might have been the Þurgrim who held land at Wiveton worth £2.
Early sources: DB.

ÞURSTAN (Ðurstan, Þurstan, Ðorstan)
Career: the senior moneyer working at Norwich 1050-67.

ULF (Ulf, Wulf, Þulf)
Career: he either had a very long career at Lincoln 1042-96 or was two separate men, the earlier ending 1067 and the later beginning in 1074. He might have been one of the lawmen of Lincoln mentioned in the Domesday Book.
Early sources: DB
Modern references: Smart 1968.

ULFCYTEL (Ulfcytel, Ulfcetel, Ulfceetel, Ulfcetl, Ulfcutel, Ulfctel, Ulfctl, Ulfcte, Ulfcel, Ulfkel, Ulfcil, Ulfkecel, Ulfkec, Ulcetel, Ulketl, Ulfctl Ðegii, Ulfctl Ðaginc, Ulfctel Ðeginc; DB Vlchil, Vlchel)
Career: minted at York 1040-71 (he might have been the senior moneyer, but see Earncytel). His by-name might be derived from *þegn* (thane), and indicate either his own status or that of his father.
Lands: Ulfcytel was a common name and it is impossible to determine whether he was one of the thanes holding land in 1066, and, if so, which thane.
Modern references: Smart 1986.

WICING (Wicing)
Career: based at Worcester 1048-71(possibly the senior moneyer).

WIHTSIGE (Wixie)
Career: minted at Ilchester 1067-83 and is likely to have minted under Harold II.

WILGRIP (Wilgrip)

Career: worked at Hertford 1050-66, and either he or Sæman were minting there under Harold II. Freeman suggested that Wilgrip moved at various times between Stamford, Leicester and Hertford over a career between 1038 and 1066.

WINE (Winus)

Career: worked at Wilton 1062-67.

WUDUMAN (Wudeman, Wudman)

Career: minted at Shrewsbury 1059-66 and is likely to have continued under Harold II.

WULFGAR (Wulgar)

Career: he was based at Lincoln 1046-66, and may have carried on there under Harold II. Was he one of the Wulfgars minting at London?

WULFGAR (Wulfgar, Wulgar)

Career: at least two, may be more, moneyers at London 991-1067. He shared an obverse die in 1066 with Leofsige of London (also ended 1067) and Ælfwine of Ipswich (1062-71).
Modern references: Pagan 1990.

WULFGEAT (Wulfgeat, Wulfget, Wulfgt, Wulegeat, Ufgæt; DB Vlfiet)

Career: worked at Gloucester 1053-87.
Lands: A Wulfgeat held half of Pebworth worth £3 10/-.
Early sources: DB.

WULFMÆR (Wulmær, Wulmer)

Career: minted at Lincoln 1066-67.

WULFMÆR (Wulfmær, Wulmær)

Career: worked at Romney 1042-96.

WULFMÆR (Wulmær, DB Vlmer)

Career: the senior moneyer at Shrewsbury 1040-80.
Lands: possibly held a quarter of Harley worth in total 21/-.
Early sources: DB.

WULFNOÐ (Wulnoð, DB Vlnod)

Career: worked at Exeter 1065-66 and might have minted under Harold II.
Lands: a Wulfnoð was recorded as having £26 worth of land in 1066. This need not have been the same person.
Early sources: DB.

WULFNOÐ (Wulfnoð)
Career: minted at Stafford 1068-71, and possibly also under Harold II.

WULFRED (Wulfred)
Career: worked at Canterbury 1050-86. He could have moved there from London where a Wulfred minted 1038-59.

WULFRIC (Wulfric, DB Vluric)
Career: minted at Chichester 1053-66, and either he or Brunman minted there under Harold II.
Lands: a powerful local thane Wulfric held Charlston, Linch and Pulborough in Sussex worth £33, the latter two of which were near Chichester.
Early sources: DB.

WULFRIC (Wulfric)
Career: occurs on coins from Leicester 1044-66 and might have continued under Harold II as the senior moneyer.

WULFSIGE (Wulfsi, Wulsige, Wulsi, Wulsiiie)
Career: minted at London 1044-66 and might have carried on after this.

WULFWARD (Wulfward, Wulfwurd, DB Wluuard)
Career: he minted at London 1042-67 and might have been the same man who minted at Dover 1062-67.
Lands: Waldershare in Kent worth £2 10/- (2s).
Early sources: DB.

WULFWARD (Wulfward, Wulfword)
Career: worked at Stamford 1066-93.

WULFWIG (Wulfwig, Wulfwi, Wulwi, Wulnwig)
Career: was based at Bedford 1048-67 (senior moneyer), but might have begun at Huntingdon, minting there 1042-46.

WULFWIG (Wulfwi)
Career: minted at Cambridge 1066-67, possibly having moved there from Thetford where he minted 1059-62. He might also have minted at Colchester (but see Wulfwine).

WULFWIG (Wulfwi, Wulfi)
Career: minted at Oxford 1062-96. A Wulfwig the fisherman had a dwelling in Oxford worth 32d (DB). Was this the moneyer, engaging in a varied suite of activities?

WULFWINE (Wulfwine)
Career: worked at Warwick 1062-80, and at Droitwich 1066-67.

WULFWINE (Wulfwine, Wulfwne, Wulwine)
Career: there may well have been an early Wulfwine at Colchester 991-1003, followed by two further moneyers of this name 1018-93. Was one of these the Wulfwig of 1066-67? He might have expanded to Ipswich 1068-71.

WULFWINE (Wulfwine, Wulfwne, Ulfwine, DB Vluuin)
Career: minted at Exeter 1065-83.
Lands: possibly held Bray and Sutton, worth £2 in 1066.
Early sources: DB.

THE GREATER MONEYERS IN 1066

There were 32 moneyers who had minting rights in more than one borough. They fall into three groups: those based in London, those working from the main regional centres, and those whose mints were smaller and more local in importance. As might be expected, London was the mint with the largest number of moneyers working at more than one mint, 8 out of the 32 (25%). The regional centres together provided a further 14 men, leaving the lesser boroughs with the 10 remaining (Table 5). It may be that these 32 men were among the wealthier members of the urban elite. With economic interests in more than one borough, their trading networks must have been extensive. In most cases, they were also the more long-established of the moneyers at their mints (22, or possibly 24, were minting for more than 10 years before 1066), suggesting a lengthy period of accumulating wealth that might confirm their status as an upper layer of moneyers.

Some of the boroughs seem to have had well-established links: London and Canterbury, which shared four moneyers between them, Hereford and Shrewsbury with two moneyers, Winchester and Chichester also with two. A more elastic identification of moneyers could modify the list, e.g. was the Swetman who minted at Oxford and Northampton the same as the moneyer of that name who was port reeve of London?

Main centre	Moneyers	Dates	Other Centres in 1066
London	Ælfward	1044-66	Canterbury
	Ælfwine	1040-77?	Canterbury
	Deorman	1044-59	Colchester & Steyning
	Eadward	1050-62	Canterbury (1044-68)
	Eadwine	1042-96	Canterbury
	Godric	?	Southwark (1062-65) & Sandwich (1062-65)
	Osmund	1053-67	Southwark
	Wulfward	1042-67	Dover
Winchester	Ælfwine	1036-71	Chichester
	Godwine	?	Chichester & Lewes (1050-67)
	Leofwold	1059-90	Guildford
Hereford	Ægelric	1046-68	Shrewsbury
	Earnwig	1046-66	Shrewsbury
	Leofnoð	1030-66	Chester
Thetford	Ælfwine	1059-87	Ipswich
	Godwine	1062-74	Norwich
Exeter	Brihtric	1066-68	Taunton (1056-77)
Gloucester	Leofwine	1050-80	Bristol
Lincoln	Oþgrim	1038-71	York
Norwich	Manna	1066-68	Nottingham (1066-87)
Oxford	Swetman	1050-87	Northampton
Shrewsbury	Godwine	1059-66	Stafford
Bridport	Hwateman	1036-80	Dorchester
Canterbury	Leofwine	1018-65	Rochester
Huntingdon	Godwine	1050-83	Cambridge & Maldon
Ilchester	Ægelwine	1053-83	Shaftesbury
Ipswich	Brihtric	1053-65	Cambridge
Salisbury	Godric	1056-86	Shaftesbury
Stamford	Leofric	1036-74	Leicester & Huntingdon
	Leofwine	1046-80	Huntingdon
Tamworth	Coling	1056-93	Stafford
Warwick	Wulfwine	1062-80	Droitwich

Table 5: Moneyers working at more than one mint in 1066

CASUALTIES OF THE CONQUEST

The boroughs were not an isolated part of English life in 1066. They were linked closely to the rest of the economic and social life of the country. However, discussion of politics and society of the time tends to treat the urban and landed elite as separate spheres. Moreover, it is the landed elite which is most visible in the records of the time and which tends to dominate modern analyses of events. The impact of the succession of Harold and the Conquest by Willelm must have had its effects on urban society, and the financial facilities of the burgesses must have played a part in financing, and profiting from, the military adventures of the day.

If we ignore the moneyers who were only optionally minting under Harold (the 29 alternatives for 18 minting places), and take only the 179 moneyers who were probably or definitely working in 1066, we find that 50 do not appear under Willelm I. A further seven make their last appearance in the first issue of Willelm, 17 disappear after 1071 and 11 after 1074. This left only 52.5% of the 179 moneyers still at work after 1074.

Last issue	Moneyers	Cumulative	%	In areas of revolt	% of moneyers
1066-67	50	50	27.9	25	50
1067-68	7	57	31.8	5	71
1068-71	17	74	41.3	11	65
1071-74	11	85	47.5	5	45
TOTAL	85			48	56

Table 6: Moneyers under Harold II

The real number of moneyers who stopped work in 1066-74 will be less than this since some will undoubtedly appear under Willelm when more coins come to light in future. A small number will also have either died naturally or retired at this time, e.g. possibly Ælfwine at Bristol and certainly Snæbeorn at York. The increased financial burden born by the moneyers might also account for some of the decrease (Stafford 1989: 216). However, this still leaves a large number of people who seem to have been casualties of the Conquest. The increase in numbers whose last minting occurred during the issue of 1068/71 (Table 6) must surely represent displacement after the revolts of these years, as must the high percentage of moneyers from areas of revolt who disappeared between 1067 and 1071.

The disappearance of moneyers was especially high at some of the boroughs situated in areas where revolts had broken out before 1071. Lincoln and York had the highest rate of disappearance with 17 out of 23 definite or probable moneyers (74%) ending their minting activity by 1074. Around the Fens, Cambridge and Stamford lost six out of nine (67%) and in the Welsh marches, Chester and Hereford lost nine out of 12, although one of the Hereford moneyers who ceased work there carried on at Shrewsbury so only eight out of 12 actually stopped minting (67%). Mints in East Anglia and around the Fens also seem to have suffered; Thetford lost four out of nine, Cambridge four out of five. Not all the mints in the rebellious areas suffered to the same degree. Shrewsbury only lost one moneyer, Exeter two, and Ilchester, the nearest mint to the unrest at Montacute, lost none of its personnel. Some boroughs which were not obviously connected with areas of revolt suffered heavily. Wilton lost four out of five moneyers, while London lost eight out of 15. However, most boroughs that were not in or near regions of revolt suffered very little attrition. Winchester saw only one out of six moneyers disappear by 1074. Oxford lost only one out of eight moneyers. Slightly higher figures can be seen at Wallingford, one (or two including alternatives) out of four, and Gloucester, two (or three) out of seven, but these are still low compared with mints like York or Chester which were at the heart of revolts. There is enough of a pattern to suggest that some moneyers were involved in the resistance to Willelm and were dispossessed as a result. Among the greater moneyers, only five do not seem to have minted under Willelm, and a further two disappeared by 1074. This is a much lower proportion than for the moneyers as a whole. It could have been the lesser moneyers who were more prepared to take the risk of supporting revolts against Willelm and paid the price. Those whose position was less established might well have been looking to take advantage of the situation to advance themselves.

FOREIGN-BORN ENGLISH

There had always been people of foreign birth in England. It would be wrong to see any country in 11th century Europe as a single ethnic unit or as mindful of the movements of its citizens as a modern state. England in 1066 had a cosmopolitan element within its ruling class, both clerical and lay. The legal position of such people after the Conquest by Willelm of Normandy was that they were to be regarded in the same way as native-born English. Such a legal distinction cut across ethnic divisions and even families. The legally English but ethnically Norman priest Osbeorn was brother of the newly arrived Earl Willelm, legally and ethnically Norman. Osbeorn's promotion to be Bishop of Exeter could be seen as increasing Norman influence in the church. However, he became noted as a champion of traditional English practices and against Norman innovation. The death of Bishop Wulfstan in 1095 is often said to mark the end of the native episcopate but it might be more realistic to regard this as being signalled by Osbeorn's death in 1103. The mix of foreign-born English men and women included mainly Normans, Danes, Lotharingians, Germans, Bretons and Flemings.

There is a great deal of difficulty in identifying foreign-born English men and women. Without biographical information, we are forced to rely on personal names, which are highly unreliable as indicators of nationality (see Introduction). Many continental names shared common elements with English, and the spelling of such names was often 'normalised' to their English equivalent (Smart 1986). However, the presence of foreigners in England is undeniable. The laws of King Æþelred (IV Æþelred 5) refer to foreigners (*transmarinus*) among the moneyers, traders and forgers, which make it plain they were to be expected among the urban population.

Many of the foreign settlers have already been recorded in other categories above. These are merely listed in this chapter, without repetition of their details. However, there were others who do not readily fall into the categories already dealt with and whose existence was noted in historical sources of the time, being more than mere names. Details are given about each of them below. Information is also given about people who had been active in Eadward III's reign but who were either dead or had left England by 1066, since many of them influenced or took part in the events leading to the Conquest.

LAY MEN AND WOMEN

Those in office or holding land in 1066 and who have already been mentioned above were:

Royal family – *Agatha* (Prince Eadgar's mother)

King's household – Alan (Steward), Hugo (Chamberlain), Rodbert FitzWymarc (Constable)

Earls' families – *Gyða* (Harold's mother)

Moneyers – Anderboda, Baldric, Eorlwine, Folcard, Folcwine, Godesbrand, Godleof, Heregod, Sigeboda, Sigebrand, Þeodred

Thanes – Baldwine FitzHerluin, Earnsige, Fitel, Iohan, Tolig, Þurcyll Hwit

Details for each of these can be found in the appropriate section above. Others known to be in England in 1066 but were either not holding high office or were not among the top rank of landowners were:

ÆLFRED (DB Alured)

Life: Ælfred was the King's equerry, one of the Norman followers of Eadward III allowed to remain in England after the reinstatement of Earl Godwine and his family in 1052.

Lands: in Cornwall worth £15 (+ lands in Devon to total £36 according to Lewis 1995).

Early sources: W.

Modern references: Barlow 1970, Lewis 1995.

EOFERWACER (DB Eureuuacre, Euuacre, Euroac)

Life: his name is German and occurred as a charter witness under Eadward.

Lands: his lands in Devon and Somerset amounted to £18.

Early sources: DB: witnessed charter S1034 (1061), S1042 (1065).

Modern references: Oleson 1955.

MATHILD (DB Mathild, Matheld, Mathila)

Life: a lady in waiting of Queen *Eadgyð*. She married a thane, Ælfward.

Lands: in Devon worth £3 according to Lewis 1995.

Early sources: Hm.

Modern references: Barlow 1970, Lewis 1995.

RICARD FITZ SCROB (DB Ricard)

Life: Ricard was one of the Normans who were allowed to stay in England after the exile of Archbishop Rodbert in 1052. After the Conquest, he was involved in disputes with Eadric Wilde which led to the latter's revolt against Willelm. His son Osbeorn was Sheriff of Hereford. Ricard was described as a housecarl of Eadward III.

Lands: in Worcester, Hereford and Shropshire worth £21 according to Lewis 1995 (with £7 held also by his son Osbeorn).

Early sources: O: addressed in writs H116, H117.
Modern references: Round 1895, Harmer 1952, Williams 1995, Lewis 1995.

ÞEODRIC (DB Teodric)

Life: this man, of German name, was listed in the Domesday Book as a goldsmith and *cuneator*. It has been suggested that he was the man responsible for the design of Eadward III's great seal (of German inspiration), and the sovereign type coin issue of 1056, although this not undisputed (Talvio 1990). He witnessed a sale of land in 1072, and was still listed among the landowners of 1086 in the Domesday Book. He seems to have profited from the Conquest, increasing his estate to £28.
Lands: in Surrey worth £3, his wife holding lands in Oxfordshire worth £2 10/-.
Early sources: DB: witnessed charter P56.
Modern references: Dolley & Elmore Jones 1961, Nightingale 1982, Keynes 1997.

ÞUROLD (DB Turold)

Life: he was Sheriff of Lincolnshire after 1069 and might have been in England before the Conquest, although not listed by Lewis (1995) among the Frenchmen holding land in 1066. It has been suggested that he might have been the Þurold who founded Spalding Priory in 1051, and even that he was actually English (Green 1983).
Early sources: DB: R430.
Modern references: Round 1895, Green 1983.

WILLELM MALET (DB Willelm)

Life: it has been suggested that he held Alkborough and other lands in Lincolnshire before the Norman Conquest, although this is disputed (Hart 1997). It would however accord with the possibility that he had an English mother (Green 1983). Willelm's family came from Graville, near Le Havre. He was entrusted with the burial of Harold II after Hastings, and was made Sheriff of York in 1068, being given the lands of various Yorkshire thanes who had presumably fallen at Stamford Bridge. York fell twice to Eadgar II in 1069, Willelm being captured on the first occasion and escaping on the second. He possibly died in the campaign against Hereward at Ely in 1071. His son Rodbert became Sheriff of Suffolk.
Lands: in Lincolnshire worth £11 according to Lewis 1995.
Early sources: O, SD: DB.
Modern references: Round 1895, Douglas 1964, Green 1983, Fleming 1991, Williams 1995, Lewis 1995, Hart 1997.

A lesser stratum of French landowners has also been identified (Lewis 1995) who did not hold more than £40 of land and cannot be allocated any offices in the King's household (as yet, no similar work has been done to identify Danish and German thanes among the lesser landowners in 1066). It is likely that these were among the followers of Eadward III on his return to England in 1041, or might have come over since then in search of favour and employment. These are listed below as noted in Lewis 1995, according to the size of their landholding.

£10-£25: Alfred of Marlborough (£24), Pagen (£15), Erlebald (£11), Ernold (£10), Girald of Wilton (£10)

£5-£10: Frederic (£9), Alberic (£8), Iudichel (£7), Vital (£6), Durand of Offton (£6), Howard (£5)

£1-£5: Waland (£4), Walter (£4), Azelin (£4), Willelm of Nottingham (£4), Willelm of Kent (£4), Willelm of Essex (£4), Willelm the falconer, Kent (£3), Ansfrid of Surrey (£3), Engelbric (£3), Clarenbold (£2), Erneis (£2), Henri (£2), Herlwine (£2), Mainard (£2), Willelm of Nottingham (£2), Burde (£2), Gundulf of Sussex (£2), Hermer (£2), Hugo thane (£2), Ricard of Nottingham (£1), Anselm (£1), Maino (£1), Eburard (£1), Adelelm (£1), Ansfrid of Hampshire (£1), Durand of Hampshire (£1), Godbold (£1), *Gundrada* (£1), Hardwine (£1), Tiselin (£1)

under £1: Raulf of Lincoln (13/4), Gislebert (13/-), Adelo (12/-), Raulf of Wiltshire (12/-), Fulbert (10/-), Fulcard (10/-), Fulcwi (10/-), Luvet (10/-), Ricard of Worcester (10/-), Winemar (10/-), Gundulf of Gloucester (8/-), Waldin (3/4), Willelm of Cambridge (2/10), Bodin (2/-), Durand of Nottingham (2/-), Hereman (1/8)

Other French thanes with lands of unknown value were Girald of Hampshire, Gerin, Rainer and Willelm of York

Dead or No Longer in England in 1066

The following had settled in England but were either dead, or had left before 1066:

ÆLFGYFU-YMME (Ælfgifu, Ælfgyfa, Ælfgiue, Ælfgiua, Ymma, Imme)

Life: *Ymme* was the daughter of Ricard I of Normandy and married King Æþelred in 1002, adopting the English name *Ælfgyfu*. She went into exile in the face of the Danish invasion in 1013-14 and again after Cnut's conquest in 1016. However, she returned to England to marry Cnut in 1017, abandoning her children by Æþelred (Eadward, Ælfred and *Godgyfu*). After Cnut's death she struggled to have her son by him, Harðacnut, accepted as King. However, on Harold I's acceptance by the whole of England she was forced again into exile in Flanders. She returned with Harðacnut in 1040. On his death, her eldest son Eadward succeeded but feelings between them cannot have been cordial. He had refused to help her in exile in 1038 and she had abandoned him to a life of exile in 1017. Eadward deprived her of her lands and position in 1043, but they were reconciled in the following year. Little is heard of her after this. *Ymme* died on 7th March 1052.

Early sources: EE: Chr C, D (1002, 1003, 1013, 1017, 1035, 1036, 1037, 1043, 1052), E, F (1002, 1003, 1013, 1017, 1035, 1037, 1043, 1052): witnessed charters

S902 (1002), S909 (1004), S910, S911 (1005), S915, S916 (1007), S918 (1008), S926 (1012), S950, S951, S952 (1018), S955, S956 (1019), S957 (1020), S977, S980 (1021/23), S958 (1022), S960 (1023), S1221, S962 (1026), S963 (1031), S964 (1032), S967, S968 (1033), S975, S976 (1035), S981, S995 (1038/39), S993, S994 (1042), S998 (1042), S999, S1000 (1043), S1001, S1002, S1006 (1044), S1011 (1045).
Modern references: Campbell 1949, Barlow 1958, Campbell 1971, Searle 1989.

ANFRID

Life: he was one of the Norman followers of Eadward III allowed to remain in England after the reinstatement of Earl Godwine and his family in 1052. He had the byname Cocksfoot.
Early sources: W.
Modern references: Barlow 1970.

HUGO

Life: a Norman comrade of Osbern Pentecost, settled in Herefordshire. With Osbern, he was exiled in 1052 and made his way to Scotland to serve King Macbeth.
Early sources: W.
Modern references: Barlow 1970.

OSBEORN

Life: known as Osbern Pentecost, he was one of the Norman settlers in Herefordshire, exiled along with Archbishop Rodbert in 1052. He went to Scotland to serve King Macbeth. His nephew, Ælfred of Marlborough held land in Worcester and Hereford in 1066, and became a major landowner after the Norman Conquest.
Early sources: W.
Modern references: Barlow 1970.

RAULF (Raulf, Rawulf)

Life: the French born nephew of King Eadward. Raulf was the second son of Eadward's sister *Godgyfu* and her husband Drogo, Count of the Vexin, born somewhere around 1027. He probably came to England with Eadward in 1041. Eadward made him an earl, most likely in 1050. He died in 1057; his widow *Gyða* and son Harold were still living in 1066, although Harold was under age (see above under the Royal Family). He had been a benefactor of Peterborough and Ramsey Abbeys. His earldom of 1050 might have been in south east Mercia, although he was certainly in charge of Hereford also by 1055 and Oxford sometime between 1053 and 1057.
Early sources: Chr C (1055), D (1052, 1055, 1057), E (1052); D, W, Ra: witnessed charters S1020, S1021, S1022 (1050), S1023 (1052), S1478 (1053/55), S1025 (1054), S1055: addressed in writ H55 (1053/57).
Modern references: Barlow 1970, Williams 1989a, Fleming 1991.

RODBERT OF RHUDDLAN

Life: Rodbert was brought to England by his father, Hunfrið de Tilleuil, to serve in Eadward's household. He returned to his parents after his education was complete and came back to England with Willelm in 1066. His cousin Hugo was made Earl of Chester and Rodbert began an attempt to conquer north Wales. He was killed fighting the Welsh in 1093. Hunfrið de Tilleuil was granted the castle of Hastings at the Conquest but later returned to Normandy.

Early sources: O, DB.

Modern references: Barlow 1970, Williams 1995.

CLERICS

Those in office or holding land in 1066 and who have already been mentioned above were:

Bishops – Gisa (Wells), Hereman (Sherborne and Ramsbury), Walter (Hereford), Willelm (London)

Abbots – Baldwine (St Edmund's), Siward (Thorney)

King's priests – Albert, Bernard, Engelric, Osbeorn, Peter, Radulf, Reinbald ('Chancellor'), Rodbert, Uitalis.

Details for each of these can be found in the appropriate section above. Others known to be in England in 1066 but not holding high office were:

ADALARD

Life: he came from Liege in Lotharingia and had been educated at Utrecht. Adalard was brought over to England by Earl Harold to reform his minster at Waltham.

Early sources: Wþ.

Modern references: Keynes 1997.

BALDWINE (DB Balduin)

Life: Baldwine, godson of Eadward III, was mentioned in connection with the lands of Westminster Abbey. He may have been a monk of that house but it is also possible that the reference is to the layman Baldwine FizHerluin.

Early sources: DB.

Modern references: Barlow 1970.

FOLCARD

Life: Folcard was a monk of St Bertin's in Flanders who was appointed as ruling Prior of Thorney 1068-85, never being consecrated as abbot. Little is known of his life, other than that he may have left St Bertin's because of dissension among the community and then found refuge with Queen *Eadgyð* before finding help from Archbishop Ealdred. He wrote Lives of St Botwulf and St John of Beverley, and possibly other works. He may have been the author of the *Vita Aedwardi Regis*.

Early sources: O: own works.
Modern references: Barlow 1962.

GOSCELIN

Life: Goscelin was another monk of St Bertin's in Flanders who joined Bishop Hereman, either in his household or in the cathedral priory at Sherborne. He was also a chaplain to the nuns of Wilton Abbey. After Hereman's death, he visited several abbeys before settling down at St Augustine's in Canterbury. He was a learned scholar and skilful writer who wrote a large number of lives of English saints. He died some time after 1107.
Early sources: M: own works.
Modern references: Barlow 1962.

Dead or No Longer in England in 1066

The following had settled in England but were either dead, or had left before 1066:

DUDUC (Duduce, Dudoc, Dudoce)

Life: a Lotharingian King's priest under Cnut, Duduc was consecrated as Bishop of Wells on 11th June 1033. He attended the Council of Rheims in 1049. Duduc died on 18th January 1060.
Early sources: W: Chr D (1060), E (1049, 1061), F (1049): witnessed charters S969 (1033), S1392 (1038), S993, S994, S998, S1396 (1042), S999 (1043), S1391 (1043/44), S1001, S1002, S1003, S1004, S1005, S1006 (1044), S1007, S1008, S1010, S1011, S1012 (1045), S1014 (1046), S1017 (1048), S1019 (1049), S1020, S1021, S1022 (1050), S1475 (1051/53), S1025 (1054), S1027 (1059): addressed in writ H53 (1033/35).
Modern references: Harmer 1952, Oleson 1955, Hart 1975.

LANDBERT

Life: a Lotharingian priest of Bishop Leofric, sent by him on a mission to the Pope in 1049.
Early sources: LM.
Modern references: Barlow 1979.

RODBERT (Rodbert, Rodbeard, Rotbeard, Hrodberd)

Life: the Norman Abbot of Jumieges in 1037, he was made Bishop of London in 1044 and Archbishop of Canterbury in 1051 (enthroned on 29th June). He was an opponent of Earl Godwine, being instrumental in his exile in 1051 but fled England at Earl Godwine's return in 1052. Rodbert was at St Denis in 1052/3 and Fécamp sometime before 1055. He died at Jumieges but the date of his death is unknown (possibly before 1058).

Early sources: VÆ, Chr C, D, E, F (1051, 1052): witnessed charters S1014 (1046), S1017 (1048), S1025 (1049/50), S1020, S1021, S1022 (1050), S1055 (1044/47, spurious): addressed in writ H77 (1044/46).
Modern references: Harmer 1952, Oleson 1955, Hart 1975, Barlow 1979.

RODBERT

Life: Rodbert was a deacon who (with his son-in-law) was one of the Norman followers of Eadward III allowed to remain at court after the flight of Rodbert of Jumieges in 1052. It is not known if he was living in 1066.
Early sources: W.
Modern references: Barlow 1970.

RODULF (Roðulf)

Life: Abbot of Abingdon 1051-1052. He was an elderly Norwegian bishop, said to be a kinsman of Eadward III.
Early sources: W, Ab: Chr E (1051).
Modern references: Knowles et al 1972.

ULF

Life: a King's priest, Bishop of Dorchester 1049-1052. He was a Norman associate of Rodbert of Jumieges who fled with him in 1052.
Early sources: W: Chr C (1049, 1052, 1053), D (1049, 1052), E (1049, 1052), F (1049): witnessed charters S1025 (1049/50), S1020, S1022 (1050), S1023 (1052): addressed in writ H59 (1050/52).
Modern references: Harmer 1952, Oleson 1955, Barlow 1979.

PROPORTIONS OF SETTLERS FROM ABROAD

The proportion of people from abroad varied greatly within the different lay and clerical categories (Table 7). King Eadward's influence is apparent in the higher numbers found among the King's household and the bishops. In other areas of society, the proportion of foreigners was between 4% and 6%, but among the household and bishops it was 36%. With Eadward's long period of exile between 1016 and 1041 (aged 11 to 36), he clearly established close links with many people which he continued when King. How to categorise particular individuals can be a problem. Prince Eadgar, and his sisters *Margareta* and *Cristina*, were Hungarian born but to describe them as foreigners would conflict with their royal family origins and later strong affiliation with England. It seems best to exclude them from the list, although the point can be argued. The proportion among the moneyers is highly uncertain. Most with Danish names were probably English but some might have been Scandinavian by birth.

Category	Total	Foreign	%
King and his family	6	1	17
Earls and their families	20	1	5
Bishops	14	4	29
Greater thanes	84	6	7
Abbots and Abbesses	40	2	5
Sheriffs	26	1	4
King's household	14	4	29
King's priests	15	8	53
Moneyers	215	11	5

Table 7: The proportions of settlers from abroad

The two main nationalities among the settlers from abroad were French and Germans with lesser numbers of Danes (Table 8). However, they were not all equally represented in the various categories. Danes were found mostly among the thanes rather than appointed officials, reflecting Eadward's early antipathy towards the Danish conquest that had led to his exile. These Danes were presumably the elderly survivors from among the followers of Cnut. Germans were found either in the church or among the moneyers, in both of which categories they were the dominant group of foreigners. The most widespread group were the French (mainly Normans but also Bretons). They were the only group to find appointment as secular officials (largely in the King's household), which reflects Eadward's upbringing in exile in northern France. In particular, he seems to have leant towards Normandy for laymen while continuing England's longstanding connections with Lotharingia in the church (Table 9).

Category	Total	French	German	Flemish	Norse	?
King and his family	1		1			
Earls and their families	1				1	
Bishops	4	1	2	1		
Abbots and Abbesses	2	1			1	
Greater thanes	5	2			4	
Sheriffs	1	1				
King's household	4	4				
King's priests	8	1	5			2
Moneyers	11	2	7	2		
TOTAL	37	11	15	3	6	2

Table 8: Place of origin of settlers from abroad

Category	French	German	Flemish	Danes	?
lay officials	5				
clerical officials	3	7	1	1	2
thanes	2			4	
moneyers	2	7	2		

Table 9: Summary of ethnic origins by category

ENGLISH EXILES ABROAD

The Anglo-Saxon Chronicle contains numerous references to exile as a punishment in pre-Conquest England. These outnumber instances of execution or imprisonment. Prominent examples since 1016 include Earls Ægelward (1020), Þurcyll (1021), Swegn (1047), Godwine and Harold (1051), Ælfgar (1055 & 1058) and Tostig (1065). Others of note were Cnut's niece *Gunnhild* (1044) and the Constable Osgod in (1046). It is a moot point whether all the instances were as a result of judicial sentence or from flight, e.g. *Ymme* in 1037. Some of those exiled made efforts to return by military force. In the case of Godwine in 1051, and Ælfgar in 1055 and 1058, these were successful. For Osgod after 1046, they were not. Other prominent people could find themselves abroad as hostages and two members of Harold's family had been held as such in Normandy.

The advantages of exile were in ridding the kingdom of potential trouble within without leading to blood feud or a desire for vengeance by any kin of an executed or murdered man. The disadvantage of exile was that it left a potential troublemaker free to associate with England's enemies, as did Ælfgar with the Welsh and Norwegians, and Tostig was to do with Harald of Norway.

COPSIG
Life: Copsig was a follower of Tostig and had been his deputy in the government of Northumbria up to 1065. After the Norman Conquest, he returned to England and secured appointment as Earl of Northumberland in February 1067, but was killed by his predecessor Oswulf on 12th March.
Early sources: SD.
Modern references: Freeman 1869-75 (Vol. 4), Barlow 1970, Williams 1995.

SPIRITES (DB Spirites)
Life: Spirites was a King's priest who was disgraced and exiled before 1066. He had a brother Earnwig and had served as chaplain since at least 1040. He was made a canon of St Martin's in Dover and in Bromfield, Shropshire.
Lands: He held lands in Shropshire, Hereford, Somerset, Wiltshire and Hampshire worth £54.
Early sources: Hm, DB: witnessed charter S993 (1042).
Modern references: Barlow 1970.

Tostig (Tostig, Tosti, Tostinus; DB Tosti)

Life: Tostig was the younger brother of Earl Harold, appointed as Earl of Northumbria and Mid Anglia in 1055. He probably had held a position at court before this, signing charters as first or second among the thanes. His wife was *Iudith*, sister of Count Baldwine V of Flanders. On his family's exile in 1051, he sought refuges at Bruges before returning in 1052. He also went abroad in 1061, on a visit to Rome. As Earl of Northumbria, he forged close relations with King Mælcolm of Scotland. His rule over Northumbria was strict and he became involved in feuds with the local nobility (having his sister Queen *Eadgyð* arrange the murder of an enemy at court), which led to a revolt against his rule in October 1065. His brother, Harold mediated a settlement, which resulted in his exile. Tostig saw this as a betrayal by Harold, even accusing Harold of conniving with the rebels. After this, he sought support from Willelm in Normandy and based himself in his wife's home Flanders. In May 1066, he attacked the Isle of Wight from there, moving to Sandwich and thence to the Humber where his force was beaten by Earl Eadwine. He then took refuge in Scotland with King Mælcolm and joined Harold of Norway's fleet in September, taking part in the Norwegian invasion of England. Tostig was killed fighting his brother Harold II at the Battle of Stamford Bridge on 25th September 1066. He was described as prudent but strong minded and inflexible. His steadfastness of purpose made him persevere vigorously with any action, although he was cunning and secretive about his intentions. He was especially close to his sister Queen *Eadgyð*.

Early sources: VÆ, SD, O: Chr C (1051, 1053, 1065, 1066), D (1051, 1061, 1063, 1065, 1066), E (1049, 1063, 1065, 1066): witnessed charters S1000 (1043), S1002 (1044), S1055 (1044/47), S1017 (1048), S1019 (1049), S1025 (1049/50), S1020, S1021, S1022 (1050), S1023 (1052), S1026 (1055), S1060 (1055/60), S1028 (1059), S1033, S1034 (1061), S1036 (1062), S1037a, S1038 (1065): addressed in writs H7, H119 (1060/65), H62: mentioned in writ H93 (1058/66).

Modern references: Freeman 1869-75, Harmer 1952, Douglas 1966, Barlow 1970, Williams 1995.

Wulfnoð

Life: the younger brother of Harold II, born around 1036, he was held as a hostage in Normandy since 1051. Wulfnoð was freed at Willelm's death in September 1087, but was imprisoned again by Willelm II at Winchester in October the same year. He died in 1094, aged 58.

Early sources: W, O, WP.

Modern references: Barlow 1970, Walker 1997.

CONCLUSION

This book lists less than 500 people at the apex of English society in 1066. This was not the extent of the ruling elite of the time, merely its most visible tip. While we have details about the lives of many, others are but names. Unfortunately, since we do not have much information about their family and political relationships, we cannot fully reconstruct the factions that must have existed and which provided the political dynamics of the day. However, the story of the Norman Conquest of England is the story of the dispossession and disappearance of this highest part of society and it is worth investigating in more detail.

THE SOCIAL PYRAMID

All medieval and later European societies were pyramids with access to power and wealth being limited to fewer and fewer people at the higher levels. The people listed in this book belonged to the very upper reaches of the social hierarchy. Our knowledge of those lower down the social scale at this period is very limited in the absence of widespread manorial and other records. Out of a total population of at least 1,700,000, there might be just over 500,000 adult males (the politically and economically active part of the population). This is assuming that just over half the population were men, and that about 60-65% of these would be over 15 years old (Russell 1969, Cipolla 1976). We can never hope to know the names, let alone the life stories of more than a tiny fraction of these. For women, the position is even worse. Our attempts to reconstruct the precise shape of the social pyramid are hampered by the lack of data until the censuses of the 19th century. One early attempt to do this for pre-industrial England was that of Gregory King in 1696 (Clark 1946). Social and economic conditions had changed greatly of course between 1066 and 1696 but the broad outlines might have been similar. King estimated that the gentry, superior clergy and merchants accounted for just over 4% of the population, with most of the people (58%) belonging to the poorer sections of society: the cottagers, artisans, labourers and paupers. Our view of 11th century society is dominated by its wealthier sections: the greater clergy, earls and thanes. Even if we cast the net wider to include all thanes, we end up with an estimated 4-5,000 families (Fleming 1991), about 1½% of the total number of families in the kingdom. This agrees well with King's estimate of 1·2% for the equivalent groups of the 17th century, the lords, bishops, baronets, knights and gentry.

A person's position in society was largely determined by his or her place in the system of landholding and lordship within rural society (Faith 1997). Boroughs could offer opportunities to sidestep the system but even there the links between rural manors and their lords with urban landholdings makes any rigid distinction between urban and rural hard to maintain. The social system of the 11th century was marked by legal differences between classes. At the base of the pyramid was a class not to be found later, slaves. These were without civil rights, being unable to plead in the courts and were the property of their owners. However, they were accorded some protection in law from complete exploitation and their owners had an obligation to feed and shelter them. This would give them some protection during times of famine that a free man might envy. The lowest of the free classes were the cottagers, townsmen (the town being the rural township), and other commoners divided into various grades according to the amounts of land they held and their relationships to the lords of their lands. Many held their lands in return for rents and services whose level would vary from place to place. Some among them (freemen or sokemen) held land freely, able to buy and sell without reference to a lord. However, they might still owe service for that land and be under the jurisdiction of a lord's court. With greater freedom came responsibility to provide for themselves and their families with little outside help. Many freemen held small amounts of land and were economically less well off than those bound to lords by service for land (Loyn 1991: 356-367). The top of the social scale was formed by the thanes, a term that covered the whole range of what would later be differentiated into lesser gentry, knights and barons. Thanes either held land directly of the King (king's thanes) or through a greater lord, an earl or bishop, or even another thane (ordinary or mediated thanes). The same principle of service in return for land was applied to thanes as to lower classes. The service expected of thanes was usually threefold: service in the army, contribution to the upkeep of fortifications and of bridges. Other services of a non-military nature might have been attached to particular lands, e.g. minting coins, which would later be known as serjeanties. The whole system can be seen as one of rights and responsibilities. Thanes' rights included their land, possible judicial powers over their tenants, access to high office, a high *wer* (monetary compensation for death) and being able to swear oaths in court of greater value than those of commoners. Their responsibilities included the service due from their lands, being accountable for the actions of their men, being subject to greater fines for wrongdoing in line with their increased *wer* and increased heriots (death duties). They will also have had responsibilities to their tenants. A tract on estate management written at this time made the point that the reeve (steward) of an estate should know not just the rights of the lord but also the rights of it people (Swanton 1975: 25).

The terminology applied to the nobility at this date was rather underdeveloped. There were numerous grades within the aristocracy but, as yet, no way of describing these simply as would come later (eg baron, knight, serjeant, esquire). There were three broad avenues for preferment whereby people could advance up the social scale: land ownership, church office and mercantile activity. Within each of these there were various grades in a hierarchical system, which would have rough equivalences with each other, e.g. earls with bishops, or thanes with greater merchants. Within grades, the evidence of charters and of mints, seems to show some respect being paid to seniority by length of service. The degree of wealth would also determine position relative to others.

The Leading Englishmen in January 1066

The actors in the drama that would settle the succession and the fate of England after Harold II's death at Hastings were the uppermost parts of the social pyramid. This would include (Table 10) the earls, bishops, abbots, greater thanes, leading officials of the King's household, his priests and, the important link between the national and local elites, the sheriffs, some of whom were greater thanes in their own right (there were 34 shires, six of which were held in pairs by three sheriffs). It might also have included the most important moneyers, representatives of the mercantile urban elite, those with interests in more than one borough, and whose outlook was presumably more than purely local.

Category	People	Notes
Royal family	6	King, Queen, *Agatha* & children
Earls and family	9	7 earls, *Gyða*, Harold Raulf's son
Greater thanes	102	
King's household	6	
Sheriffs	26	19 known + 7 unknown
Greater moneyers	32	Total lay 181
Bishops	14	
Abbots and Abbesses	44	32 abbots, 8 abbesses, 4 provosts
King's priests	16	Total clerical 74
TOTAL	255	

Table 10: The elite in 1066

A total ruling elite of 255 people is not a large group and is vulnerable to defeat, death and dispossession as the events of 1066-71 were to show.

Power came from access to wealth, either through trade or from the land, and appointment to positions within the state. We perhaps know most about landed wealth as a source of power at this period. There were wide differences in the amount of land held by an individual or corporation like a monastery. The top 50 landowners were those with lands worth over £170 and are listed in Table 11. Earl Harold and

Archbishop Stigand were staggeringly wealthy, holding more than twice the amount of landed wealth as their nearest rivals and more than four times the amount held by the wealthiest of the thanes. If Harold had charge of most of the lands assigned to his father, Earl Godwine, in the Domesday Book then his wealth would have reached the awesome level of £3,570, dwarfing all but the King himself. The importance of the earls is readily apparent from the table, with only 7 thanes holding more land than the weakest of the earls. Bishops were generally at the same level as the lesser earls and were more than matched by the number of wealthy abbeys. The greatest of the abbeys were Ely and Glastonbury, wealthier than most bishops or any of the thanes. Particular abbots might accumulate several monasteries and advance themselves up the list, e.g. Leofric who held Burton, Coventry, Peterborough and Thorney, none of which on their own would have placed him in the top 50.

Earls and Kin	Thanes	Bishops	Abbots
Harold 2850		Stigand 2830	
Eadgyð 1670 Eadwine 1420 Morcere 1120			
			Wulfric 730 Ægelnoð 670
Gyða 590	Bu. Brihtric 560 Co. Esgar 450	<u>Hereman</u> 510 <u>Willelm</u> 490 Wulfstan 440	Ordric 430 Ægelsige 420
Walþeof 350	Ulf 390 *Eadgyfu* 370 Osbern the priest 330	Wulfwig 360 Ealdred 350	Eadwine 390 Ælfwine 390 <u>Baldwine</u> 320 *Ælfgyfu* 310
Leofwine 290 Gyrð 250	Bu. Ælfstan 290 Ætsere 270 Ægelnoð 260 Eadric 230 Wulfward 220 Sh. Mærleswegn 210 Co. <u>Rodbert</u> 200 Co. <u>Raulf</u> 200	<u>Walter</u> 270 Leofric 250 Ægelmær 220 <u>Gisa</u> 200	Ælfwig 280 *Leofgyfu* 280 Wulfwold 270 Ecgfrið 260 Leofric 260
(Harold) 170	Wihtgar 180 Co. Bondig 180		Brihtric 170 Eadward 170 *Ælfgyfu* 170

Table 11: The top 50 landowners in 1066
Note: foreign-born English are underlined. Co = constable, Sw = steward,
Bu = butler, Sh = sheriff. The value of land is given to the nearest £10

It can be seen from Table 11 that status and wealth did not always match exactly. This is made more apparent in Table 12, which is extended to all owning lands worth more than £40, and is arranged according to the classes of wealth used by Corbett in his analysis of the Norman baronage (Corbett 1926). In this way, the late Anglo-Saxon nobility can be compared with the Norman baronage that replaced it. There were more Norman barons than there had been English thanes of similar degree, but the shape of the pyramid among this upper layer of society was remarkably similar. However, wealth and power are not exactly the same thing. The involvement of leading figures in the government of the kingdom might provide for the exercise of power and influence out of proportion to their actual wealth. The Bishop of Dorchester was fifth on the list of bishops in terms of wealth, but his duties included presiding at the courts of nine shires, more than any other of his episcopal colleagues.

Wealth	Bishop	Abbey	Earl	Thane	Lay Total	%	Corbett	%
+£750	1	-	3	-	3	3	8	4
+£400	3	4	1	2	3	3	10	6
+£200	7	8	3	10	13	12	24	14
+£100	3	8	1	22	23	21	36	21
-£100	-	14	-	67	67	61	95	55
TOTAL	14	34	8	101	109		173	

Table 12: Categories of landowner in 1066 grouped by wealth

The Geography of Power

The geography of England allowed a strong central government to rule within borders that were naturally secure to the east and south, and over an area that was within practical travelling distance from the King's household. However, the great diversity of landscape, soils and climate ensured regional variation and permitted local identities and sources of power.

There are many ways of looking at the geographical distribution of power. Power as exercised through institutions and office is simply analysed by looking at the boundaries of earldoms and bishoprics. However, power also has social and economic dimensions. If we analyse the pattern of landholding in each shire, we can isolate four power groupings, each of which was the largest landowner within particular shires.

- the King
- Earl Harold and his family
- the family of Earls Eadwine and Morcere
- the church

The King was dominant in two areas: Wessex and south Mercia (Berkshire, Dorset, Gloucester, Oxford, Somerset, Wiltshire), and central Mercia (Bedford, Derby, Leicester, Northampton). The former area was the heartland of the King's power but the King also had large amounts of land elsewhere. However, 75% of the King's lands lay in the old kingdom of Wessex (England south of the Thames) along with Gloucester and Oxford. His position in this area was challenge only by Earl Harold in the far south west and Sussex, and by Archbishop Stigand in Kent and Hampshire.

Earl Harold's family also dominated two areas: the far south west (Cornwall, Devon) and the south east (Buckingham, Essex, Norfolk, Surrey, Sussex). They held land throughout most of the kingdom but Sussex was the family's home shire. Although Harold and his father were Earls of Wessex, it was the south east that was the core of their interests, based on the coastal shires around the Thames and their links with Flanders. Harold himself patronised the minster at Waltham within this area, where he was later buried.

The family of Eadwine and Morcere held the leading position in two regions: north west Mercia (Chester, Shrewsbury, Stafford, Warwick) and the Humber/Trent and North Sea (Lincoln, Nottingham, York East and North Ridings). The Mercian area was the source of their power, where the family had long been earls and aldermen. This brought them into contact with the Welsh Kings, hence the alliance between Eadwine's father, Earl Ælfgar and Gruffydd of Gwynedd. Their presence in Northumbria was more recent and resulted from the fall of Tostig. Opposition to Tostig's return ensured their defence of the north at the Battle of Fulford.

For the church, five bishops held the dominant position as follows: Archbishop Ealdred (York West Riding), Archbishop Stigand (Kent and Hampshire), Bishop Walter (Hereford), Bishop Willelm (Middlesex) and Bishop Wulfstan (Worcester). Abbeys were dominant in four shires, all in East/Mid Anglia: Ely Abbey (Cambridge), St Alban's Abbey (Hertford), Ramsey Abbey (Huntingdon) and St Edmund's Abbey (Suffolk).

Church and State

The wealth and power of the church was considerable. The church owned nearly one third of the landed wealth in England; £13,876 compared to £25,990 owned by the King, earls and greater thanes. The total amount of lay landholdings would be greater than this when the lands of the lesser thanes and freemen were added. The church held the majority of land in three shires: Kent, Worcester and Huntingdon with further shires in which single church interests were the largest landowner (see above). Moreover, the 'top 50' landowners were split nearly in half with 23 laymen and 27 from the church. Bishops presided jointly with the earls over the twice-yearly shire courts. Their lands (and those of the abbeys) were liable to taxation and levy of men for the army. In some cases, bishops took an active part in military campaigns. Appointment of senior clerics was still effectively in the King's hands as the Papal reforms were so far largely ignored. The church was thus a potentially powerful ally for any King in the face of over mighty nobles. For instance, it may be that King Eadward's endowment of the Norman priest Osbeorn with the valuable estate of Bosham church was an attempt to balance the power of Earl Harold's family in Sussex. Likewise, the leading lay families would have sought to influence church appointments. Bishops Ealdred and Wulfstan were noted associates of Earl Harold and both found preferment in areas outside his area of direct power.

Race and Gender

The elite in 1066 was largely an Anglo-Saxon male preserve. However, there were both foreigners from the continent and women among most powerful in the land. Foreigners accounted for 9% of those holding land worth over £40 or holding office (household or sheriff). In the same categories only 4% (but 6 out of the 'top 50') were women, although only some positions were open to them (lay landholders and abbeys). In these, their proportion rose to 11%. In deciding who should be classified as foreign I have chosen those who were born abroad of foreign parents. Thus, Osbeorn FitzRicard I count as English, although his father was Norman. Likewise, the Constable Raulf is classified as English, having been born in Norfolk.

Category	Foreign	Women	Out of
King's family	-	4	6
Earls' families	1	9	20
Bishops	4	-	14
Abbots/Abbesses	2	7	41
Greater thanes	6	4	102
Sheriffs	-	-	19
King's household	2	-	6
King's priests	8	-	15
Moneyers	11	-	210
TOTAL	34	24	433

Table 13: Foreigners and women among the elite

Note: Sheriffs or household officials only include those who were not already listed among the greater thanes. In all categories, only those holding office in January 1066 have been included. The total for abbots includes cathedral provosts.

THE SUCCESSION

The great political question of the day was the succession to Eadward III, which must have exercised the minds of the elite to a great degree. There were several potential claimants to the throne (Fig. 7). Eadward was the son of King Æþelred and Queen *Ymme.* He had no children of his own, and his nearest full blood relation was Harold, grandson of his sister *Godgyfu.* Harold had two disadvantages – being only a child in 1066 and his connection with Eadward was through the female line. The most obvious heir to the throne was Prince Eadgar, the grandson of Edward's elder half-brother, King Eadmund II. Eadgar was thus a full blood member in the male line of the royal house. Unfortunately, he was only around 14 in 1066 and so borderline as to whether he would be of age to rule. More importantly, he would not have had time to build up a network of political alliances among the nobility. The person who could have done so on his behalf was his mother, *Agatha.* However, she was German with no family in England to rely on, and seems to have remained an isolated figure. Eadward had other half-relations through the daughters of Æþelred's first marriage, but these do not seem to have been considered part of Eadward's close family network.

Eadward also had a number of relations by marriage who could have had a claim on the throne. His mother's second husband was King Cnut, whose nephew, Sveinn, was currently ruling in Denmark and was later to claim that Eadward had promised him the throne. As a relation of Cnut, Sveinn would naturally want to recombine his uncle's empire. However, the English had been in no hurry to help Sveinn in his wars with Norway, and there was no longer a party of Danish nobility in the higher reaches of power on whom he could rely for support (Eadward had purged the leading Danes at court early in his reign). Eadward's mother had come from the Norman ducal family, and he himself had spent a time in exile in Normandy and had Norman followers with him in England. The current ruler of the duchy was Willelm II, the grandson of *Ymme's* brother and so Eadward's great-nephew. Willelm had received an offer of the succession during the political upheaval of 1051/2. However, this must have been rescinded after the political revolution that brought Earl Godwine back to power by the end of 1052, accompanied by the expulsion of some of the leading Normans from England. The most powerful of the potential claimants was undoubtedly Earl Harold, Eadward's brother-in-law. He was by far the wealthiest layman in England, with land in most shires, and hence many followers and allies. Since the death of Earl Ælfgar, his position was politically secure as the elder statesman of the nation, loyally serving the King. Even in the revolt against his brother, Earl Tostig, he was careful not to side with Tostig and mediated a settlement that handed Tostig's earldom to Morcere, and so preserved the harmony of the kingdom. Furthermore, his military prowess had been established by the conquest of north Wales (with the disgraced Earl Tostig).

Prince Eadgar's family had spent some years in exile in Hungary, and it is Hungary that provided the most recent parallel for the situation facing England at Eadward's death (Ronay 1989). When Istvan (Stephen) of Hungary died in 1038, he had no children and the succession went to his nephew Peter, the son of his sister. Peter was later expelled and the throne was taken by Istvan's brother-in-law, Aba. Meanwhile, the representatives of the male line of the royal house, the sons of Istvan's uncle, were in exile in Russia. After Aba had been killed by Peter, the sons were invited to return and Peter was again deposed (in 1046), the eldest son Andras becoming King. Eadgar's father had probably joined Andras in his expedition to Hungary and the story of these events would have been known in England. Eadgar's family must have been nervous about seeing history repeat itself. Would the throne go to the King's sister's son, Harold son of Raulf (= Peter), to the King's brother-in-law, Earl Harold (= Aba) or to the King's nearest male relative, Eadgar (= Andras)?

The English political world would also no doubt have been aware of recent precedents for succession crises among its near neighbours. The most recent was the death of Henry II of Germany without direct heirs in 1024. The solution adopted was the election of the most senior representative of the royal family in the female line, Conrad of Franconia. Earlier experience involved different principles. On the extinction of the legitimate Carolingian line at the death of Ludwig III in 911, the Germans elected a Duke with no links to the royal family, another Conrad of Franconia. A crisis on his death without heirs in 919 was avoided by Conrad nominating as his successor the most powerful of the remaining dukes, Henry of Saxony, a man well able to make good his claim. France had experienced a similar crisis in 987 on the death of the Carolingian Louis V. Rather than accept a German Carolingian, the French opted to keep their independence by offering the crown to the most powerful of the French nobles, Duke Hugh Capet. The fact that Hugh was from the same family that had produced two earlier Kings of France during earlier political upheavals was an added factor. The option of giving the crown to an in-law of a King had also been tried in France; on the death of Hugh's grandfather Robert I when the crown went to his son-in-law. One further, and more recent, example of in-law succession was the selection of King Stenkil of Sweden to succeed his father-in-law, Emund, in 1060.

There were thus several models for the English to adopt in the succession crisis of 1066. The chief actors in the drama would no doubt be aware of the precedents and be ready to marshal arguments supporting one option or another. The current example of Germany would no doubt have been quoted as an example of the dangers of minority, where the currently underage King had been prey to the conflicting ambitions of rival prelates and a weak maternal guardianship. The results of any discussions and arguments would result from the interplay between the ambitions, personalities, abilities, alliances and feuds of the elite listed in this book. We have enough information to make a start on reconstructing the pattern of alliances between people in 1066. It is immediately obvious that Earl Harold had by far the greatest connection of allies and supporters. His faction included:

family   Queen *Eadgyð*, Earls Gyrð, Leofwine, Abbot Ælfwig (New Minster)
bishops Ægelwine (Durham), Walter (Hereford), Wulfstan (Worcester)
abbots   Ælfwold (St Benet's), Brihtric (Malmesbury), Sihtric (Tavistock)

thanes Esgar the Constable, Ætsere the Steward, Ægelnoð Cild, Mærleswegn, Eadmær, Cypping, Eadward Cild, Osgod & Brihtric, Godwine the priest, Eadnoð the Constable, Þurcyll Hwit, Ælfwold of Stevington, Gautig, Dunna

The position of the Queen was ambivalent. Although she was Harold's sister, her affection towards Eadward III was genuine and she was the guardian of his nephew, Harold son of Raulf. She had also been closely allied to the disgraced Earl Tostig, who harboured a grudge against his brother Harold for not supporting him during the northern revolt of 1065. Her own connection included Bishops Gisa of Wells, and Hereman of Sherborne & Ramsbury, as well as the thanes Wulfward Hwit, Hearding, Brihtric, *Wulfgyfu*, and Ætsere Totig's son.

The two archbishops had their own connections. Archbishop Ealdred was an ally of Earl Harold and could count on the support of Abbots Ægelwig of Evesham and Wulfstan of Gloucester. The only thane who was known to have been connected with Ealdred was Baldwine.

Stigand on the other hand was a power in his own right and steered his own course independently of the family of Godwine. His known empire included:

bishops Ægelmær (Elmham), Ægelric (Selsey), Siward (Rochester)
abbots Ægelsige (St Augustine's), Ecgfrið (St Alban's)
thanes Cytel Alder

Earl Eadwine was head of a family that included Earl Morcere and Abbot Leofric. He could also probably count on Bishop Leofwine of Lichfield and Abbot Ulfcytel of Crowland. In no way was his following as powerful as that of Harold. Although Eadwine's father had a longstanding feud with Harold, he himself was (or would shortly become) Harold's brother-in-law. The major unknowns were Earls Walþeof and Oswulf; Bishops Leofric (Exeter), Willelm (London), and Wulfwig (Dorchester); and Abbots Baldwine (St Edmund's), Eadwine (Westminster), and Wulfric (Ely). Among the major thanes Brihtric, Ælfgar's son, Ulf Fenisc, *Eadgyfu* Fæger, Ælfstan of Boscombe, and the Constables, Raulf, Rodbert, and Bondig were also of uncertain affiliation.

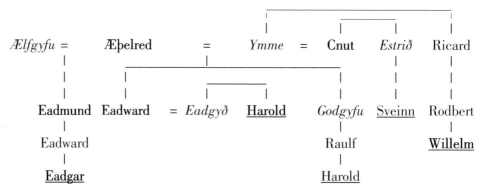

Fig. 7: Successors and claimants to the throne after 1066
Kings of England are shown in **bold**

SURVIVAL OF THE ENGLISH AFTER 1066

At the beginning of Willelm I's reign, we find native English alongside Normans in the highest positions. Had events proceeded differently, a mixed Anglo-Norman elite might have coexisted, as had the mixed Anglo-Danish elite under Cnut 50 years before. An important feature of the later situation under Willelm was the existence already in England of foreigners (eg Bishop Willelm, Constable Rodbert, Priest Osbeorn, Constable Raulf, Bishop Gisa, Bishop Walter, Abbot Baldwine), some of them Norman, who could have acted as a bridge between the natives and the newcomers. Unfortunately, Willelm as Duke of Normandy had relied on a closely knit circle of family and friends, whose help he could rely upon in the turbulent early years of his rule: Bishop Odo, Count Rodbert of Mortain, Willelm FitzOsbern, Count Alan of Brittany, Roger of Montgomerie, Willelm of Warenne, Hugo of Avranches, Ricard of Clare. These men, along with Count Eustatius of Boulogne, Goisfrið of Mandeville and Bishop Goisfrið of Coutances were to receive about half the lay land in England (Douglas 1966: 269). He had grown to manhood in an atmosphere of distrust and reaching out to people who had hardly welcomed his accession with open arms was not in his nature. As for the English, they had inherited a belief that revolt was a way of airing grievances that a King would listen to and redress in order to preserve harmony in the state. The Northumbrian revolt of 1065 had shown the effectiveness of such a tactic. Being accepted and trusted by the new King was clearly not going to be easy for the leading survivors among the English (Eadgar, Queen *Eadgyð*, Archbishops Stigand and Ealdred, Earls Eadwine & Morcere, and thanes like Brihtric, Ulf, *Eadgyfu* and Gospatric).

Some of the English elite were killed at Hastings or died of wounds shortly thereafter: Harold II, Earls Gyrð and Leofwine, Abbots Ælfwig of New Minster and Leofric of Burton, Coventry and Peterborough, Sheriff Godric of Berkshire and possibly Constable Esgar. Others had died from natural causes during 1066: Abbots Wulfric of Ely and Ordric of Abingdon. Those who died naturally between 1066 and 1074 were: Archbishop Ealdred, Bishops Wulfwig and Leofric, Abbots Eadwine of Westminster, Brand of Peterborough, Wulfstan of Gloucester, Þurstan of Ely and Siward of Thorney. In addition, Constable Eadnoð was killed in Willelm's service repelling an attack by Harold's sons in the south west.

Several people were removed from office in the same period: Archbishop Stigand, Bishops Ægelmær, Leofwine and Ægelric, Abbots Godric of Winchcombe, Wulfric of New Minster, and Ecgfrið of St Alban's. Brihtric, Abbot of Malmsbury, was translated to the much smaller house of Burton. Earl Eadwine had parts of his earldom granted to others before his own downfall. Others were involved in revolts against Willelm and forfeited their position or much of their lands. These included: Earls Eadwine, Morcere, Oswulf and Walþeof (also Earl Gospatric appointed by Willelm), Bishop Ægelwine of Durham, Abbots Ægelsige of St Augustine's, Ealdred of Abingdon, Þurstan of Ely and Ælfwold of St Benet's, thanes Mærleswegn (£210), Siward of Maldon (£150), Siward Barn (£140), Eadric the Wild (£100), Siward (£70), Þurcyll

(£40) and among the lesser thanes, Wulfwine Cild, Arncyll, the sons of Carl (Gamal, Þorbrand, Cnut, Sumorled) and Hereward. Of these, Abbot Þurstan paid a heavy fine to remain in office, and Abbots Ægelsige and Ælfwold were later pardoned. Eadric the Wild was also pardoned and took part in the King's expedition to Scotland in 1072.

From the beginning of his reign, Willelm showed a marked bias against appointing native English to office. In fact, none was appointed earl or bishop after 1069 and appointments as abbots or sheriffs were rare. The two new English earls he appointed (before 1069) were both for the far north, where Normans had yet to settle. His raising of Copsig to the Earldom of Bamburgh can only be seen as inept. Copsig had been Tostig's deputy and shared in his overthrow by the revolt of the northern thanes in 1065. They would hardly welcome him back so soon afterwards. Appointing Gospatric after his death was more realistic as the new earl was a member of the traditional family of Bamburgh. Unfortunately for Willelm, Gospatric was a cousin and close friend of Prince Eadgar and joined him in opposition to Willelm in 1069. The only other native English appointments before 1074 were of Abbots Leofwine of Coventry and Wulfric of New Minster.

Foreigners in England before 1066 were legally treated as native English by Willelm. However, their race gave them advantages not possessed by the native born English. Those promoted by Willelm by 1074 included the Constable R aulf (made Earl of East Anglia), the priests Osbeorn and Peter (Bishops of Exeter and of Lichfield), and the monk Folcard made Abbot of Thorney. In all, eight 'Englishmen' were appointed to high office by 1074, compared with 25 newcomers from the continent (Table 14).

Category	Native English	Foreign English	Foreign
Earls	2	1	6
Bishops	-	2	7
Abbots	2	1	12
TOTAL	4	4	25

Table 14: Appointments made by Willelm by 1074

By 1074, the number of English survivors was limited to the following (foreign born English are underlined):
Earls: Raulf, Walþeof
Bishops: Gisa, Hereman, Osbeorn, Siward, Peter, Walter, Willelm, Wulfstan
Greater Abbots (over £170): Ælfwine (Ramsey), Ægelnoð (Glastonbury), Baldwine (St Edmund's), Eadward (Cerne), Wulfwold (Chertsey & Bath)
Lesser Abbots (less than £170): Ælfwold (St Benet's), Æsward (Abbotsbury), Ægelwig (Evesham), Brihtric (Burton), Eadmund (Pershore), Ealdwine (Milton), Fulcard (Thorney), Leofward (Muchelney), Leofwine (Coventry), Osric (Horton), Sihtric (Tavistock), Ulfcytel (Crowland); possibly Ælfwine (Buckfast), Ægelwine (Cranborne), Wulfgeat (Athelney)

Cathedral Priors: Ælfstan (Worcester), Wulfric (Sherborne)
Sheriffs: probably Eadward (Wilton), Hearding (Derby & Nottingham), Swegn (Essex), Þurold (Lincoln); possibly Ælfric (Huntingdon), Norðman (Northampton), Tofig (Somerset), Þurcyll (Stafford)

The major thanes are not well enough known to list fully those who survived. Those known to heave been still in possession of their lands by 1074 (or handed them on to their heir) included: Ælfsige, Barð, Eadric, Gospatric, Orm, Osferð, Raulf (became an earl, and handed on his position to his heir Raulf), Rodbert (heir Swegn), Siward, Swegn, Þor, Wigod, Wulfward, *Wulfwynn* (heir Eadward). It has been suggested that some thanes survived as median tenants, often in reduced circumstances and often farming manors, and that the rate of survival was paradoxically greater in the more rebellious western Mercia and Northumbria (Williams 1995). By 1086, less than a quarter of greater thanes had survived or handed on their lands to children or other near kinsmen (Appendix 4). It can be shown by detailed studies of particular localities (eg Michelmore 1981) that the Domesday Book only partially recorded mesne tenancies in 1086. Many cases of seeming transference of lands from one English thane to a new Norman tenant in chief were thus in reality a case of intruding the Norman lord as superior over the head of the existing English owner who continued in possession of the land. Using only the evidence of the Domesday Book will therefore greatly underestimate the degree of survival of English thanes as landowners.

By 1074, the ethnic balance among lay and clerical officials had swung decisively in favour of the Normans and other newcomers (Table 15). This was surely a major factor in persuading Eadgar II to give up his hopes of ousting Willelm and regaining the crown by leading a nationalist reaction against the Normans. Of course, not all the English survivors would have necessarily welcomed such a move in any case.

Category	1069				1074				1087			
	NE	FE	NF	?	NE	FE	NF	?	NE	FE	NF	?
Earls	4	1	3	0	1	1	4	0	0	0	3	0
Bishops	8	4	1	1	2	6	7	0	1	3	11	0
Greater abbots	13	1	1	1	4	1	9	2	0	1	11	4
Lesser abbots	16	1	2	5	11	1	4	8	4	0	10	10
New abbeys	0	0	2	0	0	0	2	0	0	0	6	1
Cathedral priors	3	0	0	1	2	0	2	0	2	0	3	1
Sheriffs	11	2	9	10	3	1	16	11	3	0	26	1
TOTAL	55	9	18	18	23	10	44	21	10	4	70	18

NE = native English, FE = foreign born English, NF = new foreign,
? = holder/origin unknown or position vacant

Table 15: The ethnic balance 1069-1087

English loyalty after 1075 did not bring any rewards and by the end of Willelm's reign the ethnic balance was tilted even further away from native born English (Table 16). By then, the only survivors at a high level were Prince Eadgar, Harold son of Raulf, Bishop Wulfstan of Worcester, Abbots Ælfwold of St Benet's, Ægelric of Milton, Leofward of Muchelney, Þurstan of Pershore, Priors Ælfric of Sherborne and Þurgod of Durham, and Sheriffs Eadward in Wiltshire, Earnwig in Derby & Nottingham, and possibly Swegn in Oxford. Foreign born English were Bishops Osbern of Exeter, Rodbert of Hereford, Gisa of Wells, Abbot Baldwine of St Edmund's. The Domesday survey likewise shows a low level of English landholding in the upper levels of society. Corbett (1926) reckoned that the English held £4,000 worth of land compared with £30,350 held by Norman newcomers (i.e. only 11½% of lay baronial land). Although secure identification of ethnic origin is not always possible, the major English thanes are listed in Table 16, and treated in more detail in Appendix 4.

Name	Total Lands	Held Directly
	£	£
Edward of Salisbury	421	333
Swegn, Robert's son	339	193
Ælfred of Marlborough	236	119
Þurcyll of Warwick	120	24
Osbeorn FitzRicard	107	55
Colswegn of Lincoln	88	52
Ælfred of Lincoln?	73	39
Harold, Raulf's son	65	65
Godric the steward	60	60
Ælfsige of Faringdon	52	52
Oda of Winchester	52	47

Table 16: The main English thanes by 1086

It has become clear that native English did survive at lower levels among the landowning class, e.g. among local officials like reeve and beadle, and what would later be termed lesser 'gentry'. They were often in reduced circumstances and held their land under new Norman and other landlords, but nevertheless continued as an important part of the social scene, ensuring that English social and cultural norms would survive at the highest level (Williams 1995). A few managed to prosper. One, Leofgeat in Kent, took the Norman name Rodbert Latimer (i.e. the interpreter), and made himself useful to the new aristocracy to such an extent that he paid £114 a year for the farm of several manors (Williams 1995: 83-84). Detailed work at local level on 12th century sources makes it plain that the Domesday Book underestimates the survival of English families and many would appear in the 12th century as knightly families, as in parts of Yorkshire (Michelmore 1981: 251-253). They were also the essential cogs in the administrative machine that enabled English society and law to function effectively after the Conquest (Fleming 1998). While society at a national level became dominated by foreigners, it remained English at local level, especially among the local officials of the King and sheriff.

Another arena where native English survived to a greater extent was the mercantile world of the boroughs. This is clearly seen in the names of moneyers, which continue to be overwhelmingly English for many years after the Conquest. It may be that there was a turnover of moneyers though. Many of the moneyers active under Harold disappear from the record after 1074 (see above). What is significant is that their replacements and the survivors continued to be native English. The urban Anglo-Saxon component in the 12th century Norman state is always liable to be ignored in studies that focus on the landed elite and its political or administrative role under the King. However, much of the wealth of the kingdom came from trade and mercantile activity. In this, the role of the towns and their Anglo-Saxon upper strata played a key role.

However, the distinction between native English and foreigner cannot be maintained as a hard-and-fast distinction for any length of time after 1066. The children of the first generation of settlers would be born in England and could be considered English, albeit that their cultural norms were those of the dominant French speaking ruling elite. Furthermore, there would soon be a proportion of families of mixed descent. Inter-marriage between newcomers and native English began soon after the Conquest and occurred in all strata of society (Williams 1995). It can be seen also in the second or third generation. The most notable example is perhaps King Henry I marrying a representative of the old Anglo-Saxon royal family, *Eadgyð* (daughter of Prince Eadgar's sister *Margareta*), later renamed *Mathild*. Even bishops were not immune, e.g. Bishop Ranulf of Durham (1099-1128) had an English concubine, *Ælfgyfu*. Two notable results of mixed marriage were the 12th century historians Orderic Vitalis and William of Malmesbury.

WHAT IF?

Historians are usually loath to play the game of *what if?* and quite rightly. It is an exercise of imagination and opinion rather than sober fact and interpretation. As such, speculation about what might have happened can only be supposition and cannot tell us anything about the past as it was. However, if accepted for what it is, the game can afford some amusement and force us to think about past events in a new light.

So, what if Eadgar's campaign in the north in 1069 had succeeded? Perhaps, a determined defence of the river crossing at Castleford might have inflicted defeat on the Normans. Perhaps, Earl Morcere might have joined Eadgar and raised greater forces for his cause. Let us assume that Willelm was killed during the campaign against Eadgar in the north and that the Normans then evacuated the country. Who would have formed England's ruling group and what would have been its dynamics? The various categories within the ruling elite could have been as follows:

Royal family: King Eadgar II, his sisters *Margareta* (married to Mælcolm of Scotland) and *Cristina*. The King's position would have been immensely strong having the lands of Harold and his family now in his hands in addition to the royal demesne. His most pressing problem would have been to find a wife and produce an heir. Unfortunately, we know little about the female members of the leading families, but tradition would dictate that he marry the sister or daughter of one of his Earls. Any female relative of Eadwine and Morcere would be a prime candidate. Unfortunately, the obvious such person was the dead Harold's widow (*Ealdgyð*), already married previously to the dead Welsh King Gruffydd. Could she have been persuaded to repeat the performance? Were there other members of the family who could have been introduced to Eadgar instead? We would dearly love to know in more detail the family connections of Eadgar. For instance, one of his main supporters in his opposition to Willelm was his cousin Gospatric. Was this family loyalty, or self interest? Could Eadgar have built up a following based on extended family relations?

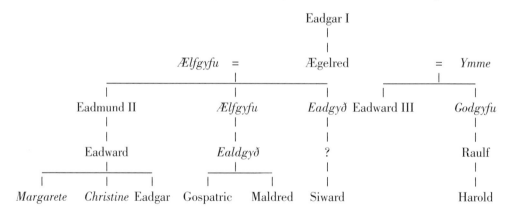

Fig. 8: Eadgar's family connections

Bishops: the only change had been the death of Wulfwig of Dorchester and his replacement by Remigius of Fécamp. Archbishop Ealdred had only just died and Wulfstan of Worcester might expect promotion to York. His rival, Abbot Ægelwig, might then have bid for the see of Worcester. Stigand's death in 1072 would free two sees for promotion – Canterbury and Winchester. The most obvious candidates for promotion to Canterbury would have been Hereman of Ramsbury, Walter of Hereford or Gisa of Wells. The others were probably too elderly or otherwise unsuitable (eg Leofwine of Lichfield being married). Wulfsige, the provost of the cathedral, might have been in a good position for appointment as Bishop of Winchester.

Earls: these would have been Eadwine (Mercia), Morcere (York), Walþeof (Mid Anglia), Gospatric (Bamburgh), Raulf (East Anglia). Eadwine would have been the senior Earl and would seek to establish a link with the new King to bolster his position. He had been Harold II's brother in law, and might have been promised a marriage link with Willelm. What better way than to become Eadgar II's brother in law by marrying the available *Cristina*? Of course, *Cristina* might have had her own views about this, but these did not necessarily count in the world of marriage politics at the highest level. A possible source of tension among the earls might have been Gospatric occupying the northern earldom to which Walþeof might feel he had a better claim. The Norman earls Willelm FitzOsbern (Wessex) and Bishop Oda (Kent) would presumably have fled back to Normandy leaving vacancies available for English thanes to be promoted. The earldoms of Hugo (Chester) and Roger (Shrewsbury) would most likely have been reabsorbed by Eadwine.

Constables: there would be two surviving constables; Bondig, Rodbert. Vacancies for three positions would be open to ambitious thanes.

Thanes: thanes loyal to Eadgar II and expecting promotion would include Mærleswegn and Siward Barn. Mærleswegn's lands in the south west would make him a prime candidate for Earl of Wessex. The powerful thane Brihtric would dominate Gloucester and could have added Hereford to this, or have been a rival for Mærleswegn in the south west. Central Wessex could have gone to the Constable Bondig, the Butler Wigod or thane Ælfstan, while the other Constable Rodbert could have been a rival for the south east (based on his position in Essex) with the Steward Ætsere (based in Sussex) and Ægelnoð Cild (based in Kent). Siward Barn and others could then have been appointed as the new constables and other household officials.

The Reign of Eadgar II

We cannot know how the reign of Eadgar II would have developed. We have too little information on his character and abilities. However, there are certain themes that would have formed the international framework for the period that must have had an influence on events. A clash with the newly reformed Papacy over the investiture of bishops and other issues would have been unavoidable. English participation in the First Crusade would have been likely given Eadgar's actual involvement as a individual. The revival of learning in the early 12th century did involve English scholars and this involvement would most likely still have occurred. A more remote possibility is the revival of the concept of 'empire' within Britain. A desire to restore the fortunes of the royal house of Wessex and look back to a golden age of Eadgar's namesake, Eadgar I, might have led to a revival of an imperial English crown based on dominance over the two satellite Kings established by Harold in Wales and marriage alliance with Mælcolm of Scotland.

A disruptive theme might have been rivalries within the nobility, between the old established family of Eadwine and Morcere and the newer families promoted by Eadgar, and between Gospatric and Walþeof. As a young ruler, Eadgar would have been at the mercy of conflicting interests. His mother, *Agatha*, might have been a useful shield against over-ambitious nobles. Alternatively, he could have found himself drawn to supporting one faction at the expense of another, like his great grandfather Æþelred before him. Threats to his rule would have come from the Danes. Swegn of Denmark attacked England in 1069/70 and there is no reason to think that he would have been any less aggressive with Eadgar on the throne instead of Willelm. The sons of Earl Harold were in exile and could have been an irritant; seeking to return and claim back the family land. Harold's younger son could have become a claimant to the throne, waiting in the wings should there be discontent against Eadgar in the years to come.

In Eadgar's favour would have been his longevity. He is known to have been still alive in the 1120s and would have outlived most of the key players of his early reign. Of course, an elderly King in his dotage would also be prey to rivalries erupting between established interests and rising new figures based around an heir to the throne. We know that Eadgar went on the First Crusade. As King he might still have felt the call and sent an English contingent to take part. Would he have still gone himself if he had the kingship to provide him with activity and honour? At any rate, involvement in the crusade could have provided an outlet for any restless souls among the aristocracy and it could have helped provide stability at home. Loyalty to the traditional royal family cannot be discounted. A yearning for a return to the golden age of Eadgar I under Eadgar II might well have been undertaken with positive effect. We could even postulate a celebration of the 100th year since the death of the first Eadgar in 1075 and a cult of Eadmund II (Eadgar's grandfather), the leader of heroic resistance to foreign conquest as propaganda tools in support of the King and his family.

Much would have depended on Eadgar's character. The earliest surviving direct reference to him occurs in an entry for 1086 in the E version of the Anglo-Saxon Chronicle. This is a copy made for Peterborough Abbey in 1121 of an original chronicle written at Canterbury. The original has all the signs of being contemporary for the years after the Norman Conquest. A reference to Eadgar for the year 1086 ends:

> "... *ac se ælmihtiʒa ʒod him ʒife purðscipe on þam topeardan.*"
> "... but may the almighty God give him honour in the life to come"

The chronicler clearly thought of him with respect. The Anglo-Norman Orderic Vitalis, writing in 1114 (*Historia Ecclesiastica*), provided us with the only description of Eadgar's appearance or character and mixed seeming praise with a less flattering attitude:

> *"ille uero quia idem puer mitis et sincerus erat"*
>
> *"Hic corpore speciosus, lingua disertus, liberalis et generosus, ... , sed dextare segnis erat"*
>
> "since he was a boy who was gentle and honourable"
>
> "he was handsome in appearance, eloquent, generous and nobly born, ..., but indolent too"

William of Malmesbury, another Anglo-Norman writer, amplified the negative assessment of Eadgar's character in his *Gesta Regum Anglorum* of 1125:

> *"pluribusque annis in curia manens, pedetemptim pro ignavia, et, ut mitius dictum sit, pro simplicitate, contemptui haberi coepit."*
>
> "remaining at court for many years silently sunk into contempt through his indolence, or more mildly speaking his simplicity"

William's judgement on Eadgar was based on his failure to successfully oppose the Norman Conquest. It also reflected the perception of his position at court as someone outside Willelm I's inner circle. As a description of his personality, it was somewhat lacking in balance or regard for the facts of his life. However, William of Malmesbury provided a reason for Eadgar's 'indolence' that might receive a more sympathetic reading today:

> *"omnia pro natalis soli desiderio sprevit; quosdam enim profecto fallit amor patriæ, ut nihil eis videatur jocundum nisi consuetum hauserint cælum."*
>
> "he gave up everything through regard to his native soil; for truly the love of their country deceives some men to such a degree that nothing seems pleasant to them unless they can breath their native air."

History does not look kindly on failures and Eadgar has been seen very much as a failure ever since his own time. However, his character and actions suggest he might have made a good job as King. He was loyal to his friends, not afraid of adventure and action (taking part in the Crusade and leading a successful invasion of Scotland), and loved his country. His sister *Margareta* undoubtedly was highly conscious of her royal ancestry, an attitude probably shared by Eadgar. Would Eadgar have been a good King? Would England have prospered under his rule? We can never know. However, it is fun to speculate and I have provided some suggestions above to help the reader to make up their own mind and play out the dynamics of a 60-year reign.

APPENDIX 1

PERSONAL NAMES

The replacement of the Anglo-Saxon upper class during the reign of Willelm I left a social gulf between those using continental names and those of lower status using traditional English names. The way to social respectability was to provide your children with names acceptable in 'polite society'. The replacement of traditional Old English and Old Norse names by continental Germanic (i.e. Norman and Flemish) and Biblical/Christian names proceeded rapidly (Clark 1992b). Urban areas led the way with towns like Winchester having only 35% of identified burgesses using traditional native names by 1101. The proportion had fallen as low as 6% by 1207 (Feilitzen 1976). A similar picture was presented by the urban tenants of London and Canterbury Cathedrals (Clark 1976). In rural areas, most names were still of traditional type during the first half of the 12th century. However, by the second half of the 12th century, traditional names were in the minority and by 1250 had fallen to the same low figure of less than 5% as the towns. The commonest of the newer names among the aristocracy and royal family by 1154 were Goisfrið, Henri, Ricard, Rodbert, Roger, Walter and Willelm. Among Winchester burgesses in 1148, Herbert, Hugo, Raulf, Ricard, Rodbert, Roger and Willelm accounted for over 25% of individuals. By 1207, nearly 60% of burgesses shared 11 names: Adam, Goisfrið, Henri, Iohan, Peter, Raulf, Ricard, Rodbert, Roger, Walter and Willelm (Feilitzen 1976).

Only a few native names survived as modern first names, although some were revived in the Victorian era. However, many names have survived into later times as surnames (Skeat 1907).

Given below are the modern equivalents of the English names in this book. In most cases only the commonest or closest version of the modern name is given.

Anglo-Saxon

Ælfgar	- Algar/Elgar	Ælfgeat	- Elliot	Ælfmær	- Elmer
Ælfnoð	- Allnatt	Ælfred	- Alfred	Ælfric	- Aldrich
Ælfsige	- Elsey	Ælfstan	- Allston	Ælfward	- Allward
Ælfwig	- Elvey	Ælfwine	- Alwin	Ælfwold	- Elwood
Ægelberht	- Allbright	Ægelfrið	- Alfrey	Ægelmær	- Aylmer

Ægelnoð	- Allnatt	Ægelric	- Etheridge	Ægelward	- Aylward
Ægelwig	- Alaway	Ægelwine	- Aylwin	Blacman	- Blackman
Brihtmær	- Brihtmore	Brihtsige	- Brixey	Brihtwine	- Brightween
Bruning	- Browning	Brunwine	- Brunwin	Burhred	- Burrett
Cenric	- Kerrich	Cild	- Childs	Coling	- Colling
Cyneward	- Kenward	Cypping	- Kipping	Deorman	- Dearman
Dodda	- Dodd	Duning	- Downing	Dunna	- Dunn
Dunstan	- Dunstan	Eadgar	- Edgar	*Eadgyð*	- Edith
Eadmund	- Edmund	Eadred	- Errett	Eadric	- Edrich
Eadward	- Edward	Eadwig	- Eddy	Eadwine	- Edwin
Ealdgyð	- Aldith	Ealdred	- Aldred	Ealdwine	- Alden
Earnwig	- Arneway	Eastmær	- Eastmure	Garwulf	- Gorrell
Goda	- Good	Godcild	- Goodchild	*Godgyfu*	- Goodeve
Godleof	- Goodliffe	Godric	- Goodrich	Godwine	- Goodwin
Goldman	- Goldman	Goldstan	- Goldstone	Goldwine	- Goldwin
Hearding	- Harding	Hereward	- Hereward	Hwateman	- Whatman
Leofa	- Leaves	Leofgeat	- Levet	Leofric	- Leveridge
Leofsige	- Lewsey	Leofward	- Livard	Leofwine	- Lewin
Leofwold	- Leavold	Lyfing	- Levinge	Manna	- Mann
Norðman	- Norman	Ordgar	- Orgar	Ordric	- Orrick
Osgod	- Osgood	Osmær	- Osmer	Osmund	- Osmond
Oswold	- Oswald	Sæfara	- Seavers	Sæman	- Seaman
Sæward	- Seward	Sæwold	- Sewell	Selewine	- Selwyn
Sideman	- Seedman	Sigered	- Sirett	Spracling	- Sprackling
Swetman	- Sweetman	Wihtgar	- Widger	Wine	- Winn
Wuduman	- Woodman	Wulfgar	- Woolgar	Wulfgeat	- Woolvett
Wulfgyfu	- Wolvey	Wulfmær	- Woolmer	Wulfnoð	- Woolnoth
Wulfric	- Wooldridge	Wulfsige	- Wolsey	Wulfstan	- Woolston
Wulfward	- Woollard	Wulfwig	- Woolaway	Wulfwine	- Woolven

Norse

Arncyll	- Arkell	Arncytel	- Arkettle	Beorn	- Barne
Bondig	- Bond	Brand	- Brand	Carl	- Carl
Colbein	- Colban	Copsig	- Copsey	Cytel	- Kettle
Eglaf	- Elliff	Gamal	- Gamble	*Gunnhild*	- Gunnell
Harold	- Harold	Hrolf	- Rolf	Ingware	- Inger
Magnus	- Magnus	Orm	- Orme	Osbeorn	- Osborn
Oscyll	- Askell	Oscytel	- Axtell	Osgod	- Osgood
Siward	- Seward	Stigand	- Styan	Storig	- Storey
Sumorled	- Summerlad	Sutere	- Suter	Swegn	- Swain
Tocig	- Tookey	Tofig	- Tovey	Tolig	- Tooley
Þurberht	- Turbett	Þurcyll	- Thirkell	Þurcytel	- Thirkettle
Þurgod	- Thurgood	Þurold	- Thorold	Þurstan	- Thurston
Ulf	- Ulph	Ulfcytel	- Uncle	Walþeof	- Waddilove
Wicing	- Wicking	Wigod	- Wiggett		

APPENDIX 2

SHIRE BY SHIRE

To focus on the national scene when considering medieval politics is to miss much of the dynamic interplay between magnates and lesser figures, and their followers that was played out at local level. For most of the landowners, the most important arena for political action would have been the shire and hundred courts. While we cannot reconstruct the network of alliances and enmities that motivated politics of the period in any detail at this level, we can use the data of the Domesday Book to reconstruct the pattern of landholding shire by shire. This allows us to identify the key players and their likely strengths or weaknesses in any one shire. What are missing below are the names of the lesser landowners, the backbone of the county community. These would be the thanes with more purely local interests, many of whom would no doubt have been tenants of, or were commended to, greater landlords. Information about these awaits detailed work on each shire. The figures for each landowner below take no account of men who had commended themselves to various lords, e.g. Earl Eadwine held no land in Buckingham but did have followers in the shire (Clarke 1994). One feature of interest is the often extensive holding of lands by earls and bishops in areas outside their own spheres of office, as well as the wide spread of lands held by the thanes and abbeys. The landholding community was truly national at the uppermost levels, even if it did have local concentrations of power. A bishop may have presided at the shire court, yet a rival bishop might have been a powerful landowner in that same shire. Likewise, the earl might have faced the followers of a rival while having his own followers present at the shire courts presided over by others.

Names of bishoprics and abbeys that are underlined are those whose churches were situated in that shire. In the case of thanes, any that are underlined only had lands within that shire and so straddle the divide between the local aristocracy and the national. Names in italics are those of women or nunneries. Brackets indicate earls either dead or in exile. A minster church is indicated by an asterisk. All earls, bishops and abbeys holding land in each shire are shown, but greater thanes are only shown if they had at least £25 in the shire (unless there were none with that amount, in which case all greater thanes are shown). Unfortunately, this means that some major thanes do not appear below as their lands were widely spread and did not amount to more than £25 in any one shire, e.g. Wigod of Wallingford. Values are given to the nearest £ unless under 20/-. The situation presented below is that for 5th January 1066, the day that Eadward III died.

WESSEX

Berkshire Earl Harold, Bishop Hereman, Sheriff Godric
Royal family King £560, *Queen* £94
Earls Harold £165, Gyrð £10, (Raulf) £10, (Tostig) £10
Bishops Ramsbury £51, Winchester £48, Exeter £16
Abbeys <u>Abingdon</u> £356, Glastonbury £35, *Amesbury* £25, New Minster £8, Chertsey £8, Westminster £5, Waltham* £3
Greater thanes Constable Esgar £52, Siward Barn £48, Baldwine £27, Osgod £28, Brihtric (Osgod's brother) £32, Sheriff Godric £31
Moneyers Wallingford: Brand, Brihtmær, Burhwine, Sweartling

Cornwall Earl Harold, Bishop Leofric, Sheriff ?
Royal family King £10, Queen £4
Earls Harold £104, *Gyða* £2
Bishops Exeter £52
Abbeys <u>St Petroc</u>* £45, Tavistock £12, <u>Launceston</u> £8
Greater thanes Mærleswegn £32, Brihtmær £62, Brihtric £30

Devon Earl Harold, Bishop Leofric, Sheriff Heca
Royal family King £250, *Queen* £120
Earls Harold £182, *Gyða* £173, Leofwine £43
Bishops <u>Exeter</u> £169, York £3
Abbeys <u>Tavistock</u> £48, <u>Buckfast</u> £16, Horton £9, Glastonbury £4, Cranborne £3, <u>Hartland</u>* £2, <u>Plympton</u>* £2, (St Petroc) £2
Greater thanes Brihtric £164, Mærleswegn £36, Brihtmær £46, Ordwulf £50, <u>Brihtric</u> of Devon £43, Osferð £22
Moneyers Exeter: Brihtric, Leofwine, Lyfing, Sæwine, Wulfnoð?, Wulfwine

Dorset Earl Harold, Bishop Hereman, Sheriff Ælfred
Royal family King £490, *Queen* £90
Earls Harold £225, *Gyða* £40, Leofwine £10
Bishops <u>Sherborne</u> £133, Stigand £66
Abbeys <u>Cerne</u> £168, *Shaftesbury* £90, <u>Milton</u> £90, Glastonbury £82, Abbotsbury £69, <u>Sherborne</u> £66, New Minster £28, <u>Cranborne</u> £18, *Wilton* £9, Tavistock £7, <u>Horton</u> £4
Greater thanes Brihtric £93, Ælfstan £30, Constable Bondig £40, Eadmær £38, *Wulfwynn* £50, Tolig £42, Ætsere £40, Ægelferð £38, Ælfmær £27

Moneyers	Bridport: Hwateman; Dorchester: Blæcman, Hwateman; Shaftesbury: Ælfnoð, Ægelwine, Godric; Wareham: Ægelric?, Sideman

Kent — Earl Leofwine, Bishops Stigand & Siward, Sheriff Osward

Royal family	King £350, *Queen* £6
Earls	(Godwine) £236, Leofwine £63
Bishops	<u>Canterbury</u> £557, <u>Rochester</u> £112, Stigand £40
Abbeys	<u>St Augustine's</u> £421, <u>Canterbury</u> £293, <u>Dover</u>* £61, <u>Lewisham</u> £16
Greater thanes	Ægelnoð £71, Sheriff Osward £93, Brihtsige Cild £47, Norþman £34, <u>Eadric</u> of Elmham £66, <u>Sigered</u> £66, <u>Osbeorn</u> Bicga £49
Moneyers	Canterbury: Ælfward, Ælfwine, Eadward, Eadwine, Gildwine, Manna, Sigered, Wulfred + one of Eadric, Leofstan, Leofwine; Dover: Ceolwig, Cynstan, Manwine, Wulfward; Hythe: Goldwine; Rochester: Leofstan, Leofwine, Leofwine Horn; Romney: Wulfmær; Sandwich: either Godric or Ære-inne

Somerset — Earl Harold, Bishop Gisa, Sheriff Tofig

Royal family	King £500, *Queen* £311
Earls	Harold £146, *Gyða* £70, (Tostig) £11, Leofwine £10
Bishops	<u>Wells</u> £202, Winchester £85
Abbeys	<u>Glastonbury</u> £365, <u>Bath</u> £63, <u>Muchelney</u> £44, <u>Athelney</u> £22, *Shaftesbury* £6
Greater thanes	Ælfstan £43, Mærleswegn £41, Ægelwig £47, Ælfwold £50, Siward £29, Ægelsige £32
Moneyers	Bath: Eorlwine?, Osmær; Ilchester: Ægelwine, Wihtsige; Taunton: Brihtric; Watchet: either Godcild or Sigewulf

Southampton — Earl Harold, Bishop Stigand, Sheriff Eadsige

Royal family	King £450, *Queen* £36
Earls	Harold £147, (Tostig) £137, (Godwine) £64, *Gyða* £57, Gyrð £8
Bishops	<u>Winchester</u> £376, Stigand £61, Hereford £4, York £4
Abbeys	<u>Winchester</u> £342, <u>New Minster</u> £155, *Wherwell* £41, *Romsey* £39, *Nunminster* £38, <u>Twynham</u>* £7, *Wilton* £3, Glastonbury £1, Milton 3/4
Greater thanes	Ægelnoð £25, Constable Bondig £28, Cypping £128, *Wulfgyfu* £66, Seaxig £40, Fitel £23
Moneyers	Winchester: Ælfwine, Anderboda, Godwine, Leofwold, Lyfing, Spræcling

Surrey — Earl Leofwine, Bishop Stigand, Sheriff ?

Royal family	King £117, *Queen* £76
Earls	Harold £175, Leofwine £17, *Gyða* £16, (Godwine) £15

Bishops	Canterbury £66, Winchester £55
Abbeys	<u>Chertsey</u> £189, Westminster £8, London £6, Waltham* £6, New Minster £5, *Barking* £3
Greater thanes	Ætsere £61, Ægelnoð £40, Sheriff Osward £26
Moneyers	Guildford: Leofwold; Southwark: Osmund + either Godric or Leofwine

Sussex — Earl Harold, Bishop Ægelric, Sheriff ?

Royal family	King £240, *Queen* £59
Earls	(Godwine) £425, Harold £280, *Gyða* £107, Leofwine £60, (Tostig) £6
Bishops	<u>Selsey</u> £160, Canterbury £143
Abbeys	<u>Bosham</u>* £329, *Wilton* £86, New Minster £25, *Shaftesbury* £10, <u>Arundel</u>* £7, Westminster £4, <u>Malling</u>* £3
Greater thanes	Ætsere £171, Ægelnoð £58, Brihtsige £38, Godwine the priest £58, Norþman £33
Moneyers	Chichester: Ælfwine, Godwine + either Brunman or Wulfric; Hastings Colswegn, Duning, Þeodred; Lewes: Godwine, Leofward, Oswold; Steyning: Deorman

Wilton — Earl Harold, Bishop Hereman, Sheriff Eadric

Royal family	King £660, *Queen* £181
Earls	Harold £259, *Gyða* £117, (Tostig) £42
Bishops	<u>Ramsbury</u> £250, Winchester £167
Abbeys	*Wilton* £209, *Shaftesbury* £176, <u>Malmesbury</u> £166, Glastonbury £165, New Minster £89, *Romsey* £85, <u>Amesbury</u> £29, Cranborne £16, *Nunminster* £15, Westminster £9
Greater thanes	Ælfstan £90, Ætsere £30, Constable Bondig £25, Hearding £58, Carl £92, Ætsere (Þored's son) £87, Spirites the priest £38, Fitel £6
Moneyers	Bedwyn: Cild; Cricklade: Leofred; Malmesbury: Brihtwig; Salisbury: Godric + either Sæfara or Sigeboda; Wilton: Ælfwold, Centwine, Owig?, Sæwine, Wine

ENGLISH MERCIA

Chester — Earl Eadwine, Bishop Leofwine, Sheriff ?

Royal family	King £145
Earls	Eadwine £134, Morcere £10, Harold £1, *Godgyfu* 5/-
Bishops	Lichfield 10/-
Abbeys	<u>St Werburh</u>* £15
Greater thanes	none
Moneyers	Chester: Ælfsige, Bruning, Duning, Ealhsige, Huscarl, Leofnoð, Þrond

Note: the King's lands lay between the Ribble and Mersey (what would later become south Lancashire). They were administered as six royal manors, probably as an anomalous part of the shire of Chester annexed from York in 919, and allowed to keep its own local customs.

Gloucester	Earl Harold, Bishops Wulfstan & Walter, Sheriff Brihtric
Royal family	King £420, *Queen* £35
Earls	Harold £59, (Raulf) £40, (Tostig) £12, *Gyða* £7
Bishops	Stigand £51, York £50, Hereford £16
Abbeys	Worcester £127, <u>Winchcombe</u> £59, Westminster £41, <u>Gloucester</u> £40, Evesham £37, <u>Deerhurst</u> £27, Pershore £21, Glastonbury £20, Abingdon £12, Eynsham £10, (Gloucester) £10, Bath £9, Coventry £8, Malmesbury £3, <u>Cirencester</u>* £2
Greater thanes	Brihtric £237, Ælfstan £31, Baldwine £38, Osgod £45, Earnsige £60, Eadric £27, Ulf the Housecarl £38, Ælfwine £64
Moneyers	Bristol: Ælfwine, Ceorl; Gloucester: Ælfsige, Brihtnoð, Leofwine, Ordric, Seolhwine, Sigelac, Wulfgeat; Winchcombe: Goldwine

Hereford	Earl Harold, Bishop Walter, Sheriff Osbeorn
Royal family	King £60, *Queen* £141
Earls	Harold £142, Eadwine £10, Morcere £6, (Tostig) £3
Bishops	<u>Hereford</u> £207
Abbeys	<u>St Guðlac</u>* £20, Gloucester £5
Greater thanes	Þurcyll Hwit £44, Ælfwine £2
Moneyers	Hereford: Ælfwig, Ægelric, Eadric, Eadwig, Leofnoð + two of Ægelwine, Brihtric, Earnwig

Oxford	Earl Gyrð, Bishop Wulfwig, Sheriff Sæwold
Royal family	King £370, *Queen* £24
Earls	(Tostig) £78, Eadwine £56, Harold £46, (Ælfgar) £36
Bishops	<u>Dorchester</u> £262, Winchester £34, Winchcombe £20, Stigand £16, Ramsbury £15, Canterbury £11, Exeter £4
Abbeys	Abingdon £62, <u>Eynsham</u> £10, Deerhurst £10, <u>Oxford</u>* £5, St Edmund's 6d
Greater thanes	Ægelnoð £50
Moneyers	Oxford: Ælfwig, Ægelwine, Brihtred, Brihtwold, Godwine, Heregod, Swetman, Wulfwig

Shrewsbury	Earl Eadwine, Bishops Leofwine & Walter, Sheriff ?
Royal family	King £50
Earls	Eadwine £147, Morcere £53, (Leofric) £21, *Godgyfu* £9, Harold £8
Bishops	Hereford £38, Lichfield £8

Abbeys	St Alhmund* £12, Bromfield* £5, St Chad*, Shrewsbury £3, Lapley 0/8, St Juliana* 8/-
Greater thanes	Eadric Wild £98, Siward the Fat £68
Moneyers	Shrewsbury: Ægelric, Earnwig, Godesbrand, Godwine?, Wuduman, Wulfmær

Stafford — Earl Eadwine, Bishop Leofwine, Sheriff Þurcyll

Royal family	King £20
Earls	(Ælfgar) £147, Morcere £10, Eadwine £9, Harold £5, *Godgyfu* £5
Bishops	Lichfield £41
Abbeys	Burton £16, St Chad*, Lichfield £11, Wolverhampton* £6, Westminster £2, Stafford* £1, Lapley 18/-, St Werburh* 15/-
Greater thanes	none
Moneyers	Stafford: Godwine + either Coling or Wulfnoð; Tamworth: Bruning, Coling

Warwick — Earl Eadwine, Bishops Leofwine/Wulfstan, Sheriff Ælfwine

Royal family	King (17 hides)
Earls	Eadwine £67, *Godgyfu* £35, (Harold) £16, (Ælfgar) £10, (Raulf) £2, (Leofric) £2
Bishops	Worcester £20, York £8, Lichfield £7
Abbeys	Coventry £81, Worcester £9, Evesham £5, Winchcombe £3, Burton £2, Malmesbury £2
Greater thanes	Baldwine £37, Ælfwine £7
Moneyers	Warwick: Lyfing, Þurcytel, Wulfwine

Worcester — Earl Eadwine, Bishop Wulfstan, Sheriff Cyneward

Royal family	King £20
Earls	Eadwine £54, Harold £12, *Godgyfu* £4, (Harold) £2
Bishops	Worcester £191, York £7, Lichfield £5, Hereford £2
Abbeys	Worcester £96, Evesham £94, Pershore £84, Westminster £83, Coventry £2, Deerhurst 1 hide, Gloucester ½ hide, St Guðlac* 17/8, Wolverhampton* 15/-
Greater thanes	Brihtric Ælfgar's son £3, Earnsige £10, Brihtric (*Eadgyð's* man) £1
Moneyers	Droitwich: Godric, Heaþuwulf, Wulfwine; Worcester: Baldric, Eastmær, Garwulf, Leofric, Wicing

SOUTHERN DANELAW

Bedford — Earl ?, Bishop Wulfwig, Sheriff Ælfstan

Royal family	King £240
Earls	(Tostig) £36, Gyrð £30, Walþeof £4
Bishops	Stigand £23, Dorchester £4

Abbeys	Ramsey £70, *Barking* £12, Waltham* £11, Westminster £5, St Edmund's £4, Thorney £3, Peterborough £2
Greater thanes	Ælfstan £37, Wulfward £30, Leofnoð £62, Oscyll £59, Wulfmær £43, <u>Ælfwold</u> of Stevington £47
Moneyers	Bedford: Sigegod, Wulfwig + either Leofþegn or Sigebrand

Buckingham	Earl Leofwine?, Bishop Wulfwig, Sheriff ?
Royal family	King £70, *Queen* £65
Earls	(Tostig) £56, Harold £48, (Ælfgar) £41, Leofwine £40, *Gyða* (Raulf's wife) £19
Bishops	Dorchester £37, Winchester £33
Abbeys	St Alban's £27, Westminster £10, *Barking* £6, Oxford* £6
Greater thanes	*Eadgyfu* (Wulfward's wife) £38, *Wulfwynn* £28, Brihtric (*Eadgyð's* man) £79, Burgred & sons £36, Ætsere (Toti's son) £35, Ælfric Goding's son £46, Eadward Cild £73

Cambridge	Earl ?, Bishop Wulfwig, Sheriff Blacwine
Royal family	King £130
Earls	(Ælfgar) £58, Harold £37, Gyrð £24
Bishops	Stigand £35, Winchester £31, Dorchester £11, Rochester £2
Abbeys	<u>Ely</u> £379, Ramsey £85, Crowland £16, *Chatteris* £14, <u>Thorney</u> £7, St Edmund's 8/-
Greater thanes	*Eadgyfu* £235, Wulfwine £62, Tocig £39
Moneyers	Cambridge: Brihtric, Eadwine, Godwine, Sæcoll, Wulfwig

Essex	Earl Leofwine, Bishop Willelm, Sheriff Ordgar?
Royal family	*Queen* £62
Earls	Harold £253 (+ 16 farms), (Ælfgar £113), Leofwine £40, Walþeof £15, Gyrð £6
Bishops	London £157, Hereford £1
Abbeys	*Barking* £143, Ely £82, London £82, Canterbury £65, <u>Waltham</u>* £35, <u>Mersea</u> £26, St Edmund's £20, Westminster £20
Greater thanes	Constable Esgar £148, *Eadgyfu* £26, Constable Rodbert £104, Wihtgar £76, Siward of Maldon £113, Wulfwine £74, *Ægelgyð* £53, Wulfmær £36, Ingwar £61, Ælfric £46, Guðmund £39, <u>Ægelmær</u> £63, Gautig £25
Moneyers	Colchester: Brihtric, Deorman, Goldman, Goldstan, Wulfwine; Maldon: Godwine

Hertford	Earl Leofwine, Bishops Willelm & Wulfwig, Sheriff Eadmund
Royal family	King£20
Earls	Harold £118, (Tostig) £20, *Ælfgyfu* £15
Bishops	Stigand £63, London £27, Winchester £3

Abbeys	<u>St Alban's</u> £233, Westminster £78, Ely £50, London £24, Ramsey £12, Waltham* £9, *Chatteris* £4
Greater thanes	Constable Esgar £68, *Eadgyfu* £57, Ælfstan £47, Eadmær £28, *Wulfwynn* £25, Oscyll £50, Engelric (priest) £25
Moneyers	Hertford: either Sæman or Wilgrip

Huntingdon   Earl Walþeof, Bishop Wulfwig, Sheriff Ælfric

Royal family	King £100
Earls	(Ælfgar) £40, (Tostig) £12, Walþeof £2
Bishops	Dorchester £37
Abbeys	<u>Ramsey</u> £184, Thorney £44, Peterborough £12, Crowland £6
Greater thanes	Ulf Fenisc £17, Constable Robert £32, Ingware £10, Ælfwine £2
Moneyers	Huntingdon: Godric, Godwine + either Leofric or Leofwine

Middlesex   Earl Leofwine, Bishop Willelm, Sheriff Ælfgeat?

Royal family	King £1, *Queen* £12
Earls	(Ælfgar) £120, Leofwine £60, Harold £30, Walþeof £26, (Harold) £12
Bishops	<u>London</u> £135, Canterbury £30
Abbeys	<u>Westminster</u> £111, <u>London</u> £61, Ely £34, *Barking* £5
Greater thanes	Constable Esgar £102, Wulfward £42
Moneyers	London: Ælfsige, Ælfward?, Ælfwine?, Ægelric?, Eadwine, Ealdgar, Godric, Leofsige, Osmund, Sibwine?, Swetman, Wulfgar, Wulfsige, Wulfward + either Ægelwine or Eadward

Norfolk   Earl Gyrð, Bishop Ægelmær, Sheriff Ægelwig

Royal family	King £70
Earls	Gyrð £81, Harold £59 (+ 6 farms)
Bishops	<u>Elmham</u> £152, Stigand £13
Abbeys	Ely £87, <u>St Benet's</u> £80, St Edmund's £52, Ramsey £30
Greater thanes	Constable Raulf £43, Eadric of Laxfield £33, *Ægelgyð* £42, Tocig £60, <u>Bondig</u> £49, Cytel £41
Moneyers	Norwich: Cenric, Eadwine, Godfrið, Godwine, Manna, Þurgrim, Þurstan; Thetford: Ælfwine, Ægelwine, Folcard, Goda, Godleof, Godric, Godwig, Godwine, Þurgod

Northampton   Earl Walþeof, Bishop Wulfwig, Sheriff Norþman

Royal family	King £260, *Queen* £35
Earls	*Gyða* (Raulf's wife) £32, Walþeof £24, (Tostig) £17, (Ælfgar) £12, Morcere £11, *Ælfgyfu* £7, (Raulf) £2
Bishops	none
Abbeys	<u>Peterborough</u> £70, Crowland £14, Westminster £11, Coventry £7, Ramsey £4, Thorney £3, Lapley £3, St Edmund's £2
Greater thanes	Leofnoð £47, Burgred & sons £35

Moneyers	Northampton: Leofstan, Sæwine, Swetman

Suffolk Earl Gyrð, Bishop Ægelmær, Sheriff Tolig
Royal family King £90, *Queen* £37
Earls *Ælfgyfu* £33, Harold £30, Gyrð £24, (Ælfgar) £11
Bishops Stigand £85, Elmham £65, Ægelmær £5
Abbeys <u>St Edmund's</u> £241, Ely £132, Canterbury £42, <u>Clare</u>* £40, Ramsey £8, *Chatteris* £4
Greater thanes *Eadgyfu* £34, Constable Robert £53, Eadric of Laxfield £199, Wihtgar £108, Siward £34, Guðmund £31
Moneyers Bury St Edmunds: Morcere; Ipswich: Ælfwine, Brunman, Leofstan + one of Ægelberht, Brihtric, Bruning and Leofwold; Sudbury: Folcwine

NORTHERN DANELAW

Derby Earl Eadwine?, Bishop Leofwine, Sheriff Hearding
Royal family King £100
Earls (Ælfgar) £38, Eadwine £11, Walþeof £5, (Siward) £4, Morcere £1
Bishops Lichfield £15
Abbeys Burton £6
Greater thanes Tocig (Otta's son) £38, Siward Barn £35 (+4 ploughlands), Leofnoð (Leofric's brother) £47
Moneyers Derby: Colbein, Froma

Leicester Earl Eadwine?, Bishop Wulfwig, Sheriff ?
Royal family King £40, *Queen* £29
Earls Harold £40, (Raulf) £31, Morcere £22, *Ælfgyfu* £11, Walþeof £8, *Godgyfu* £2
Bishops none
Abbeys Crowland £4, Coventry £2
Greater thanes Tocig (Otta's son) £8, Ægelric £6
Moneyers Leicester: Ægelwine, Godric, Leofric + two of Ægelric, Oþwulf, Wulfric

Lincoln Earl Eadwine, Bishop Wulfwig, Sheriff Mærleswegn
Royal family *Queen* £140
Earls Morcere £214, Harold £201, (Ælfgar) £68, Eadwine £24
Bishops Dorchester £12
Abbeys Peterborough £36, <u>Crowland</u> £10, Ramsey £2
Greater thanes Ulf Fenisc £189, Mærleswegn £62, Constable Raulf £137, Tocig (Otta's son) £50, Tonnig £60, Ægelric £60, Hrolf £58, Þurgod £47, <u>Storig</u> £46, <u>Ægelstan</u> £45

Moneyers	Lincoln: Agmund, Ælfgeat, Ælfmær, Ælfnoð, Ægelmær, Eadric, Garfin, Gifel, Oþgrim, Ulf, Wulfmær + four out of Ælfwine, Osbeorn, Otta, Sigeferð; Stamford: Brunwine, Leofric, Leofwine, Wulfward + either Osward or Swartcol

Nottingham   Earl Morcere?, Bishop Ealdred, Sheriff Hearding

Royal family	King £70
Earls	*Godgyfu* £59, Morcere £27, (Tostig) £18, (Ælfgar) £5, Harold £3
Bishops	none
Abbeys	Peterborough £12, <u>Southwell</u>* £9
Greater thanes	Ulf Fenisc £45, Tocig (Otta's son) £28
Moneyers	Nottingham: Forna, Manna

Rutland   Earl ?, Bishop Wulfwig, Sheriff Hearding

Royal family	*Queen* £132
Earls	Walþeof £28, Harold £5
Bishops	none
Abbeys	none
Greater thanes	Ulf Fenisc £4

THE NORTH

Northumberland   Earl Oswulf, Bishop Ægelwine, Sheriff ?

Royal family	?
Earls	Oswulf £?
Bishops	<u>Durham</u> £?
Abbeys	?
Greater thanes	?

York East Riding   Earl Morcere, Bishop Ealdred, Sheriff Gamal

Royal family	King £40
Earls	Morcere £499, (Tostig) £58, Harold £52, Walþeof £7
Bishops	<u>York</u> £119 (+1.6 ploughlands), Durham £10
Abbeys	<u>Beverley</u>* £23 (+103.4 ploughlands), <u>York</u>* £2 (+10.2 ploughlands)
Greater thanes	Ulf Fenisc £88, Þurcyll £30 (+17.2 ploughlands), Gamal £39 (+13.2 ploughlands), <u>Carl</u> £34 (+7.4 ploughlands)

York North Riding   Earl Morcere, Bishop Ealdred, Sheriff Gamal

Royal family	King £10
Earls	(Siward) £208, Eadwine £144, Morcere £123, (Tostig) £56, Walþeof £5 (+21 ploughlands)
Bishops	Durham £5
Abbeys	<u>York</u>* £7 (+12.4 ploughlands), Durham £6

Greater thanes	Orm £36 (+14 ploughlands), Arncyll & Gospatric £45 (+43.3 ploughlands), Þorr £30 (+27 ploughlands)
Moneyers	York: Anlaf, Earncytel, Iocytel, Oþbeorn, Oþgrim, Oþwulf, Roscytel, Snæbeorn, Sutere, Sweartcol, Þorr, Ulfcytel

York West Riding	Earl Morcere, Bishop Ealdred, Sheriff Gamal
Royal family	King £87
Earls	Eadwine £51 (+74 ploughlands), (Tostig) £18 (+38 ploughlands), Harold £18, Walþeof £9, Morcere £1
Bishops	York £89
Abbeys	York* £12, Christ Church* £5 (+2.4 ploughlands)
Greater thanes	Arncyll & Gospatric £42 (+46.1 ploughlands), Ælfsige £61 (+5 ploughlands), Swegn £33 (+5.6 ploughlands), Orm £36, Ligulf £31, Barð £36 (+3.4 ploughlands)

Note: Amounderness and the area to the north (what would later become north Lancashire) were only partially incorporated into the local government structure of Yorkshire. In this area, Earl Tostig was recorded in the Domesday Book as having 420 ploughlands.

APPENDIX 3

COINS AND MINTS

It is usually accepted that there were 19 coin types issued by Kings Eadward, Harold and Willelm, the weight of coins varying between 17 and 26 grains (15.432 grains = 1 gram). The difficulty of distinguishing coins of Willelm I from his son Willelm II makes it difficult to decide exactly how many types belong to the father and how many to the son. It is generally accepted that the PAXS type was the last issued by Willelm I, although the precedents of Eadward and Harold would suggest that a type bearing such a legend would be the first to be issued by a new King at the beginning of his reign. A series of regular issues every three years, beginning in 1067 would place the PAXS type in 1088 and would conveniently form the first issue of Willelm II. However, this would both challenge the assumption made about the dating of certain hoards (Dolley 1966) and leave too many issues to be squeezed into the reign of Willelm II. The dates given below (Table 17) are based on my own assumption of a possible regular three-year cycle, and should be treated with appropriate caution (see Stewart 1990).

Type	Date	Obverse	Reverse
PACX	1042	diademed bust, facing left	long cross with PACX in the angles
Radiate	1044	radiate crowned bust, facing left	small cross pattée
Trefoil quadrilateral	1046	diademed bust, facing left	short cross, quadrilateral in centre with pellets in the angles
Small flan	1048	diademed bust, facing left	short cross, no outer circle
Expanding cross	1050	diademed bust, facing left	short cross with expanding arms
Pointed helmet	1053	helmeted bust with beard, facing right	short cross, each arm ending in three crescents
Sovereign	1056	king enthroned	short cross, a bird in each angle
Hammer cross	1059	crowned bust with beard, facing right	short cross, each arm ending in an incurved line

Type	Date	Obverse	Reverse
Facing bust	1062	crowned bust with beard, face-on	small cross pattée
Pyramids	1065	crowned bust with beard, facing right	short cross with pyramid facing inwards in each angle
PAX	1066	crowned bust, facing left	PAX between two lines
Cross fleury	1067	crowned bust, facing left	short cross fleury
Bonnet	1068	crowned bust, face-on	short cross each arm ending in two crescents, pyramid facing outwards in each angle
Canopy	1071	crowned bust face-on underneath canopy	quadrilateral, fleury at each point
Two sceptres	1074	crowned bust face-on with two sceptres	short cross fleury over a saltire
Two stars	1077	crowned bust face-on between two stars	short cross over a large quadrilateral
Sword	1080	crowned bust face-on holding sword	short cross over fleury quadrilateral
Trefoil	1083	crowned bust, facing right	short cross with trefoil in each angle
PAXS	1086	crowned bust face-on with sceptre	short cross with PAXS in a circle in each angle

Table 17: Coin types of Eadward III, Harold II and Willelm I

The weights of coins at the beginning of Eadward's reign centred around 16-17 grains. Two weight standards seem to have been adopted for the issue of 1050: the normal 16-17 grains and a heavier standard of 26 grains. Later issues had just one standard, and this was 20-21 grains, with a reversion to the lighter 16-17 grain standard for the 1062-65 issue. The standard was raised again to its final level of 22½ grains in 1080.

Information about mints is contained in the Domesday Book, but only for selected boroughs. A summary of this information is given below.

Bridport: 1 moneyer, each paid 1 silver mark and 20/- when the coinage was changed

Chester: 7 moneyers who paid £7 to the King and Earl when the coinage was changed

Colchester: the moneyers paid £4 towards the upkeep of the King's soldiers, Colchester and Maldon pay £20 for the mint (1086)

Dorchester: 2 moneyers, each paid 1 silver mark and 20/- when the coinage was changed

Gloucester: the King had £20 from the mint (1086)

Hereford: 7 moneyers (1 belonging to the Bishop), each gave 18/- for dies at a change of issue followed by a further 20/- within one month, also paid 20/- relief at death

Huntingdon: 3 moneyers who paid £2 shared between the King and Earl

Ipswich: moneyers paid £4 a year for the mint (£20 in 1086), the Earl having one third

Leicester: £20 a year from the moneyers (1086), two thirds to the King, one third to Hugo Grandmesnil

Malmesbury: the borough paid £5 for the mint (1086)

Thetford: the town pays £40 from the mint (1086)

Oxford: a moneyer has a free house paying 40d (1086)

Shaftesbury: 3 moneyers, each paid 1 silver mark and 20/- when the coinage was changed

Shrewsbury: the King had 3 moneyers who paid 20/- for dies at change of type on the 15th day

Wallingford: 1 moneyer had a plot (*haga*) free of customary dues as long as he minted coins

Wareham: 2 moneyers, each paid 1 silver mark and 20/- when the coinage was changed

Worcester: each moneyer paid 20/- for dies at a change of type

To allow readers to make their own analysis of the moneyers in 1066, this appendix lists all the moneyers for each mint between 1042 and 1087, according to the current state of knowledge as found in Jonsson & Van Der Meer (1990) and Harris (1983-88), supplemented with the latest volumes of the *Syllogue of Coins of the British Isles* and the Fitzwilliam Museum's *Early Medieval Corpus*. Readers may be able to update this listing for themselves in the light of new discoveries. Figures in brackets after the name of the mint indicate the number of moneyers assigned there for 1066 in the Domesday Book. The minting of a coin of a particular type is shown by 'x'. If a moneyer minted coins earlier and later than an individual type then he may also have minted that type although none have yet been found. This is indicated by '\'. The identification of moneyers is complicated by the variations in spelling used on the coins and the similarity of many English name elements which can, for example, confuse names in -wig and – wine, or see the reduction of the first element of names in Ælf- and Ægel- to Al-/Ail-. The number of moneyers given as working at a mint is the total of possible moneyers. The actual number may well be less than this. I have been generous in allowing continuity of names between Eadward III and Willelm I, which may not actually be justified in all cases.

mint/moneyer	Eadward										Harold	Willelm							
	1	2	3	4	5	6	7	8	9	10	1	1	2	3	4	5	6	7	8
Aylesbury	0	1	1	0	0	1	1	1	0	0	0	0	0	0	0	0	0	0	0
Leofwine	-	x	x	-	-	-	-	-	-	-	-	-	-	-	-	-	-	-	-
Wulfred	-	-	-	-	-	x	\	x	-	-	-	-	-	-	-	-	-	-	-
Barnstaple	0	2	1	1	1	1	1	1	0	0	0	0	0	0	0	1	1	1	2
Ælfric	-	x	\	\	x	x	x	x	-	-	-	-	-	-	-	-	-	-	-
Ægelmær	-	x	-	-	-	-	-	-	-	-	-	-	-	-	-	-	-	-	-
Godesbrand	-	-	-	-	-	-	-	-	-	-	-	-	-	-	-	-	-	-	x
Sæword	-	-	-	-	-	-	-	-	-	-	-	-	-	-	-	x	x	\	x
Bath	2	2	2	3	2	2	2	3	2	1	1	1	1	2	1	1	1	1	2
Ægelmær	x	x	x	x	x	-	-	-	-	-	-	-	-	-	-	-	-	-	x
Brungar	-	-	-	-	-	-	-	-	-	-	-	-	-	x	-	-	-	-	-
Eorlwine	-	-	-	-	-	-	-	x	x	-	-	-	-	-	-	-	-	-	-
Godric	-	-	-	x	x	x	x	x	-	-	-	-	-	-	-	-	-	-	-
Osmær	-	-	-	-	-	x	x	x	x	\	\	x	\	\	\	x	\	\	x
Wædel	x	x	\	x	-	-	-	-	-	-	-	-	-	-	-	-	-	-	-
Bedford	5	3	3	4	5	3	4	4	4	3	2	2	2	2	2	2	1	1	1
Ægelman	x	x	x	x	x	-	-	-	-	-	-	-	-	-	-	-	-	-	-
Godric	-	-	-	-	-	-	x	-	-	-	-	-	-	-	-	-	-	-	-
Godwine	-	-	-	-	-	-	x	x	-	-	-	-	-	-	-	-	-	-	-
Leofþegn	-	-	-	-	-	-	x	x	x	-	-	-	-	-	-	-	-	-	-
Lyfing	x	-	-	-	-	-	-	-	-	-	-	-	-	-	-	-	-	-	-
Sigebrand	-	-	-	-	-	-	-	-	-	-	-	x	\	x	\	x	\	\	x
Sigegod	-	-	-	-	-	-	x	x	x	x	x	\	x	x	x	x	-	-	-
Sweta	\	x	\	x	x	\	x	-	-	-	-	-	-	-	-	-	-	-	-
Swetric	x	-	-	-	-	-	-	-	-	-	-	-	-	-	-	-	-	-	-
Ulfcytel	x	\	\	x	\	x	-	-	-	-	-	-	-	-	-	-	-	-	-
Wulfmær	-	-	-	-	-	x	-	-	-	-	-	-	-	-	-	-	-	-	-
Wulfwig	-	-	-	x	x	x	x	x	\	x	x	-	-	-	-	-	-	-	-
Wulfwine	-	-	-	-	-	-	-	x	-	-	-	-	-	-	-	-	-	-	-
Bedwyn	0	0	1	1	1	1	1	1	1	1	1	1	0	0	0	0	0	0	0
Cild	-	-	x	x	x	x	x	x	x	x	\	x	-	-	-	-	-	-	-
Berkeley	1	0	1	1	1	1	0	0	0	0	0	0	0	0	0	0	0	0	0
Eadgar	-	-	x	\	\	x	-	-	-	-	-	-	-	-	-	-	-	-	-
Ulfcytel	x	-	-	-	-	-	-	-	-	-	-	-	-	-	-	-	-	-	-
Bridport (1)	1	1	1	1	1	1	1	1	1	1	1	1	1	1	1	1	0	0	2
__fric	-	-	-	-	-	-	-	-	-	-	-	-	-	-	-	-	-	-	x
Brihtwine	-	-	-	-	-	-	-	-	-	-	-	-	-	-	-	-	-	-	x
Hwateman	\	\	\	x	\	\	\	\	\	x	x	\	\	\	\	x	-	-	-
Bristol	7	4	4	3	4	4	4	3	2	2	3	2	2	2	2	2	2	3	5
Ælfric	-	-	-	-	-	x	x	x	-	-	-	-	-	-	-	-	-	-	-
Ælfward	x	x	x	x	x	-	-	-	-	-	-	-	-	-	-	-	-	-	-
Ælfwig	x	-	-	-	-	-	-	-	-	-	-	-	-	-	-	-	-	-	-
Ælfwine	x	\	\	\	\	\	x	x	x	x	x	-	-	-	-	-	-	-	-
Ægelstan	x	\	x	x	x	x	x	-	-	-	-	-	-	-	-	-	-	-	-
Ægelwine	\	x	-	-	-	-	-	-	-	-	-	-	-	-	-	-	-	-	-
Brihtword	-	-	-	-	-	-	-	-	-	-	-	-	-	-	-	-	x	x	x
Brunstan	-	-	-	-	-	-	-	-	-	-	-	-	-	-	-	-	-	-	x
Ceorl	-	-	-	-	-	-	-	-	-	x	x	x	\	x	x	x	-	-	-
Colblac	-	-	-	-	-	-	-	-	-	-	-	-	-	-	-	-	-	-	x

Appendix 3

mint/moneyer	Eadward 1	2	3	4	5	6	7	8	9	10	Harold 1	Willelm 1	2	3	4	5	6	7	8
Godwine	-	-	-	-	x	x	\	x	x	-	-	-	-	-	-	-	-	-	-
Leofwine	-	-	-	-	-	-	-	-	-	-	x	x	x	x	x	x	x	\	x
Sæwine	x	-	-	-	-	-	-	-	-	-	-	-	-	-	-	-	-	-	-
Smeawine	-	-	x	-	-	-	-	-	-	-	-	-	-	-	-	-	-	-	-
Swegn	-	-	-	-	-	-	-	-	-	-	-	-	-	-	-	-	-	x	x
Wulfwine	x	-	-	-	-	-	-	-	-	-	-	-	-	-	-	-	-	-	-
Bruton	1	1	0	0	0	0	0	0	0	0	0	0	0	0	0	0	0	0	0
Godric	x	x	-	-	-	-	-	-	-	-	-	-	-	-	-	-	-	-	-
Buckingham	1	1	1	1	1	0	1	1	0	0	0	0	0	0	0	0	0	0	0
Ægelstan	-	-	-	-	-	-	-	x	-	-	-	-	-	-	-	-	-	-	-
Leofwine	x	x	x	\	x	-	-	-	-	-	-	-	-	-	-	-	-	-	-
Þeodred	-	-	-	-	-	-	x	-	-	-	-	-	-	-	-	-	-	-	-
Bury St Edmunds	0	0	0	1	1	1	1	1	1	0	0	0	0	1	0	0	0	0	0
Goding	-	-	-	-	-	-	-	-	-	-	-	-	-	x	-	-	-	-	-
Morcere	-	-	-	x	x	x	x	x	x	-	-	-	-	-	-	-	-	-	-
Cambridge	4	5	5	5	6	5	5	4	6	3	5	1	0	0	2	2	1	1	2
Ælfwig	\	\	\	\	x	x	x	-	-	-	-	-	-	-	-	-	-	-	-
Ægelmær	-	-	-	-	-	-	-	-	-	-	-	-	-	x	x	-	-	-	-
Brihtric	-	-	-	-	-	-	-	-	-	-	x	-	-	-	-	-	-	-	-
Eadstan	-	x	x	x	x	-	-	-	-	-	-	-	-	-	-	-	-	-	-
Eadward	-	-	-	-	x	x	\	x	x	-	-	-	-	-	-	-	-	-	-
Eadwine	-	-	-	-	-	-	-	-	-	-	x	-	-	-	-	-	-	-	-
Gil	-	-	-	-	-	-	-	-	-	-	-	-	-	-	-	-	-	-	x
Godlamm	-	-	-	-	-	-	-	x	x	-	-	-	-	-	-	-	-	-	-
Godric	-	-	-	-	-	-	-	-	-	-	-	x	-	-	-	-	-	-	-
Godsunu	x	x	x	x	x	x	-	-	-	-	-	-	-	-	-	-	-	-	-
Godwine	\	\	\	\	\	x	x	\	x	\	x	-	-	-	-	-	-	-	-
Oþbeorn	-	-	-	-	-	-	-	-	-	-	-	-	-	x	-	-	-	-	-
Sæcoll	-	-	-	-	-	-	x	x	x	\	x	-	-	-	-	-	-	-	-
Ulfcytel	-	-	-	-	-	-	-	-	-	-	-	-	-	-	-	x	\	x	x
Wigbearn	-	-	-	-	-	-	-	x	-	-	-	-	-	-	-	-	-	-	-
Wulfwig	-	-	-	-	-	-	-	-	-	-	x	-	-	-	-	-	-	-	-
Wulfwine	\	\	x	x	x	\	\	x	x	-	-	-	-	-	-	-	-	-	-
Canterbury	7	8	9	7	8	9	7	10	12	9	7	5	4	4	6	6	5	7	8
Ælfred	x	x	x	x	x	x	x	x	\	\	\	\	\	\	x	x	x	x	x
Ælfric	-	-	-	-	-	-	-	x	-	-	-	-	-	-	-	-	-	-	-
Ælfward	-	-	-	-	-	-	x	x	x	-	-	-	-	-	-	-	-	-	-
Ælfwine	-	-	-	-	-	-	-	-	x	\	x	-	-	-	-	-	-	-	-
Brihtwold	-	-	-	-	-	-	-	-	-	-	-	-	-	-	-	-	-	-	x
Brunman	x	x	x	x	-	-	-	-	-	-	-	-	-	-	-	-	-	-	-
Burgnoð	-	-	-	-	-	-	-	-	-	-	-	-	-	-	-	-	-	-	x
Cytel	x	-	-	-	-	-	-	-	-	-	-	-	-	-	-	-	-	-	-
Eadmær	-	-	-	-	-	x	-	-	-	-	-	-	-	-	-	-	-	-	-
Eadric	-	-	-	-	-	-	-	x	-	-	-	-	-	-	-	-	-	-	-
Eadward	-	x	x	x	x	x	x	x	x	x	x	x	-	-	-	-	-	-	-
Eadwine	-	-	-	-	-	-	-	-	-	-	x	-	-	-	-	-	-	-	-
Godric	-	-	-	-	-	-	-	-	-	-	-	-	-	-	-	-	-	x	x
Gildwine	x	x	x	x	x	x	x	x	x	x	-	-	-	-	-	-	-	-	-
Godsunu	-	-	x	-	-	-	-	-	-	-	-	-	-	-	-	-	-	-	-

mint/moneyer	Eadward										Harold	Willelm							
	1	2	3	4	5	6	7	8	9	10	1	1	2	3	4	5	6	7	8
Leofstan	x	x	x	x	x	x	x	x	x	-	-	-	-	-	-	-	-	-	-
Leofwine	x	x	x	x	x	x	x	x	x	-	-	-	-	-	-	-	-	-	-
Manna	x	\	x	x	x	x	x	x	x	x	x	x	x	x	x	x	-	-	-
Rodcarl	-	-	x	-	-	-	-	-	-	-	-	-	-	-	-	-	-	-	-
Sigemær	-	-	-	-	-	-	-	-	-	-	-	-	-	-	-	-	-	x	x
Sigered	-	-	-	-	-	-	-	x	x	-	-	-	-	-	-	-	-	-	-
Winedi	-	-	-	-	-	-	-	-	-	-	-	-	-	-	x	\	\	\	x
Wulfbold	-	-	-	-	-	-	-	-	-	-	-	-	-	-	-	-	-	x	x
Wulfgeat	-	x	-	-	-	-	-	-	-	-	-	-	-	-	-	-	-	-	-
Wulfred	-	-	-	-	x	\	\	\	\	\	x	x	\	\	\	\	\	x	-
Wulfric	-	-	-	-	-	-	-	-	-	-	-	-	-	-	x	x	\	\	x
Wulfstan	-	-	-	-	x	x	-	-	-	-	-	-	-	-	-	-	-	-	-
Wulfwine	-	-	-	-	-	-	-	x	\	\	\	\	\	x	\	\	x	-	-
Cardiff	0	0	0	0	0	0	0	0	0	0	0	0	0	0	0	0	0	0	1
Ælfsige	-	-	-	-	-	-	-	-	-	-	-	-	-	-	-	-	-	-	x
Chester (7)	10	10	8	9	11	12	13	11	6	7	5	3	5	2	3	2	2	2	3
Ælfgar	-	-	-	-	-	x	-	-	-	-	-	-	-	-	-	-	-	-	-
Ælfsige	x	x	x	x	x	x	x	x	x	x	\	\	x	\	\	x	\	x	x
Ælfsige Alda	-	-	-	-	x	\	\	x	-	-	-	-	-	-	-	-	-	-	-
Ælfward	-	-	-	-	-	-	-	-	-	-	-	-	x	-	-	-	-	-	-
Ælfwine	-	-	-	x	x	x	\	x	-	-	-	-	-	-	-	-	-	-	-
Ægelwine	x	x	\	\	\	\	\	x	-	-	-	-	-	-	-	-	-	-	-
Bruning	x	x	x	x	x	x	x	x	x	x	\	x	-	-	-	-	-	-	-
Colbrand	-	x	x	x	x	x	x	-	-	-	-	-	-	-	-	-	-	-	-
Colþegn	x	-	-	-	-	-	-	-	-	-	-	-	-	-	-	-	-	-	-
Croc	x	x	-	-	-	-	-	-	-	-	-	-	-	-	-	-	-	-	-
Duning	-	-	-	-	-	-	x	x	\	x	-	-	-	-	-	-	-	-	-
Dunstan	-	-	-	-	-	x	-	-	-	-	-	-	-	-	-	-	-	-	-
Ealhsige	-	-	-	-	x	x	x	x	\	x	x	\	x	-	-	-	-	-	-
Fargrim	x	x	\	\	x	-	-	-	-	-	-	-	-	-	-	-	-	-	-
Friþugist	-	-	-	-	-	-	-	-	-	-	-	-	x	-	-	-	-	-	-
Huscarl	-	x	\	x	x	x	x	x	x	x	x	-	-	-	-	-	-	-	-
Leofnoð	x	x	x	x	x	x	x	x	x	x	-	-	-	-	-	-	-	-	-
Leofwig	x	-	-	-	-	-	-	-	-	-	-	-	-	-	-	-	-	-	-
Leofwine	x	x	x	x	x	-	-	-	-	-	-	-	-	-	-	-	-	-	x
Ordric	-	-	-	-	-	-	x	-	-	-	-	-	-	-	-	-	-	-	-
Snell	x	x	-	-	-	-	-	-	-	-	-	-	-	-	-	-	-	-	-
Sprot	-	-	-	-	-	-	x	-	-	-	-	-	-	-	-	-	-	-	-
Sweartcol	-	-	-	-	x	x	x	-	-	-	-	-	-	-	-	-	-	-	-
Sunwulf	-	-	-	-	-	-	-	-	-	-	-	-	x	\	\	\	\	\	x
Ulf	-	-	-	-	-	-	-	-	-	-	-	-	-	-	x	-	-	-	-
Wigal	-	-	-	-	-	-	x	-	-	-	-	-	-	-	-	-	-	-	-
Þrond	-	-	-	-	-	-	-	-	x	-	x	-	-	-	-	-	-	-	-
Chichester	1	1	2	1	1	3	3	3	3	3	2	2	2	2	2	2	2	2	3
Ælfwine	-	-	x	x	x	x	x	x	x	x	x	-	-	-	-	-	-	-	-
Brunman	-	-	-	-	-	-	-	-	-	-	-	x	\	x	x	x	x	x	x
Eadwine	-	-	-	-	-	-	-	-	-	-	-	-	-	-	-	-	-	-	x
Godwine	-	-	-	-	-	x	x	x	\	\	x	\	\	\	\	x	x	\	\
Leofwine	\	x	x	-	-	-	-	-	-	-	-	-	-	-	-	-	-	-	-

mint/moneyer	Eadward										Harold	Willelm							
	1	2	3	4	5	6	7	8	9	10	1	1	2	3	4	5	6	7	8
Wulfric	-	-	-	-	-	x	x	x	x	x	-	-	-	-	-	-	-	-	-
Christchurch	0	0	0	0	0	0	0	0	0	0	0	0	0	0	0	0	0	1	0
Colman	-	-	-	-	-	-	-	-	-	-	-	-	-	-	-	-	-	x	-
Colchester	2	4	6	5	5	6	5	6	5	4	6	5	5	2	2	2	3	3	5
Ælfric	-	-	-	-	-	-	-	-	-	-	-	-	-	-	-	-	-	-	x
Ælfsige	-	-	-	-	-	-	-	-	-	-	-	-	-	-	-	-	-	-	x
Ælfwine	-	-	x	-	-	-	-	-	-	-	-	-	-	-	-	-	-	-	-
Brihtric	-	-	x	x	x	x	x	x	x	\	x	x	x	-	-	-	-	-	-
Brunhyse	x	x	x	x	x	x	x	x	x	-	-	-	-	-	-	-	-	-	-
Deorman	-	-	-	-	-	x	\	x	\	\	\	\	\	\	\	x	x	\	x
Godwine	-	-	-	-	-	-	-	x	-	-	-	-	-	-	-	-	-	-	-
Goldman	-	-	-	-	-	x	x	\	x	-	x	x	x	-	-	-	-	-	-
Goldstan	-	-	-	-	-	-	-	-	-	-	x	x	x	-	-	-	-	-	-
Leofward	-	x	x	x	x	x	-	-	-	-	-	-	-	-	-	-	-	-	-
Stanmær	-	x	x	x	x	x	-	-	-	-	-	-	-	-	-	-	-	-	-
Wulfric	-	-	-	-	-	-	-	-	-	-	-	-	-	-	-	-	-	-	x
Wulfward	-	-	-	-	-	-	-	-	-	-	-	-	-	-	-	-	x	x	-
Wulfwig	-	-	-	-	-	-	-	-	-	-	x	-	-	-	-	-	-	-	-
Wulfwine	x	x	x	x	\	x	x	x	x	x	x	\	\	x	x	x	\	x	x
Cricklade	2	1	1	1	1	2	2	2	1	1	1	1	1	1	1	2	1	1	1
Ælfwine	x	-	-	-	-	-	-	-	-	-	-	-	-	-	-	-	-	-	x
Ægelwine	x	x	x	x	x	x	x	x	-	-	-	-	-	-	-	-	-	-	-
Leofred	-	-	-	-	-	x	x	x	\	x	x	\	x	\	x	x	-	-	-
Wulfstan	-	-	-	-	-	-	-	-	-	-	-	-	-	-	x	\	x	-	-
Derby	4	4	2	3	3	3	2	2	3	2	2	2	2	2	1	1	0	1	2
Blacman	x	-	-	-	-	-	-	-	-	-	-	-	-	-	-	-	-	-	-
Colbein	-	-	-	-	-	-	-	-	x	\	\	x	x	x	-	-	-	-	-
Froma	-	x	\	x	x	x	\	x	x	x	x	x	x	\	x	x	-	-	-
Godric	\	x	-	-	-	-	-	-	-	-	-	-	-	-	-	-	-	-	-
Godwine	-	-	-	-	-	-	-	-	-	-	-	-	-	-	-	-	-	x	x
Leofwine	-	-	-	x	x	\	\	x	x	-	-	-	-	-	-	-	-	-	x
Swearting	\	\	x	\	x	x	-	-	-	-	-	-	-	-	-	-	-	-	-
Wulfheah	x	-	-	-	-	-	-	-	-	-	-	-	-	-	-	-	-	-	-
Wynric	-	x	-	-	-	-	-	-	-	-	-	-	-	-	-	-	-	-	-
Dorchester (2)	3	3	3	2	2	1	1	1	1	1	1	0	0	0	1	2	2	2	3
Blæcman	x	x	\	x	\	x	\	x	x	x	x	-	-	-	-	-	-	-	-
Godwine	\	\	x	-	-	-	-	-	-	-	-	-	-	-	x	x	x	\	\
Hwætman	\	\	x	\	x	-	-	-	-	-	-	-	-	-	-	-	-	-	-
Leofric	-	-	-	-	-	-	-	-	-	-	-	-	-	-	-	-	-	-	x
Otter	-	-	-	-	-	-	-	-	-	-	-	-	-	-	-	x	x	x	x
Dover	5	5	3	3	3	3	3	3	4	4	3	2	3	3	3	3	1	4	4
Boga	x	x	-	-	-	-	-	-	-	-	-	-	-	-	-	-	-	-	-
Brunman	-	-	-	-	-	-	-	-	-	-	-	-	x	x	x	x	-	-	-
Ceolwig	-	-	-	-	x	x	x	x	\	x	-	-	-	-	-	-	-	-	-
Cynstan	x	x	x	x	x	x	x	x	x	\	x	\	\	\	\	\	\	x	-
Eadsige	\	\	x	-	-	-	-	-	-	-	-	-	-	-	-	-	-	-	-
Eadward	-	-	-	-	-	-	-	-	-	-	-	-	-	-	-	-	-	x	x
Eadwine	x	x	-	-	-	-	-	-	-	-	-	-	-	-	-	-	-	-	-
Godwine	-	-	-	-	x	x	x	x	-	-	-	-	-	-	-	-	-	-	x

mint/moneyer	Eadward 1	2	3	4	5	6	7	8	9	10	Harold 1	Willelm 1	2	3	4	5	6	7	8
Leofric	-	-	-	-	-	-	-	-	-	-	-	-	-	-	-	-	-	x	x
Leofwine	\	x	x	x	-	-	-	-	-	-	-	-	-	-	-	-	-	x	x
Manwine	-	-	-	-	-	-	-	-	x	x	\	x	x	x	x	x	-	-	-
Wulfward	-	-	-	-	-	-	-	-	x	x	x	-	-	-	-	-	-	-	-
Wynstan	-	-	-	x	-	-	-	-	-	-	-	-	-	-	-	-	-	-	-
Droitwich	0	0	0	0	0	0	0	1	2	2	3	0	0	0	0	0	0	0	0
Godric	-	-	-	-	-	-	-	-	x	\	x	-	-	-	-	-	-	-	-
Heaþuwulf	-	-	-	-	-	-	-	x	x	\	x	-	-	-	-	-	-	-	-
Wulfwine	-	-	-	-	-	-	-	-	-	-	x	-	-	-	-	-	-	-	-
Durham	0	0	0	0	0	0	0	0	0	0	0	0	0	0	0	0	0	0	1
Cuþberht	-	-	-	-	-	-	-	-	-	-	-	-	-	-	-	-	-	-	x
Exeter	8	7	6	6	10	6	6	7	5	5	5	9	5	6	6	5	4	3	3
Ælfric	-	x	x	x	\	x	x	x	-	-	-	-	-	-	-	-	-	-	-
Ælfwine	\	x	x	-	-	-	-	-	-	-	-	x	x	x	x	x	-	-	-
Brihtric	-	-	-	-	-	-	-	-	-	-	x	x	-	-	-	-	-	-	-
Brihtwine	-	-	-	-	-	-	-	-	-	-	-	x	-	-	-	-	-	-	-
Dodda	x	x	-	-	-	-	-	-	-	-	-	-	-	-	-	-	-	-	-
Eadmær	x	x	-	-	-	-	-	-	-	-	-	-	-	-	-	-	-	-	-
Eadsige	-	-	-	-	x	-	-	-	-	-	-	-	-	-	-	-	-	-	-
Eadwig	-	-	-	-	x	-	-	-	-	-	-	-	-	-	-	-	-	-	-
Eadwold	x	-	-	-	-	-	-	-	-	-	-	-	-	-	-	-	-	-	-
Goda	-	-	-	-	-	-	-	-	-	-	-	x	-	-	-	-	-	-	-
Godwine	x	-	-	-	-	-	-	-	-	-	-	-	-	-	-	-	-	-	-
Hunwine	-	-	-	x	x	-	-	-	-	-	-	-	-	-	-	-	-	-	-
Leofwine	x	x	\	\	\	\	\	x	x	\	x	x	\	\	\	\	\	\	x
Lyfing	x	\	x	\	x	x	x	x	x	\	x	x	-	-	-	-	-	-	-
Man	-	-	-	-	-	-	-	-	-	-	-	x	-	-	-	-	-	-	-
Semier	-	-	-	-	-	-	-	-	-	-	-	-	-	-	-	-	x	x	x
Sæwine	-	-	-	-	x	x	x	\	x	x	\	\	\	\	x	x	x	x	x
Sæwulf	-	-	-	-	x	-	-	-	-	-	-	-	-	-	-	-	-	-	-
Siward	-	-	-	-	-	-	-	-	-	-	-	-	x	x	\	x	-	-	-
Sweting	-	-	-	-	-	-	-	-	-	-	-	-	x	x	-	-	-	-	-
Wicing	-	-	-	-	-	-	-	x	-	-	-	-	-	-	-	-	-	-	-
Wulfmær	-	-	x	x	x	x	x	x	x	-	-	-	-	-	-	-	-	-	-
Wulfnoð	x	\	\	\	\	\	\	\	\	x	-	-	-	-	-	-	-	-	-
Wulfwine	-	-	-	-	-	-	-	-	x	\	\	\	\	x	x	x	x	-	-
Frome	1	1	1	0	0	0	0	0	0	0	0	0	0	0	0	0	0	0	0
Brihtwine	x	\	x	-	-	-	-	-	-	-	-	-	-	-	-	-	-	-	-
Gloucester	5	5	5	7	7	7	12	9	7	7	7	5	5	4	4	4	3	3	3
Ælfsige	x	\	x	x	x	x	x	x	\	x	x	-	-	-	-	-	-	-	-
Ægelric	x	x	x	x	x	x	-	-	-	-	-	-	-	-	-	-	-	-	-
Brihtnoð	-	-	-	-	-	-	-	x	x	\	x	\	\	\	\	\	\	\	x
Eadwig	-	-	-	-	-	-	x	-	-	-	-	-	-	-	-	-	-	-	-
Eadwulf	-	-	-	x	x	-	-	-	-	-	-	-	-	-	-	-	-	-	-
Godric	x	x	\	x	x	x	-	-	-	-	-	-	-	-	-	-	-	-	-
Godwine	-	-	-	-	-	-	x	-	-	-	-	-	-	-	-	-	-	-	-
Leofnoð	x	\	x	x	x	x	x	x	-	-	-	-	-	-	-	-	-	-	-
Leofstan	-	-	-	-	-	-	x	-	-	-	-	-	-	-	-	-	-	-	-
Leofwine	-	-	-	-	x	\	x	x	x	\	x	\	\	x	\	x	-	-	-

mint/moneyer	Eadward 1	2	3	4	5	6	7	8	9	10	Harold 1	Willelm 1	2	3	4	5	6	7	8
Ordric	-	-	-	-	-	-	-	x	x	\	\	x	x	-	-	-	-	-	-
Seolhwine	-	-	-	-	-	-	-	x	x	x	\	x	-	-	-	-	-	-	-
Sigelac	-	-	-	-	-	-	x	x	x	x	\	x	x	\	\	x	\	x	x
Wulfgeat	-	-	-	-	-	x	x	x	\	\	x	\	x	x	x	x	\	\	x
Wulfric	-	-	-	-	-	-	x	-	-	-	-	-	-	-	-	-	-	-	-
Wulfward	\	x	x	x	x	x	x	x	-	-	-	-	-	-	-	-	-	-	-
Wulfwig	-	-	-	x	-	-	-	-	-	-	-	-	-	-	-	-	-	-	-
Guildford	0	1	1	1	1	1	1	2	2	1	1	0	0	0	1	1	1	1	1
Ælfric	-	-	-	-	-	-	-	x	x	-	-	-	-	-	-	-	-	-	-
Blacman	-	x	\	x	x	x	x	x	-	-	-	-	-	-	-	-	-	-	-
Godwine	-	-	-	-	-	-	-	x	-	-	-	-	-	-	-	-	-	-	-
Leofwold	-	-	-	-	-	-	-	-	x	-	x	-	-	-	-	-	-	-	-
Særic	-	-	-	-	-	-	-	-	-	-	-	-	-	-	x	x	\	\	x
Hastings	2	2	2	3	3	3	3	4	3	3	3	3	1	1	1	1	1	1	2
Brid	x	x	x	x	x	x	x	x	-	-	-	-	-	-	-	-	-	-	-
Colswegn	-	-	-	-	-	-	-	-	x	x	x	x	-	-	-	-	-	-	-
Cypping	-	-	-	-	-	-	-	-	-	-	-	-	-	-	-	-	-	-	x
Duning	-	-	-	x	\	x	x	x	x	x	x	x	x	\	\	x	\	\	x
Leofwine	x	x	x	x	x	-	-	-	-	-	-	-	-	-	-	-	-	-	-
Wulfric	-	-	-	-	-	x	x	x	-	-	-	-	-	-	-	-	-	-	-
Þeodred	-	-	-	-	-	-	-	x	x	x	x	x	-	-	-	-	-	-	-
Hereford (7)	5	5	7	5	5	7	7	7	6	6	5	3	3	3	3	2	1	1	3
Ælfwig	-	-	-	-	-	-	x	x	x	x	\	x	-	-	-	-	-	-	-
Æstan	-	-	-	-	-	-	-	-	-	-	-	-	-	x	-	-	-	-	-
Ægelric	-	-	x	x	\	\	x	x	\	\	x	x	-	-	-	-	-	-	-
Ægelstan	-	-	-	-	-	-	x	\	x	-	-	-	-	-	-	-	-	-	-
Ægelwine	-	-	-	-	-	-	-	-	-	-	-	x	x	x	x	\	\	-	x
Brihtric	-	-	-	-	-	-	-	-	-	-	-	x	\	x	-	-	-	-	-
Eadric	-	-	-	-	-	-	x	x	\	x	x	-	-	-	-	-	-	-	-
Eadwig	-	-	-	-	x	\	\	x	\	\	x	\	x	-	-	-	-	-	-
Earnwig	\	\	x	x	\	x	x	x	x	x	-	-	-	-	-	-	-	-	-
Heaðuwig	-	-	-	-	-	-	-	-	-	-	-	-	-	-	x	-	-	-	-
Leofnoð	x	x	\	x	x	x	x	x	\	\	x	-	-	-	-	-	-	-	-
Leofstan	-	-	-	-	-	-	-	-	-	-	-	-	-	-	-	-	-	-	x
Ordric	x	x	-	-	-	-	-	-	-	-	-	-	-	-	-	-	-	-	-
Ordwig	-	-	-	-	-	-	-	-	-	-	-	-	-	-	-	-	-	-	x
Rædwulf	-	-	x	x	-	-	-	-	-	-	-	-	-	-	-	-	-	-	-
Wulfsige	\	x	-	-	-	-	-	-	-	-	-	-	-	-	-	-	-	-	-
Wulfstan	-	-	x	-	-	-	-	-	-	-	-	-	-	-	-	-	-	-	-
Wulfwig	-	-	x	-	-	-	-	-	-	-	-	-	-	-	-	-	-	-	-
Wulfwine	x	x	\	\	\	x	-	-	-	-	-	-	-	x	-	-	-	-	-
Hertford	3	5	6	4	1	1	1	2	2	1	0	1	1	1	1	1	1	1	2
Ælfwine	-	-	x	-	-	-	-	-	-	-	-	-	-	-	-	-	-	-	-
Deorsige	x	x	x	-	-	-	-	-	-	-	-	-	-	-	-	-	-	-	-
Eadwig	x	x	-	-	-	-	-	-	-	-	-	-	-	-	-	-	-	-	-
Godman	\	x	x	-	-	-	-	-	-	-	-	-	-	-	-	-	-	-	-
Godwine	-	x	x	x	-	-	-	-	-	-	-	-	-	-	-	-	-	-	-
Goldwine	-	-	x	-	-	-	-	-	-	-	-	-	-	-	-	-	-	-	-
Lyfing	-	-	-	x	-	-	-	-	-	-	-	-	-	-	-	-	-	-	-

mint/moneyer	Eadward										Harold	Willelm							
	1	2	3	4	5	6	7	8	9	10	1	1	2	3	4	5	6	7	8
Sæman	-	-	-	-	-	-	-	-	-	-	-	x	\	\	\	\	\	x	x
Sæmær	-	-	-	-	-	-	x	-	-	-	-	-	-	-	-	-	-	-	-
Wihtred	-	-	-	x	-	-	-	-	-	-	-	-	-	-	-	-	-	-	-
Wilgrip	-	-	-	-	x	x	\	x	x	x	-	-	-	-	-	-	-	-	-
Wulfric	-	-	-	-	-	-	-	x	-	-	-	-	-	-	-	-	-	-	-
Þeodred	x	\	\	x	-	-	-	-	-	-	-	-	-	-	-	-	-	-	-
Þeodric	-	-	-	-	-	-	-	-	-	-	-	-	-	-	-	-	-	-	x
Horndon	0	0	0	0	0	0	1	0	0	0	0	0	0	0	0	0	0	0	0
Duding	-	-	-	-	-	x	-	-	-	-	-	-	-	-	-	-	-	-	-
Huntingdon (3)	4	4	1	2	3	2	2	4	2	2	2	2	2	2	2	1	1	1	1
Ælfwine	\	\	x	x	x	-	-	-	-	-	-	-	-	-	-	-	-	x	x
Godric	-	-	-	-	x	x	x	x	x	\	\	x	x	x	x	-	-	-	-
Godwine	-	-	-	-	x	x	x	x	x	\	x	\	x	x	x	x	x	-	-
Leofric	-	-	-	-	-	-	x	-	-	-	-	-	-	-	-	-	-	-	-
Leofwine	-	-	-	-	-	-	x	-	-	-	-	-	-	-	-	-	-	-	-
Ulfcytel	-	-	-	x	-	-	-	-	-	-	-	-	-	-	-	-	-	-	-
Wulfstan	\	x	-	-	-	-	-	-	-	-	-	-	-	-	-	-	-	-	-
Wulfwig	x	x	-	-	-	-	-	-	-	-	-	-	-	-	-	-	-	-	-
Wulfwine	x	x	-	-	-	-	-	-	-	-	-	-	-	-	-	-	-	-	-
Hythe	0	1	0	1	0	1	0	1	0	0	0	0	0	0	0	1	1	1	1
Ælfwine	-	x	-	-	-	-	-	-	-	-	-	-	-	-	-	-	-	-	-
Eadred	-	-	-	-	-	-	-	-	-	-	-	-	-	-	-	x	\	\	x
Goldwine	-	-	-	-	-	-	-	x	-	-	-	-	-	-	-	-	-	-	-
Guðred	-	-	-	-	-	x	-	-	-	-	-	-	-	-	-	-	-	-	-
Leofwine	-	-	-	x	-	-	-	-	-	-	-	-	-	-	-	-	-	-	-
Ilchester	2	1	1	1	2	2	2	2	1	1	1	2	2	2	2	2	3	1	1
Ælfward	-	-	-	-	-	-	-	-	-	-	-	-	-	-	-	-	x	x	x
Ægelwine	-	-	-	-	-	x	\	x	x	x	x	x	\	\	\	x	x	-	-
Dunbeard	x	-	-	-	-	-	-	-	-	-	-	-	-	-	-	-	-	-	-
Godric	\	\	\	\	\	x	x	x	-	-	-	-	-	-	-	-	-	-	-
Osward	-	-	-	-	x	-	-	-	-	-	-	-	-	-	-	-	-	-	-
Wihtsige	-	-	-	-	-	-	-	-	-	-	-	x	x	x	\	\	x	-	-
Ipswich	2	3	3	5	5	5	5	5	6	3	3	2	4	3	5	5	4	4	5
Ælfric	-	-	-	-	-	-	-	-	-	-	-	-	-	-	-	x	\	\	x
Ælfwine	-	-	-	-	-	-	-	x	x	-	x	\	x	-	-	-	-	-	-
Ægelberht	-	-	-	-	-	-	-	-	-	-	-	-	x	\	x	x	-	-	-
Ægelwine	-	-	-	-	-	-	-	-	-	-	-	-	-	-	-	-	-	x	x
Brihtric	-	-	-	-	-	x	x	x	x	-	-	-	-	-	-	-	-	-	-
Bruning	-	x	x	x	x	x	\	x	x	-	-	-	-	-	-	-	-	-	-
Brunman	-	-	-	-	-	-	x	x	x	x	x	-	-	-	-	-	-	-	-
Eadwig	-	-	-	x	-	-	-	-	-	-	-	-	-	-	-	-	-	-	-
Leofstan	x	x	\	\	\	\	\	\	\	\	x	\	x	x	\	x	x	-	-
Leofwine	-	-	-	-	-	-	-	-	-	-	-	-	-	-	-	-	x	\	x
Leofwold	-	-	-	-	x	x	x	x	x	-	-	-	-	-	-	-	-	-	-
Lyfing	x	x	x	x	x	-	-	-	-	-	-	-	-	-	-	-	-	-	-
Manstan	-	-	-	-	-	-	-	-	-	-	-	-	-	-	-	x	-	-	-
Swegn	-	-	-	-	-	-	-	-	-	-	-	-	-	-	-	-	-	-	x
Wulfric	-	-	-	-	-	-	-	-	-	-	-	-	-	-	-	x	-	-	-
Wulfsige	-	-	-	x	x	x	-	-	-	-	-	-	-	-	-	-	-	-	-

mint/moneyer	Eadward										Harold	Willelm							
	1	2	3	4	5	6	7	8	9	10	1	1	2	3	4	5	6	7	8
Wulfward	-	-	-	-	-	-	-	-	-	-	-	-	-	-	-	x	-	-	-
Wulfwine	-	-	-	-	-	-	-	-	-	-	-	-	x	\	\	\	\	\	x
Langport	0	0	0	0	1	0	0	0	0	0	0	0	0	0	0	0	0	0	0
Ægelwine	-	-	-	-	x	-	-	-	-	-	-	-	-	-	-	-	-	-	-
Launceston	0	0	0	0	0	0	0	0	0	0	0	0	0	0	0	0	1	1	1
Godric	-	-	-	-	-	-	-	-	-	-	-	-	-	-	-	-	x	x	x
Leicester	3	5	4	4	5	5	5	7	6	6	3	3	3	2	2	2	2	2	1
Ægelric	-	-	-	-	-	x	x	x	x	x	-	-	-	-	-	-	-	-	-
Ægelwine	-	-	-	-	-	-	x	x	x	x	x	\	\	x	x	x	\	x	-
Blæcman	-	x	-	-	-	-	-	-	-	-	-	-	-	-	-	-	-	-	-
Bruning	-	-	-	-	-	-	x	-	-	-	-	-	-	-	-	-	-	-	-
Eadwine	-	-	-	-	x	\	\	\	x	-	-	-	-	-	-	-	-	-	-
Godric	-	-	x	x	x	x	x	x	x	x	x	\	\	\	\	\	\	\	x
Leofric	-	-	-	-	-	-	-	x	\	\	\	\	x	-	-	-	-	-	-
Oþwulf	-	-	-	-	-	-	-	-	x	-	-	-	-	-	-	-	-	-	-
Sæwine	\	x	x	x	x	-	-	-	-	-	-	-	-	-	-	-	-	-	-
Wulfnoð	x	\	x	x	x	x	-	-	-	-	-	-	-	-	-	-	-	-	-
Wulfric	-	x	\	x	\	x	\	\	x	x	-	-	-	-	-	-	-	-	-
Wulfwine	\	x	-	-	-	-	-	-	-	-	-	-	-	-	-	-	-	-	-
Lewes	3	3	7	9	6	4	4	4	3	3	3	1	1	2	3	3	3	3	3
Ælfric	-	-	-	-	-	-	-	-	-	-	-	-	-	-	x	\	\	\	x
Ælfsige	-	-	-	-	x	-	-	-	-	-	-	-	-	-	-	-	-	-	-
Dyring	-	-	-	x	-	-	-	-	-	-	-	-	-	-	-	-	-	-	-
Eadward	-	-	x	x	x	x	x	-	-	-	-	-	-	-	-	-	-	-	-
Eadwig	-	-	-	x	-	-	-	-	-	-	-	-	-	-	-	-	-	-	-
Eadwine	x	x	x	x	\	x	x	-	-	-	-	-	-	-	-	-	-	-	-
Godric	-	-	x	-	-	-	-	-	-	-	-	-	-	-	-	-	-	-	-
Godwine	\	\	\	\	x	x	x	x	x	x	x	-	-	-	-	-	-	-	-
Leofman	-	-	-	x	-	-	-	-	-	-	-	-	-	-	-	-	-	-	-
Leofnoð	-	-	x	-	-	-	-	-	-	-	-	-	-	-	-	-	-	-	-
Leofward	-	-	-	-	-	-	x	x	x	-	x	-	-	-	-	-	-	-	-
Leofwine	-	-	-	x	x	-	-	-	-	-	-	-	-	-	-	-	-	-	-
Norðman	x	-	-	-	-	-	-	-	-	-	-	-	-	-	-	-	-	-	-
Osmund	-	-	x	x	-	-	-	-	-	-	-	-	-	-	-	-	-	-	-
Oswold	-	x	x	\	x	x	x	x	x	x	x	\	x	\	x	x	\	\	x
Wulfwine	-	-	-	-	-	-	x	-	-	-	-	-	-	-	-	-	-	-	-
Wynred	-	-	-	-	-	-	-	-	-	-	-	-	-	x	x	x	x	x	x
Lincoln	23	19	18	18	17	16	15	14	14	14	13	11	10	7	6	7	6	4	3
Agmund	-	-	-	-	-	-	-	-	x	x	x	x	x	-	-	-	-	-	-
Ælfgeat	-	-	-	-	-	-	-	-	-	x	x	-	-	-	-	-	-	-	-
Ælfmær	-	-	-	-	-	-	-	-	-	-	x	x	x	-	-	-	-	-	-
Ælfnoð	\	x	x	x	x	x	x	x	\	\	\	\	\	x	-	-	-	-	-
Ælfwine	-	-	x	x	\	\	\	x	\	x	-	-	-	-	-	-	-	-	-
Ægelmær	-	-	-	-	-	-	-	-	x	x	x	-	-	-	-	-	-	-	-
Brihtric	x	x	x	x	x	-	-	-	-	-	-	-	-	-	-	-	-	-	-
Bruning	-	x	-	-	-	-	-	-	-	-	-	-	-	-	-	-	-	-	-
Colgrim	x	x	x	x	x	x	-	-	-	-	-	-	-	-	-	-	-	-	-
Eadmund	x	-	-	-	-	-	-	-	-	-	-	-	-	-	-	-	-	-	-
Eadric	x	x	x	x	\	\	\	\	x	x	x	-	-	-	-	-	-	-	-

mint/moneyer	Eadward 1	2	3	4	5	6	7	8	9	10	Harold 1	Willelm 1	2	3	4	5	6	7	8
Garfin	-	-	-	-	-	-	-	-	x	\	x	x	-	-	-	-	-	-	-
Gifel	-	-	-	-	-	-	-	x	x	\	\	x	x	x	-	-	-	-	-
Gilcrist	x	-	-	-	-	-	-	-	-	-	-	-	-	-	-	-	-	-	-
Godric	x	x	x	x	x	x	x	x	x	x	\	\	\	x	-	-	-	-	-
Guðfrið	x	x	-	-	-	-	-	-	-	-	-	-	-	-	-	-	-	-	-
Hildwulf	\	x	-	-	-	-	-	-	-	-	-	-	-	-	-	-	-	-	-
Leofnoð	\	x	\	x	-	-	-	-	-	-	-	-	-	-	-	-	-	-	-
Leofwig	x	-	-	-	-	-	-	-	-	-	-	-	-	-	-	-	-	-	-
Leofwine	x	x	x	\	\	\	\	\	x	\	\	\	\	\	\	\	\	x	\
Manna	-	-	-	x	x	x	x	-	-	-	-	-	-	-	-	-	-	-	-
Osbeorn	-	-	-	-	-	-	-	-	-	-	-	x	-	-	-	-	-	-	-
Osferð	x	x	x	x	x	x	x	-	-	-	-	-	-	-	-	-	-	-	-
Oslac	\	\	\	\	x	\	\	x	x	-	-	-	-	-	-	-	-	-	-
Otta	-	-	-	-	x	x	x	x	x	x	-	-	-	-	-	-	-	-	-
Oþbeorn	\	\	\	\	x	x	-	-	-	-	-	-	-	-	-	-	-	-	-
Oþgrim	\	\	\	x	x	x	x	x	x	x	x	\	x	x	-	-	-	-	-
Sigeferð/Siward	-	-	-	-	-	-	-	-	-	-	-	x	x	x	x	x	x	\	x
Sumorled	x	-	-	-	-	-	-	-	-	-	-	-	-	-	-	-	-	-	-
Swafi	x	-	-	-	-	-	-	-	-	-	-	-	-	-	-	-	-	-	-
Swearting	x	x	-	-	-	-	-	-	-	-	-	-	-	-	-	-	-	-	-
Ulf	x	x	x	x	x	\	x	x	x	x	x	\	\	\	x	x	\	x	x
Ulfbeorn	\	\	\	\	\	\	x	x	x	-	-	-	-	-	-	-	-	-	-
Unspac	-	-	-	-	-	-	-	-	-	-	-	-	-	-	x	x	x	-	-
Wælrafn	x	-	-	-	-	-	-	-	-	-	-	-	-	-	-	-	-	-	-
Wihtric	-	-	-	-	-	-	-	-	-	-	-	-	-	-	x	x	-	-	-
Wilgrip	-	-	-	x	-	-	-	-	-	-	-	-	-	-	-	-	-	-	-
Wineman	-	-	x	-	-	-	-	-	-	-	-	-	-	-	-	-	-	-	-
Wulfgar	-	-	x	\	\	\	\	x	\	x	-	-	-	-	-	-	-	-	-
Wulfmær	-	-	-	-	-	-	-	-	-	-	x	-	-	-	-	-	-	-	-
Wulfric	x	\	\	\	\	\	x	x	-	-	-	-	-	-	-	-	-	-	-
Wulfsige	-	-	-	-	-	-	-	-	-	-	-	-	x	-	-	-	-	-	-
Wulfstan	-	-	-	-	-	-	-	-	-	-	-	-	-	-	x	x	-	-	-
Þurcytel	-	-	-	-	-	-	x	x	-	-	-	-	-	-	-	-	-	-	-
Þurgrim	x	x	x	-	-	-	-	-	-	-	-	-	-	-	-	-	-	-	-
Þurstan	-	-	-	-	-	-	-	-	-	-	-	-	-	-	x	x	\	x	-
London	51	59	55	57	51	46	30	25	21	20	17	13	13	16	15	10	9	9	9
Ælfgar	-	x	x	\	x	-	-	-	-	-	-	-	-	-	-	-	-	-	-
Ælfgeat	-	-	-	x	-	-	-	-	-	-	-	-	-	-	-	-	-	-	-
Ælfnoð	\	\	\	x	-	-	-	-	-	-	-	-	-	-	-	-	-	-	-
Ælfred	\	x	x	x	x	x	x	x	\	\	\	\	\	\	x	\	\	\	x
Ælfric	\	\	x	x	-	-	-	-	-	-	-	-	-	-	-	-	-	-	-
Ælfsige	-	x	x	\	x	x	x	x	\	x	\	x	x	x	-	-	-	-	-
Ælfstan	-	-	-	x	-	-	-	-	-	-	-	-	-	-	-	-	-	-	-
Ælfward	\	x	\	\	\	x	x	x	x	x	-	-	-	-	-	-	-	-	-
Ælfwig	x	\	x	x	x	x	-	-	-	-	-	-	-	-	-	-	-	-	-
Ælfwine	x	x	x	x	x	x	\	x	\	\	\	x	x	\	x	\	\	x	\
Ælfwold	\	\	\	x	-	-	-	-	-	-	-	-	-	-	-	-	-	-	-
Ægelgar	-	x	-	-	-	-	-	-	-	-	-	-	-	-	-	-	-	-	-
Ægelman	-	x	-	-	-	-	-	-	-	-	-	-	-	-	-	-	-	-	-

mint/moneyer	Eadward										Harold	Willelm							
	1	2	3	4	5	6	7	8	9	10	1	1	2	3	4	5	6	7	8
Ægelric	-	x	x	x	x	x	\	\	\	\	\	\	x	x	-	-	-	-	-	-
Ægelsige	\	x	\	\	\	\	x	-	-	-	-	-	-	-	-	-	-	-	-	-
Ægelward	x	x	\	\	x	x	x	-	-	-	-	-	-	-	-	-	-	-	-	-
Ægelwig	\	x	x	x	\	x	-	-	-	-	-	-	-	-	-	-	-	-	-	-
Ægelwine	x	\	\	x	x	x	\	x	x	\	\	\	x	\	x	-	-	-	-	-
Æwig	-	-	-	-	-	-	-	-	-	-	-	-	-	-	-	-	-	-	-	x
Blacsunu	-	-	-	-	-	-	-	-	-	-	-	-	-	-	x	-	-	-	-	-
Brihtmær	x	x	\	\	x	x	-	-	-	-	-	-	-	-	-	x	-	-	-	-
Brihtred	\	x	x	x	x	x	-	-	-	-	-	-	-	-	-	-	-	-	-	-
Brihtric	-	-	-	-	-	-	-	-	-	-	-	-	-	x	\	x	-	-	-	-
Brihtsige	-	-	-	-	x	-	-	-	-	-	-	-	-	-	-	-	-	-	-	-
Brihtwine	x	\	\	\	x	x	-	-	-	-	-	-	-	-	-	-	-	x	x	
Bruna	\	\	\	x	-	-	-	-	-	-	-	-	-	-	-	-	-	-	-	-
Brungar	x	x	x	\	\	x	x	-	-	-	-	-	-	-	-	-	-	-	-	-
Bruning	\	\	x	-	-	-	-	-	-	-	-	-	-	-	-	-	-	-	-	x
Brunman	\	\	x	-	-	-	-	-	-	-	-	-	-	-	-	-	-	-	-	-
Burgred	-	x	\	x	x	-	-	-	-	-	-	-	-	-	-	-	-	-	-	-
Colswegn	-	-	-	-	-	-	-	-	-	-	-	-	-	-	x	-	-	-	-	-
Corf	x	-	-	-	-	-	-	-	-	-	-	-	-	-	-	-	-	-	-	-
Cynemær	-	-	-	x	-	-	-	-	-	-	-	-	-	-	-	-	-	-	-	-
Deorman	\	x	\	x	\	\	x	-	-	-	-	-	-	-	-	-	-	-	-	-
Duding	x	x	\	x	x	-	-	-	-	-	-	-	-	-	-	-	-	-	-	-
Dyring	-	-	-	-	-	-	-	x	-	-	-	-	-	-	-	-	-	-	-	-
Eadgar	-	-	-	-	-	-	-	x	-	-	-	-	-	-	-	-	-	-	-	-
Eadmund	x	x	x	\	x	-	-	-	-	-	-	-	-	-	-	-	-	-	-	-
Eadred	\	\	x	\	x	x	-	-	-	-	-	-	-	-	-	-	-	-	-	-
Eadric	x	x	x	x	x	x	-	-	-	-	-	-	-	-	x	\	\	x	x	
Eadsige	-	-	-	-	x	-	-	-	-	-	-	-	-	-	-	-	-	-	-	-
Eadward	\	\	\	\	x	x	\	x	\	\	\	\	\	\	\	x	x	-	-	
Eadwig	\	\	\	x	x	\	x	\	\	\	\	\	\	\	\	\	\	x	-	
Eadwine	\	x	x	x	x	x	x	x	x	x	x	x	x	x	x	x	x	x	x	
Eadwold	x	x	x	x	\	x	-	-	-	-	-	-	-	-	-	-	-	-	-	-
Eadwulf	-	-	-	-	-	x	-	-	-	-	-	-	-	-	-	-	-	-	-	-
Ealdgar	x	x	\	x	x	x	x	\	x	x	x	x	x	x	x	-	-	-	-	
Ealdred	-	-	-	-	x	-	-	-	-	-	-	-	-	-	-	-	-	-	-	-
Ealdwine	-	x	x	-	-	-	-	-	-	-	-	-	-	-	-	-	-	-	-	-
Ealdwulf	-	-	-	-	-	x	-	-	-	-	-	-	-	-	-	-	-	-	-	-
Eastmær	-	x	-	-	-	-	-	-	-	-	-	-	-	-	-	-	-	-	-	-
Eastmund	-	-	-	-	-	x	\	\	x	-	-	-	-	-	-	-	-	-	-	-
Eawig	-	x	x	\	x	-	-	-	-	-	-	-	-	-	-	-	-	-	-	-
Goda	x	-	-	-	-	-	-	-	-	-	-	-	-	-	-	-	-	-	-	-
Godhere	-	-	-	-	-	x	-	-	-	-	-	-	-	-	-	-	-	-	-	-
Goding	-	-	-	-	-	-	-	-	-	-	-	-	x	\	x	-	-	-	-	
Godman	\	x	\	\	\	x	-	-	-	-	-	-	-	-	-	-	-	-	-	-
Godric	x	x	x	x	x	x	x	x	x	x	x	x	x	x	\	x	x	\	x	
Godsunu	-	x	x	x	x	-	-	-	-	-	-	-	-	-	-	-	-	-	-	-
Godwig	x	\	x	x	\	x	-	-	-	-	-	-	-	-	-	-	-	-	-	-
Godwine	x	x	x	x	x	x	x	x	\	\	\	\	x	x	x	x	x	x	x	
Golda	-	-	-	x	-	-	-	-	-	-	-	-	-	-	-	-	-	-	-	-

mint/moneyer	Eadward										Harold	Willelm							
	1	2	3	4	5	6	7	8	9	10	1	1	2	3	4	5	6	7	8
Goldsige	x	x	x	x	x	x	-	-	-	-	-	-	-	-	-	-	-	-	-
Goldwine	-	x	x	\	\	\	x	-	-	-	-	-	-	-	-	-	-	-	-
Leofnoð	-	-	-	x	-	-	-	-	-	-	-	-	-	-	-	-	-	-	-
Leofred	x	x	x	x	x	x	-	-	-	-	-	-	-	-	-	-	-	-	-
Leofric	x	x	x	\	\	x	-	-	-	-	-	-	-	-	-	-	-	-	-
Leofsige	-	-	-	-	x	x	\	\	\	\	x	-	-	-	-	-	-	-	-
Leofstan	x	x	-	-	-	-	-	-	-	-	-	-	-	-	-	-	-	-	-
Leofwig	\	\	x	x	-	-	-	-	-	-	-	-	-	-	-	-	-	-	-
Leofwine	\	\	x	x	x	x	x	x	-	-	-	-	-	-	-	-	-	-	-
Leofwold	-	-	-	-	-	-	-	-	x	-	-	-	-	-	-	-	-	-	-
Lyfing	x	x	x	x	x	\	x	x	-	-	-	-	-	-	-	-	-	-	-
Manning	-	-	-	-	-	-	-	-	-	-	-	-	-	-	-	-	x	-	-
Ordlaf	x	-	-	-	-	-	-	-	-	-	-	-	-	-	-	-	-	-	-
Osmund	-	-	-	-	-	x	x	x	x	x	x	-	-	-	-	-	-	-	-
Sibwine	-	-	-	-	-	-	-	-	-	x	-	-	-	-	-	-	-	-	-
Sigebod	-	-	-	-	-	-	-	-	-	-	-	-	-	x	-	-	-	-	-
Sigered	-	-	-	-	-	x	-	-	-	-	-	-	-	-	-	-	-	-	-
Spræcling	-	-	-	x	-	-	-	-	-	-	-	-	-	-	-	-	-	-	-
Sweting	-	-	-	x	-	-	-	-	-	-	-	-	-	-	-	-	-	-	-
Swetman	\	x	x	x	x	x	\	\	x	x	x	x	-	-	-	-	-	-	-
Uhtred	-	-	-	-	-	-	-	-	-	-	-	-	-	x	-	-	-	-	-
Wihtred	-	-	x	-	-	-	-	-	-	-	-	-	-	-	-	-	-	-	-
Wulfgar	x	x	\	\	\	x	x	x	x	x	x	-	-	-	-	-	-	-	-
Wulfnoð	-	-	-	-	-	-	x	-	-	-	-	-	-	-	-	-	-	-	-
Wulfred	x	x	x	x	x	\	x	-	-	-	-	-	-	-	-	-	-	-	-
Wulfric	x	x	x	x	\	x	x	\	\	\	\	\	\	\	x	-	-	-	-
Wulfsige	\	x	x	x	\	\	\	\	x	x	-	-	-	-	-	-	-	-	-
Wulfstan	x	-	-	-	-	-	-	-	-	-	-	-	-	-	-	-	-	-	-
Wulfward	x	\	\	\	x	\	\	\	x	x	x	-	-	-	-	-	-	-	-
Wulfwig	-	x	\	x	-	-	-	-	-	-	-	-	-	-	-	-	-	-	-
Wulfwine	x	x	x	x	x	x	x	\	\	\	\	x	x	x	x	\	\	x	-
Þeodred	x	x	-	-	-	-	-	-	-	-	-	-	-	-	-	-	-	-	-
Þorr	-	-	-	x	-	-	-	-	-	-	-	-	-	-	-	-	-	-	-
Þurferð	-	-	-	-	-	-	x	-	-	-	-	-	-	-	-	-	-	-	-
Lydford	1	1	1	1	0	0	0	0	0	0	0	0	0	0	0	0	0	0	0
Ælfric	x	x	x	x	-	-	-	-	-	-	-	-	-	-	-	-	-	-	-
Maldon	0	1	1	1	1	3	3	2	1	1	1	0	0	1	1	1	1	1	3
Ælfward	-	-	-	-	-	-	-	-	-	-	-	-	-	-	-	-	-	-	x
Ælfwine	-	-	-	-	-	-	-	-	-	-	-	-	-	-	-	-	-	-	x
Dægniht	-	x	\	x	x	x	x	-	-	-	-	-	-	-	-	-	-	-	-
Godric	-	-	-	-	-	x	x	x	-	-	-	-	-	-	-	-	-	-	-
Godwine	-	-	-	-	-	x	x	x	x	\	x	-	-	-	-	-	-	-	-
Leofsunu	-	-	-	-	-	-	-	-	-	-	-	-	-	x	\	x	\	x	x
Malmesbury	2	2	2	1	2	2	2	1	1	1	1	1	1	1	1	1	0	1	2
Brihtwig	-	-	-	-	x	\	\	x	x	x	x	\	x	x	x	x	-	-	-
Brihtwine	x	x	x	-	-	-	-	-	-	-	-	-	-	-	-	-	-	-	-
Ealdwig	-	-	-	-	x	x	-	-	-	-	-	-	-	-	-	-	-	-	-
Ealdwine	-	-	-	-	-	-	x	-	-	-	-	-	-	-	-	-	-	-	-
Godesbrand	-	-	-	-	-	-	-	-	-	-	-	-	-	-	-	-	-	x	x

mint/moneyer	Eadward										Harold	Willelm							
	1	2	3	4	5	6	7	8	9	10	1	1	2	3	4	5	6	7	8
Huna	x	x	\	x	-	-	-	-	-	-	-	-	-	-	-	-	-	-	-
Sæward	-	-	-	-	-	-	-	-	-	-	-	-	-	-	-	-	-	-	x
Marlborough	0	0	0	0	0	0	0	0	0	0	0	0	0	1	1	1	1	1	1
Cild	-	-	-	-	-	-	-	-	-	-	-	-	-	x	x	x	x	x	x
Newport	0	0	0	0	1	1	0	1	0	0	0	0	0	0	0	0	0	0	0
Sæman	-	-	-	-	-	-	-	x	-	-	-	-	-	-	-	-	-	-	-
Sigered	-	-	-	-	x	x	-	-	-	-	-	-	-	-	-	-	-	-	-
Northampton	2	2	2	2	2	5	5	4	5	3	3	2	2	1	2	1	1	1	1
Ælfwine	x	x	x	x	x	x	x	x	x	-	-	-	-	-	-	-	-	-	-
Ceolwine	-	-	-	-	-	x	-	-	-	-	-	-	-	-	-	-	-	-	-
Godwine	-	-	-	-	-	-	-	-	-	-	-	-	-	-	x	-	-	-	-
Leofric	-	-	-	-	-	x	x	-	-	-	-	-	-	-	-	-	-	-	-
Leofstan	-	-	-	-	-	-	-	-	x	-	x	-	-	-	-	-	-	-	-
Leofwine	x	x	\	\	x	\	\	\	x	-	-	-	-	-	-	-	-	-	-
Sæwine	-	-	-	-	-	-	x	x	x	x	x	\	x	x	x	x	\	\	x
Swetman	-	-	-	-	-	-	-	x	x	x	x	\	x	-	-	-	-	-	-
Wulfnoð	-	-	-	-	-	x	x	x	x	-	-	-	-	-	-	-	-	-	-
Norwich	5	6	5	6	8	7	7	9	7	6	7	5	4	3	4	5	4	5	7
Ægelric	-	-	-	-	-	-	-	-	-	-	-	-	-	-	-	x	-	-	-
Ælfwine	-	-	-	-	-	-	x	-	-	-	-	-	-	-	-	-	-	-	-
Cenhelm	-	-	-	-	x	-	-	-	-	-	-	-	-	-	-	-	-	-	-
Cynric	-	-	-	-	-	-	-	-	-	-	x	-	-	-	-	-	-	-	-
Dægfin	-	-	-	-	x	-	-	-	-	-	-	-	-	-	-	-	-	-	-
Eadwald	-	-	-	-	-	-	-	-	-	-	-	-	-	-	-	x	\	\	x
Eadwine	-	-	-	-	-	-	-	x	x	\	\	x	x	\	\	\	\	\	x
Godfrið	-	-	-	-	-	-	-	x	\	-	x	x	-	-	-	-	-	-	-
Godman	-	-	-	-	-	x	-	-	-	-	-	-	-	-	-	-	-	-	-
Godric	-	-	-	-	-	-	-	-	-	-	-	-	-	-	x	x	x	x	x
Godwine	-	x	\	\	\	\	\	\	x	x	x	\	\	\	x	x	x	\	x
Haward	-	-	-	-	-	-	-	-	-	-	-	-	-	-	-	-	-	-	x
Hringwulf	x	x	\	\	\	x	x	-	-	-	-	-	-	-	-	-	-	-	-
Inhune	-	-	-	-	-	-	-	-	-	-	-	-	-	-	-	-	-	-	x
Leofric	-	-	-	-	-	-	-	x	-	-	-	-	-	-	-	-	-	-	-
Leofwig	x	\	\	x	-	-	-	-	-	-	-	-	-	-	-	-	-	-	-
Leofwine	x	x	x	\	x	x	\	x	x	-	-	-	-	-	-	-	-	-	-
Leofwold	-	-	-	-	-	-	-	-	-	-	-	-	x	-	-	-	-	-	-
Manna	x	x	\	\	\	\	\	\	\	\	x	x	-	-	-	-	-	-	-
Osmund	x	x	-	-	-	-	-	-	-	-	-	-	-	-	-	-	-	-	-
Price	-	-	-	-	-	-	-	-	x	-	-	-	-	-	-	-	-	-	-
Ulfcyll	-	-	-	-	-	-	-	-	-	-	-	-	-	-	-	-	-	-	x
Wideman	-	-	-	-	-	-	-	-	-	-	-	-	-	-	-	-	-	x	-
Wulfsige	-	-	-	-	-	x	x	-	-	-	-	-	-	-	-	-	-	-	-
Wulfstan	-	-	-	-	-	-	x	-	-	-	-	-	-	-	-	-	-	-	-
Þurferð	-	-	-	x	x	x	x	-	-	-	-	-	-	-	-	-	-	-	-
Þurgrim	-	-	-	-	-	-	-	-	x	-	x	x	x	x	x	-	-	-	-
Þurstan	-	-	-	-	x	x	x	x	x	x	x	-	-	-	-	-	-	-	-
Nottingham (2)	5	5	4	6	3	2	2	2	2	1	2	2	2	2	2	1	1	1	2
Acere	-	-	-	-	-	-	-	-	-	-	-	-	-	-	-	-	-	-	x
Blacman	x	x	x	x	x	-	-	-	-	-	-	-	-	-	-	-	-	-	-

mint/moneyer	Eadward 1	2	3	4	5	6	7	8	9	10	Harold 1	Willelm 1	2	3	4	5	6	7	8
Ealhmund	-	-	-	x	-	-	-	-	-	-	-	-	-	-	-	-	-	-	-
Earngrim	-	-	-	-	-	-	-	-	x	-	-	-	-	-	-	-	-	-	-
Forna	-	-	-	-	-	x	x	x	x	\	x	x	x	x	x	-	-	-	-
Healfdene	x	\	\	x	x	-	-	-	-	-	-	-	-	-	-	-	-	-	-
Leofsige	x	\	x	x	-	-	-	-	-	-	-	-	-	-	-	-	-	-	-
Manna	-	-	-	-	-	-	-	-	-	-	x	x	x	x	x	x	\	x	x
Sægrim	\	x	-	-	-	-	-	-	-	-	-	-	-	-	-	-	-	-	-
Snotor	-	-	-	x	-	-	-	-	-	-	-	-	-	-	-	-	-	-	-
Wulfnoð	\	x	\	\	x	\	\	x	-	-	-	-	-	-	-	-	-	-	-
Oxford	7	10	7	7	8	9	9	9	9	9	8	6	7	6	6	5	3	3	3
Ælfwig	-	x	\	x	x	x	x	x	x	x	x	\	x	\	x	x	-	-	-
Ægelric	x	x	-	-	-	-	-	-	-	-	-	-	-	-	-	-	-	-	-
Ægelwig	x	x	x	x	x	x	x	x	x	x	-	-	-	-	-	-	-	-	-
Ægelwine	x	x	x	x	x	x	x	x	\	\	\	\	x	x	x	-	-	-	-
Brihtred	-	-	-	-	-	-	-	x	\	\	\	\	x	x	\	x	x	x	x
Brihtwold	x	x	x	x	x	x	x	x	\	x	x	-	-	-	-	-	-	-	-
Eadwig	\	x	-	-	-	-	-	-	-	-	-	-	-	-	-	-	-	-	-
Eadwine	-	-	-	-	-	x	x	-	-	-	-	-	-	-	-	-	-	-	-
Godric	-	x	-	-	-	-	-	-	-	-	-	-	-	-	-	-	-	-	-
Godwine	x	x	x	x	\	\	x	\	\	\	x	x	x	x	x	-	-	-	-
Healfdene	x	-	-	-	-	-	-	-	-	-	-	-	-	-	-	-	-	-	-
Heregod	-	x	x	x	\	\	x	x	x	x	\	x	x	x	x	x	\	x	-
Manna	-	-	-	-	-	-	-	-	-	-	-	-	x	-	-	-	-	-	-
Swetman (DB)	-	-	-	-	x	x	x	x	\	\	\	\	\	\	\	\	\	\	x
Wulfwig	-	x	\	\	\	\	\	\	x	x	\	x	x	x	x	\	x	x	x
Pershore	0	0	0	0	0	0	0	1	0	0	0	0	0	0	0	0	0	0	0
Wulfric	-	-	-	-	-	-	-	x	-	-	-	-	-	-	-	-	-	-	-
Petherton	0	1	1	0	0	0	0	0	0	0	0	0	0	0	0	0	0	0	0
Brihtric	-	x	x	-	-	-	-	-	-	-	-	-	-	-	-	-	-	-	-
Pevensey	0	0	0	0	0	0	0	0	0	0	0	0	0	0	0	1	1	1	1
Ælfheah	-	-	-	-	-	-	-	-	-	-	-	-	-	-	-	x	\	\	x
Reading	0	2	1	0	0	0	0	0	0	0	0	0	0	0	0	0	0	0	0
Brihtric	-	x	-	-	-	-	-	-	-	-	-	-	-	-	-	-	-	-	-
Corf	-	x	x	-	-	-	-	-	-	-	-	-	-	-	-	-	-	-	-
Rhuddlan	0	0	0	0	0	0	0	0	0	0	0	0	0	0	0	0	0	0	1
Ælfwine	-	-	-	-	-	-	-	-	-	-	-	-	-	-	-	-	-	-	x
Rochester	2	3	3	2	2	2	4	4	3	3	3	2	2	2	2	2	2	2	2
Eadwine	-	x	x	\	\	x	x	-	-	-	-	-	-	-	-	-	-	-	-
Godwine	x	x	x	\	\	x	x	x	-	-	-	-	-	-	-	-	-	-	-
Leofstan	-	-	-	-	-	-	x	\	\	\	x	\	x	\	x	\	\	\	x
Leofwine	-	-	-	-	-	-	x	x	\	\	x	-	-	-	-	-	-	-	-
Leofwine Horn	-	-	-	-	-	-	-	x	x	x	\	\	\	\	\	x	\	\	x
Wulfric	\	\	x	-	-	-	-	-	-	-	-	-	-	-	-	-	-	-	-
Romney	1	1	1	1	1	1	1	1	1	1	1	1	1	1	1	2	3	2	2
Ælfmær	-	-	-	-	-	-	-	-	-	-	-	-	-	-	-	x	x	-	-
Winedi	-	-	-	-	-	-	-	-	-	-	-	-	-	-	-	-	-	x	x
Wulfmær	x	\	x	x	\	x	x	x	x	x	x	x	\	\	\	x	\	\	x
Wulfnoð	-	-	--	-	-	-	-	-	-	-	-	-	-	-	-	-	x	-	-
St Davids	0	0	0	0	0	0	0	0	0	0	0	0	0	0	0	0	0	0	3

mint/moneyer	Eadward										Harold	Willelm							
	1	2	3	4	5	6	7	8	9	10	1	1	2	3	4	5	6	7	8
Godesbrand	-	-	-	-	-	-	-	-	-	-	-	-	-	-	-	-	-	-	x
Leofwine	-	-	-	-	-	-	-	-	-	-	-	-	-	-	-	-	-	-	x
Þurig	-	-	-	-	-	-	-	-	-	-	-	-	-	-	-	-	-	-	x
Salisbury	4	3	3	2	0	0	1	1	1	2	1	2	1	1	1	1	1	2	3
Ælfwold	-	-	x	x	-	-	-	-	-	-	-	-	-	-	-	-	-	-	-
Ealdwine	-	-	-	-	-	-	-	-	-	-	-	-	-	-	-	-	-	-	x
Godric	-	-	-	-	-	-	x	x	\	\	\	x	\	\	\	x	\	x	-
Godwine	x	x	x	x	-	-	-	-	-	-	-	-	-	-	-	-	-	-	x
Leofstan	\	x	-	-	-	-	-	-	-	-	-	-	-	-	-	-	-	-	-
Osbeorn	-	-	-	-	-	-	-	-	-	-	-	-	-	-	-	-	-	x	x
Sæfara	-	-	-	-	-	-	-	-	-	-	-	x	-	-	-	-	-	-	-
Sigeboda	-	-	-	-	-	-	-	-	x	-	-	-	-	-	-	-	-	-	-
Wineman	x	x	x	-	-	-	-	-	-	-	-	-	-	-	-	-	-	-	-
Wynstan	x	-	-	-	-	-	-	-	-	-	-	-	-	-	-	-	-	-	-
Sandwich	1	2	2	2	2	2	2	2	1	0	0	0	1	0	2	2	3	3	3
Adalbot	-	-	-	-	-	-	-	-	-	-	-	-	-	-	x	-	-	-	-
Ælgeat	-	-	-	-	-	-	-	-	-	-	-	-	-	-	x	x	x	\	x
Ælfheah	-	-	-	-	-	-	-	-	-	-	-	-	-	-	-	x	x	x	x
Ære--nne	-	-	-	-	-	-	-	-	-	-	-	-	x	-	-	-	-	-	-
Godric	-	x	\	\	\	\	\	\	x	-	-	-	-	-	-	-	-	-	-
Godwine	-	-	-	-	-	-	-	-	-	-	-	-	-	-	-	-	x	x	x
Leofwine	x	x	x	x	\	x	\	x	-	-	-	-	-	-	-	-	-	-	-
Shaftesbury (3)	1	2	2	3	4	3	2	2	1	1	3	1	2	2	2	3	3	3	3
Ælfnoð	-	-	-	-	-	-	-	-	-	-	x	\	\	\	\	x	x	x	x
Ælfward	-	x	\	\	\	\	\	x	-	-	-	-	-	-	-	-	-	-	-
Ægelwine	-	-	-	-	-	-	-	-	-	-	x	-	-	-	-	-	-	-	-
Cnihtwine	-	-	-	-	-	-	-	-	-	-	-	-	-	-	-	x	x	x	x
Eadric	-	-	-	x	-	-	-	-	-	-	-	-	-	-	-	-	-	-	-
Godesbrand	-	-	-	-	-	-	-	-	-	-	-	-	x	\	\	\	x	x	x
Godric	-	-	-	-	-	-	-	x	x	-	x	-	-	-	-	-	-	-	-
Wuducoc	-	-	-	x	\	x	-	-	-	-	-	-	-	-	-	-	-	-	-
Wulfric	x	x	x	x	x	x	x	x	-	-	-	-	-	-	-	-	-	-	-
Shrewsbury	5	5	4	4	5	5	5	7	6	6	4	4	4	4	4	4	3	3	3
Ælfgeat	-	-	-	-	-	-	x	-	-	-	-	-	-	-	-	-	-	-	-
Ælfheah	\	x	\	\	x	x	-	-	-	-	-	-	-	-	-	-	-	-	-
Ægelric	-	-	-	-	-	-	x	\	x	x	x	\	x	\	x	-	-	-	-
Earnwig	-	-	-	-	-	x	x	x	x	x	x	\	x	\	x	x	x	\	x
Godesbrand	-	-	-	-	x	x	x	x	x	x	x	\	\	\	\	\	\	\	x
Godwine	-	-	-	-	-	-	x	x	x	-	-	-	-	-	-	-	-	-	-
Leofstan	\	x	x	x	x	x	x	-	-	-	-	-	-	-	-	-	-	-	-
Leofwine	\	\	x	\	x	x	-	-	-	-	-	-	-	-	-	-	-	-	-
Sægrim	-	-	-	-	-	-	-	-	-	-	-	-	-	-	-	x	\	\	x
Wuduman	-	-	-	-	-	-	-	x	x	x	-	-	-	-	-	-	-	-	-
Wulfgeat	x	x	-	-	-	-	-	-	-	-	-	-	-	-	-	-	-	-	-
Wulfmær	x	x	x	x	x	x	x	x	\	x	x	\	x	\	x	x	-	-	-
Southwark	4	3	1	2	1	3	3	2	2	1	1	1	2	2	2	2	2	3	4
Ælfric	x	x	-	-	-	-	-	-	-	-	-	-	-	-	-	-	-	-	-
Ælfwine	-	-	-	x	-	-	-	-	-	-	-	-	-	-	-	-	-	-	-
Brunman	x	-	-	-	-	-	-	-	-	-	-	-	-	-	-	-	-	-	-

mint/moneyer	Eadward 1	2	3	4	5	6	7	8	9	10	Harold 1	Willelm 1	2	3	4	5	6	7	8
Brunred	x	-	-	-	-	-	-	-	-	-	-	-	-	-	-	-	-	-	-
Burgred	x	x	-	-	-	-	-	-	-	-	-	-	-	-	-	-	-	-	-
Ealdwulf	-	-	-	-	-	-	-	-	-	-	-	-	-	-	-	-	-	-	x
Godman	-	-	-	-	-	x	-	-	-	-	-	-	-	-	-	-	-	-	-
Godric	-	-	-	-	-	-	-	-	x	\	\	\	\	\	\	\	\	x	x
Leofred	-	-	-	-	x	x	-	-	-	-	-	-	-	-	-	-	-	-	-
Leofward	-	-	-	-	-	-	-	-	-	-	-	-	-	-	-	-	-	-	x
Leofwine	-	-	x	x	\	\	\	\	\	\	\	\	x	\	\	x	x	\	\
Osmund	-	-	-	-	-	x	x	x	x	x	x	\	x	\	\	\	\	x	x
Swetman	-	-	-	-	-	x	\	x	-	-	-	-	-	-	-	-	-	-	-
Wulfwine	-	x	-	-	-	-	-	-	-	-	-	-	-	-	-	-	-	-	-
Stafford	0	0	0	0	1	2	0	1	0	1	1	1	2	1	1	1	1	1	2
Ælfric	-	-	-	-	x	x	-	-	-	-	-	-	-	-	-	-	-	-	-
Coling	-	-	-	-	-	x	-	-	-	-	-	-	-	-	-	-	-	-	-
Godric	-	-	-	-	-	-	-	-	-	-	-	-	-	-	-	-	-	-	x
Godwine	-	-	-	-	-	-	-	-	x	\	-	x	x	\	\	\	\	\	x
Osmund	-	-	-	-	-	x	-	-	-	-	-	-	-	-	-	-	-	-	-
Wulfnoð	-	-	-	-	-	-	-	-	-	-	-	-	x	-	-	-	-	-	-
Stamford	16	13	12	10	10	10	7	8	7	5	4	4	5	5	2	2	2	2	3
Ælfheah	x	x	x	\	\	\	\	x	-	-	-	-	-	-	-	-	-	-	-
Ælfwine	-	-	-	-	-	-	-	-	-	-	-	-	-	x	-	-	-	-	-
Baldwine	-	x	x	-	-	-	-	-	-	-	-	-	-	-	-	-	-	-	-
Brinit	x	-	-	-	-	-	-	-	-	-	-	-	-	-	-	-	-	-	-
Brunstan	-	-	-	-	-	-	-	-	-	-	-	-	-	-	-	-	-	x	x
Brunwine	x	\	x	\	\	x	x	x	x	x	x	x	x	x	-	-	-	-	-
Deoring	-	-	-	-	-	-	-	-	-	-	-	-	x	-	-	-	-	-	-
Eadwine	-	-	x	-	-	-	-	-	-	-	-	-	-	-	-	-	-	-	-
Earnfrið	-	-	x	x	x	x	-	-	-	-	-	-	-	-	-	-	-	-	-
Earngrim	x	-	-	-	-	-	-	-	-	-	-	-	-	-	-	-	-	-	-
Fargrim	\	\	\	x	x	-	-	-	-	-	-	-	-	-	-	-	-	-	-
Godleof	-	-	-	-	-	-	-	-	-	-	-	-	-	-	-	-	-	-	x
Godric	x	x	-	-	-	-	-	-	-	-	-	-	-	-	-	-	-	-	-
Godwine	x	x	\	x	x	x	x	x	-	-	-	-	-	-	-	-	-	-	-
Harcin	\	x	x	\	\	x	\	\	x	-	-	-	-	-	-	-	-	-	-
Leofric	x	x	x	x	x	x	x	x	x	x	x	\	x	x	-	-	-	-	-
Leofwine	\	\	x	x	x	\	x	x	x	\	x	x	x	x	x	x	x	-	-
Osward	-	-	-	-	-	-	-	x	x	x	-	-	-	-	-	-	-	-	-
Sweart	x	\	x	-	-	-	-	-	-	-	-	-	-	-	-	-	-	-	-
Sweartcol	-	-	-	-	-	-	-	-	x	x	-	-	-	-	-	-	-	-	-
Wilgrip	\	x	x	x	\	\	x	x	x	-	-	-	-	-	-	-	-	-	-
Wulfnoð	x	-	-	-	-	-	-	-	-	-	-	-	-	-	-	-	-	-	-
Wulfric	-	-	-	-	-	x	-	-	-	-	-	-	-	-	-	-	-	-	-
Wulfward	-	-	-	-	-	-	-	-	-	-	x	\	\	\	\	\	x	\	x
Wulfwine	x	\	\	x	x	x	-	-	-	-	-	-	-	-	-	-	-	-	-
Þorulf	x	-	-	-	-	-	-	-	-	-	-	-	-	-	-	-	-	-	-
Þurstan	\	x	-	-	-	-	-	-	-	-	-	-	-	-	-	-	-	-	-
Steyning	2	2	2	2	2	1	1	1	1	1	1	1	1	1	1	1	1	1	2
Deorman	-	-	-	-	-	-	-	x	x	x	x	\	x	\	x	x	x	\	x
Friþuwine	x	x	x	-	-	-	-	-	-	-	-	-	-	-	-	-	-	-	-

mint/moneyer	Eadward										Harold	Willelm							
	1	2	3	4	5	6	7	8	9	10	1	1	2	3	4	5	6	7	8
Þorbeorn	-	-	-	-	-	-	-	-	-	-	-	-	-	-	-	-	-	-	x
Wulfgeat	-	-	-	x	x	-	-	-	-	-	-	-	-	-	-	-	-	-	-
Wulfric	x	\	\	x	x	x	x	-	-	-	-	-	-	-	-	-	-	-	-
Sudbury	1	0	0	0	0	1	1	1	1	1	1	1	1	0	0	0	1	1	1
Brunman	x	-	-	-	-	-	-	-	-	-	-	-	-	-	-	-	-	-	-
Folcwine	-	-	-	-	-	x	x	x	x	\	\	\	x	-	-	-	-	-	-
Wulfric	-	-	-	-	-	-	-	-	-	-	-	-	-	-	-	-	x	\	x
Tamworth	0	1	1	1	2	1	2	2	2	2	2	2	2	2	2	2	2	2	2
Ægelwine	-	-	-	-	x	-	-	-	-	-	-	-	-	-	-	-	-	-	-
Bruning	-	x	x	x	\	\	\	x	x	\	\	\	x	\	\	\	\	\	x
Coling	-	-	-	-	-	-	x	x	\	x	\	\	x	\	\	\	\	\	x
Taunton	2	1	1	1	0	1	1	1	1	1	1	1	2	1	1	1	1	1	1
Ælfwine	-	-	-	-	-	-	-	-	-	-	-	-	-	-	-	x	x	x	x
Boga	x	\	x	x	-	-	-	-	-	-	-	-	-	-	-	-	-	-	-
Brihtric	-	-	-	-	-	x	x	x	\	x	x	\	x	x	x	-	-	-	-
Gilcrist	x	-	-	-	-	-	-	-	-	-	-	-	-	-	-	-	-	-	-
Leofwine	-	-	-	-	-	-	-	-	-	-	-	-	x	-	-	-	-	-	-
Thetford	7	9	8	7	9	8	6	10	9	7	7	7	9	9	6	7	6	6	6
Ælfric	-	-	-	x	x	-	-	-	-	-	-	-	-	-	-	-	-	-	-
Ælfwine	-	-	-	-	-	-	-	x	x	x	x	\	\	\	\	\	\	\	x
Ætsere	-	-	-	-	-	-	x	x	x	-	-	-	-	-	-	-	-	-	-
Ægelsige	-	x	x	x	x	x	-	-	-	-	-	-	-	-	-	-	-	-	-
Ægelwine	-	-	-	-	-	-	-	-	x	\	x	-	-	-	-	-	-	-	-
Blæcere	-	-	-	x	x	x	x	x	-	-	-	-	-	-	-	-	-	-	-
Blacsunu	-	-	-	-	-	-	-	-	-	-	-	-	x	x	-	-	-	-	-
Brunstan	x	x	x	-	-	-	-	-	-	-	-	-	-	-	-	-	-	-	-
Cynric	-	-	-	-	-	-	-	-	-	-	-	x	x	x	x	x	\	x	-
Eadric	x	x	\	\	x	x	-	-	-	-	-	-	-	-	-	-	-	-	-
Eadwig	-	-	-	-	-	x	-	-	-	-	-	-	-	-	-	-	-	-	-
Eastmund	-	x	x	x	x	x	-	-	-	-	-	-	-	-	-	-	-	-	-
Folcard	-	-	-	-	-	-	-	x	\	\	\	\	\	\	x	x	x	x	x
Goda	-	-	-	-	-	-	-	-	-	-	-	x	x	x	-	-	-	-	-
Godleof	-	-	-	-	x	x	x	x	x	x	x	\	\	\	\	\	\	\	x
Goding	-	-	-	-	-	-	-	-	-	-	-	-	-	-	-	-	-	-	x
Godred	-	-	-	-	-	-	-	-	-	-	-	-	-	-	-	x	x	x	x
Godric	-	-	-	-	-	-	-	x	x	x	x	x	x	x	x	x	x	x	x
Godwig	-	-	-	-	-	-	-	-	x	-	-	-	-	-	-	-	-	-	-
Godwine	x	\	\	\	\	\	\	\	x	\	x	x	x	x	-	-	-	-	-
Leofred	-	-	x	-	-	-	-	-	-	-	-	-	-	-	-	-	-	-	-
Leofric	\	\	\	x	x	-	-	-	-	-	-	-	-	-	-	-	-	-	-
Leofwine	x	x	x	x	x	x	-	-	-	-	-	-	-	-	-	-	-	-	-
Manna	-	x	-	-	-	-	-	-	-	-	-	-	-	-	-	-	-	-	-
Osbeorn	-	-	-	-	-	-	-	-	-	-	-	-	x	x	x	x	-	-	-
Sægrim	x	-	-	-	-	-	-	-	-	-	-	-	-	-	-	-	-	-	-
Sumorled	-	-	-	-	-	-	x	x	x	-	-	-	-	-	-	-	-	-	-
Tidred	x	x	-	-	-	-	-	-	-	-	-	-	-	-	-	-	-	-	-
Wulfwig	-	-	-	-	-	-	x	-	-	-	-	-	-	-	-	-	-	-	-
Þurferð	-	-	-	-	-	-	x	x	-	-	-	-	-	-	-	-	-	-	-
Þurgod	-	-	-	-	-	-	-	-	-	-	x	-	-	-	-	-	-	-	-

mint/moneyer	Eadward										Harold	Willelm							
	1	2	3	4	5	6	7	8	9	10	1	1	2	3	4	5	6	7	8
Wallingford	8	9	7	7	7	5	5	5	4	4	4	3	3	3	2	2	2	2	2
Ælfwig	-	x	-	-	-	-	-	-	-	-	-	-	-	-	-	-	-	-	-
Ægelwig	x	x	x	\	x	-	-	-	-	-	-	-	-	-	-	-	-	-	-
Ægelwine	-	-	-	-	-	-	-	-	-	-	-	-	-	-	-	-	-	-	x
Brand	-	-	-	-	x	x	x	x	x	x	x	x	x	x	x	x	x	-	-
Brihtmær	-	-	-	-	-	-	-	x	x	x	x	x	x	x	-	-	-	-	-
Brihtric	\	x	x	\	x	x	x	x	-	-	-	-	-	-	-	-	-	-	-
Brihtwine	\	\	x	x	\	x	x	-	-	-	-	-	-	-	-	-	-	-	-
Brunwine	\	x	\	x	x	x	x	x	\	x	-	-	-	-	-	-	-	-	-
Burhwine	\	\	\	\	\	x	\	x	x	x	x	-	-	-	-	-	-	-	-
Eadward	\	x	x	x	-	-	-	-	-	-	-	-	-	-	-	-	-	-	-
Leofwine	x	x	-	-	-	-	-	-	-	-	-	-	-	-	-	-	-	-	-
Sweartling	-	-	-	-	-	-	-	-	-	-	x	x	x	x	x	x	x	x	x
Wideman	-	-	-	-	-	-	-	-	-	-	-	-	-	-	-	-	-	x	-
Wulfwine	\	\	\	\	x	-	-	-	-	-	-	-	-	-	-	-	-	-	-
Wareham (2)	2	1	1	1	1	1	1	2	2	2	2	3	3	3	2	3	3	3	4
Ægelric	-	-	-	-	-	-	-	-	-	-	-	x	\	\	x	x	x	x	x
Beorn	-	-	-	-	-	-	-	x	\	\	\	\	\	\	\	x	\	\	x
Godwine	-	-	-	-	-	-	-	-	-	-	-	-	-	-	x	x	x	x	x
Sideloc	-	-	-	-	-	-	-	-	-	-	-	-	-	-	-	-	-	-	x
Sideman	\	x	x	\	x	x	x	x	x	x	x	x	\	x	-	-	-	-	-
Wulfric	x	-	-	-	-	-	-	-	-	-	-	-	-	-	-	-	-	-	-
Warminster	1	1	1	1	0	0	0	0	0	0	0	0	0	0	0	0	0	0	0
Wulfstan	\	\	\	x	-	-	-	-	-	-	-	-	-	-	-	-	-	-	-
Warwick	4	3	2	2	2	2	3	3	3	4	3	3	3	3	3	3	2	2	4
Ælfsige	-	x	-	-	-	-	-	-	-	-	-	-	-	-	-	-	-	-	-
Ægelric	-	-	-	-	-	-	-	-	-	-	-	-	-	-	-	-	-	-	x
Ægelstan	-	-	-	-	-	x	\	x	-	-	-	-	-	-	-	-	-	-	-
Leofric	\	x	x	x	x	-	-	-	-	-	-	-	-	-	-	-	-	-	x
Leofwig	x	-	-	-	-	-	-	-	-	-	-	-	-	-	-	-	-	-	-
Leofwine	x	-	-	-	-	-	-	-	-	-	-	-	-	-	-	-	-	-	-
Lyfing	x	\	x	x	x	x	x	\	\	\	x	\	\	\	x	x	\	\	x
Wulfwine	-	-	-	-	-	-	-	-	x	x	x	\	x	\	\	x	-	-	-
Þeodric	-	-	-	-	-	-	-	-	-	x	x	-	-	-	-	-	-	-	-
Þurcytel	-	-	-	-	-	x	x	x	x	x	x	x	x	x	x	x	\	\	x
Watchet	1	1	1	1	1	1	0	0	0	0	0	0	0	0	0	0	1	1	1
Godcild	x	x	x	x	x	x	-	-	-	-	-	-	-	-	-	-	-	-	-
Sigewulf	-	-	-	-	-	-	-	-	-	-	-	-	-	-	-	-	x	\	x
Wilton	3	4	4	2	3	3	6	8	6	5	5	3	5	4	5	3	3	3	3
Ælfstan	x	x	x	x	-	-	-	-	-	-	-	-	-	-	-	-	-	-	-
Ælfward	-	-	-	-	-	-	-	x	-	-	-	-	-	-	-	-	-	-	-
Ælfwine	x	x	x	\	x	x	x	x	x	\	\	\	\	\	\	x	\	x	x
Ælfwold	-	-	-	-	x	x	x	x	x	x	x	-	-	-	-	-	-	-	-
Brihtsige	-	-	-	-	-	-	-	x	-	-	-	-	-	-	-	-	-	-	-
Centwine	-	-	-	-	-	-	-	-	x	-	x	-	-	-	-	-	-	-	-
Godric	-	-	-	-	-	-	-	-	-	-	-	-	x	x	x	-	-	-	-
Herered	-	-	-	-	-	x	x	x	-	-	-	-	-	-	-	-	-	-	-
Leofwine	-	-	-	-	-	-	-	x	-	-	-	-	-	-	-	-	-	-	-
Lyfing	x	x	x	-	-	-	-	-	-	-	-	-	-	-	-	-	-	-	-

mint/moneyer	Eadward 1	2	3	4	5	6	7	8	9	10	Harold 1	Willelm 1	2	3	4	5	6	7	8
Owig	-	-	-	-	-	-	-	-	-	-	-	x	x	-	-	-	-	-	-	-
Ricard	-	-	-	-	-	-	-	-	-	-	-	-	-	-	x	-	-	-	-
Sæfare	-	-	-	-	-	-	-	-	-	-	-	-	x	x	\	\	\	\	x
Sæwine	-	-	-	-	-	-	x	x	\	\	\	x	x	x	x	x	\	x	x
Swetric	-	-	-	-	-	-	x	x	-	-	-	-	-	-	-	-	-	-	-
Wine	-	-	-	-	-	-	-	-	x	x	x	-	-	-	-	-	-	-	-
Wineman	-	x	x	-	-	-	-	-	-	-	-	-	-	-	-	-	-	-	-
Þurcytel	-	-	-	-	x	x	x	x	-	-	-	-	-	-	-	-	-	-	-
Winchcombe	0	0	0	1	1	1	1	1	1	1	1	1	1	1	1	1	1	1	1
Goldwine	-	-	-	x	x	\	\	x	x	x	x	\	\	\	x	x	\	x	x
Winchester	19	17	16	17	18	11	8	7	6	6	6	6	8	8	6	6	7	7	8
Ælfstan	\	\	\	x	\	\	x	-	-	-	-	-	-	-	-	-	-	-	-
Ælfwine	\	x	x	x	x	x	x	x	x	x	x	x	x	-	-	-	-	-	-
Anderboda	-	-	-	-	-	x	x	x	x	x	x	x	x	x	x	x	x	-	-
Æstan	-	-	-	-	-	-	-	-	-	-	-	-	-	-	-	x	x	x
Ægelstan	x	x	x	x	x	x	x	-	-	-	-	-	-	-	-	-	-	-	-
Ægelstan Loc	\	\	x	x	x	-	-	-	-	-	-	-	-	-	-	-	-	-	-
Ægelwine	x	x	\	x	x	-	-	-	-	-	-	-	-	-	-	-	-	-	-
Brand	-	-	-	-	x	-	-	-	-	-	-	-	-	-	-	-	-	-	-
Brihtmær	-	x	\	\	\	x	x	x	-	-	-	-	-	-	-	-	-	-	-
Brihtwold	-	-	-	-	x	-	-	-	-	-	-	-	-	-	-	-	-	-	-
Bruning	-	-	-	-	-	-	-	-	-	-	-	-	-	-	-	-	-	x	x
Coll	-	-	-	x	-	-	-	-	-	-	-	-	-	-	-	-	-	-	-
Eadwine	\	\	\	x	x	-	-	-	-	-	-	-	-	-	-	-	-	-	-
Friþumund	x	-	-	-	-	-	-	-	-	-	-	-	-	-	-	-	-	-	-
Godman	x	\	x	\	\	x	-	-	-	-	-	-	-	-	-	-	-	-	-
Godnoð	-	-	-	-	-	-	-	-	-	-	-	-	x	x	-	-	-	-	-
Godric	-	x	x	x	x	-	-	-	-	-	-	-	-	-	-	-	-	-	-
Godwine	x	x	x	x	x	x	x	x	\	x	\	\	\	x	x	x	x	x	x
Godwine Ceoca	x	\	x	\	\	x	-	-	-	-	-	-	-	-	-	-	-	-	-
Godwine Widia	\	x	\	\	x	x	-	-	-	-	-	-	-	-	-	-	-	-	-
Golding	-	-	-	-	-	-	-	-	-	-	-	-	-	x	-	-	-	-	-
Ifing	x	x	\	x	-	-	-	-	-	-	-	-	-	-	-	-	-	-	-
Leodmær	x	x	x	x	x	x	-	-	-	-	-	-	-	-	-	-	-	-	-
Leofstan	x	-	-	-	-	-	-	-	-	-	-	-	-	-	-	-	-	-	-
Leofwine	\	x	x	x	x	-	-	-	-	-	-	-	-	-	-	-	-	-	-
Leofwine Riclaf	-	x	-	-	-	-	-	-	-	-	-	-	-	-	-	-	-	-	-
Leofwold	-	-	-	-	-	-	-	x	x	x	x	x	x	x	x	x	x	x	x
Lyfing	x	x	x	x	x	x	x	x	x	x	x	x	x	x	x	x	x	\	x
Sæward	x	-	-	-	-	-	-	-	-	-	-	-	-	-	-	-	-	-	-
Sæwine	x	-	-	-	-	-	-	-	-	-	-	-	-	-	-	-	-	-	-
Siward	-	-	-	-	-	-	-	-	-	-	-	-	x	x	x	x	x	x	x
Spileman	x	-	-	-	-	-	-	-	-	-	-	-	-	-	-	-	-	-	-
Spræcling	-	-	-	-	-	x	x	x	x	x	x	\	\	\	\	\	\	\	x
Wigmund	-	-	-	-	-	-	-	-	-	-	-	-	-	-	-	-	-	-	x
Wynstan	-	-	-	-	x	-	-	-	-	-	-	-	-	-	-	-	-	-	-
Worcester	3	3	3	6	5	6	5	5	6	5	5	5	7	6	5	4	3	3	3
Ælfgeard	-	-	-	-	-	-	-	-	-	-	-	-	-	x	x	\	x	x	x
Ælfwine	-	-	-	-	-	-	-	-	x	-	-	-	-	-	-	-	-	-	-

mint/moneyer	Eadward										Harold	Willelm							
	1	2	3	4	5	6	7	8	9	10	1	1	2	3	4	5	6	7	8
Ægelric	-	-	-	-	-	x	-	-	-	-	-	-	-	-	-	-	-	-	-
Ægelwine	x	x	x	\	x	\	x	x	-	-	-	-	-	-	-	-	-	-	-
Baldric	-	-	-	-	-	-	-	-	x	\	\	\	\	\	x	x	\	x	-
Eadwine	-	-	-	-	-	-	-	-	-	-	-	-	x	-	-	-	-	-	-
Eastmær	-	-	-	-	-	-	-	-	-	x	x	x	x	x	\	\	x	\	x
Garwulf	-	-	-	-	x	x	x	x	x	x	\	x	\	x	\	\	x	-	-	-
Godwine	-	-	-	x	-	-	-	-	-	-	-	-	-	-	-	-	-	-	-
Heaþuwulf	-	-	-	-	-	-	-	-	-	-	-	-	-	-	x	-	-	-	-
Leofric	\	\	\	x	\	\	\	x	\	\	x	x	x	x	-	-	-	-	-
Leofstan	x	x	\	x	x	\	x	x	x	-	-	-	-	-	-	-	-	-	-
Reafwine	-	-	-	-	-	-	-	-	-	-	-	-	x	x	-	-	-	-	-
Sæwine	-	-	-	-	-	-	-	-	-	-	-	-	-	-	-	-	-	-	x
Wicing	-	-	-	x	x	x	x	x	x	\	x	x	x	-	-	-	-	-	-
Wulfwig	-	-	-	x	-	-	-	-	-	-	-	-	-	-	-	-	-	-	-
York	20	22	17	16	16	12	12	12	11	11	13	10	11	5	5	5	4	4	4
Agin	-	x	-	-	-	-	-	-	-	-	-	-	-	-	-	-	-	-	-
Ælfhere	x	x	x	x	-	-	-	-	-	-	-	-	-	-	-	-	-	-	-
Ælfwine	\	x	x	x	x	-	-	-	-	-	-	-	-	-	-	-	-	-	-
Anlaf	-	-	-	-	-	-	-	-	x	x	x	\	x	\	x	x	x	\	x
Arþulf	-	-	-	-	-	-	-	-	-	-	-	-	x	\	\	x	-	-	-
Ægelwine	x	x	-	-	-	-	-	-	-	-	-	-	-	-	-	-	-	-	-
Beorn	x	x	-	-	-	-	-	-	-	-	-	-	-	-	-	-	-	-	-
Col	-	-	x	x	x	-	-	-	-	-	-	-	-	-	-	-	-	-	-
Cytel	x	x	-	-	-	-	-	-	-	-	-	-	-	-	-	-	-	-	-
Earncytel	x	x	x	x	x	x	\	x	x	x	x	\	x	-	-	-	-	-	-
Earngrim	x	x	x	x	x	x	x	x	x	-	-	-	-	-	-	-	-	-	-
Earngrim Coa	-	-	-	-	x	-	-	-	-	-	-	-	-	-	-	-	-	-	-
Eltan	-	-	x	x	-	-	-	-	-	-	-	-	-	-	-	-	-	-	-
Godric	x	-	-	-	-	-	-	-	-	-	-	-	-	-	-	-	-	-	-
Godwine	-	-	-	-	x	-	-	-	-	-	-	-	-	-	-	-	-	-	-
Grimwulf	x	x	-	-	-	-	-	-	-	-	-	-	-	-	-	-	-	-	-
Gunnulf	-	x	-	-	-	-	-	-	-	-	-	-	-	-	-	-	-	-	-
Hrafn	\	x	x	x	x	x	-	-	-	-	-	-	-	-	-	-	-	-	-
Iocytel	-	x	x	x	\	x	x	x	x	x	x	-	-	-	-	-	-	-	-
Ioli	x	x	x	x	x	x	x	x	-	-	-	-	-	-	-	-	-	-	-
Leising	-	-	-	-	-	-	-	-	-	-	x	\	x	\	\	\	\	x	x
Leofnoð	-	-	x	x	x	x	x	-	-	-	-	-	-	-	-	-	-	-	-
Leofwine	x	x	-	-	-	-	-	-	-	-	-	-	-	-	-	-	-	-	-
Lyfing	-	-	-	x	-	-	-	-	-	-	-	-	-	-	-	-	-	-	-
Manna	-	x	-	-	-	-	-	-	-	-	-	-	-	-	-	-	-	-	-
Oþbeorn	-	-	-	-	-	-	-	x	x	x	x	\	x	\	x	x	x	\	x
Oþgrim	-	-	-	-	-	x	x	x	x	x	x	x	x	x	x	-	-	-	-
Oþhun	\	x	x	-	-	-	-	-	-	-	-	-	-	-	-	-	-	-	-
Oþwulf	-	-	-	-	-	-	-	-	x	x	x	x	x	-	-	-	-	-	-
Roscytel	-	-	-	-	-	-	-	-	-	-	x	x	x	-	-	-	-	-	-
Sæfugl	x	x	x	x	-	-	-	-	-	-	-	-	-	-	-	-	-	-	-
Scule	x	x	x	x	x	x	x	x	x	x	-	-	-	-	-	-	-	-	-
Snæbeorn	-	-	-	-	-	-	x	x	x	x	x	-	-	-	-	-	-	-	-
Styrcol	\	x	x	\	x	x	-	-	-	-	-	-	-	-	-	-	-	-	-

mint/moneyer	Eadward 1	2	3	4	5	6	7	8	9	10	Harold 1	Willelm 1	2	3	4	5	6	7	8
Sutere	-	-	-	-	-	-	-	-	-	-	x	-	-	-	-	-	-	-	-
Sweartcol	-	-	-	-	x	x	x	x	x	x	x	\	x	-	-	-	-	-	-
Swegn	x	-	-	-	-	-	-	-	-	-	-	-	-	-	-	-	-	-	-
Ulfcytel	x	x	x	x	x	x	x	x	x	x	x	x	x	-	-	-	-	-	-
Ulfcytel Þaginc	-	-	-	-	-	-	x	x	-	-	-	-	-	-	-	-	-	-	-
Unnulf	x	x	-	-	-	-	-	-	-	-	-	-	-	-	-	-	-	-	-
Wetrfugl	-	-	-	-	x	x	-	-	-	-	-	-	-	-	-	-	-	-	-
Þor	-	-	x	x	x	x	x	x	x	x	\	\	x	-	-	-	-	-	-
Þurgrim	x	x	x	-	-	-	-	-	-	-	-	-	-	-	-	-	-	-	-
Þurig	-	-	-	-	-	-	-	-	-	-	-	-	-	-	-	x	x	\	x
'Derne'	0	0	0	0	0	1	1	1	0	0	0	0	0	0	0	0	0	0	0
Wulfsige	-	-	-	-	-	x	\	x	-	-	-	-	-	-	-	-	-	-	-
'Dyr'	1	0	0	1	0	0	0	0	0	0	0	0	0	0	0	0	0	0	0
Bruning	x	-	-	-	-	-	-	-	-	-	-	-	-	-	-	-	-	-	-
Wulfgar	-	-	-	x	-	-	-	-	-	-	-	-	-	-	-	-	-	-	-
'Maint'	0	0	0	0	0	0	0	0	0	0	0	0	1	0	0	0	0	0	0
Brihtwig	-	-	-	-	-	-	-	-	-	-	-	-	x	-	-	-	-	-	-
'Spes'	1	0	0	0	0	0	0	0	0	0	0	0	0	0	0	0	0	0	0
Lyfing	x	-	-	-	-	-	-	-	-	-	-	-	-	-	-	-	-	-	-
'tes'	0	1	0	0	0	0	0	0	0	0	0	0	0	0	0	0	0	0	0
Brihtric	-	x	-	-	-	-	-	-	-	-	-	-	-	-	-	-	-	-	-

APPENDIX 4

ENGLISH LANDOWNERS IN 1086

This section includes all English landowners in 1086 with more than £20 of land (English as defined in law, i.e. both native and foreign born but resident before 1066), also English sheriffs, survivors from the greater thanage of 1066, and close relatives of the greater thanes in 1066. It must be an underestimate of the total number of English survivors of the Conquest, since the Domesday survey was inconsistent in recording undertenancies. Later evidence suggests that many English survived as tenants of the new Norman landlords (Michelmore 1981). Even those listed below as holding from the King, often also held lands from other lords (included in the totals given). Some survivors had moved into other spheres of society, e.g. Orm, whose son Gamal was a lawman of York in 1106, and Þurgod Lah who went into the church and eventually became Bishop of St Andrews. Some work has been done already (e.g. Williams 1995), but a great deal of detailed work has yet to be done on all the local evidence of the 11th and 12th centuries which will shed light on just who survived and prospered among the native-born English after 1066.

In the lists below, a name with an asterisk * is that of someone who has already been given an entry in an earlier section. Modern references for this section include the Phillimore edition of the Domesday Book and Williams 1995.

The Royal Family

PRINCESS *CRISTINA** (DB Cristina)
Lands: in Oxford and Warwick worth £55, and 1 dwelling in the borough of Warwick.

PRINCE EADGAR* (DB Edgar)
Lands: in Hertford worth £10, held from him by Godwine. Prince Eadgar had given up his lands shortly before the survey was undertaken and Hertford was the only shire to note which lands he had held. It is likely that he had held lands elsewhere. Two estates in Huntingdon were noted as having been held by an Eadgar in 1066 (held by Earl Hugo in 1086). This Eadgar is not identified as the Prince and might have been someone else.

Thanes Holding of the King

ÆLFRED OF LINCOLN (DB Alvred, Alvered)

Life: it is possible that Ælfred was not English but Breton, coming over after the Conquest. The name Ælfred was common in Brittany as well as England and his son was named Alan, a distinctively Breton name.

Lands: in Bedford, Lincoln and Rutland worth £38 6/-, with a further £33 14/4 held by tenants. He had not held any land in 1066.

ÆLFRED OF MARLBOROUGH (DB Alvred)

Life: his daughter possibly married Harold*, son of Earl Raulf. Some of his lands had been held by his uncle, the Norman Osbeorn Pentecost, before 1052.

Lands: in Hampshire, Hereford, Somerset, Surrey, Wiltshire and Worcester worth £118 17/-, with a further £117 held from him by tenants.

ÆLFRED (DB Alvred)

Life: he was the nephew of Wigod* of Wallingford, and had inherited some of Wigod's lands.

Lands: in Middlesex and Oxford worth £14 10/-.

ÆLFSIGE (DB Alsi)

Life: he was the son-in-law of Wulfward* Hwit.

Lands: in Buckingham worth £7 10/-. His brother Leofwine held 10/- worth of land also in Buckingham.

ÆLFSIGE OF FARINGDON (DB Alsi)

Lands: in Berkshire, Gloucester and Oxford worth £52 (+2 hides). His son Ælfwig held Milton in Oxfordshire.

BALDWINE* FITZHERLUIN (DB Balduin, Baldeuin)

Lands: in Buckingham, Gloucester, Northampton and Worcester £10 9/4.

BARÐ* (DB Baret)

Lands: in the West Riding of York worth £4 10/7.

BRIHTRIC OF TROWBRIDGE (DB Brictric)

Life: it is possible that he was related to Eadward of Salisbury.

Lands: in Wiltshire worth £34, with a further £3 15/- held from him by his brother Ælfwig. He had inherited most of his lands from his father.

BRIHTWINE (DB Brictuin, Brictvin)

Lands: in Dorset worth £22 17/7 (+1½ hides), with a further 7/- held by tenants. He had been a landowner in 1066 also.

COLGRIM OF GRANTHAM (DB Colegrim)

Lands: in Lincoln worth £24 3/- (+4 pl. 7 oxgangs), with a further £4 6/- held by tenants. He also held part of the borough of Grantham. He had held a small amount of land in 1066 and increased his holdings by 1086.

COLSWEGN OF LINCOLN (DB Colsvain)

Life: he had a son Picot and nephew Cola, and a daughter *Muriel* who married Rodbert de la Haye (who inherited his lands).
Lands: in Lincoln worth £51 11/4, with a further £35 13/- held from him by tenants. He held no land before 1066. He also held 4 tofts in Lincoln and had recently built 36 houses and 2 churches on wasteland near the city.

EADWARD OF SALISBURY (DB Edward, Eduuard)

Life: he was most likely the son of greater thane *Wulfwynn** and was Sheriff of Wiltshire, and his son Walter after him. Eadward married *Mathild*, daughter of Raulf FitzHubert. Green (1983) suggests that his father might have been a Norman, Gerald of Roumare (presumably resident before 1066).
Lands: in Buckingham, Dorset, Gloucester, Hampshire, Hertford, Middlesex, Oxford, Somerset, Surrey, Wiltshire worth £333 4/-, with a further £88 held by tenants. He might have held Alton, Etchilhampton and Wilcot in 1066. He held also 3 dwellings in the borough of Malmesbury and 2 dwellings in the borough of Oxford.

EALDGYÐ, m Rodbert de Oilgi

Life: she was the daughter of Wigod* of Wallingford, and had married Rodbert de Oilgi. Their daughter *Mathild* had married Miles Crispin, who held much of Wigod's lands (worth £51), presumably by right of this marriage.
Lands: in Berkshire, Buckingham and Oxford worth £43. Her husband Rodbert held much more land than this.

EALDRED (DB Aldred)

Life: he was the brother of Oda of Winchester and seems to have prospered alongside him, both possibly as officials of the New Minster or the Bishop.
Lands: in Hampshire, Sussex and Wiltshire worth £22 16/-, some of which he held through his wife who had held them in 1066.

EARNWIG THE SHERIFF (DB Ernui)

Lands: he was Sheriff of Derby and Nottingham and held land in both shires worth £1 8/-. Although he had held land in 1066, and become Sheriff, he does not seem to have enriched himself after the Conquest.

EARNWINE THE PRIEST (DB Ernuin, Ernui)

Life: his father had held Harrowden in Bedfordshire in 1066, and his kinsman Godric had held a church in Lincoln which Earnwine was claiming in 1086.

Lands: in Bedford, Lincoln, Nottingham, the East and West Ridings of York worth £10 10/8 (+55½ ploughlands). He had held lands himself in 1066 but these were largely exchanged for others by the time of the Domesday survey. His urban properties included 1 dwelling in Lincoln and 7 tofts in Grantham (although these were claimed from him by the Bishop of Durham). He had held 22 dwellings and 2 churches in Stamford in 1066 but had lost these by 1086.

GODRIC THE STEWARD (DB Godric)

Life: he might have been the son of Ælfwine and brother of Cytel. Much of his own lands had come from his maternal uncle Eadwine. He later became Sheriff of Norfolk and Suffolk under Willelm II. It is possible that he had been a steward of Earl Raulf of East Anglia and was kept on to manage the earl's estates after his disgrace. Is it significant that his own son was named Raulf?
Lands: in Norfolk, Suffolk and the North Riding of York worth £60 (+1 ploughland). He administered £161 12/7 worth of Raulf's former lands for the King in Cambridge, Essex and Suffolk.

GOSPATRIC* (DB Gospatric)

Life: he was the son of greater thane Earncyll*.
Lands: in the East, North and West Ridings of York worth £18 13/6, with a further +100 ploughlands.

HAROLD*, SON OF EARL RAULF (DB Harold, Herald)

Lands: in Gloucester, Warwick and Worcester worth £64 10/-. He also had 2 dwellings in Warick borough, and 20 burgesses in his own borough of Droitwich. Harold's lands were much less extensive than he had held in 1066.

HEARDING* OF WILTON (DB Harding, Herding)

Lands: in Berkshire, Dorset, Hampshire, Somerset and Wiltshire worth £32 12/-.

HEARDING (DB Harding)

Life: he was the son of Eadnoð* the Constable, and was still living 1118/25. Hearding was ancestor of the later Berkeley family.
Lands: in Gloucester and Somerset worth £10 10/-, with a further £1 held by a tenant, Godwine.

LEOFRIC (WILLELM) (DB Leuric)

Life: he was the son of Osgod, and had brothers Brihtric and Eadmund. He had accommodated himself to the new regime by adopting the Norman name Willelm.
Lands: in Berkshire, Essex, Gloucester and Oxford £20 6/8, with a further £3 held by tenants.

LEOFWINE (DB Leuuin)
Lands: in Oxford worth £22. He was also a landowner in 1066.

LIGULF* (DB Ligulf)
Lands: in the West Riding of York worth £2.

ODA OF WINCHESTER (DB Ode, Odo)
Life: Oda was a steward and had obviously made himself useful in local administration. His brother Ealdred also held land in Hampshire, Sussex and Wiltshire (see above).
Lands: in Berkshire, Hampshire, Sussex and Wiltshire worth £46 10/-, with a further £5 held by tenants. He also had 8 properties in Wichester and 3 burgesses in Cricklade (and had held property in Southampton in 1066). He had a claim on Hatch Warren in Hampshire, pledged to him for £10 by Ælfsige.

OSBEORN* FITZRICARD (DB Osbern)
Life: he married *Nest* the daughter of Queen *Ealdgyð* by her first husband, Griffin of Wales.
Lands: in Bedford, Gloucester, Hereford, Nottingham, Oxford, Shropshire, Warwick and Worcester worth £54 15/- (+30 hides 2 yardlands), and a further £52 8/- held from him by tenants. His urban properties included 1 dwelling in Warwick and 8 houses in Worcester. He also had 13 burgesses in Droitwich.

REINBALD* OF CIRENCESTER (DB Reinbald, Reimbald, Rainbald)
Life: he had been chancellor of Eadward III (see under King's priests above).
Lands: in Berkshire and Oxford worth £31.

SWEGN OF ESSEX (DB Svain, Suen)
Life: he was the son of Rodbert* the Constable, and one time Sheriff of Essex.
Lands: in Essex, Huntingdon, Oxford and Suffolk worth £193 5/-, with a further £146 9/- held by tenants. He also received £6 5/- in pleas from Clavering and Rochford hundreds in Essex.

SWEGN* (DB Suuen, Suuan)
Lands: in the West Riding of York worth £2 15/-.

ÞEODRIC* THE GOLDSMITH (DB Teodric)
Lands: in Berkshire, Oxford and Surrey £28.

ÞOR* (DB Tor)
Lands: in the West Riding worth £2.

ÞURCYLL OF WARWICK (DB Turchil)

Life: he was the son of greater thane Ælfwine*, and had made a formal submission to Willelm in 1067. His brothers were Cytelbeorn and Guðmund, and his uncles Ælfmær and Ægelric.

Lands: in Warwick worth £9 15/-, with £13 16/- held from him by members of his family, and a further £95 16/- held from him by tenants. Þurcyll's urban properties included 4 dwellings in Warwick.

Holding Only of Other Lords

ÆÞELWOLD THE CHAMBERLAIN (DB Adelold)

Life: the spelling of his name would be unusual (but not impossible) for 1066 in England and he might have been of continental rather than native origin.

Lands: in Kent worth £21 held from Bishop Oda. He appears to have gained a great deal of land after the Conquest but had lost much of it by 1086, some of it going to Rodbert Latimer.

EADRIC* OF ELHAM (DB Edric, Ederic)

Lands: Williams 1995 suggests that Eadric was farming the manor of Elham, worth, (for £50) from Bishop Oda.

EADRIC* WILDE (DB Edric)

Lands: in Shrewsbury worth £4 6/-. Eadric's holdings have been partially reconstructed using 12th century evidence of the holdings of his descendants (Williams 1995).

EADRIC* OF WILTSHIRE'S WIDOW

Lands: in Wiltshire worth £6 from Ernulf de Hesdin. Eadric had been a greater thane in 1066. His widow also held one dwelling in the borough of Malmesbury.

OSFERÐ* (DB Offers)

Lands: in Cornwall worth £8 7/- from Count Rodbert of Mortain.

RODBERT LATIMER (LEOFGEAT) (DB Rotbt., Robt.)

Life: Rodbert was the son of Ægelric the priest and *Godgyfu*, and had a brother Ælfwine. He and his brother were sheriff's officers, and Rodbert's byname of Latimer shows him to have acted as an interpreter. His adoption of Rodbert instead of his English name (probably Leofgeat) shows an early willingness to accommodate himself to his new masters.

Lands: in Kent worth £82 from Bishop Oda, the Archbishop and St Augustine's Abbey.

SIWARD* THE FAT (DB Siuuard, Seuuard, Seuuar)

Lands: in Shrewsbury worth £4 1/2¼ from a variety of lords – Earl Roger, Walkelin, Osbern FitzRicard and Roger de Laci. His brother Ealdred still held Acton Scott and part of Aldon from Earl Roger, worth c.£1.

ÞUROLD (DB Turold)

Life: he was the son of Osmund, and brother-in-law of Wigod of Wallingford.
Lands: in Hampshire, Surrey and Wiltshire worth £42 from Earl Roger. All his lands had been held by his father in 1066.

Survivors, Kin and New Men

The landowners listed above comprise just 14 with lands worth over £40 (but only 11 held from the King), and 14 worth over £20. The only people listed with lands worth less than £20 are survivors and close kinsmen of greater thanes. In all, just 12 of the greater thanes of 1066 were still holding lands in 1086. There were also four sons, one nephew and a brother in law who had inherited lands from a greater thane of 1066. In two cases, some of the thane's lands had passed to a son-in-law. Of those holding more than £40 in 1086, three had moved into this category by increasing their holdings after the Conquest: Ælfred of Marlborough, Osbeorn FitzRicard and Ælfsige of Faringdon. Four men were new landowners: Rodbert Latimer, Godric, Colswegn and Oda of Winchester. The most successful of the survivors was undoubtedly Eadward of Salisbury, whose lands made him a major tenant in chief of the King. Indeed, his descendants would become Earls of Salisbury. Apart from Swegn and Ælfred of Marlborough, the other major landowners were all of lesser wealth and influence. Some of those listed were lords of lesser tenants, whose lands added up to a sizable proportion of the lord's total holdings. One interesting, and extreme, example of this is Þurcyll of Warwick, son of Ælfwine, the majority of whose lands were in the hands of tenants, many of them English (some of them his own family).

For ease of comparison, the 41 landowners are listed below in order of value of the lands they held directly themselves. Greater thanes in 1066 are marked with an asterisk *.

Holdings worth more than £40	held directly	from others	by tenants
Eadward, son of *Wulfwynn**	£333	£88	
Swegn , son of Rodbert*	£193	£146	
Ælfred of Marlborough	£113	£6	£117
Rodbert Latimer			£82
Harold*, son of Earl Raulf	£65		
Godric the Steward	£56	£4 (+1 pl.)	
Princess *Cristina*		£55	
Osbeorn FitzRicard	£55 (+30½ h.)	£52	

	held directly	from others	by tenants
Ælfsige of Faringdon	£52 (+2 h.)		
Colswegn of Lincoln	£43	£9 (1½ pl.)	£36
Oda of Winchester	£44	£3	£5
Ealdgyð, daughter of Wigod*	£43		
Þurold, br.-in-law of Wigod*		£42	
Eadric* of Elham			£40

Holdings worth more than £20	**held directly**	**from others**	**by tenants**
Ælfred of Lincoln?	£39		£34
Brihtric of Trowbridge	£34		£4
Hearding* of Wilton	£25	£8	
Reinbold of Cirencester	£31		
Þeodric the goldsmith	£28		
Colgrim of Grantham	£6 (+5pl.)	£18	£4
Þurcyll, son of Ælfwine*	£24		£96
Brihtwine	£15	£8	7/-
Ealdred, brother of Oda	£16	£7	
Leofwine	£22		
Æþelwold the Chamberlain?		£21	
Leofric (Willelm)		£20	£3
Gospatric*, son of Earncyll*	£11 (+55½ pl.)		£8 (+44½ pl.)
Earnwine the Priest	£4 (+49 pl.)	£7 (+6 pl.)	

Holdings worth less than £20	**held directly**	**from others**	**by tenants**
Ælfred, nephew of Wigod*	£6	£9	
Hearding, son of Eadnoð*	£11		£1
Baldwine* FitzHerluin	£7	£3	
Osferð*		£8	
Ælfsige, son-in-law of Wulfward*		£8	
widow of Eadric* of Wiltshire		£6	
Barð*	10/-	£4	
Eadric* Wilde		£4	
Siward* the Fat		£4	
Swegn*	15/-	£2	
Ligulf*	10/-	30/-	
Þor*	£2		
Earnwig the Sheriff	£1		

APPENDIX 5

NEWCOMERS AFTER 1066

The Norman Conquest brought many newcomers to England. Those listed below, are the major land and office holders that can be identified as being in England by 1074, or who formed the inner circle of Willelm's government. Willelm relied on a close-knit circle of family and friends as his core group of supporters. Early in his reign, these included Count Alan of Brittany, Hugo d'Avranches, Bishop Odo of Bayeux, Ricard of Clare, Count Rodbert of Mortain, Roger de Montgomerie, Willelm FitzOsbern, Willelm de Warenne. Only summaries of lives and careers are given below. Further information about those listed can be found in Barlow 1979, Bates 1997, Fleming 1991, Green 1990, Knowles et al 1972, Lewis 1991, Loyn 1994. The best biography of Duke Willelm II is probably still that of Douglas 1966. Accounts of the Norman Conquest are too numerous to mention, but ones that form good introductions and starting points for further reading are Allen Brown 1985 and Golding 1994. Van Houts 1997 should be consulted for information about those who accompanied Willelm to England. Introductions to the history of Normandy before 1066 can be found in Bates 1982 and Searle 1988.

The Ducal Family of Normandy

WILLELM II (Willelm, Willem, Wilgelm, Wyllelm, DB Willelm)

He was born in 1028, the illegitimate son of Duke Rodbert I (at this period, the rulers of Normandy were known as either Counts or Dukes). There was weak central government during his youth and he had to overcome serious revolts when he came of age and tried to assert his authority. His position was secured with the help of King Henri of France. However, this changed after 1052 when Henri formed an alliance with Willelm's opponent the Count of Anjou. Internal opposition in Normandy was ruthlessly put down and he relied on a close-knit circle of relatives and supporters that he could trust. The deaths of the King of France and Count of Anjou in 1060 removed external threats to his power and he took over the county of Maine in 1063. Normandy was a noted centre of monasticism during his rule, attracting clerics from elsewhere in Europe, such as Lanfranc from Italy.

MATHILD (Mathild, Mattildis, Mahthild, Mathildis, DB Mathildis)

The daughter of Baldwine V of Flanders; her proposed marriage to Willelm was forbidden by the Pope in 1049 but the marriage went ahead at Eu, probably in 1051/2. The Papacy agreed to sanction the marriage in 1059. She ruled Normandy in Willelm's absence in 1066, and came over to England in 1068 to be crowned as Queen. She died on 2nd November 1083.

BALDWINE (Baldewine, DB Balduin)

The son of Count Gislebert of Brionne (grandson of Duke Ricard I and one of Willelm's guardians), he was made Sheriff of Devon and held £350 of land in England after the Conquest. However, his brother Ricard was more important politically.

IUDITH (DB Iudita)

She was the daughter of Willelm's sister *Adela* and was married to the English Earl Walþeof, who was executed in 1076.

BISHOP ODO (Odo)

The half-brother of Willelm, Odo was born c1030, and became Bishop of Bayeux in 1049/50. As a member of Willelm's inner circle, he became Earl of Kent and regent of England with Willelm FitzOsbern in 1067-68. He was arrested and imprisoned in 1082, but was released at Willelm's death in 1087, dying in 1090. His lands in England after the Conquest amounted to £3,240. Odo was patron of Þurstan (later Abbot of Glastonbury), Willelm (later Abbot of Fécamp), Thomas (later Archbishop of York) and Samson (later Bishop of Worcester).

RICARD (DB Ricard)

Known as Ricard of Clare, he was the son of Count Gislebert of Brionne (grandson of Duke Ricard I and one of Willelm's guardians). Ricard's Norman lands were based on Orbec. He was one of the inner circle of landowners endowed by Willelm with a large number of English lands, worth £794. He was part of the commission enquiring into the conduct of sheriffs in 1076/77 and served as regent of England in Willelm's absence, dying in 1090. The Clares later became Earls of Hertford and Pembroke.

COUNT RODBERT OF EU (Rotbertus)

He was the grandson of Duke Ricard I, and was Count of Eu. Rodbert helped defend Normandy against invasion in 1054, and guarded Lindsey against revolt and invasion in 1069 before taking part in the suppression of the northern revolt in 1069-70. He was given the rape of Hastings in Sussex in succession to Hunfrið de Tilleul, and was appointed to the commission enquiring into the conduct of sheriffs in 1076/77. He died in 1090.

COUNT RODBERT OF MORTAIN (Rodbert, Rotbert, Rodbeart, Rodbeart, Rotbryht, Robertus)

Rodbert was the half-brother of Willelm and Count of Mortain since 1055/56. He was a key member of Willelm's inner circle, guarded Lindsey with Rodbert of Eu against revolt and invasion in 1069, and helped to put down the northern rebellion in 1069-70. He was given the rape of Pevensey in Sussex and large estates in Cornwall after 1070 with lands worth £1,794. He died in 1091.

WILLELM

He was the son of Count Ricard of Evreux (grandson of Duke Ricard I), and succeeded his father in 1067. Willelm died in 1118.

WILLELM'S CHILDREN

Rodbert (born 1052, died 1134), was designated heir to Normandy, secured by an oath of the barons in 1066. He assumed responsibility for Normandy in 1068, rebelling against his father in 1078-80, and from 1083. Ricard, the second son was killed c1069/74. Willelm, born c1060, became King of England after his father's death. The youngest son Henri was born in 1068 and was King in turn after Willelm II, and took over Normandy from Rodbert in 1106. Willelm's daughters were *Adela*, who married Count Stephen of Blois, *Constance* who married Count Alan of Brittany, and *Cecily*, Abbess of Caen. Other daughters existed and were possibly *Agatha?*, *Adeliza* and *Mathild*.

EARLS

GERBOD

A Fleming, Gerbod was Advocate of St Bertin's Abbey in Flanders. His sister *Gundrada* married Willelm de Warenne, and he was appointed Earl of Chester, probably in 1069, but in late 1070 or early 1071 surrendered the earldom and returned to Flanders. His brother Frederic was killed by Hereward in the Fens in 1070.

HUGO D'AVRANCHES (DB Hugo)

Hugo was the son of Ricard, Viscount of Avranches. He was left behind to assist *Mathild* in governing Normandy in 1066-67. Appointed Earl of Chester in 1070/71, he extended Norman power into north Wales and held £794 of land in England by 1086. Hugo died in 1101.

ODO

see under the Ducal Family

RODBERT DES COMMINES

He was made Earl of Northumberland in December 1068, but was killed on 28th January 1069 in Durham at the start of the revolt against Willelm I.

ROGER DE BRETEUIL (Rogcer)

The son of Willelm FitzOsbern, he succeeded to his father's English lands and was made Earl of Hereford in 1071. His father had probably been Earl of Wessex, and he was disappointed to only be given Hereford. His sister *Ymme* married Earl Raulf of East Anglia and he took part in the revolt of 1075, losing his earldom and lands, and was imprisoned for life.

ROGER DE MONTGOMERIE (Rocger, DB Roger)

Roger was part of Willelm's inner circle, and had been with Willelm in the campaign at Domfront 1051/52. He was Viscount of Hiémois, and was left behind to assist *Mathild* in governing Normandy in 1066-67. After the Conquest, he was given the rape of Arundel in Sussex, and made Earl of Shrewsbury, possibly as early as May 1068. He would come to hold £2,078 of land in England. Roger died in 1094.

WILLELM FITZ OSBERN (Willelm, Wilhelm)

He was Willelm's steward, and part of his inner circle (his father had been one of Willelm's guardians). His brother was Osbeorn, a chaplain of Eadward III. Willelm was active in the campaign at Domfront 1051/52, was entrusted with the fortification of Breteuil in 1054/55, and was instrumental in persuading the Norman barons to support the invasion of England. He was appointed Earl of Wessex and Hereford in 1067 in succession to Harold and was regent of England with Bishop Odo in 1067-68. The English revolt at Exeter was put down by him in 1069 after he had helped suppress the northern revolt under Eadgar earlier in the year. Willelm was killed invading Flanders in support of the claimant to the County, Arnulf, on 22nd February 1071. He held £1,750 of land in England after the Conquest.

BISHOPS

HERFAST (Arfast, Erfast, DB Arfast, Erfast, Eruast, Ærefast)

Bishop of Elmham

Herfast was a chaplain of Willelm who was appointed chancellor in England shortly after December 1067, and was made Bishop of Elmham in 1070. His successor as chancellor was Osmund, under whom writs were to be written in Latin rather than English. Herfast moved his see to Thetford in 1075 and died in 1085.

LANFRANC (Landfranc, DB Lanfranc)

Archbishop of Canterbury

Lanfranc was an Italian, born c1007, who had been renowned for his teaching in Italy and at Avranches, becoming Prior of Le Bec c1044, and Abbot of Caen in 1063. He had been estranged from Willelm by supporting the Papal opposition to his marriage, but they were reconciled by Willelm FitzOsbern. He was appointed to Canterbury in 1070, and was part of Willelm's inner circle. Appointed to the commission enquiring into the conduct of sheriffs in 1076/77, he also acted at times as regent during Willelm's absences from England.

REMIGIUS (DB Remigius)

Bishop of Dorchester

A monk from Fécamp, he had contributed ships to the invasion in 1066 and was made Bishop of Dorchester in 1067, being consecrated by Archbishop Stigand. His appointment was queried in 1072 by the Pope on grounds of simony and his consecration by Stigand, but he was defended by Lanfranc. Remigius moved the see to Lincoln in 1072, and established territorial archdeaconries in his geographically large diocese. He died in 1092.

STIGAND

Bishop of Selsey

Appointed in 1072, he transferred the cathedral to Chichester in 1075 and died in 1087.

THOMAS (Thomas, DB Thomas)

Archbishop of York

Thomas, the son of Osbert, was educated at Liege and became a canon at Bayeux, before being made Archbishop of York in 1069. His brother Samson would become Bishop of Worcester in 1096. He objected to making a written submission of York to the primacy of Canterbury but was forced to give way on this. Thomas attempted to have this reversed by the Pope and laid claim to the inclusion in his province of Lichfield, Dorchester and Worcester but this was refused in 1072. His primacy over the Scottish sees was recognised and he consecrated a Bishop of Orkney in 1073, although this primacy would be difficult to enforce. The chapter of York was reorganised and he established prebends for the canons to replace their communal rule. Territorial archdeacons were also established. He died in 1100.

WALCELIN (DB Walchelin)

Bishop of Winchester

A secular canon at Rouen, he was appointed in 1070, and at first wanted to abolish the monastic cathedral chapter soon but changed his mind. He acted as regent of England for Willelm II in 1097, and died in 1098.

WALCHER (DB Walcher)

Bishop of Durham

He was from Lotharingia and was appointed in 1071. He acted as Earl of Northumberland from 1075, but was killed in 1080 during a dispute involving his deputy in the earldom. Walcher was on good terms with Earl Walþeof and fostered the monastic revival in Northumbria.

ABBOTS

ADELELM

Abbot of Abingdon
Appointed in 1071, Adelelm was a monk of Jumieges, and died in 1083. Although his name could have been English, it is as likely to have been continental. He apparently refused to honour the feast days of Saints Æþelwold and Eadmund at Abingdon because he considered them to be mere English rustics (Loyn 1994: 96).

BENEDICT (DB Benedict)

Abbot of Selby
Benedict was the Sacrist of Auxerre and was made the first Abbot of Selby in 1069/70. He retired in 1096/97, joining the community at Rochester.

EULALIA

Abbess of Shaftesbury
She was appointed in 1074 and died some time after 1106.

FREDERIC

Abbot of St Alban's
Later tradition reported that Frederic was German. He was abbot by 1072 and died some time before 1077.

GALAND

Abbot of Winchcombe
Galand was one of Willelm's first appointments in 1066/67 and came from either Chertsey or, more likely, Cerisy. He died in 1075.

GOISFRIÐ

Abbot of Westminster
He was appointed probably in 1072 and died in 1076.

RIWALLON

Abbot of New Minster
He was Abbot of New Minster from 1072 to 1088.

RODBERT BLANCHARD

Abbot of Battle
The abbey of Battle was founded on the site of the Battle of Hastings. Rodbert was appointed as its first abbot in 1067 but was drowned later the same year.

SCOLLAND

Abbot of St Augustine's
A monk of Mont St Michel, he was abbot 1070-1087.

SERLO

Abbot of Gloucester
Serlo had been a canon at Avranches and then a monk at Mont St Michel. He was appointed in 1072 at the suggestion of the Chancellor Osmund, and died in 1104.

ÞEODWINE

Abbot of Ely
He was a monk of Jumieges, appointed in 1073 and died in 1076.

ÞUROLD

Abbot of Malmesbury and Peterborough
Þurold was a monk of Fecamp, appointed to Malmesbury in 1066/67. His transfer to Peterborough in 1070, sparked off the revolt centred on Ely under Hereward. While at Peterborough, he reclaimed the relics of St Oswald from Ramsey. He died in 1098.

WARIN

Abbot of Malmesbury
Warin succeeded Þurold at Malmesbury in 1070 after being a monk at Lire. He died c1091.

OTHER IMPORTANT LANDOWNERS

COUNT ALAN THE RED (DB Alanus)

Alan was a Breton, the son of Count Eudo of Ponthièvre, and nephew of Willelm's guardian Count Goisfriδ of Brittany. He was part of Willelm's inner circle, and was given the honour of Richmond in Yorkshire among other lands, holding £1,120 in all. He died c1093.

COUNT BRIAN (Breon, Brien, Brient, DB Brien)

Brian was the brother of Count Alan and son of Count Eudo of Ponthièvre. He held some sort of command in the south west and helped to repel the attack of Harold's sons from Ireland in 1069. He also helped to put down the revolt at Exeter later in the year. Brian disappeared from the historical record after this.

COUNT EUSTATIUS (Eustatius, DB Eustachius)

Count of Boulogne, he held £915 in England. He had married Eadward III's sister *Godgyfu*, probably in 1036. She was dead by 1049. It is possible that they had a daughter, who in turn had a son approaching adulthood in 1066 (Barlow 1970: 307-308). Eustatius had visited England in 1051, and a violent confrontation between his men and the citizens of Dover had sparked off the crisis that resulted in the exile of Earl Godwine and his family. One of his sons was a hostage of Willelm and Eustatius participated fully in the Battle of Hastings. In 1067, rebels in Dover called upon him for help and he took over the town only to be forced out by troops loyal to Willelm, leaving his grandson as a prisoner of Willelm. It has been suggested that his attack on Dover was his own initiative and not part of an English revolt. He was later reconciled with Willelm and, although he held lands in England, he seems to have spent most of his time in Boulogne.

GOISFRIÐ DE MANDEVILLE (Gosfregð, DB Goisfrid)

Goisfrið was given the lands of Constable Esgar, and made Portreeve of London and Sheriff of Middlesex. He was later also Sheriff of Essex. His English lands amounted to £740. The Mandevilles were later Earls of Essex.

BISHOP GOISFRIÐ (Gosfred, Goisfridus, Goisfredus, DB Goisfridus)

A member of the Mowbray (de Montbrai) family and Bishop of Coutances since 1049, he assisted Archbishop Ealdred at Willelm's coronation. He may have been Portreeve of Bristol and put down a revolt at Montacute in Dorset in 1069, as well as helping to lead the King's forces against the revolt of Earl Raulf in 1075. On a number of occasions he acted as a justice overseeing important legal cases. He was given £788 of land in England by Willelm. Goisfrið died in 1093, having supported Rodbert against Willelm II after the death of the Willelm I.

HENRI DE BEAUMONT

The son of Roger de Beaumont, Henri assisted *Mathild* in ruling Normandy in 1066-67 while Willelm was in England, but was entrusted with the castle at Warwick in 1068. He would later be made Earl of Warwick.

HUGO DE GRANDMESNIL (DB Hugo)

He was given the castle of Winchester and was left in England to help the regents Willelm and Oda in 1067, but eventually returned to Normandy. However, he did later come back to England and received new lands in the midlands.

HUGO DE MONTFORT (DB Hugo)

The son of Hugo, he was Constable of Normandy and was entrusted with the castle at Dover. He fought at Mortemer in 1054 and at Hastings, being left in England to help the regents Willelm and Oda in 1067.

RAULF DE TOSNI (DB Radulfus)

Ranulf was the son of Roger. He helped to defend Normandy against France in 1054 and was present at the Battle of Hastings.

RODBERT DE BEAUMONT (DB Rogerius)

He was the brother of Henri de Beaumont, and was present with Willelm at the Battle of Hastings. Rodbert later became Count of Meulan and Earl of Leicester.

WALTER GIFFARD (DB Walterius)

Walter fought in defence of Normandy at the Battle of Mortemer in 1054. He became Earl of Buckingham under Willelm II and died in 1102, being buried in Normandy.

WILLELM DE BRIOUZE

Willelm was given the rape of Bramber in Sussex.

WILLELM DE WARENNE (DB Willelm)

He was part of Willelm's inner circle, and fought in defence of Normandy in 1054. Willelm was given the rape of Lewes in Sussex, and he helped to put down the revolt of Earl Raulf in 1075. He established the first Cluniac Priory in England at Lewes in 1078/80. His lands in England were worth £1,140 by 1086. Willelm served as regent in the King's absences from England and would later be made Earl of Surrey.

SHERIFFS

FROGER (DB Froger)

He was probably appointed to Berkshire soon after 1066 but replaced by c1071.

HUGO DE PORT (DB Hugo)

Hugo was a vassal of Bishop Odo. He may have been Sheriff of Kent by 1070 and was probably also appointed later to Hampshire. Hugo retired to become a monk in 1096 at Gloucester.

HUGO FITZBALDRIC (DB Hugo)

He was made Sheriff of York in 1069 and may also have been appointed to Nottingham. He helped the monk Benedict found a new monastery at Selby.

ILBERT

Sheriff of Hertford in 1072/75.

PICOT (DB Picot)

He was Sheriff of Cambridge from c1071 to after 1086.

RODBERT D'OILLY (Rodbeard, DB Robert)

Rodbert was appointed to Oxford c1071 and also Warwick. He married *Ealdgyð*, the daughter of Wigod of Wallingford.

ROGER BIGOD (DB Roger)

Roger was Sheriff of Suffolk in 1072/75 and possibly of Norfolk by 1069.

ROGER DE PÎTRES (DB Roger)

He was made Sheriff of Gloucester by c1071.

URSE D'ABETOT (Urs, DB Urso)

Urse was appointed to Worcester by 1069, and died in 1108.

WILLELM DE VAUVILLE

He was castellan of Exeter and Sheriff of Devon by 1069. Willelm helped to repel the attack by Harold's sons in 1069.

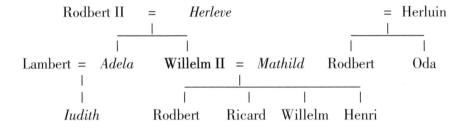

Fig. 9: The immediate family of Duke Willelm II

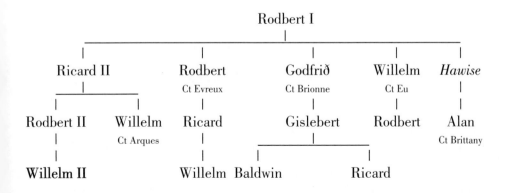

Fig 10: Duke Willelm II's cousins

APPENDIX 6

FOREIGN RULERS IN 1066

England was not an isolated state in 1066. It was a full part of the community of nations that made up European Christendom. It obviously shared the British Isles with a group of predominantly Celtic kingdoms, and its recent history was intimately bound up with that of Scandinavia. Relations across the English Channel with France and Germany (especially those parts facing England like Flanders, Normandy and Brittany) were strong in areas such as politics, learning and art, religion and economics. The legal code IV Æþelred (c2) provides a list of foreign peoples trading with London, which includes men from France (Rouen in Normandy, Flanders, Ponthieu), Lotharingia (Huy, Liege, Nivelles), and Germany. Archaeology provides evidence from a number of towns for the importing of Rhenish quernstones, honestones from Norway, silk and wine (Vince 1990: 96-103, Richards 1991:89-90). English prelates would also attend church councils in Rome (the pilgrims' route to that city had been well trodden by many English men and women before 1066). Diplomatic relations were also maintained with Hungary, the place of exile for Prince Eadgar's family before 1057. Norman rule after 1066 could not fail to lead to contacts with the other area of Norman adventure in Europe, southern Italy. English participation in the First Crusade, 30 years after Hastings, would bring Englishmen into contact with much of the eastern Mediterranean world. Some had already made their way to Byzantium as exiles after the Norman Conquest of England. Other exiles would find their way to Scandinavia and Russia.

The world of European Christendom lay between the Urals and Atlantic. It was bounded to the east by the Turkic peoples of central Asia and to the south by the Moslem Arabs and Berbers. The Moslems held most of Iberia, Sicily and the Holy Land. The latter half of the 11th century saw the beginnings of Christian advance against them with the invasion of Sicily in 1060, the Conquest of northern Toledo in 1061 and the First Crusade in 1096. Europe was on the verge of a period of expansion and self-confidence that would transform the medieval world.

The political and cultural geography of Europe is divided here into well-defined blocks for ease of reference. However, these are not hard and fast divisions and are merely done for convenience. The major kingdoms and some vassal states are included. In some parts of Europe the development of states was not yet far advanced, e.g. the still heathen Baltic states or the Turkic Pechenegs in southern Ukraine. In other parts, the smaller states were of only local importance and unable to play any significant military or political role, e.g. the Duchy of Naples. Names of rulers are given in their usual modern form.

The natural starting point for reading about Europe during this period is Previté-Orton 1953, and the longer *Cambridge Medieval History* in 8 volumes (although the latter is now very dated). Good shorter introductions are Davis 1988 and Bartlett 1993.

NORTHERN BRITAIN

The north of Britain was a patchwork of different regions with their own ethnic identities and environmental characteristics. In the south east was the English-speaking area of Lothian. This was the northern part of Northumbria, ceded to the Scots in the 10th century and long regarded as nominally part of England. The south west had been the independent, Cumbrian-speaking, kingdom of Strathclyde until the early 11th century. Within this, lay the mixed Gaelic and Norse region of Galloway. To the north was the original kingdom of the Scots, a union of Gaelic Argyll and the Pictish east (known as Alba). This was an area of semi-independent provinces ruled by officers styled *mormaers*. The task of welding these areas into one kingdom was still to be accomplished and was to be the work of Mælcolm III and his sons. The most independent of the provinces was Moray until 1130, whose rulers were descended from Macbeth's stepson Lulach. Caithness, Orkney, Shetland and the Hebrides had been settled by the Vikings and were ruled by the Norse Earls of Orkney. The Hebrides and Isle of Man had a Gaelic population with Norse rulers, but the far north was by the 11th century wholly Norse. It would be over 400 years before all these areas were incorporated into Scotland. The Isle of Man was disputed between Dublin and Orkney but was becoming independent in its own right at this time. An account of Scotland at this period can be found in Barrow 1981, while Viking Scotland is covered in Pálsson & Edwards 1978, and Crawford 1987. The Isle of Man is dealt with by Kinvig 1975.

Isle of Man

KING GODRED SIGTRYGSON 1064-1070/75

Godred may have succeeded Echmarcach (see Dublin) and kept Man independent of Dublin and Orkney until his death. The history of Man at this time is poorly known and he is often confused with his namesake and successor, Godred Crovan who founded the later ruling dynasty of Man.

Orkney

EARLS PAUL AND ERLEND 1064-1098

The sons of Earl Þorfinn, they ruled an area that included the Hebrides as well as Orkney, Shetland and Caithness. Orkney and Shetland were held under the King of Norway, and Caithness nominally under the King of Scots. Both Earls took part in the invasion of England in 1066 by Haraldr of Norway and in his defeat at Stamford Bridge. They were deposed and imprisoned in 1098 by Magnus III of Norway.

Scotland

KING MALCOLM III 1054-1093

The son of King Duncan; Malcolm was placed on the throne by the English Earl Siward of Northumbria who invaded Scotland and defeated Macbeth in 1054. Macbeth, and then his stepson Lulach, held out in the north until 1058 (Lulach's son Máel Snechta ruled Moray from 1058 to 1085). He married *Ingebiorg*, widow of Earl Þorfinn of Orkney in 1065. His relations with Northumbria were generally peaceful before 1066. Only in Tostig's absence abroad did he launch a raid into England in 1061. He sheltered Tostig in 1066 after his ejection from Northumbria and allowed him to team up with Harold of Norway for the invasion of England that ended at Stamford Bridge. When Eadgar fled England in 1068, he also found shelter in Scotland and his sister *Margareta* was married to Malcolm shortly thereafter. This opened up Scotland to English influences and personnel. *Margareta's* influence was particularly strong in the church. It also meant that Malcolm had to face the hostility of Willelm I. He raided England again in 1070, which brought Willelm to Scotland with his army in 1072 and Malcolm was forced to submit to Willelm's overlordship. Further raids on England followed in 1079, 1091 (with Eadgar again) and 1093 (after losing Cumbria to Willelm II the year before). It was on the last that he was killed near Alnwick. A number of English exiles from the Normans made their homes in Scotland, including Earl Gospatric whose family became Earls of Dunbar.

WALES

The kingdoms of the Welsh were seldom united and competing dynasties were often in conflict. Gruffydd ap Llewelyn of Gwynedd had succeeded in uniting all of Wales in 1055 and was a potent ally of the English Earl Ælfgar. After Ælfgar's death, his opponents Earl Harold and Earl Tostig mounted a successful invasion by land and sea, which led to Gruffydd's death at the hands of his own men. Wales immediately split into four kingdoms and the traditional conflict between dynasties was resumed. The most detailed account of medieval Welsh history is that of Lloyd 1912. More modern accounts can be found in Davies 1982 and Davies 1987.

Deheubarth

KING MAREDUDD 1063-1072

The son of Owain and nephew of King Hywel (died 1044), he was killed fighting Caradoc of Gwynllwg. Deheubarth covered Wales south of the Severn, and was centred on the River Tywi in Dyfed.

Gwent and Gwynllwg

KING CARADOC 1063-1081

The son of Gruffydd, he lost most of Gwent to the Norman Earl of Hereford, keeping hold only of Gwynllwg (west of Newport). However, he added Morgannwg to this in 1072. He was heavily involved in the various wars of the Welsh Kings, being successful in battle against Maredudd of Deheubarth in 1072 and his successor Rhys in 1078. He himself was killed fighting again with Deheubarth in 1081.

Gwynedd and Powys

KING BLEDDYN 1063-1075

He was the son of Cynfyn and half-brother of King Gruffydd. His younger brother Rhiwallon was associated with him as King 1063-70 (killed fighting off an attack on Gwynedd by the sons of Gruffydd). Bleddyn himself was killed fighting Rhys of Deheubarth.

Morgannwg

KING CADWGAN 1063-1072

He was the son of Meurig of Morgannwg and had ruled Gwent under his father from 1043 to 1055.

IRELAND

Ireland was divided into a great many competing dynasties. These were organised on a hierarchical basis with the small local kingdoms being grouped into larger provincial kingdoms. The title High King of Ireland conferred prestige and some limited power over other Kings and had been fought over by the two branches of the Uí Néill (Kings of Ailech and Mide) until Brian Bóruma of Mumu broke their stranglehold in 1002. Few High Kings were able to fully establish their authority and Kings after Brian were often styled as High Kings with opposition. King Diarmit of Leinster was the most powerful of the Kings in 1066 but could not establish his claim as High King. Introductions to 11th century Irish history can be found in Ó Corráin 1972, Byrne 1973, Moody et al 1984, Ó Cróinín 1995 and Duffy 1997.

Ailech

KING ÁED UA HUALGAIRG 1064-1067

Ailech covered the area of modern Ulster west of Lough Neagh and was centred on Tyrone and the important religious site of Armagh.

Connachta (Connaught)

KING ÁED IN GAÍ BERNAIG 1046-1067

He was of the Ua Conchobair, the son of King Tadg (1010-30), and succeeded Art Uallach. He was an ally of Diarmait of Leinster. Áed was killed fighting one of his under-kings, Art of Breifne (the son of his predecessor) who supplanted him on the throne.

Dublin

KING MURCHAD 1052-1070

He was the son of King Diarmait of Leinster and replaced the Norse descended Echmarcach, son of Ragnall who continued to rule the Isle of Man until 1064.

Laigin (Leinster)

KING DIARMAIT 1042-1072

Diarmait belonged to the Uí Chennselaig, and was the son of Donnchad Máel na mBó. He succeeded Murchad of the Uí Dúnlainge in Leinster, and controlled the Viking port of Wexford, which had trading links with Bristol. The sons of King Harold II found shelter and help in Leinster after 1066, as had Earl Ælfgar 11 years earlier. He fought for the High Kingship throughout his reign but without complete success, although he did establish his son Murchad as King in Dublin and overthrow his rival Donnchad of Munster. Diarmait was killed attacking his longstanding enemy, Conchobar of Meath.

Mide (Meath)

KING CONCHOBAR 1030-1073

He was of the Ua Máelsechlainn and successfully resisted attempts to reduce Meath to be subordinate to Leinster. Meath included the important site of Tara, connected with the High Kingship of Ireland but was no longer large enough to play a dominant role in Irish politics.

Mumu (Munster)

KING TAIRRDELBACH 1063-1086

He belonged to the Dál Cais, and was the son of Tadg and grandson of Brian Bóruma. With the help of Diarmait of Leinster, he overthrew his uncle Donnchad after a long campaign. After Diarmait's death, he succeeded in establishing his own supremacy over most of Ireland.

Osraige (Ossory)

KING DOMNALL 1055-1072

Domnall was of the Ui Dúnlainge, and succeeded his father Gilla Pátraic. Osraige was a small buffer state between Mumu and Laigin, covering roughly the area of the later County Kilkenny.

Ulaid (Ulster)

KING CÚ ULAD UA FLAITHRÍ 1065-1071

He was of the Dál Fiatach, but his parentage is unknown. Cú succeeded Donnchad but was deposed in 1071 and died the following year. Ulaid covered only the east of modern Ulster (Counties Antrim and Down).

SCANDINAVIA

The three parts of Scandinavia slowly achieved a sense of statehood under separate dynasties from the 10th century. Denmark was united c950, and under Sveinn I and Knutr, the Danes conquered England in a campaign lasting from 1013-1016. Norway was disputed between the native dynasty of Vestfold and the Danish Kings. Knutr of Denmark had ruled Norway from 1028 to his death in 1035. Sweden was united around the area of Uppsala and tended to look eastwards to Russia. Norse colonies abroad included the Earldom of Orkney, various towns in Ireland (chiefly Dublin), the islands of the Faroes, Iceland and Greenland. The best introduction to the development of Scandinavia during the age of the Vikings is Jones 1984. Other works of interest are Byock 1988 and Sawyer 1993.

Denmark

KING SVEINN II 1046-1074

He was the grandson of King Sveinn I, and was regent of Denmark on the death of his cousin Harðacnut in 1042, when the crown went by treaty to Magnus of Norway. As Harðacnut was also King of England, Sveinn had ambitions there and later claimed that Eadward had agreed to make Sveinn his heir. He rebelled against Magnus and spent the next four years struggling to establish himself in Denmark. Only on the death of Magnus in 1046 was he successful. A series of wars with Haraldr of Norway then followed until peace was agreed in 1064. Sveinn could then turn his attention to his claim to England. A fleet was sent in 1069-70, which linked up with Eadgar II in opposition to Willelm I but achieved little.

Iceland

Iceland had been settled between 870 and 930 by Norse families from Norway and the British Isles. The great bulk of the people came from south west Norway but there were also Irish servants and slaves among the early settlers. A constitution had been agreed c930 whereby an assembly would meet every year. This assembly was dominated of the *goðar*, the priest-chieftains (48 by 1066), who formed the island's aristocracy. The *goðar* also appointed the judges of the local and national courts, and administered their own local assemblies. The highest official of the state was the Lawspeaker, who was elected by the national assembly for a three year, renewable term. The Lawspeaker did not rule the country but was the guardian of its laws and could exercise influence. The Lawspeaker from 1063 to 1066 was Gunnarr. He was succeeded by Kolbeinn 1066-71.

Norway

KING HARALDR III 1046-1066

Haraldr was the half-brother of King Olaf and had fled Norway when the latter had been killed in 1030 trying to reverse the Danish conquest of Cnut. He first went to Russia and then on to Constantinople where he joined the Varangian guard of the Byzantine Emperors. His service there included campaigning in Sicily and Palestine. By 1046, he had returned to Norway and successfully claimed a half-share in the kingship from his nephew Magnus who died the following year, allowing Haraldr to succeed to the whole. Magnus had also ruled Denmark and Haraldr spent many years fighting its new King Sveinn. A peace treaty was concluded in 1064 and Harald's next adventure was to mount an invasion of England. Haraldr was pursuing a claim by Magnus through his treaty with Harðacnut who had died in 1042. He allied himself with Earl Tostig, King Harold II's brother, but was beaten and killed at the Battle of Stamford Bridge on 25th September 1066.

King Olafr III 1066-1093

Olafr was the son of Haraldr III, and was known as Olafr Kyrre (the peaceful) for not engaging in foreign wars and successfully keeping the peace within Norway. He had married *Ingrid*, the daughter of Sveinn of Denmark. When his brother-in-law Knutr of Denmark was preparing to invade England in 1085, Olafr contributed ships to his fleet. He was co-ruler with his brother Magnus II until the latter's death in 1069.

Sweden

King Stenkil 1060-1066

The son in law of King Emund, coming originally from Gotland, he was elected King in 1060. Although a Christian, Stenkil was either tolerant towards, or could not overcome, the strong heathen community centred on Uppsala.

King Inge 1066-1112

The history of Sweden at this time is poorly known. Inge was the son of Stenkil and may have been co-ruler with his brother Halsten, deposed in 1070. Attempts were made to depose Inge also in 1070 by Hakon and later by Svein at the head of the heathen faction.

GERMANY

Germany was the eastern part of the old Frankish state. The last attempt at Frankish unity had ended in 887 and since 916, Germany had been under the Saxon dynasty founded by Henry I. Italy was taken over by them in 965. Otto I had revived the Holy Roman Empire in 962 and henceforth the Kings of Germany were elevated to the Imperial throne upon coronation at Rome. The crown had passed to the Franconian house in 1024, which added the Slav area of Lausitz (1031) and the kingdom of Burgundy to the Empire (1032). A source of weakness was the division of Germany into large tribal duchies, whose dukes often challenged the power of the crown. Only Franconia was usually without a Duke, being held directly by the crown. Good introductions to German history of the period are Fuhrmann 1986 and Haverkamp 1988, while the classic study is that of Barraclough 1947.

Holy Roman Empire

Emperor Henry IV 1056-1105

Henry was born in 1050, the son of Emperor Henry III and was associated as King of Germany with his father in 1054. His first regent was his mother *Agnes* but she was displaced in 1062 by Archbishop Anno of Köln, who was in turn replaced by Archbishop Adalbert of Bremen in 1064. Henry was declared of age early in 1065.

He clashed with Pope Gregory VII in 1075 over the Pope's decree against the investiture of bishops by lay rulers. They both declared each other deposed and Henry had to face a rival anti-King Rudolf, elected by his enemies and supported by the Papacy. Rudolf was killed in 1080 and Henry took over Rome in 1083, being crowned Emperor the following year by his own anti-Pope Clement III (he had styled himself King of the Romans since his accession). He remained unreconciled to the Papacy and was declared deposed by his son Henry V in 1105, and died in 1106.

Bavaria

DUKE OTTO II 1061-1070

From Nordheim in Saxony, he was appointed by *Agnes* but supported Archbishop Anno in 1062 when he deposed her as guardian of the King. Henry IV deposed him in 1070 and he rebelled against the King in 1073, and later supported Rudolf as anti-King against Henry. Otto died in 1083.

Carinthia

DUKE BERHTOLD 1061-1078

He was from Zähringen in Swabia. Berhtold supported Rudolf against Henry in 1077 and was deposed the following year.

Lower Lorraine

DUKE GODFREY II 1056-1069

Godfrey was the son of Duke Gozelo of Upper Lorraine. He had been co-Duke of Upper Lorraine in 1040 and succeeded his father as sole Duke in 1044. Claiming Lower Lorraine also, he came into conflict with Emperor Henry III and was deposed in 1047. Reconciliation came after Henry's death and *Agnes* appointed him Duke in 1056. He had married *Beatrice* of Tuscany in 1054 and become Margrave in Italy, with his brother becoming Pope Stephen IX in 1057-1058. His Italian position made him an important power and he supported Archbishop Anno against *Agnes* in 1062.

Upper Lorraine

DUKE GERHARD 1048-1070

Gerhard was the brother of his predecessor Duke Adalbert.

Saxony

DUKE ORDULF 1059-1071

He succeeded his father Duke Bernhard and belonged to the powerful Billung family.

Swabia

DUKE RUDOLF 1057-1079

Rudolf was from Rheinfelden in Burgundy, and was appointed Duke by the regent *Agnes*, as well as being made governor of Burgundy. He was elected anti-King in 1077 as the brother in law of Henry IV. The attempt to replace Henry failed and he was replaced in Swabia in 1079, and died in 1080.

FRANCE

France was the western part of the old Frankish state. Its last union with Germany had ended in 887 and the throne had come to be disputed between two separate royal houses. The Capetians finally secured the crown in 987 but were left only as overlords of powerful vassals, with a secure territory of their own based on a small area around Paris and Orleans. Ethnically France was divided into two Romance speaking areas, the northern Langue d'Oil and the southern Langue d'Oc (Aquitaine, Toulouse, Barcelona). There were also minorities of Celtic speakers (Brittany), Flemings (Flanders) and Basques (Gascony). Good introductions to France at this time include Fawtier 1960 and Duby 1991.

France

KING PHILIP I 1060-1108

Philip was the son of King Henry I, born in 1052 and associated in the kingship in 1059. The regent during his youth (to 1067) was his uncle Baldwin of Flanders. His father had used a policy of exploiting the divisions of his vassals to increase his power and Philip was to continue this when he came to power. He abducted and married bigamously, *Bertrada*, the wife of the Count of Anjou in 1092. For this, he was excommunicated and relations with the Papacy were further tarnished by his refusal to follow church reform and give up his rights to appoint bishops.

Aquitaine

DUKE WILLIAM VIII 1058-1086

He was the brother of Duke William VII. Aquitaine was a strong state that had recently (1039) been combined with the Duchy of Gascony.

Brittany

DUKE CONAN II 1040-1066

The son of Duke Alan III, he succeeded when young, effectively ruling since 1057. He struggled to assert his authority over an unruly nobility, and was at war with Normandy in 1064 and Anjou in 1065-66.

DUKE HOEL 1066-1084

Hoel was the son in law of Duke Conan II and Count of Cornouailles.

Burgundy

DUKE ROBERT II 1031-1075

He was the son of King Robert II of France. Robert had only a weak authority over his vassals.

Normandy

DUKE WILLIAM II 1035-1087

see above

Anjou

COUNT GEOFFREY III 1060-1069

Geoffrey was born in 1040, the nephew of Count Geoffrey II. He was deposed, and died in 1098.

Barcelona

COUNT RAMON BERENGAR I 1035-1076

The son of Berengar Ramon, he had lands north as well as south of the Pyrenees. His son would capture Tarragona from the Moslems in 1091.

Flanders

COUNT BALDWIN V 1035-1067

He was the son of Count Baldwin IV, and regent of France since 1060. A long-standing enemy of England, although his sister was the wife of Earl Tostig, he sheltered many exiles from there (Eadward III had blockaded the Flemish coast in support of the Emperor Henry III). Baldwin was father in law of Willelm II of Normandy. His wife *Adela* was the daughter of King Robert of France, which made Baldwin the uncle in law of Philip I. He sought to increase Flemish lands to the east in opposition to the Emperor and he established his sons as rulers of Hainault and Friesland. Flanders was a strongly centralised state with a wealthy urban merchant class and was actively reclaiming fertile land from the sea.

ITALY

The north of Italy formed the kingdom of Italy whose ruler was also King of Germany and Holy Roman Emperor. The south had been divided among Lombard states of Capua, Benevento and Salerno, the Byzantine provinces of Apulia and Calabria, and the city states of Naples, Gaeta and Amalfi. Between the two were the Papal States. The Western Empire and Byzantium were struggling for mastery over the area and in 1017 Norman troops arrived to take part in the fighting. Their military prowess won them lands and titles; the County of Aversa in 1030 and County of Apulia in 1042. The Count of Aversa became Prince of Capua in 1058, and the Count of Apulia was raised to a Duke in 1059. More details about the Normans in Italy can be found in Norwich 1967, Douglas 1969 and Matthew 1992. Accounts of the 11th century Papacy can be found in Daniel-Rops 1957, Ullmann 1972 and Morris 1989.

Papacy

POPE ALEXANDER II 1061-1073

Anselm of Lucca. He was a leading reformer whose chief minister was the radical Cardinal Hildebrand. The reform process was begun by Pope Leo IX in 1049 who began to travel outside Rome exercising direct authority over the church by holding councils and appointing legates. His aim had been to eliminate simony, and interference in church affairs by laymen, and to enforce clerical celibacy. One result of this was the permanent schism with the Orthodox church in Byzantium in 1054. Another was a quarrel with the Emperor over the right of the right of rulers to control episcopal appointments. Alexander's own appointment was opposed by the Empire and a rival anti-Pope was set up, Honorius II. His position was affirmed in 1064 but Honorius remained free and based at his own diocese at Parma until his death in 1072. To further reform, he gave a Papal banner to Duke Willelm II of Normandy to use in his invasion of England (continuing the Papal policy of support for the Normans, so far followed in Italy).

Apulia

DUKE ROBERT I (GUISCARD) 1059-1085

Son of Tancred of Hauteville in Normandy and half-brother of the first three Counts of Apulia. He came to Italy in 1046 and succeeded as Count in 1057. In return for providing military help to the reform faction in the Papacy, he was enfeoffed by Pope Nicholas as Duke of Apulia, Calabria and Sicily in 1059. He completed the Conquest of the Byzantine provinces by taking Reggio in 1060 and Bari in 1071, and took over the Lombard state of Salerno in 1077. Robert's brother Roger conquered Moslem Sicily on his behalf in 1061-91. His ambition took him further, to the Balkans in 1081-85 to campaign against the Byzantine Empire and although he had initial success, this was eventually a failure.

Capua

PRINCE RICHARD I 1049-1078

Richard was the son of Asclettin of Normandy and nephew of Count Rainulf I of Aversa. He arrived in Italy in 1046 and took full part in the unrest of the time before being imprisoned by Drogo of Apulia. His freedom came in 1048 when the Prince of Salerno brought about his appointment as regent of Aversa for his young cousin, Herman. The following year Richard himself became Count. He took part with Apulia in the defeat of Papal forces at Civitate in 1053. Richard invaded and took the Principality of Capua in 1058 and the following year helped the reform party of the Papacy overthrow Pope Benedict X and was formally recognised as Prince of Capua by the new Pope Nicholas. Military help was also given to Pope Alexander II in his struggle against the Imperial nominee Honorius II in 1061. However in 1066 he marched against Rome and had to be beaten off by Papal forces. Relations with Apulia were generally peaceful, except for a period between 1072 and 1076. He died while besieging Naples in 1078.

IBERIA

Most of Iberia had been taken over by Moslem invaders in the 8th century. The Moslem Caliphate reached its peak under the chief minister Al Mansur (978-1002). The Caliphate itself was abolished in 1031 and the Moslems split into rival kingdoms (Toledo, Saragossa, Badajoz, Valencia, Seville, Granada, Murcia). Christian states were limited to the northern coast and Pyrenees. The kingdom of Asturias was created out of the wreckage of Gothic Spain, maintaining its independence against the Moors. By the 10th century, it had been joined by the kingdom of Pamplona to the east. Sancho III of Pamplona divided his kingdom into three for his sons in 1035, creating Castile and Aragon alongside Pamplona. Castile was combined with Asturias in 1037 by Ferdinand, who conquered northern Toledo (1062) and northern Portugal (1057-64) from the Moslems. This new state was in turn divided on his death in 1065 into Castile, Leon (Asturias), and Galicia. In the far east, Barcelona was a County under the King of France. Those wishing to read more about Spain at this time could begin with MacKay 1977, Reilly 1992 and Reilly 1993.

Aragon

KING SANCHO I 1063-1094

He was the son of King Ramiro I and grandson of Sancho III of Pamplona. Sancho took over Pamplona in 1076, having already expanded his territory by the capture of Barbastro from the Moslems in 1065. He helped Castile conquer Toledo in 1085, and was himself making further advances against the Moslems of Saragossa when he was killed at the siege of Huesca.

Castile

KING SANCHO II 1065-1072

He was born c1038, son of King Ferdinand, and grandson of Sancho III of Pamplona. Sancho was murdered while besieging his sister *Urraca*.

Galicia

KING GARCIA 1065-1071

The son of King Ferdinand of Castile, he was deposed by his brother Sancho II of Castile and died in 1090.

Leon

KING ALFONSO VI 1065-1109

Alfonso was born 1040, a son of King Ferdinand of Castile, succeeding to Castile in 1072. He conquered Toledo from the Moors in 1085, and created the County of Portugal in 1097. Further advance southwards was blocked by the newly installed Almoravid dynasty after 1086. One of his nobles was Rodrigo Diaz, known as El Cid, who left Alfonso's service and eventually took Valencia from the Moslems in 1094.

Pamplona (Navarre)

KING SANCHO IV 1054-1076

The son of King Garcia III and grandson of Sancho III, he was deposed by Sancho of Aragon.

CENTRAL AND EASTERN EUROPE

This was an area of Slav and Magyar domination. Bohemia, Poland and Hungary were struggling to find unity and independence in the face of growing German power to the west. Croatia straddled east and west with its links to Byzantium. Russia had by now largely left its Scandinavian past behind. It was a weakened state, divided among many principalities. However, they were all united in their Orthodox religion, and so split from their Slav cousins to the west. More about Russia during this period can be found in Franklin and Shepard 1996, and Martin 1995. Croatia is covered by Guldescu 1964.

Bohemia

DUKE VRATISLAV II 1061-1092

Bohemia had been a vassal of Germany 950-1034 and since 1041. Vratislav was brother of Prince Spytihnev II, and was granted the title of King of Bohemia in 1085 by the Emperor. His alliance with Germany was a useful counter against Poland (Bohemia had lost Silesia to Poland in 1054).

Croatia

KING KRESIMIR IV 1058-1074/75

Croatia had been a kingdom since 988 and had recently incorporated the area of Slavonia. Kresimir was the son of Stjepan I. He secured his position as an Adriatic power by securing appointment as the representative of the Byzantine Emperor in Dalmatia in 1069.

Hungary

KING SALAMON 1063-1074

The Magyars had occupied Hungary from the east shortly before 900 and were troublesome nomad raiders of the west until their defeat by Germany in 955. Salamon was born in 1052, son of King Andras I, and he married Judith, daughter of Emperor

Henry III. He had succeeded his uncle Bela, who had deposed Andras I. Continued rivalry within the royal family led to his own deposition in 1074, and he died in 1087.

Poland

DUKE BOLESLAW II 1058-1079

Poland had become Christian in 967 and its dynasty had aimed to bring all the western Slavs under its leadership. After the death of Boleslaw I, Polish power was reduced and the authority of its rulers faded. Boleslaw II was born in 1039, the son of Duke Kazimiersz I who had recreated Poland as a western style state. Under Boleslaw II, Poland pursued an aggressive foreign policy against its neighbours in Germany, Bohemia and Russia. He took the title King of Poland in 1076, but was deposed in 1079 and died in 1081. He was a supporter of the Papacy against the Emperor in the investiture contest.

Russia

PRINCE IZYASLAV I 1054-1078

Viking rulers, known as Rus, had been established in the eastern Slav lands since the early 9th century, controlling the trade routes between Scandinavia and central Asia and Byzantium. They were consolidated into a single state in 882 and became Christians as part of the Orthodox church after 988. By this time, the links with Byzantium had become more important than with Scandinavia and the Viking character of the rulers was merged with that of their Slav subjects. However, some links with the north remained, and as late as 1041, a Swedish expedition came to Russia to fight against the Moslems near the mouth of the Volga. Izyaslav was the son of Prince Yaroslav I who was the last strong ruler of a united early medieval Russia. He faced opposition from other members of the ruling family who had divided the state among themselves. Izyaslav had control over the capital at Kiev. He was deposed in 1068-69 and 1073-77. An invasion of the steppes by the Cumans (Polovtsy) in 1068 prevented effective Russian control over the Black Sea coast.

SOUTH-EASTERN EUROPE

The major power in south eastern Europe was the Byzantine Empire, the lineal heir of ancient Rome, which had recently undergone a revival and was once more a great power. Over the last 100 years, it had accomplished the Conquest of Bulgaria, and spread Orthodox Christianity to Russia. The Empire was currently in the process of absorbing the divided Christian states of Armenia. However, the religious division between Rome and Constantinople, which had become an open breach in 1054, was a source of weakness, isolating Byzantium from the west. External threats included the growing power of Islamic Turks in Asia Minor, and attacks by Russians and

Pechenegs to the north in the 1040s. Good introductions to Byzantine history are Sewter 1966, Ostrogorsky 1968, Angold 1984 and Treadgold 1997. The Balkans in this period are covered by Fine 1981.

East Roman Empire (Byzantium)

EMPEROR CONSTANTINE X 1059-1067

The power of the Emperor was undermined by the intrigues and rivalries of civilian and military factions around the joint Empresses *Zoe* and *Theodora* from 1028 to 1056. Constantine had been chosen as successor by Isaac I and, although a soldier, followed the civilian faction at court. The Turks under Seljuk leadership would inflict a major defeat on the Empire in 1071 at the Battle of Manzikert. Byzantine lands in southern Italy were under threat from the Normans with few strongholds left by the end of Constantine's reign.

Duklja

KING MICHAEL 1046-1081/82

Later known as Zeta, the state of Duklja was centred on modern Montenegro. The son of Vojislav, Michael had ruled jointly with his brothers since 1043 but had become sole ruler with the title of King in 1046. Duklja had only recently secured its independence from Byzantium and he sought to enlarge its territory while helping rebels against the Empire. He turned to the west to buttress his position against Byzantium, becoming a Papal vassal in 1077.

Georgia

KING BAGRAT IV 1027-1072

Born in 1018, the son of King Girogi I, he was under the regency of his mother during his youth. His half-brother attempted to depose him from 1039 to 1041 but the most serious threat to his rule was from Girogi II in 1050-53, during which time Bagrat was in exile in Constantinople. Bagrat was eventually successful in subduing the nobility and increasing the power of the crown. However, Georgia was coming under pressure from the Seljuk Turks and from the 1060s there was a series of invasions and attacks that would force Bagrat's son and successor to pay tribute to the Seljuks.

References

EARLY SOURCES

Ab   Abingdon Abbey Chronicle (1154/64)
   Stevenson, J 1858 *Chronicon Monasterii de Abingdon* (Rolls Series)

AB   Adam of Bremen (1070s)
   Schmeidler, B 1917 *Magistri Adam Bremensis Gesta Hammaburgensis Ecclesiae Pontificum*
   Tschan, F J 1959 *History of the Archbishops of Hamburg-Bremen*

AL   Acts of Lanfranc (within the Anglo-Saxon Chronicle A)
   Earle, J & Plummer, C 1892-99 *Two of the Saxon Chronicles Parallel* 1: 287-292

AR   Ailred of Rievaulx – "De Genealogiae Regum Anglorum"
   Migne, J P 1844-64 "Ailred of Rievaulx: De Genealogiae Regum Anglorum", *Patrologia Latina* 195: 711-738

Æ   Life of Abbot Æþelwig (c1077, within the Evesham Abbey Chronicle)
   Macray, W D 1863 *Chronicon Abbatiae de Evesham ad annum 1418* (Rolls Series 83)

B   Bayeux Tapestry (1066/90)
   Bernstein, D J 1986 *The Mystery of the Bayeux Tapestry*
   Grape, W 1994 *The Bayeux Tapestry*

BT   Brut Chronicles of Wales (c1285)
   Jones, T 1952 *Brut y Tywysogyon: Peniarth Ms20 Version*
   Jones, T 1955 *Brut y Tywysogyon: Red Book of Hergest Version*
   Jones, T 1971 *Brenhinedd y Saesson*

Chr Anglo-Saxon Chronicles (versions A c1070, C 1046-66, D 1051-80, E 1121, F c1070)
   Thorpe, B 1861 *The Anglo-Saxon Chronicle* (Rolls Series 23, the only one to print all the versions in parallel)
   Plummer, C 1892-99 *Two of the Saxon Chronicles Parallel*
   Garmonsway, G N 1954 *The Anglo-Saxon Chronicle* (the main popular version)
   Whitelock, D 1961 *The Anglo-Saxon Chronicle*
   Swanton, M 1996 *The Anglo-Saxon Chronicles*
   Dumville, D 1995 *The Anglo-Saxon Chronicle, Volume 1: Ms F*

Bately, J 1986 *The Anglo-Saxon Chronicle, Volume 3: Ms A*

Taylor, S 1983 *The Anglo-Saxon Chronicle, Volume 4: Ms B*

Cubbin, G P 1996 *The Anglo-Saxon Chronicle, Volume 6: Ms D*

Cw Crowland Chronicle (a 15th century forgery purported to be by Ingulf)

Gransden, A 1982 *Historical Writing in England II: c1307 to the early sixteenth century*

D   Durham Chronicle (copy of the Anglo-Saxon Chronicle attributed to Simeon of Durham 1096/1119)

Arnold, T 1882 *Symeonis Monachi Opera Omnia* (Rolls Series)

DB Domesday Book (1086)

Morris, J (Gen. ed.) 1969-86 *The Domesday Book*

DM "Domesday Monachorum" (c1100, based on earlier information)

Douglas, D C 1944 *The Domesday Monachorum of Christchurch Canterbury*

E   Eadmer – "Historia Novorum" (1095-1123)

Bosanquet, G 1964 *Eadmer's History of Recent Events in England*

Rule, M 1884 *Eadmeri Historia Novorum in Anglia* (Rolls Series 81)

EE "Encomium Emmae" (1037/41)

Campbell, A 1949 *Encomium Emmae Reginae*

EG Eadmer's letter to Glastonbury (c1120)

Sharpe, R 1991 "Eadmer's letter to the monks of Glastonbury concerning St Dunstan's disputed remains", in Abrams, L & Carley, J P *The Archaeology and History of Glastonbury Abbey*

Ev Evesham Chronicle (including Life of Æþelwig) (1200/12)

Macray, W D 1863 *Chronicon Abbatiae de Evesham ad annum 1418* (Rolls Series 83)

Fl   John Flete – "History of Westminster Abbey" (1420/65)

Armitage Robinson, J 1909 *The History of Westminster Abbey by John Flete*

GA Guy of Amiens – "Carmen de Hastingae Proelio" (c1067)

Morton, C & Muntz, H 1972 *The Carmen de Hastingæ Proelio of Guy, Bishop of Amiens*

GG Geoffrey Gaimar – "L'Estoire des Engleis" (c1140)

Bell, A 1960 *Geoffrey Gaimar's L'Estoire des Engleis* (Anglo-Norman Text Society 14-16)

Duffus Hardy, T & Trice Martin, C 1888-89 *Lestoire des Engles solum la Translacion Maistre Geffrei Gaimar* (Rolls Series, 2 vols.)

GP William of Malmesbury – "Gesta Pontificum" (1124/25)

Hamilton, N E S A 1870 *De Gestis Pontificum Anglorum* (Rolls Series)

GW Life of Gisa of Wells (1066/88)

Hunter, J 1840 *Ecclesiastical Documents* (Camden Soc.)

H   Hyde Abbey – "Liber Vitae Hyda" (from 1031)

Birch, W de G 1892 *Liber Vitae: Register and Martyrology of New Minster and Hyde Abbey Winchester*

Hm Hemming's Cartulary (c1095)

Hearne, T 1723 *Hemingi Chartularium Ecclesiae Wigorniensis*

Thorn, C; Thorn, F; Whitelaw, E & Wood, S 1982 *Domesday Book, Vol. 16: Worcestershire*

HR   Hariulf of St Riquier
Lot, F 1894 *Chronique de l'abbaye de Saint-Riquier*

JF   John of Fordun – "Chronica Gentis Scotorum" (1363)
Skene, W F 1872 *John of Fordun's Chronicle of the Scottish Nation*

JO   St Benet's Chronicle – "Chronica de Johannes Oxenedes" (c1292)
Ellis, H 1859 *Chronica de Johannes Oxenedes* (Rolls Series)

LE   "Leges Edovardi Confessoris"
Wilkins, D 1721 *Leges Edovardi Confessoris*
Riley, H T 1853 *The Annals of Roger de Hoveden*
Liebermann, F 1896-1912 *Die Gesetze der Angelsachsen*

Lf   Life of Leofric of Exeter (c1072)
Chambers, R W, Forster, M & Flower, R 1933 *The Exeter Book of Old English Poetry*

LibE   Ely Chronicle – "Liber Eliensis" (1169/74)
Blake, E O 1962 *Liber Eliensis* (Camden Soc. 3rd series 92)

LM   Leofric Missal
Warren, F E 1883 *The Leofric Missal*

M   William of Malmesbury – "Gesta Regum Anglorum" (1124/25)
Stephenson, J 1854 *William of Malmesbury* (Church Historians of England)
Stubbs, W 1887-89 *Willelmi Malmesbiriensis Monachi de Gestis Regum Anglorum Libri Quinque* (Rolls Series 90) 2 vols
Mynors, R A B, Thomson, R M & Winterbottom, M 1998 *William of Malmesbury: Gesta Regum Anglorum, the History of the English Kings*

O   Orderic Vitalis – "Historia Ecclesiastica" (1114/15)
Chibnall, M 1969-80 *Orderic Vitalis: Historia Ecclesiastica Libri Tredecim*

Pb   Hugh Candidus – "Peterborough Chronicle" (c1175)
Mellows, W T 1949 *The Chronicle of Hugh Candidus*

Ra   Ramsey Chronicle (c1170)
Macray, W D 1886 *Chronicon Monasterii de Rameseia* (Rolls Series)

SB   St Benet's Abbey Cartulary
West, J R 1932 *St Benet of Holme, 1020-1210* (Norfolk Record Society)

SD   Simeon of Durham – "Historia Dunelmensis Ecclesiae"
Arnold, T 1882-85 *Symeonis Monachi Opera* (Rolls Series 75) 2 vols
Stephenson, J 1858 *The Works of Simeon of Durham* (The Church Historians of England vol 3:2)

SE   St Edmund's Chronicle (c1212)
Arnold, T 1890-96 *Memorials of St Edmund's Abbey* (Rolls Series)

TÆ   The "Translation of St Ælfheah" by Osbern (c1075)
Wharton, H 1691 *Anglia Sacra*

TE   Thomas of Elmham – "History of St Augustine's" (c1410)
Hardwick, C 1858 *Historia Monasterii S Augustini Cantuariensis* (Rolls Series)

Th   William Thorne's Chronicle (1397)
       Davis, A H 1934 *William Thorne's Chronicle*
Ty   Thorney Annals (12th-15th centuries)
       Caley, J, Ellis, H & Bandinel, B (eds) 1817-30 *Monasticon Anglicanum* Vol.
          2: 611-612
VÆ   "Vita Ædwardi Regis" (1065/67)
       Barlow, F 1962 *The Life of King Edward who Rests at Westminster*
VBE   Osbert of Clare – "Vita Beati Eadwardi Regis Anglorum" (1138)
       Bloch, M 1923 "La vie de S. Edouard le Confesseur par Osbert de Clare",
          Analecta Bollandiana 41: 5-131
VD   Eadmer – "Vita Dunstani" (1095/1125)
       Stubbs, W 1874 *Memorials of St Dunstan* (Rolls Series)
VH   "Vita Haroldi" (anon of Waltham Abbey)
       Swanton, M 1984 *Three Lives of the Last Englishmen*
VM   Þurgod – "Vita Margareta" (1100/07)
       Anderson, A O 1922 *Early Sources for Scottish History AD 500-1286* II: 59-88
       Hinde, J H 1868 *Turgot: The Life of Margaret Queen of Scotland*, Surtees
          Society 51
VSE   Ailred of Rievaulx – "Vita Sancti Edwardi Regis" (1161-63)
       Migne, J P *Patrologia Latina* 115: 737-790
VW   "Vita Wulfstani" (1095/1113)
       Darlington, R R 1928 *The Vita Wulfstani of William of Malmesbury*, Camden
          Soc. 3rd Ser. XL
       Peile, J H F 1934 *William of Malmesbury's Life of St Wulfstan*
W   John of Worcester – "Chronicon ex Chronicis" (1090-1117)
       Thorpe, B. 1848-49 *Florentii Wigorniensis Monachi Chronicon ex Chronicis*
          2 vols
       Stephenson, J. 1853 *Florence of Worcester: A History of the Kings of
          England*
       Darlington, R R & McGurk, P 1995 *The Chronicle of John of Worcester*
WC   Worcester cartulary
       Darlington, R R 1968 *The Cartulary of Worcester Cathedral Priory* (Pipe Roll
          Society 76)
Wc   Winchcombe Chronicle (c1230)
       Darlington, R R 1962 "Winchcombe Annals 1049-1181", in P M Barnes & C
          F Slade *A Medieval Miscellany for Doris Mary Stenton*: 111-137
Wi   Abbesses of Wilton
       Wilmart, A 1938 *Annalecta Bollandiana* 56: 99, 295-296.
WJ   William of Jumieges – "Gesta Normannorum Ducum" (1050s-70)
       van Houts, E M C 1992-95 *The Gesta Normannorum Ducum* 2vols.
WP   William of Poitiers – "Gesta Guillelmi Ducis" (1073/75)
       Foreville, R 1952 *Guillaume de Poitiers: Histoire de Guillaume le Conquerant*
       Douglas, D C & Greenaway, G W 1981 *English Historical Documents II
          1042-1189*

Ws   Goscelin – "Life of St Wulfsige" (1077/79)
      Talbot, C H 1959 "Goscelin, life of St Wulsin", in *Revue Bénédictine* 69: 68-
      85
Wþ   Waltham Chronicle (c1180)
      Stubbs, W 1861 *The Foundation of Waltham Abbey*
w   Whitelock, D 1930 *Anglo-Saxon Wills*

Charters and Writs

B – Bates, D   1998   *Regesta Regum Anglo-Normannorum: the Acta of William I
      (1066-1087)*
C – van Caeneghem, R C 1990-91   *English Lawsuits from William I to Richard I*
      (Selden Society 106-107)
F – Fauroux, M 1961 *Recueil des Actes des Ducs de Normandie de 911 à 1066*
Farrer, W H 1914 *Early Yorkshire Charters* Vol.1
H – Harmer, F E 1989 *Anglo-Saxon Writs*
P – Pelteret, D A E 1990 *Catalogue of English Post-Conquest Vernacular Documents*
R – Davis, W H C 1913 *Regesta Regum Anglo-Normannorum* vol.1
S – Sawyer, P H 1968 *Anglo-Saxon Charters*, Royal Historical Society Handbook 8
Wilkins, D 1737 *Concilia Magnae Britanniae et Hiberniae* Vol 1: 364

Information about Anglo-Saxon charters, including the texts of many and an updated
version of Sawyer 1968, are available in the Internet through the work of the Joint
Committee on Anglo-Saxon Charters, at http://www.trin.cam.ac.uk/chartwww/.

Domesday Book

The Domesday Book has been made accessible in original text and translation in a
series of volumes under the general editorship of John Morris and published by
Phillimore & Co. Ltd. of Sussex.

Vol. 1 Morgan, P & Sankaran, V 1983 *Kent*
Vol. 2 Morris, J & Mothersill, J 1976 *Sussex*
Vol. 3 Morris, J & Wood, S 1975 *Surrey*
Vol. 4 Munby, J; Mothersill, J; Osmund, P & Jenkyns, J 1982 *Hampshire*
Vol. 5 Morgan, P & Hawkins, A 1979 *Berkshire*
Vol. 6 Thorn, C & F 1979 *Wiltshire*
Vol. 7 Thorn, C; Thorn, F & Newman, M 1983 *Dorset*
Vol. 8 Thorn, C & F 1980 *Somerset*
Vol. 9 Thorn, C; Thorn, F & O'Driscoll, A 1985 *Devon* (2 parts)
Vol. 10 Thorn, C; Thorn, F & Padel, O 1979 *Cornwall*
Vol. 11 Morris, J & Wood, S 1975 *Middlesex*
Vol. 12 Morris, J; Newman, M & Wood, S 1976 *Hertfordshire*
Vol. 13 Morris, J; Teague, E & sankaran, V 1978 *Buckinghamshire*
Vol. 14 Morris, J & Caldwell, C 1978 *Oxfordshire*
Vol. 15 Moore, J S 1982 *Gloucestershire*

Vol. 16 Thorn, C; Thorn, F; Whitelaw, E & Wood, S 1982 *Worcestershire*

Vol. 17 Thorn, C; Thorn, F & Sankaran, V 1983 *Herefordshire*

Vol. 18 Rumble, A; Fellows, J & Keynes, S 1981 *Cambridgeshire*

Vol. 19 Morris, J & Hervey, S 1975 *Huntingdonshire*

Vol. 20 Morris, J; Sankaran, V & Sherlock, D 1977 *Bedfordshire*

Vol. 21 Thorn, C; Thorn, F; Jones, M; Morgan, P & Plaister, J 1979
    Northamptonshire

Vol. 22 Morgan, P & Griffin, M 1979 *Leicestershire*

Vol. 23 Morris, J & Plaister, J 1976 *Warwickshire*

Vol. 24 Morris, J; Hawkins, A & Rumble, A 1976 *Staffordshire*

Vol. 25 Thorn, C; Thorn, F & Parker, C 1986 *Shropshire*

Vol. 26 Morgan, P & Rumble, A 1978 *Cheshire*

Vol. 27 Morgan, P & Wood, S 1978 *Derbyshire*

Vol. 28 Morris, J: Parker, C & Wood, S 1977 *Nottinghamshire*

Vol. 29 Thorn, C & Parker, C 1980 *Rutland*

Vol. 30 Faull, M L & Stinson, M 1986 *Yorkshire* (2 parts)

Vol. 31 Morgan, P, Thorn, C & Woods, S 1986 *Lincolnshire* (2 parts)

Vol. 32 Rumble, A; Plaister, J & Sankaran, V 1983 *Essex*

Vol. 33 Brown, P; Hepplestone, M; Mothersill, J & Newman, M 1984 *Norfolk* (2
    parts)

Vol. 34 Rumble, A; Hepplestone, M; Hodge, B; Jones, M; Plaister, J; Coutts, C;
    Bowers, F & Teague, E 1986 *Suffolk* (2 parts)

Vol. 36 Dodgson, J M & Palmer J J N 1992 *Index of Places*

Vol. 37 Dodgson, J M & Palmer, J J N 1992 *Index of Persons*

Vol. 38 Foy, J D 1992 *Index of Subjects*

Volume 35 covers the 12th century Boldon Book for Durham.

Coins

Details of coins can be found in the major series of volumes that form the *Sylloge of
Coins of the British Isles* (SCBI). Information about the sylloge and its volumes,
published since 1958 and still ongoing, can be found on the website of the
Fitzwilliam Museum, Cambrige (http://www.fitzwilliam.ca.ac.uk/SCBI). The sylloge
itself deals with collections of coins. Single finds of coins are being catalogued as
part of the *Early Medieval Corpus*, also on the Fitzwilliam website
(http://www.fitzwilliam.cam.ac.uk/coins). The sylloge volumes containing materials
from the reign of Eadward III, Harold II and Willelm I are:

Vol. 1 Grierson, P 1958 *Fitzwilliam Museum, Cambridge: ancient British and
    Anglo-Saxon coins*

Vol. 2 Robertson, A S 1961 *Hunterian Museum, Glasgow: Anglo-Saxon coins*

Vol. 4 Galster, G 1964 *Royal Collection, Copenhagen: Part I, ancient British and
    Anglo-Saxon coins*

Vol. 5 Pirie, E J E 1964 *Grosvenor Museum, Chester: coins with the Chester mint-signature*

Vol. 6 Stevenson, R B K 1966 *National Museum of Antiquities of Scotland, Edinburgh: Anglo-Saxon coins*

Vol. 9 Thompson, J D A 1967 *Ashmolean Museum, Oxford: Part I, Anglo-Saxon pennies*

Vol. 11 Blunt, C E & Dolley, M 1969 *Reading University: Anglo-Saxon and Norman coins & Royal Coin Cabinet, Stockholm: Part VI, Anglo-Norman pennies*

Vol. 16 Blunt, C E, Elmore-Jones, F & Mack, R P 1971 *Norweb Collection: ancient British and English coins to 1180*

Vol. 17 Gunstone, A J H 1971 *Midland Museums: ancient British, Anglo-Saxon and Norman coins*

Vol. 18 Galster, G 1972 *Royal Collection, Copenhagen: Part IV, Anglo-Saxon coins from Harold I and Anglo-Norman coins*

Vol. 19 Grinsell, L V, Blunt, C E & Dolley, M 1972 *Bristol and Gloucester Museums: ancient British coins and coins of the Bristol and Gloucestershire mints*

Vol. 20 Mack, R P 1973 *Mack Collection: ancient British, Anglo-Saxon and Norman coins*

Vol. 21 Pirie, E J E 1975 *Yorkshire Collections: coins from Northumbrian mints, c895-1279; ancient British and later coins from other mints to 1279*

Vol. 24 Gunstone, A J H 1977 *West Country Museums: ancient British, Anglo-Saxon and Anglo-Norman coins*

Vol. 25 Talvio, T 1978 *National Museum, Helsinki: Anglo-Saxon and Anglo-Norman coins*

Vol. 26 Clough, T H McK 1980 *Museums in East Anglia: Morley St Peter hoard, and Anglo-Saxon, Norman and Angevin coins, and later coins of the Norwich mint*

Vol. 27 Gunstone, A J H 1981 *Lincolnshire Collections: coins from Lincolnshire mints, and ancient British and later coins to 1272*

Vol. 29 Warhurst, M 1982 *Merseyside County Museums: ancient British and later coins to 1279*

Vol. 30 Brady, J D 1982 *American Collections: ancient British, Anglo-Saxon and Normans coins*

Vol. 36 Kluge, B 1987 *State Museum, Berlin: Anglo-Saxon, Anglo-Norman, and Hiberno-Norse coins*

Vol. 37 Mikolajczyk, A 1987 *Polish Museums: Anglo-Saxon and later medieval British coins*

Vol. 42 Gunstone, A J H 1992 *South-Eastern Museums: ancient British, Anglo-Saxon and later coins to 1279*

Vol. 45 Berga, T 1996 *Latvian Collections: Anglo-Saxon and later British coins*

Vol. 48 Booth, J 1997 *Northern Museums: ancient British, Anglo-Saxon, Norman and Plantagenet coins to 1279*

The two index volumes for the series so far are:

Vol. 28 Smart, V J 1981 *Cumulative Index of Vols. 1-20*

Vol. 41 Smart, V J 1992 *Cumulative Index of Vols. 21-40*

MODERN WORKS

Listed below is a selection of books and articles. It is not a comprehensive list but covers the major works. More detailed bibliographies are available in many of the works cited. Bibliographies are given for every year since 1971 in the journal *Anglo-Saxon England*. Both that and the journal *Anglo-Norman Studies* have many important articles for this period

Abels, R P 1988 *Lordship and Military Obligation in Anglo-Saxon England*

Allen Brown, R 1984 *The Normans* (Documents of Medieval History 5)

Allen Brown, R 1985 *The Normans and the Norman Conquest*

Anderson, A O 1990 (1922) *Early Sources for Scottish History AD 500-1286*

Angold, M 1984 *The Byzantine Empire 1025-1204*

Barlow, F 1958 "Queen Emma's disgrace in 1043", *English Historical Review* 73: 651-655

Barlow, F 1970 *Edward the Confessor*

Barlow, F 1979 *The English Church 1000-1066*

Barlow, F 1979 *The English Church 1066-1154*

Barlow, F 1983 *The Norman Conquest and Beyond*

Barraclough, G 1947 *The Origins of Modern Germany*

Barrow, G W S 1981 *Kingship and Unity: Scotland 1000-1306*

Bartlett, R 1993 *The Making of Europe: conquest, colonization and cultural change 950-1350*

Bates, D 1982 *Normandy before 1066*

Bates, D 1997 "The prosopographical study of Anglo-Norman royal charters", in K S B Keats-Rohan (ed) *Family Trees and the Roots of Politics*: 89-102

Bates, D 1998 *Regesta Regum Anglo-Normannorum: the Acta of William I (1066-1087)*

Biddle, M (ed) 1976 *Winchester Studies I*

Biddle, M & Keene, D J 1976 "Winchester in the eleventh and twelfth centuries: the mint", in M Biddle (ed) *Winchester Studies I*: 396-421

Blackburn, M & Lyon, S 1986 "Regional die production in Cnut's *Quatrefoil* issue", in M Blackburn (ed) *Anglo-Saxon Monetary History*: 223-272

Brooks, N 1984 *The Early History of the Church at Canterbury*

Byock, J L 1988 *Medieval Iceland: society, sagas, and power*

Campbell, M W 1971 "Queen Emma and Ælfgyfu of Northampton: Canute the Great's women", *Medieval Scandinavia* 4: 66-79

Cheney, C R 1981 *Handbook of Dates for Students of English History* (Royal Society Handbook 4)

Cipolla, C M 1981 *Before the Industrial Revolution: European society and economy 1000-1700*

Clark, C 1976 "People and languages in post-Conquest Canterbury", *Journal of Medieval History* 2: 1-34

Clark, C 1992a "Onomastics", in R M Hogg (ed) *The Cambridge History of the English Language I: the beginnings to 1066*: 452-489

Clark, C 1992b "Onomastics", in N Blake (ed) *The Cambridge History of the English Language 2: 1066 -1476*: 558-563

Clark, G N 1946 *The Wealth of England from 1496 to 1760*

Clarke, P A 1994 *The English Nobility under Edward the Confessor*

Corbett, W J 1926 "The development of the duchy of Normandy and the Norman Conquest of England", in J R Tanner, C W Previte Orton, Z N Brooke (eds) *Cambridge Medieval History* vol 5: 481-520

Craig, Sir J 1953 *The Mint*

Crawford, B E 1987 *Scandinavian Scotland*

Cutler, K E 1973 "Edith, Queen of England, 1045-1066", in *Medieval Studies* 35: 222-231

Daniel-Rops, H (trans. J Warrington) 1957 *Cathedral and Crusade*

Darlington, R R 1933 "Aethelwig, abbot of Evesham", *English Historical Review* 48: 1-22, 177-198

Davies, H W C 1913 *Regesta Regum Anglo-Normannorum*

Davies, R R 1987 *Conquest, Coexistence and Change: Wales 1063-1415*

Davies, W 1982 *Wales in the Early Middle Ages*

Davis, R H C 1988 *A History of Medieval Europe: from Constantine to St Louis*

De Vries, K 1999 *The Norwegian Invasion of England in 1066*

Dodgson, J M 1985 "Some Domesday personal names, mainly post-Conquest", *Nomina* 9: 41-51

Dolley, R H M 1964 *Anglo-Saxon Pennies*

Dolley, R H M 1966 *The Norman Conquest and the English Coinage*

Dolley, R H M & Elmore Jones, F 1961 "A new suggestion concerning the so-called 'martlets' in the 'arms of St Edward'", in R H M Dolley *Anglo-Saxon Coins*: 215-226

Douglas, D C 1964 *William the Conqueror*

Douglas, D C 1969 *The Norman Achievement 1050-1100*

Douglas, D C and Greenaway, G W 1981 *English Historical Documents II 1042-1189*

Duby, G (trans. J Vale) 1991 *France in the Middle Ages 987-1460*

Duffy, S 1997 *Ireland in the Middle Ages*

Faith, R 1997 *The English Peasantry and the Growth of Lordship*

Faull, M L & Stinson, M 1986 *Domesday Book 30: Yorkshire*

Fawtier, R (trans. L Butler & R J Adam) 1960 *The Capetian Kings of France*

Feilitzen, O von 1937 *The Pre-Conquest Personal Names of Domesday Book*

Feilitzen, O von 1976 "The personal names and bynames of the Winton Domesday", in M Biddle (ed) *Winchester Studies I*: 143-230

Fell, C 1973 "The Icelandic saga of Edward the Confessor: its version of the Anglo-Saxon emigration to Byzantium", *Anglo-Saxon England* 3

Fellows Jensen, G 1968 *Scandinavian Personal names in Lincolnshire and Yorkshire*

Finberg, H P R 1942-46 "Abbots of Tavistock", *Devon and Cornwall Notes and Queries* 22: 159-197

Finberg, H P R 1943 "The house of Ordgar and the foundation of Tavistock Abbey", *English Historical Review* 58: 190-201

Finberg, H P R 1964 *Lucerna*

Fine, J V A 1981 *The Early Medieval Balkans*

Fleming, R 1991 *Kings and Lords in Conquest England*: 105-231

Fleming, R 1998 *Domesday Book and the Law*

Forssner, T 1916 *Continental Germanic Personal Names in England in Old and Early Middle English Times*

Franklin, S & Shepard, J 1996 *The Emergence of the Rus 750-1157*

Freeman, A 1985 *The Moneyer and the Mint in the Age of Edward the Confessor 1042-1066*, BAR 145

Freeman, E A 1869-75 *The History of the Norman Conquest of England*

Fryde, E B, Greenway, D E, Porter, S and Roy, I 1986 *Handbook of British Chronology* (Royal Society Handbook 2, 3rd ed.)

Fuhrmann, H 1986 *Germany in the High Middle Ages c1050-1200*

Garmonsway, G N 1954 *The Anglo-Saxon Chronicle*

Gibbs, V & Doubleday, H A 1916 *The Complete Peerage, Volume IV*

Gneuss, H 1972 "The origin of standard Old English and Æthelwold's school at Winchester", *Anglo-Saxon England* 1: 63-84

Godfrey, J 1978 "The defeated Anglo-Saxons take service with the Byzantine emperor", *Anglo-Norman Studies* 1

Golding, B 1994 *Conquest and Colonisation: the Normans in Britain, 1066-1100*

Gransden, A 1974 *Historical Writing in England c.550 to c.1307*

Gravett, C 1992 *Hastings 1066: The Fall of Saxon England* (Campaign Series 13)

Green, J A 1983 "The sheriffs of William the Conqueror", *Anglo-Norman Studies* 5: 129-145

Green, J A 1986 *The Government of England under Henry I*

Green, J A 1990 *English Sheriffs to 1154*, HMSO (Public Record Office Handbook 24)

Grierson, P 1940 "Les livres de l'abbé Seiwold de Bath", *Revue Bénédictine* 52: 96-116

Guldescu, S 1964 *History of Medieval Croatia*

Harmer, F E 1989 (2nd Ed.) *Anglo-Saxon Writs*

Harris, E J 1983-88 "Moneyers of the Norman Kings", *Seaby's Coin and Medal Bulletin* Jan 1983 to Mar 1988

Hart, C R 1975 *The Early Charters of Northern England and the North Midlands*

Hart, C R 1992 "Hereward the Wake and his companions", in C R Hart (ed) *The Danelaw*

Hart, C R 1997 "Willam Malet and his family", *Anglo-Norman Studies* 19: 123-165

Haverkamp, A 1988 *Medieval Germany 1056-1273*

Head, V 1995 *Hereward*

Henson, D 1998 *A Guide to Late Anglo-Saxon England: from Ælfred to Eadgar II*

Hill, D 1981 *An Atlas of Anglo-Saxon England*

Hooper, N 1985 "Edgar the Ætheling: Anglo-Saxon prince, rebel and crusader", *Anglo-Saxon England* 14: 197-214

Insley, J 1994 *Scandinavian Personal Names in Norfolk*

John, E 1982 "The end of Anglo-Saxon England" in J Campbell (ed) *The Anglo-Saxons*: 214-239

Jones, G 1984 *A History of the Vikings*

Jonsson, K & Van Der Meer, G 1990 "Mints and moneyers c973-1066, in K Jonsson (ed) *Studies in Late Anglo-Saxon Coinage* 49-136

Kapelle, W E 1979 *The Norman Conquest of the North*

Keats-Rohan, K S B 1991 "The Breton contingent in the non-Norman Conquest" *Anglo-Norman Studies* 13

Keynes, S 1980 *The Diplomas of King Æthelred 'The Unready' 978-1016*

Keynes, S 1988 "Regenbald the Chancellor", *Anglo-Norman Studies* 10: 185-222

Keynes, S 1990 "The Æthelings in Normandy", *Anglo-Norman Studies* 13: 173-206

Keynes, S 1997 "Giso, Bishop of Wells", *Anglo-Norman Studies* 19: 203-272

King, V 1996 "Ealdred, Archbishop of York: the Worcester years", *Anglo-Norman Studies* 18: 123-137

Kinvig, R H 1975 *The Isle of Man: a social, cultural and political history*

Knowles, D, Brooke, C N L & London, V C M 1972 *The Heads of Religious Houses England and Wales 940-1216*

Koerner, S 1964 *The Battle of Hastings, England and Europe*

Lamb, J W 1933 *Saint Wulfstan, Prelate and Patriot: a study of his life and times*

Larson, L M 1904 *The King's Household in England before the Norman Conquest*

Lewis, C P 1991 "The early earls of Norman England", *Anglo-Norman Studies* 13

Lewis, CP 1991 "The formation of the honour of Chester, 1066-1100", in A T Thatcher (ed) *The Earldom of Chester and its Charters*

Lewis, C P 1995 "The French in England before the Norman Conquest", *Anglo-Norman Studies* 17: 123-144

Lewis, C P 1997 "Joining the dots: a methodology for identifying the English in the Domesday Book", in KSB Keats-Rohan (ed) *Family Trees and the Roots of Politics*: 69-87

Liebermann, F 1903-16 *Die Gesetze der Angelsachsen* (3 vols)

Lloyd, J E 1912 *A History of Wales* (2 vols)

Loyn, H R 1984 *The Governance of Anglo-Saxon England 500-1087*

Loyn, H R 1991 *Anglo-Saxon England and the Norman Conquest*

Loyn, H R 1994 "Abbots of English monasteries following the Norman Conquest", in D Bates et al (ed) *England and Normandy in the Middle Ages*: 95-103

Mack, K 1982 *Kings and Thegns: Aristocratic Participation in the Governance of Anglo-Saxon England* (unpublished research paper, University of California)

Mack, K 1986 "The stallers: administrative innovation in the reign of Edward the Confessor", *Journal of Medieval History* 12: 123-134

MacKay, A 1977 *Spain in the Middle Ages: from frontier to empire, 1000-1500*

McNulty, J B 1980 "The Lady Aelfgyva in the Bayeux Tapestry", *Speculum* 55: 659-668

Martin, J 1995 *Medieval Russia 980-1584*

Mason, E 1990 *St Wulfstan of Worcester c1008-1095*

Matthew, D 1992 *The Norman kingdom of Sicily*

Maund, K L 1988 "The Welsh alliances of Earl Ælfgar of Mercia and his family in the mid-eleventh century", *Anglo-Norman Studies* 11: 181-190

Michelmore, D J H 1981 "Township and tenure", in M L Faull & S A Moorhouse *West Yorkshire: an archaeological survey to AD 1500, Vol. 2*: 231-264

Moody, T W, Martin, F X & Byrne, F J 1984 *A New History of Ireland IX: maps, genealogies and lists*

Moore, J S 1997 "Prosopographical problems of English *libri vitae*", in K S B Keats-Rohan (ed) *Family Trees and the Roots of Politics*: 165-188

Morris, C 1989 *The Papal Monarchy: the western church from 1050 to 1250*

Morris, W A 1927 *The Medieval English Sheriff to 1300*

Nightingale, P 1982 "Some London moneyers, and reflections on the organisation of English mints in the eleventh and twelfth centuries" *Numismatic Chronicle* 142: 34-50

North, J J 1980 *English Hammered Coinage I: Early Anglo-Saxon to Henry III c.600-1272*

Norwich, J J (Viscount) 1967 *The Normans in the South 1016-1130*

Ó Corráin, D 1972 *Ireland before the Normans*

Ó Cróinín, D 1995 *Early Medievbal Ireland: 400-1200*

Oleson, T J 1955 *The Witenagemot in the Reign of Edward the Confessor*

Ostrogorsky, G 1968 *History of the Byzantine State*

Pagan, H E 1990 "The coinage of Harold II", in K Jonsson (ed) *Studies in Late Anglo-Saxon Coinage*: 177-206

Pálsson, H & Edwards, P (trans) 1978 *Orkneyinga Saga*

Pelteret, D A E 1990 *Catalogue of English Post-Conquest Vernacular Documents*

Reaney, P H & Wilson, R M 1997 *A Dictionary of British Surnames* (3rd edition)

Redin, M 1919 *Uncompounded Personal Names in Old English*

Reilly, B F 1992 *The Contest of Christian and Muslim in Spain 1031-1157*

Reilly, B F 1993 *The Medieval Spains*

Reynolds, S 1981 "Eadric Sylvaticus and the English resistance", *Bulletin of the Institute of Historical Research* 54

Richards, J 1991 *Viking Age England*

Robertson, A J 1939 *Anglo-Saxon Charters*

Rogers, K H 1991 *Vikings and Surnames*

Rogers, K H 1995 *More Vikings and Surnames*

Ronay, G 1989 *The Lost King of England*

Round, J H 1895 *Feudal England*

Russell, S C 1969 *The Population of Europe 500-1500*

Sawyer B & P 1993 *Medieval Scandinavia: from conversion to reformation c800-1500*

Sawyer, P H 1968 *Anglo-Saxon Charters*, Royal Historical Society

Sawyer, P H 1979 *Charters of Burton Abbey*, British Academy: Anglo-Saxon Charters II

Scott, F S 1952 *Earl Waltheof of Northumbria*

Searle, E 1988 *Predatory Kinship and the Creation of Norman Power, 840-1066*

Searle, E 1989 "Emma the Conqueror", in C Harper-Bill, C J Holdsworth & J L Nelson (eds) *Studies in Medieval History*

Sedgefield, W J 1899 *King Alfred's Old English Version of Boethius De Consolatione Philosophiae*

Sedgefield, W J 1900 *King Alfred's Version of the Consolations of Boethius: done into English*

Sewter, E R A (trans) 1966 *Fourteen Byzantine Rulers: the* Chronographia *of Michael Psellus*

Skeat, W 1907 "On the survival of Anglo-Saxon names as modern surnames", *Transactions of the Philogical Society 1910*: 57-85

Smart, V J 1968 *Moneyers of the Late Anglo-Saxon Coinage 973-1016*

Smart, V J 1979 "Moneyers' names on the Anglo-Saxon coinage", *Nomina* 3: 20-28

Smart, V J 1986 "Scandinavians, Celts and Germans in Anglo-Saxon England: the evidence of moneyers' names", in M A S Blackburn (ed) *Anglo-Saxon Monetary History*: 171-184

Smith, M F 1994 "Archbishop Stigand and the eye of the needle", *Anglo-Norman Studies* 16: 199-220

Stafford, P 1981 "The King's wife in Wessex, 800-1066", *Past and Present* 91

Stafford, P 1983 *Queens, Concubines and Dowagers: The King's Wife in the Early Middle Ages*

Stafford, P 1997 *Queen Emma and Queen Edith*

Stewart, I 1990 "Coinage and recoinage after Edgar's reform", in K Jonsson (ed) *Studies in Late Anglo-Saxon Coinage*: 455-485

Swanton, M 1975 *Anglo-Saxon Prose*

Sweet, H 1871-72 *King Alfred's West Saxon Version off Gregory's Pastoral Care* (2 vols) Early English Texts Society 45, 50

Talvio, T 1990 "The design of Edward the Confessor's coins", in K Jonsson (ed) *Studies in Late Anglo-Saxon Coinage*: 487-499

Treadgold, W 1997 *A History of the Byzantine State and Society*

Ullmann, W 1972 *A Short History of the Papacy in the Middle Ages*

Vajay, S de 1962 "Agatha, mother of St Margaret Queen of Scotland", *Duquesne Review* (Pittsburg University)

Van Houts, E M C 1997 "Wace as historian", in KSB Keats-Rohan (ed) *Family Trees and the Roots of Politics*

Vince, A 1990 *Saxon London: an archaeological investigation*

Walker, I W 1997 *Harold: the Last Anglo-Saxon King*

Welldon Finn, R 1973 *Domesday Book: a guide*

White, G H 1949 *The Complete Peerage, Volume XI*

White, G H 1953 *The Complete Peerage, Volume XII, part 1*

Whitelock, D 1930 *Anglo-Saxon Wills*

Whitelock, D 1955 *English Historical Documents I: c500-1042*

Whitelock, D 1966 *The Norman Conquest: Its Setting and Impact*

Williams, A 1978 "Some notes and considerations on problems connected with the English royal succession 860-1066", *Anglo-Norman Studies* 1: 144-167

Williams, A 1989a "The King's nephew: the family and career of Ralph, Earl of Hereford", in C Harper-Bill, C J Holdsworth & J L Nelson (eds) *Studies in Medieval History*: 327-343

Williams, A 1989b "A vice-comital family in pre-Conquest Warwickshire", *Anglo-Norman Studies* 11

Williams, A 1995 *The English and the Norman Conquest*

Williams, A 1997 "A West Country magnate of the eleventh century: the family, estates and patronage of Beorhtric son of Ælfgar", in KSB Keats-Rohan (ed) *Family Trees and the Roots of Politics*: 41-68

Willams, A & Erskine, R W H (eds) 1989 *The Worcestershire Domesday*

Wilson, A J 1993 *St Margaret: Queen of Scotland*

INDEX

Other Titles

A Guide to Late Anglo-Saxon England: From Alfred to Eadgar II 871–1074

Donald Henson

This guide has been prepared with the aim of providing the general readers with both an overview of the period and a wealth of background information. Facts and figures are presented in a way that makes this a useful reference handbook.

Contents include: The Origins of England; Physical Geography; Human Geography; English Society; Government and Politics; The Church; Language and Literature; Personal Names; Effects of the Norman Conquest. All of the kings from Alfred to Eadgar II are dealt with separately and there is a chronicle of events for each of their reigns. There are also maps, family trees and extensive appendices.

£12·95 ISBN 1–898281–21–1 9½" x 6¾" (245 x 170mm) 6 maps & 3 family trees 208 pages

An Introduction to the Old English Language and its Literature

Stephen Pollington

The purpose of this general introduction to Old English is not to deal with the teaching of Old English but to dispel some misconceptions about the language and to give an outline of its structure and its literature. Some basic knowledge of these is essential to an understanding of the early period of English history and the present form of the language.

£4·95 ISBN 1–898281–06–8 A5 48 pages

Ærgeweorc: Old English Verse and Prose

read by Stephen Pollington

This audiotape cassette can be used with *First Steps in Old English* or just listened to for the sheer pleasure of hearing Old English spoken well.
Tracks: 1. Deor. 2. Beowulf – The Funeral of Scyld Scefing. 3. Engla Tocyme (The Arrival of the English).
4. Ines Domas. Two Extracts from the Laws of King Ine. 5. Deniga Hergung (The Danes' Harrying) Anglo-Saxon Chronicle Entry AD997. 6. Durham 7. The Ordeal (Be ðon ðe ordales weddigaþ) 8. Wið Dweorh (Against a Dwarf) 9. Wið Wennum (Against Wens) 10. Wið Wæterælfadle (Against Waterelf Sickness) 11. The Nine Herbs Charm 12. Læcedomas (Leechdoms) 13. Beowulf's Greeting 14. The Battle of Brunanburh 15. Blacmon – by Adrian Pilgrim.
£7·50 ISBN 1–898281–20–3 C40 audiotape

The English Warrior from earliest times to 1066

Stephen Pollington

This is not intended to be a bald listing of the battles and campaigns from the Anglo-Saxon Chronicle and other sources, but rather it is an attempt to get below the surface of Anglo-Saxon warriorhood and to investigate the rites, social attitudes, mentality and mythology of the warfare of those times.

The book is divided into three main sections which deal with warriorhood, weaponry and warfare respectively. The first covers the warrior's role in early English society, his rights and duties, the important rituals of feasting, gift giving and duelling, and the local and national military organizations. The second part discusses the various weapons and items of military equipment which are known to have been in use during the period, often with a concise summary of the generally accepted typology for the many kinds of military hardware. In the third part, the social and legal nature of warfare is presented, as well as details of strategy and tactics, military buildings and earthworks, and the use of supply trains. Valuable appendices offer original translations of the three principal Old English military poems, the battles of *Maldon, Finnsburh* and *Brunanburh*.

The author combines original translations from the Old English and Old Norse source documents with archaeological and linguistic evidence to present a comprehensive and wide-ranging treatment of the subject. Students of military history will find here a wealth of new insights into a neglected period of English history.

This new edition has been updated and expanded.

£14·95 ISBN 1–898281–27–0 9½" x 6¾" (245 x 170mm) over 50 illustrations 288 pages

Wordcraft: Concise English/Old English Dictionary and Thesaurus

Stephen Pollington

This book provides Old English equivalents to the commoner modern words in both dictionary and thesaurus formats. The Thesaurus presents vocabulary relevant to a wide range of individual topics in alphabetical lists, thus making it easily accessible to those with specific areas of interest. Each thematic listing is encoded for cross-reference from the Dictionary. The two sections will be of invaluable assistance to students of the language, as well as to those with either a general or a specific interest in the Anglo-Saxon period.

£11·95   ISBN 1–898281–02–5   A5   256 pages

Leechcraft: Early English Charms, Plantlore and Healing

Stephen Pollington

An unequalled examination of every aspect of early English healing, including the use of plants, amulets, charms, and prayer. Other topics covered include Anglo-Saxon witchcraft; tree-lore; gods, elves and dwarves.

The author has brought together a wide range of evidence for the English healing tradition, and presented it in a clear and readable manner. The extensive 2,000-entry index makes it possible for the reader to quickly find specific information.

The three key Old English texts are reproduced in full, accompanied by new translations.
Bald's Third Leechbook; *Lacnunga*; *Old English Herbarium*.

£35   ISBN 1–898281–23–8   10" x 6¾" (254 x 170mm)   hardcover   28 illustrations   544 pages

Dark Age Naval Power: A Reassessment of Frankish and Anglo-Saxon Seafaring Activity

John Haywood

In the first edition of this work, published in 1991, John Haywood argued that the capabilities of the pre-Viking Germanic seafarers had been greatly underestimated. Since that time, his reassessment of Frankish and Anglo-Saxon shipbuilding and seafaring has been widely praised and accepted.

In this second edition, some sections of the book have been revised and updated to include information gained from excavations and sea trials with sailing replicas of early ships. The new evidence supports the author's argument that early Germanic shipbuilding and seafaring skills were far more advanced than previously thought. It also supports the view that Viking ships and seaborne activities were not as revolutionary as is commonly believed.

'The book remains a historical study of the first order. It is required reading for our seminar on medieval seafaring at Texas A & M University and is essential reading for anyone interested in the subject.'
F. H. Van Doorninck, *The American Neptune* (1994)

£14·95   ISBN 1–898281–22–X   9½" x 6¾" (245 x 170mm)   224 pages

English Heroic Legends

Kathleen Herbert

The author has taken the skeletons of ancient Germanic legends about great kings, queens and heroes, and put flesh on them. Kathleen Herbert's encyclopaedic knowledge of the period is reflected in the wealth of detail she brings to these tales of adventure, passion, bloodshed and magic.

The book is in two parts. First are the stories that originate deep in the past, yet because they have not been hackneyed, they are still strange and enchanting. After that there is a selection of the source material, with information about where it can be found and some discussion about how it can be used. The purpose of the work is to bring pleasure to those studying Old English literature and, more importantly, to bring to the attention of a wider public the wealth of material that has yet to be tapped by modern writers, composers and artists.   This title was previously published as *Spellcraft: Old English Heroic Legends*.

£11·95   ISBN 1–898281–25–4   A5   292 pages

A Handbook of Anglo-Saxon Food: Processing and Consumption

Ann Hagen

For the first time information from various sources has been brought together in order to build up a picture of how food was grown, conserved, prepared and eaten during the period from the beginning of the 5th century to the 11th century. Many people will find it fascinating for the views it gives of an important aspect of Anglo-Saxon life and culture. In addition to Anglo-Saxon England the Celtic west of Britain is also covered. Now with an extensive index.

£9· 95   ISBN 0–9516209–8–3   A5   192 pages

A Second Handbook of Anglo-Saxon Food & Drink: Production and Distribution

Ann Hagen

Food production for home consumption was the basis of economic activity throughout the Anglo-Saxon period. This second handbook complements the first and brings together a vast amount of information on livestock, cereal and vegetable crops, fish, honey and fermented drinks. Related subjects such as hospitality, charity and drunkenness are also dealt with. Extensive index.

£14· 95   ISBN 1–898281–12–2   A5   432 pages

Looking for the Lost Gods of England

Kathleen Herbert

Kathleen Herbert sifts through the royal genealogies, charms, verse and other sources to find clues to the names and attributes of the Gods and Goddesses of the early English. The earliest account of English heathen practices reveals that they worshipped the Earth Mother and called her Nerthus. The tales, beliefs and traditions of that time are still with us and have played a part in giving us *A Midsummer Night's Dream* and *The Lord of the Rings*.

£4· 95   ISBN 1–898281–04–1   A5   64 pages

English Martial Arts

Terry Brown

By the sixteenth century English martial artists had a governing body that controlled its members in much the same way as do modern-day martial arts organisations. The *Company of Maisters* taught and practised a fighting system that ranks as high in terms of effectiveness and pedigree as any in the world.

In the first part of the book the author investigates the weapons, history and development of the English fighting system and looks at some of the attitudes, beliefs and social pressures that helped mould it.

Part two deals with English fighting techniques drawn from sources that recorded the system at various stages in its history. In other words, all of the methods and techniques shown in this book are authentic and have not been created by the author. The theories that underlie the system are explained in a chapter on *The Principles of True Fighting*. All of the techniques covered are illustrated with photographs and accompanied by instructions. Techniques included are for bare-fist fighting, broadsword, quarterstaff, bill, sword and buckler, sword and dagger.

£25   ISBN 1–898281–18–1   10" x 7½" (250 x 195mm)   220 photographs   240 pages

Anglo-Saxon Books

Frithgarth, Thetford Forest Park, Hockwold-cum-Wilton, Norfolk IP26 4NQ
Tel: +44 (0) 1842 828430   Fax: +44 (0) 1842 828332
email: sales@asbooks.co.uk

For a full list of titles and details of our North American distributor see our web site at www.asbooks.co.uk or send us a s.a.e.

We accept payment by cheque, Visa and MasterCard. Please add 10% for UK delivery, up to a maximum charge of £2· 50. For delivery charges outside the UK please contact us or see our website.

Regia Anglorum

Regia Anglorum is a society that was founded to accurately re-create the life of the British people as it was around the time of the Norman Conquest. Our work has a strong educational slant and we consider authenticity to be of prime importance. We prefer, where possible, to work from archaeological materials and are extremely cautious regarding such things as the interpretation of styles depicted in manuscripts. Approximately twenty-five per cent of our membership of over 500 people are archaeologists or historians.

The Society has a large working Living History Exhibit, teaching and exhibiting more than twenty crafts in an authentic environment. We own a forty foot wooden ship replica of a type that would have been a common sight in Northern European waters around the turn of the first millennium AD. Battle re-enactment is another aspect of our activities, often involving 200 or more warriors.

For further information see www.regia.org or e-mail kim_siddorn@compuserve.com
or write to K. J. Siddorn, 9 Durleigh Close, Headley Park, Bristol BS13 7NQ, England

Þa Engliscan Gesiðas - *The English Companions*

Þa Engliscan Gesiðas is a historical and cultural society exclusively devoted to Early English (Anglo-Saxon) history. Its aims are to bridge the gap between scholars and non-experts, and to bring together all those with an interest in the Anglo-Saxon period so as to promote a wider interest in, and knowledge of, its language, culture and traditions. The Fellowship publishes a journal, *Wiðowinde*, which helps members to keep in touch with current thinking on all relevant topics. The Fellowship enables like-minded people to keep in contact by publicising conferences, courses and meetings that might be of interest to its members.

For further details see www.kami.demon.co.uk/gesithas/ or write to:
The Membership Secretary, Þa Engliscan Gesiðas, BM Box 4336, London, WC1N 3XX England.

Sutton Hoo near Woodbridge, Suffolk

Sutton Hoo is a group of low burial mounds overlooking the River Deben in south-east Suffolk. Excavations in 1939 brought to light the richest burial ever discovered in Britain – an Anglo-Saxon ship containing a magnificent treasure that has become one of the principal attractions of the British Museum. The mound from which the treasure was dug is thought to be the grave of Rædwald, the English king who died in 624/5 AD.

For tour details contact:– The Sutton Hoo Guiding and Visits Secretary,
Tailor's House, Bawdsey, Woodbridge, Suffolk IP12 3AJ
e-mail: visits@suttonhoo.org   website: www.suttonhoo.org

The Sutton Hoo Society

Our aims and objectives focus on promoting research and education relating to the Anglo Saxon Royal cemetery at Sutton Hoo, Suffolk in the UK. The Society publishes a newsletter SAXON twice a year, which keeps members up to date with society activities, carries resumes of lectures and visits, and reports progress on research and publication associated with the site. If you would like to join the Society please write to:

Membership Secretary, Sutton Hoo Society, 258 The Pastures, High Wycombe,
Buckinghamshire HP13 5RS England, website: www.suttonhoo.org

West Stow Anglo-Saxon Village

An early Anglo-Saxon Settlement reconstructed on the site where it was excavated consisting of timber and thatch hall, houses and workshop. Open all year 10a.m.– 4.15p.m. (except Christmas). Free tape guides. Special provision for school parties. A teachers' resource pack is available. Costumed events are held at weekends, especially Easter Sunday and August Bank Holiday Monday. Craft courses are organised.

For further details see www.stedmunds.co.uk/west_stow.html or contact:
The Visitor Centre, West Stow Country Park, Icklingham Road, West Stow
Bury St Edmunds, Suffolk IP28 6HG   Tel: 01284 728718